praise for *Reason* magazine

"[*Reason* is] the libertarian magazine that's always engaging, entertaining, and unpredictable."
WASHINGTON POST

"[*Reason*] rejects labels of any sort of conservative, let alone hard-core PC leftie, which leaves readers to discover . . . a singularly lively, refreshing collection of articles."
WASHINGTON TIMES

"Loaded with sharp content. Even manages to make deregulation unboring. There is nothing remotely like this magazine."
NATIONAL JOURNAL

"This magazine does everything well: culture, politics, religion, philosophy, and while other mags redesign to simplify and commercialize, *Reason*'s redesign actually made it better."
CHICAGO TRIBUNE

"[*Reason*]'s refusal to carry water for either Democrats or Republicans is deeply refreshing in this era of partisan ugliness."
FOLIO

"[*Reason*] manages to offend leftists with its defense of bio-technology, free trade, and school choice, even as it appalls conservatives by supporting gay marriage, open immigration, and drug legalization."
COLUMBUS DISPATCH

"It's not often that those on opposite sides of the political divide find themselves seeing eye to eye, but one thing they're usually able to agree about is *Reason* magazine. They don't much like it."
MEDIA LIFE

"It's a rare thing to have one's mind changed by a magazine (or by anything, as a matter of fact) but I find this often happens with *Reason.*"
MEDIA WEEK

choice:
the best of reason

edited by

Nick Gillespie

BENBELLA

Dallas, Texas

BENBELLA

BenBella Books
6440 N. Central Expressway
Suite 617
Dallas, TX 75206

Publisher: Glenn Yeffeth
Editor: Shanna Caughey
Associate Editor: Leah Wilson
Director of Marketing/PR: Laura Watkins

Send feedback to feedback@benbellabooks.com
www.benbellabooks.com

Printed in the United States of America

10 9 8 7 6 5 4 3 2 1

Library of Congress Cataloging-in-Publication Data

Choice : the best of Reason magazine / edited by Nick Gillespie.-- 1st Benbella Books ed.
    p. cm.
 ISBN 1-932100-31-8
 1.   Social history--1970- 2.   United States--Social conditions--1960-1980. 3.   United States--Social conditions--1980- 4.   Popular culture--United States. I. Gillespie, Nick. II. Reason.

HN17.5.C4745 2004
306'.0973--dc22

                        2004008573

Cover design by Todd Michael Bushman
Interior designed and composed by Charles Colby Bence

Distributed by Independent Publishers Group
To order call (800) 888-4741
www.ipgbook.com

For special sales contact Laura Watkins at laura@benbellabooks.com

table of contents

To L.F.

An Open Letter to the Editor-In-Chief of *Reason* Magazine

Drew Carey

Dear Nick,

I've been looking over the new book celebrating 35 years of *Reason*, and it's great. We need a magazine like yours to help fight the stupid drug laws, the stupid immigration laws, and stupid big government in general. "Free Minds and Free Markets!" Right on, my man. Freedom!

What I don't get though is why your circulation is so low. You're champions of the free market system and you can only bring in around 55,000 readers a month? I'd like to offer a few suggestions to improve this.

To start with, how about some near-naked starlets? "The Girls Of *Reason*" or something like that. To justify them editorially, you could have them holding pencils between their pouty lips while reading books on privatization. You could also note how much perkier their breasts are without government interference. And think of how many hits *Reason Online* (reason.com) will get with downloadable, near-naked starlets on it. You can't lose.

I know the *Washington Post* and the *Village Voice* won't kiss your ass like they used to if you do this, but so what? You're always going on about how we can use biotechnology and stuff to help the world's poor and whatnot—don't you want to help the world's poor? Throw in some boobies and help spread the word.

It wouldn't hurt to have a crossword puzzle and a horoscope, either. People like that. Oh, and cartoons. You already have cartoons? Then better cartoons. Like *Playboy* or the *New Yorker*.

I've also noticed that a lot of magazines, even popular news magazines, dedicate an inordinate amount of space to the entertainment industry. Not the economics of the entertainment industry, but just what movies are coming out and which ones should be popular and why. Sometimes they include television coverage too. You know, what TV shows are popular and why. And of course, lots of pictures of the actors themselves: who's popular and why. America craves this kind of important information.

And don't forget the Oscars! I personally cannot let a day go by without thinking of them. Maybe Joan Rivers can do a column. Or one of those nice folks from *USA Today*?

Why, there's so many things you can do to make *Reason* better. Quotes from popular TV stars, fashion advice from the stars and the people who dress the stars, articles about what the most popular stars are doing and what they think about their latest project. . .so many fascinating things.

It's called *sizzle*, Nick. What you have here is 35 years of steak. Great steak, don't get me wrong, but still just steak. Dress it up a little, will you?

Omnia venundum, brother. It's all for sale.

Drew Carey
Hollywood, California
March 2004

Foreword

Christopher Hitchens

SOMEWHERE IN HIS MINIMA MORALIA, Theodor Adorno wrote that it would be quite possible to produce a perfectly aesthetic and dramatic motion picture that observed all the rules and guidelines of the Hays Office—but only on condition that there was no Hays Office.

The time of Hollywood censorship (at least of censorship by the Legion of Decency) has gone, but this insight remains as a guide for the self-emancipated mind. In the following pages, Dave Barry says that children should wear helmets when biking, but that they should not be compelled to do so by the government. Matt Welch points out that Vaclav Havel was opposed to the profiteering state manufacture of weapons, but in favor of using force against psychopathic dictators. Charles Paul Freund opines that people should rejoice in American junk culture as long as they are choosing it for themselves and as long as it helps free them from mullahs or bureaucrats. "No man," it used to be said on the old left, "is good enough to be another man's master." We might adapt this to say that we feel well able to make certain decisions just as well for ourselves as anyone else might, unless they are willing to prove their right to intervene. Also, that the right we claim for ourselves is one we are ready to extend to others.

The essence of the totalitarian mentality, whether it is religious or political, is the false promise of a system of all-explaining consistency: a worldview that accounts for everything and answers all questions.

Some of us, by contrast, expect our views to be contradictory or at least to contain contradictions, and welcome the opportunity for further reflection and experiment this affords.

The essence of the frivolous or trivial mentality is the taunting attitude toward principles: the jeer at the vegetarian who wears leather sandals or the socialist with a nice car or the libertarian who uses the interstate highway system. This is the sort of thing that generates easy studio applause on half-baked chat shows and promotes the wised-up and affectless cretin as the coolest cultural figure.

In negotiating these shoals, it helps to have an ironic and stoic approach that recognizes the existence of such dilemmas as inescapable. America's most celebrated Randian, Alan Greenspan, runs a huge and secretive federal bank. America's most praised "anarchist," Noam Chomsky, has mutated into an apologist for Milosevic, the Taliban, and Saddam Hussein. Probably both of the above-named gentlemen could do more to reconcile their internal opposites. But one can still hope to learn from other people's paradoxes as well as from one's own.

In the century of capitalism that produced the first industrial revolution and the first modern empires, there was a natural inclination by intellectuals to refuse the logic of the market since it seemed to foreclose any human autonomy. Those who argued that mere mortals could not be wiser than the "invisible hand" were, however elegantly, suggesting a sort of determinism. But the subsequent industrial and technological revolutions have displaced a good deal of power and initiative away from states and corporations—and the unspoken alliance between them—and toward the individual worker or producer. More than this, they have greatly attenuated the frontiers of states and nations and made it easier to be an everyday "internationalist" than many once-leftist parties would have believed possible.

In strict "policy" terms, this evidently means that it is now the planners and statists who have to justify themselves, and justify themselves each time at that. In the apparently opposite case of "terrorism" vs. free movement, how reassuring is it that our "security" services, who failed us so abysmally with enormous budgets and almost limitless power, promise to do better only if given titanic budgets and absolute power, albeit under the identical leadership as before? How useful is the thermonuclear state in the age of asymmetrical warfare? Is not the "war on drugs" a greater distraction from real tasks than any other?

As we ponder these grave and solemn questions, it is useful and encouraging to have a magazine that approaches matters with an additional dash of hedonism. Freedom might be more *efficient*, but it also might possibly be more enjoyable. The supposed ideal of a risk-free and healthy society, liberated from anxiety and responsibility but dominated by the grim idol of "liability," might be maddeningly dull as well as stultifyingly overregulated. The free citizen who turns up at the domestic airline counter with no luggage but no ID, and no credit cards but only cash, and no carry-on bag but some music and some film and some headphones, would nowadays not be allowed to fly. This unsmiling state of affairs means that mirthless officials are subtracting time from their "real" tasks in order to impose themselves where they have no business.

Such a mentality requires an eloquent and witty opposition, as well as a tough-minded one. I find that *Reason* keeps my own arteries from hardening or from flooding with adrenaline out of sheer irritation, because in the face of arbitrary power and flock-like conformism it continues to ask, in a polite but firm tone of voice, not only "why?" but "why not?"

Christopher Hitchens
Washington, DC
March 2004

Introduction

The reason for *Reason*

Nick Gillespie

"Logic, not legends. Coherance [sic], not contradictions. This is our promise; this is the reason for Reason.*"*

from the first issue, May 1968

IN A COUNTRY THAT PRIDES ITSELF on stories of humble origins, *Reason* has an especially good tale to tell. In the *annus mirabilis* (or *horribilis*, take your pick) of 1968, we came into being as a typo-ridden mimeographed publication, the brainchild of a disgruntled Boston University student named Lanny Friedlander. He was outraged equally by the demonstrators who disrupted his classes and the increasingly repressive measures used by the authorities to contain such protests.

Showing he was definitely not your average *soixante-huitard*, Friedlander penned essays such as "Animal Farm 1970," in which he averred, "We are trapped in the middle of a street war between two breeds of pigs, the police and the New Left." Illustrating the story was a wonderfully bizarre, crudely rendered drawing of a man who was part truncheon-wielding cop and part Molotov cocktail–tossing radical. That's hardly the sort of take on campus riots you would have seen in the pages of the *Nation*, the *New Republic*, *National Review*, or *Ramparts*.

From its start, *Reason* has provided a uniquely libertarian alternative to conventional right-wing and left-wing perspectives on politics and culture. As the magazine of "Free Minds and Free Markets," we champion a world of expanding choice—in lifestyles, identities, goods, work arrangements, and more—and explore the institutions, policies, and attitudes necessary for such a world. We are happy warriors against busybodies, elites, and gatekeepers who insist on how other people should live their lives. Like John Stuart Mill, we're big on "experiments in living." Within the broadest possible parameters, we believe that you should be able to think what you want, live where you want, trade for what you want, eat what you want, smoke what you want, and marry whom you want. You should also be willing to shoulder the responsibilities entailed by your actions. Those general guidelines don't explain everything and they certainly don't mean that there aren't hard choices to make. But as basic principles, they go a hell of a long way to creating a world that is tolerant, free, peaceful, prosperous, vibrant, and interesting.

Often described as socially liberal and fiscally conservative, *Reason* is surely the only publication to have won praise from both Rush Limbaugh (he's called us "a good, good magazine"—and we're pretty sure it wasn't just the OxyContin talking) and the American Civil Liberties Union (President Nadine Strossen has hailed us as a "valued ally" and a "passionate defender of free speech"). As that great American heartland newspaper, the *Columbus Dispatch*, has put it, *Reason* "manages to offend leftists with its defense of biotechnology, free trade, and school choice, even as it appalls conservatives by supporting gay marriage, open immigration, and drug legalization."

We enjoy putting forth a very different perspective on politics and culture and hope that even (or perhaps especially) readers who disagree with our views find our articles engaging and provocative. As the Nobel prize-winning economist Friedrich Hayek, one of the great intellectual inspirations of *Reason*, once said, "Society's course will be changed only by a change in ideas." We're proud that the ideas that have always animated our magazine—that economic and civil liberties are indivisible; that markets and borders and societies should be open and governments should be limited; that there is no one best way to run a country, a business, a family, a life—have moved from the fringes of the debate to the center, in some cases even becoming the conventional wisdom.

In the early '70s, Friedlander sold the magazine to three contributors, Robert W. Poole Jr., Tibor Machan, and Manuel Klausner, and *Reason* was published out of Poole's Santa Barbara, California, garage for several years. Eventually, *Reason* moved into actual offices, first in Santa Barbara and then, in 1986, Los Angeles. Although the magazine is still headquartered there, we now reside in cyberspace as much as anywhere: I edited the magazine for four years from Ohio before moving recently to Washington, D.C.; *Reason*'s publisher lives in Connecticut; our art director is in Arizona; our Web editor is in San Francisco; and most of our staff and contributors are scattered around (and far beyond) the traditional stomping grounds of political journalists, D.C. and New York.

Since its early days, *Reason* has grown in readership and stature. Each issue now goes out to around 60,000 readers and, as of this writing, *Reason Online* pulls about 1 million visits per month. We've been a finalist for a handful of National Magazine Awards, an Utne Independent Press Award for political coverage, and a Western Publications Association "Maggie" Award in the "politics and social issues" category. Earlier this year, the *Chicago Tribune* ranked us 13th in its annual list of "The 50 Best Magazines," writing, "in an era of smash-mouth, left vs. right political discourse, the libertarian *Reason* is a fresh and nuanced antidote, with a frequent a-plague-on-both-their-houses approach." (We had come in at 21 in the first list.) The trade magazine bible *Folio* dubbed us one of the "Small Magazines We Adore," noting that our "refusal to carry water for either Democrats or Republicans is deeply refreshing in this era of partisan ugliness."

While preparing this collection, I looked over the entire run of *Reason*. It was striking which hot-button issues of the day have cooled down since 1968. Some topics that once fired up the magazine's pages—the Vietnam War, the draft, the Cold War—thankfully have been swept into the ash heap of history. It was almost quaint to read about Richard Nixon's autocratic wage and price controls or "Gorbomania," the fleeting, oversized adulation of a "genius" statesman whose lasting contribution to humanity was unwittingly dismantling the Soviet Union.

Other things haven't changed much. In 1972, for example, *Reason* reported on "The New Biology," cutting-edge developments that promised to extend and enrich human lives if we could only "circumvent the recalcitrance of an antiquated culture." Today's hyperbolic fears about cloning, stem-cell research, and similar biomedical technologies testify that our society hasn't become all that less recalcitrant. In the wake of Watergate-inspired campaign finance laws, *Reason* wrote that "all of these proposals would deny fundamental rights of individuals, increase the politicians' control of elections and do nothing to eliminate the root causes of Watergate." That's an apt critique of the newest campaign finance laws, which are currently restricting explicitly political speech during this latest national election cycle. Vietnam and the Cold War may be over, but they've been replaced by Iraq and the War on Terror, both of which raise any number of hopes, fears, and doubts on both domestic and foreign fronts. Even as medical marijuana becomes the law of the land, the drug war proceeds apace, exacerbating every ill it supposedly is combating.

The most important continuity over the years has been *Reason*'s insistence that freedom is central to human flourishing. Despite the world's innumerable problems—from terrorism to war to AIDS—no one can deny that the past 35 years have seen incredible political, economic, and social progress. A higher percentage of human beings live under representative governments than ever before and the percentage of people living in poverty is declining worldwide. As important, the world we live in is dizzying in its variety, breathtaking in its riches, and wide-ranging in its options. Malcontents on the right and left will admit this much: These days we've even got a greater choice of ways to be unhappy.

The topics may have changed from those that appeared in that first mimeographed issue—and lord knows our proofreading skills have improved a bit. But more than 35 years later, these things remain unchanged about *Reason*: a commitment to free minds and free markets; to logic, not legends; and to coherence, not contradictions.

Nick Gillespie
Oxford, Ohio
March 2004

In Praise of Vulgarity

How commercial culture liberates Islam—and the West

Charles Paul Freund

WHO WILL EVER FORGET the strangeness of the first images out of post-Taliban Afghanistan, when the streets ran with beards? As one city after another was abandoned by Taliban soldiers, crowds of happy men lined up to get their first legal shave in years, and barbers enjoyed the busiest days of their lives.

Only a few months earlier, in January 2001, dozens of barbers in the capital city of Kabul had been rounded up by the Taliban's hair-and-beard cops (the Ministry for the Promotion of Virtue and Prevention of Vice) because they had been cutting men's hair in a style known locally as the "Titanic." At the time, Kabul's cooler young men wanted that Leonardo DiCaprio look, the one he sported in the movie. It was an interesting moment in fashion, because under the Taliban's moral regime movies were illegal, Leonardo DiCaprio was illegal, and his hairdo, which allowed strands of hair to fall forward over the face during prayer, was a ticket to jail. Yet thanks to enterprising video smugglers who dragged cassettes over mountain trails by mule, urban Afghans knew perfectly well who DiCaprio was and what he looked like; not only did men adopt his style, but couples celebrated their weddings with Titanic-shaped cakes.

DiCaprio was out of style, even in Kabul, by the time the Taliban's rules were being swept away along with the nation's beard clippings. Men were now measuring their freedom by the smoothness of their chins. "I hated this beard," one happy Afghan told an A.P. reporter. Being shaved was "like being free."

Although it's omitted from the monuments and the rhetoric of liberation, brutal tyrannies have ended on exactly this note before. When Paris was liberated from the Nazis, for example, one Parisian cadged a Lucky Strike from an American reporter, the first cigarette he'd had in a long, long time. As he gratefully exhaled, the Frenchman smiled and told the reporter, "It's the taste of freedom."

Afghan women, of course, removed their burqas, if they chose to, and put on makeup again. But some Afghan women had been breaking the morals laws throughout the period of Taliban bleakness; according to a memorable CNN documentary titled *Beneath the Veil*, they did so at the risk of flogging or even amputation. Courageous women had not only been educating their daughters in secret, but had also been visiting illegal underground cosmetic parlors for the simple pleasure of self-ornamentation and the assertion of self-fashioned identity that lies behind it.

Still other Afghans filled the air with music. The most frequently played tapes, according to press reports, featured the songs of the late Ahmed Zaher, a 1970s celebrity in the Western style. The *Village Voice* has described Zaher as "Afghanistan's Crosby, Presley, and Marley rolled into one," and credited him with introducing original pop compositions into the nation's culture (before Zaher, the usual practice had been to record classical verses set to traditional instrumentation). Enthusiasm for Zaher's work—including his English-language covers of American hits such as "It's Now or Never"—was one of the few things that the country's many ethnic groups had in common. The model of celebrity he established was later imitated by other local singers, including, notably, women.

Afghan shop windows suddenly displayed blow-ups of Indian actresses, who often pose for cheerful cheesecake pinup shots. India's films are very popular in Afghanistan, and Bollywood, as India's Hindi-language movie industry is known, lost almost 10 percent of its total market when the Taliban closed the theaters. When a Kabul theater quickly reopened, mobs of men assembled to see the only print of a Bollywood extravaganza remaining in the country. Crowds grew so large that soldiers had to intervene. For those who couldn't get a ticket, a video store suddenly opened to offer such fare as *Gladiator,*

Police Story, and *Independence Day.*

Other Afghans exhumed the TV sets they had buried in their yards to save them from the autos-da-fé of electronics the Taliban staged in Kabul's soccer stadium. A few Afghans examined the homemade satellite dishes—hammered out of old paint cans—that were arrayed in the streets. Those who didn't have TVs anymore ran out to see what they could get from sellers who had put their black market stocks of electronics on open display. The shoppers were looking for a boom box or for any machine that would help return pleasure to their lives.

In short, the first breath of cultural freedom that Afghans had enjoyed since 1995 was suffused with the stuff of commercially generated popular culture. The people seemed delighted to be able to look like they wanted to, listen to what they wanted to, watch what they wanted to, and generally enjoy themselves again. Who could complain about Afghans' filling their lives with pleasure after being coerced for years to adhere to a harshly enforced ascetic code?

The West's liberal, anti-materialist critics, that's who.

The High Culture Sputter

"How depressing was it," asked Anna Quindlen in a December *Newsweek* column, "to see Afghan citizens celebrating the end of tyranny by buying consumer electronics?" Apparently, if you're somebody like Quindlen—who confessed in the same column that "I have everything I could want, and then some"—the spectacle was pretty dispiriting. Liberty itself descends on the land, and the best thing its people can do is go shopping? It was just too vulgar.

Pulitzer Prize winner Quindlen had given voice to the Cultural Sputter of the *bien-pensant,* a well-known reaction afflicting people of taste forced to live in a world of vulgarities. It's an act with a very long pedigree. Eighteenth-century aristocrats by the palaceful were appalled when professional writers first appeared. Writing in exchange for money, they thought, would be the ruin of letters. John Ruskin, King of Victorian Sputterers, couldn't stand Rembrandt because the Dutch master's paintings lacked "dignity": All those paintings of self-satisfied, bulbous-nosed burghers made Ruskin gag.

The sputter is endlessly adaptable. A notorious space-age version choked Norman Mailer half to death. He was watching astronaut Alan

B. Shepard walking on the moon in 1971, when Shepard suddenly took out a secretly stowed golf club and launched a drive at the lunar horizon. Mailer was spiritually mortified. Humankind should have been humbled, literally on its knees, as it entered the cathedral of the universe; instead it drove golf balls through its windows. What's the matter with people? Give them infinity, and they make it a fairway. Give them liberty, and they reach for a Lucky. Or they go shopping.

There are a lot of sputterers like Quindlen, and they too condemn the substance of Afghanistan's national liberation celebration. Why? Because they think that cultural consumerism—whether nascent as displayed in Kabul or full-blown as in the hedonist West—is the serpent in freedom's garden. When culture and commerce meet, they believe, both democracy and prosperity are poisoned. As for true culture, it hasn't got a chance.

Hence, when Hillary Clinton, then still the first lady, addressed the World Economic Forum in Davos, Switzerland, a couple of years ago, she argued that "there is no doubt that we are creating a consumer-driven culture that promotes values and ethics that undermine both capitalism and democracy." In fact, she said, "I think you could argue that the kind of work ethic, postponement of gratification, and other attributes that are historically associated with capitalism are being undermined by consumer capitalism."

Leave aside the spectacle of making such a speech to some of the world's richest and most privileged people gathered in a highly exclusive Alpine resort. Clinton's message was actually a restatement of a well-known and highly regarded thesis. She'd lifted her text straight out of Daniel Bell's classic 1974 study *The Cultural Contradictions of Capitalism*. Capitalism was built on an ethic of work and duty, Bell argued, but it yields a culture of self-involved pleasure that undermines the attitude necessary for disciplined achievement.

The man of the hour at this nexus of culture, democracy, and commerce, however, is Benjamin R. Barber, a political science professor now at the University of Maryland. As cultural darkness descended on the Afghans, Barber published a 400-page sputter called *Jihad vs. McWorld: How Globalism and Tribalism are Reshaping the World* (1996). His argument was that tradition-bound, often blood-based anti-modernism ("Jihad") is one of two powerful forces in the world undermining true democracy. The other rogue force? "Unrestrained capitalism," especially of the sort displayed by aggressive, resource-depleting, soul-destroying multinational corporations ("McWorld"). Their encounter, he argued, would explode at the expense of the noble communitarian ideal of civil society. Barber's tome was illustrated with a striking image of a woman clad in a black burqa holding a can of Pepsi, the Western drink of "choice" throughout most of the Arab and Islamic world.

Barber's approach to this tangle of issues is in some ways the flip side of the school that derives from Daniel Bell. While Bell's group sees capitalism under threat from its own debased culture, Barber, drawing on the critique of the old Frankfort School of cultural Marxists, sees not only democracy but culture itself—in the grand sense—under siege by an inevitably debasing capitalism.

"McWorld," writes Barber, "is a product of popular culture driven by expansionist commerce. Its template is American, its form style. Its goods are as much images as materiel, an aesthetic as well as a product line. It is about culture as commodity, apparel as ideology." It is, in short, about the imposition of Americanized, commercial meaning on daily life, an act those Jihadists, who take their meaning from the transcendent, are bound to resist by any means necessary.

If one takes these complementary critiques as a set, one cannot escape an overpowering conclusion: The capitalist system is doomed, suicidal. In fact, it has been destroying itself since its appearance. These critics have isolated democracy, capitalism, and culture from one another, and have each of them surrounded by the others. Real democracy can't survive because it is choked by a capitalist "culture" driven by money and power; true culture can't survive because it is destroyed by capitalism's manufactured populism; capitalist prosperity can't survive because it is undermined by the anti-democratic forces of self-absorption that it unleashes.

In other words, whichever route one takes in this intellectual landscape, it descends into the same perdition. As for the Afghans, they're halfway to hell despite—or more precisely, because of—a national aftershave shortage.

Taste and Distaste

But wait. Barber has a solution to commercial damnation. Salvation, he has suggested, lies in good taste. Strangely enough, his good taste.

Jihad vs. McWorld made few ripples when it first appeared, but it found its readership in the wake of September 11, when it was reprinted in a large new edition. Despite its "Jihad" paradigm, and despite a cover featuring a veiled woman, Barber's book is only incidentally about Islam.

Nevertheless, as the United States began its military assault against the Taliban regime, Barber was suddenly in great demand, offering audiences and interviewers a Big Picture analysis of what was going on in the world and what we should do about it.

One of the things we should do, Barber argued, is to stop defiling the world with the crass products of our cultural machine. Why should we stop? Because Barber thinks it's all "garbage."

"I mean, we don't even export the best of our own culture," he sputtered to the *Washington Post* in November, in the course of an admiring profile. Our cultural best, thinks Barber, is "defined by serious music, by jazz, by poetry, by our extraordinary literature, our playwrights—we export the worst, the most childish, the most base, the most trivial of our culture. And we call that American."

Of course, cultural artifacts and styles that are "base" and "trivial," according to Barber and others like him, are exactly what many Afghans longed for while under the Taliban heel and what they turned to the minute they had the chance. They wanted to adorn themselves according to fleeting style, to hear pop hits, to watch escapist movies. A lot of the things Afghans sought were American products, and those that weren't are recognizably based on commercial models developed in the United States (e.g., Bollywood movies). Afghans may have thought their troubles—at least those troubles involving small pleasures—were over. Barber explains why their troubles were only beginning.

By immersing themselves in such made-for-profit vulgarity, Barber argues, people—be they Afghans or any other benighted group—undermine any hope they might have of achieving a just, civil society. Instead they enslave themselves to the West's cultural marketers (or their Eastern imitators). Instead of pursuing a democratic civil ideal, people will waste their time and money on a poisonous bath of selfish consumerism. The Afghans were buying consumer electronics before the shooting stopped; tomorrow or the next day, they'll be manipulated into wearing $200 sneakers. If there's one thing that critics of consumerism know, it's that neither Afghans nor any other people "need" such things.

The notion that there are consumerist "needs" is a founding capitalist delusion. As Barber puts it, consumer choice is a "charming fraud."

What, then, is the appropriate cultural path to democracy? Barber told the *Post* that if the U.S. must export culture it should at least export its "best." There's an obvious problem with the list Barber offers, since many of his examples of cultural quality—jazz, novels, Broadway theater—were themselves assailed as intolerably vulgar by contemporary critics who were disgusted at their appearance. But Barber surely realizes that, so we can assume he's getting at something else. He's singing in praise of culture that doesn't pander, of culture that teaches and leaves us thinking, of visionary art that lifts us morally and makes us better by challenging us. In short, he's a champion of what might be called contemplative art. That is not an art of commerce; it is an art of patronage, of enlightened taste. If you can imagine those Afghan video smugglers loading their mules with fewer copies of Titanic and more dubs of PBS programs, then you can imagine Western liberal critics being more optimistic about the prospects for Central Asian democracy.

Is Barber right? He is about one thing: The issue here is taste. But taste in this case has nothing at all to do with perceived quality. To approach it that way is to run an endless round of Hell's nine circles, only to arrive back at oneself. Thus Barber concludes that what the world should do now is attend his favorite plays.

What this taste debate is about is meaning, the meaning that style and artifacts have for those who seek them out and consume them. The reason many critics see the world devolving into vulgar chaos is that they see a world filled with artifacts, nearly all of them disposable, that have no meaning to them. It's all just "garbage": the "base," the "most trivial," the "worst." But what if these disposable artifacts actually do have meaning? Does the devolving world suddenly look any different? Do democracy, capitalism, and culture still have each other surrounded?

As it happens, the 20th century conducted a series of real-life experiments on just this subject. At various times and in various places, commerce, culture, and freedom have been isolated from one another, while taste was allowed to compete with meaning. For those who lived through some of these experiments, the experience was one of extended misery. Indeed, for some, that misery continues. But the lessons are fascinating, and the West has yet to absorb them.

The Style of Anti-Stalinism

In the 1980s, the Soviet Union was confronted by a wave of Islamism in its Central Asian Republics; it was exactly the same phenomenon that was to break the Soviets in Afghanistan. Moscow thought it knew just how to combat it. It started beaming Western rock music in Islamism's direction, the idea being that sensual degeneracy (in Soviet terms) would undermine the appeal of religious transcendence. This is Benjamin R. Barber's thesis turned inside out, but for all that it may be its best example in real life. "McWorld" was really at war with "Jihad," though the forces of McWorld had been marshaled by the anti-capitalist Soviets against a Jihad supported militarily, at least in Afghanistan, by capitalist America. Who says communism lacked a sense of irony?

The Soviets' rock gambit didn't work. Why? Because you can't export meaning the way you can export anti-aircraft Stingers. To move culture, you need an array of tricky requirements, from willing early receivers to adapters who will transmute it into local terms (like the singer Ahmed Zaher) to diffusionists who will spread it. But even with all that in place, you're still not moving meaning. You can't export meaning at all.

By the 1980s, the people who should have understood these issues better than anyone were the Soviets themselves, because they had been on the receiving end of a cultural transfer that had largely undone them. The Soviets even should have known how and where meaning can arise in such a process.

In the USSR, it was low, disruptive culture that generated a "consumerist" demand for the artifacts that embodied its values as well as a popular demand for the freedom to engage in its activities. Because neither consumerism nor democratic freedoms existed in the country, shadow versions of both eventually developed. The entire process, from beginning to end, was founded on vulgarity. Here's what happened.

Some extraordinary and totally unexpected figures appeared on the streets of Moscow in 1949 and in other major cities of the Soviet Bloc soon afterward. They wore jackets with huge, padded shoulders and pants with narrow legs. They were clean-shaven, but they let their hair grow long, covered it with grease, and flipped it up at the back. They sported unusually colorful ties, which they let hang well below their belts. What their fellow Muscovites most noticed about them, for some reason, were their shoes, which were oversized, with thick soles. There were some women in the movement as well, notable for their short, tight skirts and very heavy lipstick.

Although they were Russians, they called each other by such names as "Bob" and "Joe." In Moscow, they referred to their hangout, Gorki Prospekt, as "Broadway." They chewed gum, they affected an odd walk that involved stretching their necks as they went down the street, and they loved to listen to American jazz.

These young men were to become known in Russian as *stilyagi*, a term that is usually translated as "style hunters"; their story has been told by a number of authors, including Artemy Troitsky, Timothy W. Ryback, and S. Frederick Starr. The stilyagi constitute one of the most remarkable movements in the rich history of oppositional subcultures. What they had turned themselves into were walking cultural protests against Stalinism in one of its most paranoid periods. All that Stalin had melted into air, the stilyagi made flesh.

In the years after World War II, Stalin attempted to extirpate every aspect of American culture from Soviet life. Jazz, which had been played publicly in the USSR as recently as the war years, was now officially regarded as decadent capitalist filth; to even speak of jazz during this period was a criminal act. The same was true of anything American: It was all capitalist decadence, and it was all dangerous and usually illegal. In reaction, the stilyagi did not merely embrace American culture in secret; they actually appropriated American characters ("Joe," "Bob"), as they understood them, and took them into public. Indeed, they borrowed American cultural geography ("Broadway") and laid it over Stalin's.

But what is most striking about the American personae assumed by the stilyagi was that these alternate personalities were built out of vulgarisms. Mind you, this was not vulgarity as only the insane Stalinist cultural apparatus would define it, but a strident, studied vulgarity that made even Western elites grimace when they saw it in their own streets. The stilyagi were zoot suiters, loud-tie-wearing, gum-smack-ing, slang-using, greasy jazz-heads in need of haircuts. Their protest was not a matter of distributing banned poetry texts; it was a public act, complete with role names, costumes, and even a peculiar behav-ior that was intended to call attention to itself.

It wasn't only the authorities with whom the stilyagi had to con-tend; it was everyone. Being a stilyaga was truly isolating, and the public reaction was brutal. Their fellow Muscovites taunted them on the sidewalks and on the streetcars, loudly criticizing their appear-ance, hurling insults at them, sometimes attacking them. Obviously, the Communist press took notice of them, terming them subversive and linking them to criminal elements. Inevitably, the police also went after them. When the cops didn't arrest them, they gave the stilyagi impromptu street haircuts or, interestingly, slashed their clothes.

Improvising an Image

Where did the stilyagi get their look and behavior? They assembled their personae from the bits and pieces of low American culture to which they briefly had access. The men's hair, for example, came from Tarzan movies. Stalin had been quite taken by *Tarzan* and had previously allowed several Johnny Weismuller films into the country. Soviet critics, however, had afterward attacked the character as rep-resenting the savagery and base sexuality of the capitalist West. That was all the stilyagi had to hear. The gum chewing seems to have been borrowed from James Cagney movies that had been exhibited; as reputed celebrations of disorder and criminality, gangsterisms were naturally absorbed into the style. Other details were borrowed from disparate sources or simply made up.

But the truly impressive achievement of the stilyagi was in creating the material elements of their protest. Remember, this was the heart of Stalinist darkness: There were no marketers to exploit the stilyagi, no merchandising apparatus to lure them into the desire for false con-sumerist needs. Instead, the stilyagi had to manufacture almost every-thing themselves. Their artifacts were the expression of a pre-existing meaning, of an opposition to the stifling repression of Stalinism. The stilyagi created their hair, clothing, and slang styles as a means of achieving the identities they were struggling to assume.

To do so, they were often brilliantly resourceful. Where did they get their loud ties, for example? They weren't going to find what they wanted in the state-run GUM department store near Red Square; there were no chains of tie shops. Instead, they took whatever ties they had and literally painted over them, or they cut ties from whatever appealing swath of fabric they might locate, whether it was in the black market or hanging over their windows as a curtain. (Prague's version of the stilyagi affixed pieces of American cigarette packaging to their self-made ties.)

Who did their hair? The style wasn't merely lengthy, recall; it was flipped. There were no stylists who would sell them a look; they had to do it themselves. Using heated rods, they styled one another's hair in their kitchens; old stilyagi would later remember walking around all the time with burns on their necks. Some stilyagi obtained the leather for their notorious shoes from the black market, too. They had to peg their own pants. They couldn't even locate genuine chewing gum, so they substituted paraffin wax.

But the crowning achievement lay in their music collections. Jazz survived in the Soviet Union in some astonishing circumstances. As jazz historian S. Frederick Starr has recounted, many of the country's best musicians were actually in Siberian prison camps, but these camps were in many cases ruled by commanders who liked jazz and who organized the musicians to play for their often-lavish parties. Prison camp commanders would even exchange these jazz groups, allowing them to "tour," as it were, camps where countless prisoners were being worked, starved, and frozen to death. Other bands were exiled to remote cities, such as Kazan in the Tartar region, where they were supposed to undergo "rehabilitation." Instead, these groups, many of which had learned jazz in pre-Mao Shanghai, took advantage of the local officials' musical ignorance, and played jazz anyway. In Kazan, the courageous bands even performed on Tartar State Radio. That's how the early stilyagi kept up with the music: by monitoring Tartar broadcasts to hear exiled musicians outsmarting their cultural keepers.

But the stilyagi managed not only to hear jazz, but to assemble collections of recordings too. How? They had turntables, but they certainly couldn't buy jazz records in record stores (there weren't any). They couldn't tape what they heard on the radio. Even assuming they could get access to a reel-to-reel recorder, where were they going to get enough blank tape? The solution was a piece of genius. A jazz-loving medical student realized that he could inscribe sound grooves on the surface of a medium that was actually plentiful in the Soviet Union: old X-ray plates. He rigged a contraption that allowed him to produce "recordings" that, while obviously of low quality, at least contained the precious music and allowed its admirers to listen to it at will. He and his imitators were to make a lot of well-earned money on the black market.

The stilyagi were eventually transformed by a series of changes in their world. Stalin died in 1953, and Nikita Khrushchev inaugurated the so-called cultural thaw in 1956. In the meantime, the Voice of America began transmitting jazz to the USSR via shortwave. The surviving prisoner-musicians of the USSR were still playing big band arrangements; they—along with their "audience"—had been completely isolated from the international music scene and had no idea what had been happening. Thanks to VOA jazz DJ Willis Conover, however, the Soviet Bloc started hearing bebop. Its expressive improvisation electrified the stilyagi and their scene started going cool.

In 1957 a stilyagi dream came true. Despite Khrushchev's complaint that jazz gave him gas, American jazz musicians came to Moscow to play at a festival. The stilyagi who showed up in their notorious costume finery, however, sensed the inconsistency between their self-presentation and the cool music they were embracing. It was a bittersweet moment. They went home, put away the loud ties, and started giving each other Gerry Mulligan crew cuts.

But the cultural problems for Soviet authorities were just beginning. Russian athletes had returned from the 1956 Olympics in Melbourne, Australia, with something new: rock music. Built on the foundation prepared by the stilyagi, the Soviet Bloc rock subculture (complete with music on X-ray plates called "rock on ribs") was soon to become far, far bigger than the stilyagi scene had ever been. It was filled with innovations of its own, eventually adopting Western clothes, especially jeans. Entrepreneurs leased pictures of Western acts to fans for limited periods (remember, there were no publicly available Xerox machines under communism); exploited new technology, especially the cassette tape; and formed illegal bands that staged illegal concerts. Eventually, the Soviet Bloc rock scene grew into an alternate world, complete with a string of safe houses that one could use to inhabit the counterculture no matter where one went.

Soviet authorities tried everything to combat the rock subculture. They banned it, belittled it, and co-opted it with state-approved rock bands. They even instructed the gymnastic bureaucracy to invent "official" rock dances consistent with socialist values, which they then pushed on Soviet TV. Obviously, nothing worked, and nothing could have worked.

The point of the various musical countercultures under the Soviets was not simply to hear music. What the authorities never understood, and what many cultural critics in the West similarly don't understand, is that the fans who inhabit such "vulgar" and disruptive subcultures are not being exploited. It is the fans who are using both the music scene and the paraphernalia that surrounds it for their own expressive purposes. If there is no one to sell them the paraphernalia—the clothes, the imagery, the recordings—then the members of these subcultures will not go without it. They will create it themselves.

There was simply no way for the Soviet system to come to terms with this and remain true to its authoritarianism. In the end, it wasn't the musical subcultures that were delegitimized but Soviet authority. The inability of such a system to allow its citizens to construct their own cultural identities—that is, to meet their "consumer demands"—was a major factor in robbing communism of credibility among its own populations.

Rai Spell

Although the Soviets never understood how to use music to oppose Islamism, a segment of the Algerian populace did. Indeed, throughout the period that the USSR was vainly beaming Western pop at Central Asia's Islamists, Algerians were using their own music and their own cultural tradition in a struggle against North Africa's fundamentalists.

That struggle illustrates how broad-based culture, popular and vulgar, is far from being a mere distraction or a source of self-absorption. As Islamists have learned, it can function as a bulwark against coercion. More than that, it can even be a means of democratic resort. Here's how it worked in Algeria.

In 1994 a young man named Cheb Hasni was shot and killed outside the home he shared with his parents in the Algerian port city of Oran. His crime? He was a singer of *rai* songs, an Algerian musical style that was as controversial as it was popular. Hasni was known as the "Prince of Rai" and had recorded more than 80 cassettes of the music. His murder is often perceived as the climax of the so-called war against rai being waged by Algeria's notoriously vicious Islamists. The religious zealots see rai music as the apotheosis of a secular culture they consider lewd and impious. But nobody really knows who killed Hasni. A conspiracist view of Hasni's death maintains that he was actually assassinated by the anti-Islamist military, who then blamed his death on religious militants so as to inflame further an already seething rai world.

This much is clear: By the time of Hasni's death, rai music was a major front in the confrontation between Algerian Islamism and the secular forces it sought to overcome. What is rai? The style is at least a century old and has deep folkloric roots, but it is the late, vulgarized form that is at issue. Rod Skilbeck, one of many academics who have studied it, asserts that in its modern form rai has developed into a kind of Algerian blues, "singing of alienation, poverty, drug and alcohol abuse, and forbidden sexual desires. Hedonism, existentialism, suffering, and total inaction became major structural elements." Despite the fact that it often serves as "background" music, its content has increasingly reflected the worldly, urban concerns of its listeners.

The "rai war" erupted in earnest in the wake of the 1990 elections, when Islamists came to power in many cities. Among their first acts was to close nightclubs, prohibit alcohol, and ban rai. Some Islamists would stone rai fans when they attempted to stage concerts. In 1991 fundamentalists tried to burn down a crowded hall during a performance. In 1994 a leading Berber singer was kidnapped by Islamists; he was reportedly "tried" on religious grounds and then released. After Hasni's murder that year, many rai singers emigrated to France.

For their part, rai singers would mix provocative, supposedly pornographic lyrics with openly anti-Islamist messages in their music, and some rai fans were drawn to the scene at least in part because of the secularist meaning they perceived in it. A famous rai anthem of 1988, "To Flee, But Where?," asks: "Where has youth gone?/Where are the brave ones?/The rich gorge themselves/The poor work themselves to death/The Islamic charlatans show their true face."

In the course of its confrontation with both governmental authority and the rising Islamist challenge, the rai world took on the characteristics of an oppositional subculture, reinforcing certain aspects of its participants' identities. At least some rai cultural statements were militantly anti-Islamist. For example, the 1997 film *100 Percent Arabica*, made in France by the Algerian writer and filmmaker Mahmoud Zemmouri, uses such leading rai stars as Khaled and Cheb Mami to portray the rai world as a culture of hope beset by mullahs who are revealed as criminal hypocrites.

The Islamist campaign to take over Algeria has not succeeded. The country's military eventually took control of the government with the apparent support of many secularists who feared that the alternative was an Islamic state on the model of Iran. Islamists have massacred tens of thousands of people in the ensuing civil war.

But if democratic values are stymied in the political sphere, they remain alive culturally. Algerian rai is a vulgar form by elite standards, one that addresses "low" subjects of sexual desire through a "base" model of popular celebrity. It is diffused by way of cheap and widely available consumer electronics and is a potential means for the gradual reordering of the society around the music.

Specifically, it is capable of giving voice to powerless outgroups, and of helping to redefine the position of women and changing the relationship of the sexes. Nor would such a gradualist revolution be peculiar to Algeria. British society began a similar reordering of social roles in the 18th century using similar means. In that case, the vulgar form at issue was popular, escapist fiction of the kind that critics feared would fill women's heads with all manner of bad desires. The United States experienced a similar process of change in the 19th century. Indeed, the revolutionary change in the values of both societies was to pave the way for a series of historic humanitarian reforms.

In other words, the confluence of markets and culture has repeatedly advanced democratic values, because it has allowed a series of outgroups—women, blacks, Jews, gays, etc.—successfully to address the larger society about injustice and inequality. Such appeals have been successful precisely because of their "vulgar" forms. It is because they have involved such emotionally compelling forms as music and melodrama that they have induced their audiences to experience a given injustice through the eyes of those suffering from it. Justice's medium is empathy, and empathy's medium is more often the melodrama than it is the manifesto. In short, it is the broad-based culture that emerges from markets that frequently serves as a means of democratic self-correction.

Spice Grrls

Rai music has become a conduit for protest against the external world of authority and poverty. But it has also opened possibilities for other protests, including protest against its own world. For example, many rai songs address fantasies of illicit sex. In the tradition-bound, male-dominated world of North African societies, the women in such fantasies would be completely objectified types: women of pleasure whom one might encounter in a cabaret; women who dance, smoke, and drink alcohol. These are not prostitutes, but rather women who enjoy pleasure as a value in itself. The type, writes Danish academic Marc Schade-Poulsen, is known as a *maryula*.

In the course of rai's contemporary development, women singers have intervened in this male fantasy narrative. First, they have emerged as performers in their own right, building on the success of such Arab women singers as Asmahan and Umm Kulthum, two major Egyptian stars of earlier generations. As public celebrities, such singers provide new, assertive role models for women, in contrast to the low social status of traditional women performers. Second, they legitimize the content of their music as appropriate expressions for women.

Women rai singers do not only address love and personal happiness: Some of them have chosen to embody the personae of the female libertines that appear in male lyrics. These women perform under such professional names as Chaba "Zahouania," a word that Schade-Poulsen defines as "having the sense of being merry, joyous, fond of good living." The implication of this role playing is that the choice made by the maryula is legitimate: Women have a right to pleasure. If they have such a right, then the independence to make such a choice is a requirement. In other words, some women rai performers have used the very objectification of their role in the music to assert their right to independence.

This parallels closely what British and American women authors of escapist literature did with the concept of "virtue" in the 18th and 19th centuries. The rise of popular fiction featured the emergence of various fantasy adventures, especially the theme of "virtue in distress," in which a good and decent woman was threatened by a more powerful male villain. A series of women authors, notably the gothic specialist Ann Radcliffe, used this notion of womanly "virtue" to challenge the very idea of manly strength. As the women's-studies academic G. J. Barker-Benfield has noted, their argument was that if men too sought virtue, then they must attune themselves to what they professed to admire in feminine sensibilities. One of the results of their efforts was the emergence of the "man of feeling."

These women too were intervening in men's fantasies, turning the apparent weakness of their roles into a challenge that helped lead to moral recognition and, eventually, legal rights. Radcliffe was to intensify her argument by inventing the mechanics of suspense; she involved her readers emotionally in the fate of her virtuous characters. Radcliffe and her cohorts were overlooked in the literary histories; their lachrymose characters and creaking plots were not judged to have stood the "test of time." Yet the fact remains that they changed their time far more than did many of their more celebrated literary contemporaries.

Rai music has hardly resulted in egalitarian North African societies, but it is precisely this kind of force that will eventually facilitate social change. The potentially liberating forces that are new, by the way, are products of the market: diffusion via cheap technology. The dangerous idea that is being diffused—libertine eroticism—is not. It's been present in Islamic culture all along and is not a Western import.

In some ways, the rai scene appears to percolate with Westernisms. Ray-Ban sunglasses and backward-worn baseball caps (imported from Morocco and sold on the black market) are part of its costume. Although the music's roots are entirely Algerian, some of its modern instrumentation is obviously borrowed from Western influences. Rai owes its status as a pop form to the cassette tape recorder, and its current youth-oriented celebrity structure appears to follow a familiar model pioneered in the West.

There is a suggestion among defenders of Islamism and critics of Western culture that surviving moral traditions are being undercut by commercial baseness. Both groups are making unhistorical arguments that severely distort the cultural reality. After all, libertinism has a long tradition in North Africa.

Rod Skilbeck cites an example of the kind of lyric that angers Islamists: "Oh my love, to gaze upon you is sin/It's you who makes me break my fast . . . /It's you who makes me 'eat' during Ramadan." The same artist, Rimitti (a woman more than 70 years old), adds, "People adore God, I adore beer." Not only are the lyrics impious, they subversively use sacred references to underscore their sexuality and advance their impiety.

Here's another text, one that actually addresses Satan, demanding that the devil restore a missing lover. If he doesn't, the singer makes the following threat: "I'll read the Koran! I'll start/a Koranic Night School for Adults!/I'll make the pilgrimage to Mecca every year/and accumulate so much virtue that I'll . . . I'll . . . ." At that point, the lover is restored. "It was twice as good as before!" the singer exclaims, adding, "I've been on the best of terms/with the Father of Lies." The missing lover is identified by the male poet as "my boy."

The first text is recent; the second one, addressed to Satan and threatening Koranic virtue, is from the poet Abu Nuwas, who wrote erotic poetry to both men and women in the eighth century. Arabic poetry is extraordinarily rich, and one of its most striking strains involves the erotic in a context of religious skepticism. Even caliphs wrote erotic poetry. Indeed, there is a centuries-old tradition of Islamic poetry celebrating the pleasures of wine, sex, singing girls, and beardless young male cupbearers.

While there have certainly been periods of ascendant religious piety, there is a good case that it is modern, censorious Islamist pietism that is the newer development in the Muslim world, and that the celebration of "vulgar" pleasures predates it.

If the Hush Puppies Fit

Speaking of those reversed baseball caps worn by rai's fans, why did so many people in the West start wearing them that way in the first place? Was there an ad campaign of some kind that set the model? Was it part of a vast corporate strategy to instill a pointless "need" in stupid Western consumers and subsequently sell a lot of hats? What about those notorious, logo-heavy athletic shoes? People don't really "need" those, do they? Where did "grunge" come from? Did the flannel industry invent it because the lumberjack market was shrinking along with virgin-growth forests? What about Goth? Did some mascara factory accidentally make a batch too much and invent Goth to sell the overstock? How are such phenomena born, anyway?

Capitalism's critics in the West blame what they call "the culture industry," which makes itself rich by aggressively manipulating consumerist idiots. The latter part with their money because they have been persuaded that some truly useless but expensive object will make them hip, youthful, or desirable, or raise their status. This manipulative scheme is now a global enterprise, filling the world with what Benjamin Barber and his ilk castigate as "junk." Worse, say the Daniel Bells and Hillary Clintons, it's a threat to Western prosperity, because it instills self-absorption at the expense of the work ethic.

This critique completely misses the point of cultural commerce. The citizens of the post-subsistence world have a historically remarkable luxury: They can experiment with who they are. They can fashion and refashion their identities, and through much of their lives that is just what they do. They can go about this in a lot of ways, but one of the most important methods is what is known and reviled as "consumerism." They experiment with different modes of self-presentation, assert or mask aspects of their individuality, join or leave a series of subcultures, or oppose and adhere to centers of power. It is from this complex mix that the things of the material world become the furnishings of both a social and a personal identity. That's what meaning is.

Consumerism of this sort has been born and reborn many times. The extended and apparently open-ended chapter in which the Western world has been wallowing began in 17th-century Britain, Holland, and other European trade centers. It is still being reborn all over the world, as people grab the first opportunity to escape the traditionalist boundaries of selfhood. Yet this is the very spectacle that depresses the West's anti-consumerist critics and makes them sputter.

Far from being a drain on prosperity, the drive to create and recreate identity has proven irresistible, even in circumstances where no cultural industry exists. Where such industries do exist, self-fashioning immediately becomes an engine of the economy. As British scholars John Golby and William Purdue observed in their 1984 study of the origins of industrialist popular culture, the key factor in the increasingly positive attitude toward work in the 18th century was neither religion nor legislation but "the growth of new patterns of leisure and consumption," primed by wage increases. Generally speaking, workers didn't start punching the clock because they were forced to but because they wanted to. Regular hours—and regular wages—gave them more time and money to buy and enjoy the crass, vulgar, and base artifacts from which they fashioned their senses of self. In other words, the evidence from the beginning has been that culture, capitalism, and democracy actually reinforce one another.

The opportunity to create and revise one's identity is by its nature an anti-authoritarian enterprise, and that is nowhere more obviously demonstrated than in the reviled Western cult of "cool." Successful culture industries don't try to manipulate their customers; they long ago learned that they cannot imbue their products with meaning. Rather, they attempt to engage in "meaning" intelligence, spending vast amounts to identify rapidly changing meanings, meanings they know will change yet again the moment that the same public catches the first whiff of marketing. In other words, the most successful among the cultural industrialists are not leading their customers at all; that isn't possible. The best they can do is try to follow them.

The best description of this process is a 1997 *New Yorker* essay by Malcolm Gladwell called "The Coolhunt." Gladwell describes a telling cultural moment involving the makers of Hush Puppies shoes. A few years ago, nobody wanted the suede shoes except a dwindling number of older customers. They'd become passé. Even the manufacturers wanted to drop the old line of "Dukes" and "Columbias" and get into so-called "aspirational shoes." The company wanted to introduce something called the "Mall Walker."

"But then something strange started happening," writes Gladwell. "Two Hush Puppies executives . . . were doing a fashion shoot for their Mall Walkers and ran into a creative consultant from Manhattan named Jeffrey Miller, who informed them that the Dukes and the Columbias weren't dead, they were dead chic." People in Manhattan were scouring thrift stores for them; Hush Puppies were turning up in hip fashion shoots. Hush Puppies executives were as mystified as they were pleased. They were the beneficiaries of a process over which the market has no control: They'd become cool.

The best that the West's cultural industrialists can hope for, as Gladwell argues, is a well-timed intervention in cool. They can try to associate a product with a (temporarily) cool celebrity; they can pay to "place" their product in a film that they hope will be cool, they can try to subordinate their product to a currently cool subculture, as Sprite has done with rap music. Sometimes they succeed, but even when they do, their process begins again the next day.

More frequently, these efforts do not succeed at all, and for the same reason that Soviet teenagers rejected "official" socialist dances, and that Central Asian listeners rejected the Western music beamed at them from Moscow: Culture is built around meaning, and meaning proceeds from one's self.

Cultural Exchange

From mid-century to communism's end, the Soviet Bloc and the United States engaged in an official exchange of contemplative art forms. The U.S. actually sent its "best" abroad, exactly as Benjamin Barber wishes it would do today.

The process was largely a charade. Not that the material being exchanged wasn't good—it was often very good—but it was unrepresentative of what was going on in either country. Still, the arrangement was a good deal for the Soviets. They had under their control many extremely talented poets, filmmakers, dancers, and musicians, and—in contrast to the vulgar, commercialized West—they were thus able to position themselves as enlightened patrons of the fine arts, in the best European aristocratic tradition.

The United States, for its part, counted it as a victory when a member of the Bolshoi would hop an airport turnstile and defect. When some American would actually beat the Russians in an elitist competition— concert pianist Van Cliburn, chess master Bobby Fischer—Americans would celebrate them as national heroes. It never occurred to the West that the Soviet system was, in the meantime, being undone by the likes of Paul Anka (much more popular among Soviet fans than was Elvis, whom they simply never understood). Anyone who would have tried to make such a case would have been dismissed as simply not serious.

The West has never been comfortable with its own cultural vulgarity. Such anxiety is arguably strongest in the United States, which has long nursed a cultural inferiority complex vis-à-vis more-established British and European practitioners of high art. Popular, commercial forms are not thoughtful. Rather, they are temporary, noisy, intense, ecstatic. They are sensual and disruptive. Because they are frequently set in motion by powerless and even despised outgroups, they appear subversive. They not only threaten social morals, but challenge established power relationships.

The result is that such ecstatic forms are attacked not only by the West's left-liberal critics for their commercial origin, but by the West's conservatives for their disruptive power. Cultural ecstasy may have billions of participants, but it hardly has a single friend.

For the last 200 years, vulgar forms and subcultures have often set off a series of "moral panics" among those who perceive a threat to their own cultural power and status. The popular novel, when it first appeared, set one off. So did penny dreadfuls and pulps. So did melodramatic theater. So did the music hall. So did the tabloid press, and the waltz, and ragtime, and jazz, and radio, movies, comic books, rock music, television, rap, and computer games.

All of these—and more—led contemporary critics to declare the end of civility, to worry over some newly identified form of supposed "addiction" (to novels, to TV, to video games, to pornography, to the Internet, to Pokémon, etc.), to announce that the coming generation was "desensitized," and to rail about childishness and triviality. It's the cultural sputter that never ends.

In democratic societies, most such panics simply run their course until the media tire of them. (Drug prohibition remains a singular exception.) Thus, the generation that in the 1950s was dismissed as Elvis-loving, hot-rod-building, gum-chewing, hog-riding, leather-wearing, juvenile-delinquent barbarians eventually achieved a mature respectability in which the artifacts of their vulgarity became sought-after nostalgia, and even a beloved part of the common cultural heritage. In less than two decades, the menacing hoods of *Blackboard Jungle* became the lovable leads in *Grease*. By then, however, that same generation had become, in its turn, concerned about the disruptive social effects of rap music and violent electronic gaming.

In places where the moral order is the legal order, however, ecstatic forms and assertive ways of being remain matters for the police. In December, Cambodia's prime minister ordered tanks to raze the country's karaoke parlors. Last fall, Iran announced a new campaign against Western pop music and other "signs and symbols of depravity." And only last summer, the Central Asian Republic of Kazakhstan—just a few hundred miles north of Afghanistan—began a crackdown on dangerous "bohemian" lifestyles. The authorities went after a number of familiar outsiders—gays, religious dissidents—but even Westerners were surprised to learn that one targeted group was "Tolkienists." It turns out that there are Kazakh Hobbit wannabes who like to dress up in character costume and re-enact scenes from J.R.R. Tolkien's novels. For their trouble, they were being subjected to sustained water torture.

Hobbit re-enactors in Kazakhstan? Where do they get their paraphernalia? Are there Kazakh Tolkienist fanzines? Have fans started changing Tolkien's narratives to suit themselves, the way Western *Star Trek* subcultures turned their own obsession into soft-core pornography? Do re-enactors change roles from time to time, or are any of them trapped inside a Frodo persona? Is there no end to the identities waiting to be assumed? No end to what invention makes flesh, before it tosses it aside and starts again?

March 2003

After Socialism

Now the greatest threats to freedom come
from those seeking stability and
the 'one best way.'

Virginia Postrel

IN 1947, A SMALL GROUP OF CLASSICAL LIBERAL INTELLECTUALS gathered
in the Swiss Alps to form an international society whose purpose was
"to work out the principles which would secure the preservation of a
free society." Named for their meeting place, the Mont Pelerin Society was the brainchild of Friedrich Hayek, the economist and social
philosopher whose popular book *The Road to Serfdom* had been a sensation only a few years earlier. The 39 founding members included
future Nobel laureate economists Milton Friedman, George Stigler,
and Maurice Allais (and Hayek himself) as well as such luminaries
as philosophers Karl Popper and Michael Polanyi and Hayek's men-
tor Ludwig von Mises. Through intellectual camaraderie and rigorous
discussion, they sought to achieve "the rebirth of a liberal movement
in Europe" and, by implication, the rest of the world.

Fifty-two years later, both the society and the world have changed.
Liberal ideals of free minds and free markets have indeed enjoyed
a rebirth, not only in Europe but throughout the world. And Mont
Pelerin now boasts a membership of nearly 500, including scholars,
journalists, think tank researchers, and business people. In late August, those from the Americas met in Vancouver to take up the question, "Are we experiencing 'creeping socialism?'" In 1947, socialism's
growth was obvious. In 1999, it was a matter of much debate. In one
of the opening talks, *Reason* Editor Virginia Postrel argued that "so-

cialism" is no longer the major challenge to markets and economic freedom and that classical liberal ideals face opponents with new arguments and different values. The following is a slightly adapted version of her speech.

The theme of this conference is "Are we experiencing 'creeping socialism,'" and I am supposed to provide the optimistic answer to that question. The format presumes, however, that it is the right question, which I don't believe it is.

But I'll start with the official question. It immediately raises the issue of what we mean by *socialism*, creeping or otherwise. As a good journalist, I'll begin with an anecdote: The week of our graduation from college in 1982, my husband (who was then my boyfriend) participated in a debate between two teams of graduating seniors. The resolution was something like, "Resolved: Socialism is better than capitalism," and Steve, not surprisingly, was on the anti-socialism side.

One of the critical terms of that debate was the definition of *socialism*. Steve's team argued that socialism was the Soviet Union and therefore guilty of the terrors of the Soviet system, while the opposing side argued that socialism was Sweden, and therefore innocent of eroding political freedom. Seventeen years later, we are gathered to examine whether socialism is expanding—and I would argue that the terms of that debate suggest quite clearly that it is not. Neither the Soviet system nor the Swedish system is on the march.

That does not mean we don't have to worry about threats to liberty. It just means we don't have to worry very much about *socialism*. The issues that define our political, intellectual, and cultural coalitions are changing, and we ignore those changes to our peril.

Socialism is not simply a synonym for a large state or for government regulation of the economy. In both the nasty Soviet model and the nice Swedish one, it is particularly concerned with some issues and less concerned with others. It may be a fuzzy term, but, like an electron's quantum field, the fuzz forms around some places and not around others. The goal of socialism is a fairer allocation of economic resources, which its advocates often claim will also be a less wasteful one. Socialism is about who gets the goods and how. Socialism objects to markets because markets allocate resources in ways socialists believe to be unfair on both counts: both the who and the how.

In its pure form—what Hayek in *The Road to Serfdom* called "hot socialism"—socialism essentially turns the economy into a government monopoly, either through direct state ownership of the means of production or through complete state direction of economic life. Socialist governments nationalize industries. They set up boards governing wages and prices. They direct supply and demand.

Until the mid-1980s, this sort of socialism was common, not only in communist countries but throughout the free world—which is why it made for a good debate topic in 1982. During my teenage years, the American economy itself was marked by wage and price controls and complex schemes to allocate energy supplies; in the 1970s, you could call for the U.S. government to nationalize the oil industry and not be dismissed as a nut. (I would argue, and do in *The Future and Its Enemies*, that the U.S. regulatory system is better understood as technocracy, which substitutes the judgments of supposedly efficient experts for diffuse market decisions, than as socialism. But from time to time, the U.S. government did adopt both the methods and the goals of socialism.) Today, the remnants of hot socialism exist in the very few countries with deliberately socialist regimes, of which North Korea is the purest example, and in a few industries within otherwise nonsocialist countries. But few remnants remain.

Hot socialism disappeared so quickly, both as a policy and as an ideal, that we have forgotten how utterly common its assumptions used to be. That's one reason we can seriously debate whether our contemporary situation represents "creeping socialism," a term that dates back to the 1950s, when socialism really was on the march.

The other sort of "socialism" is what I, like Steve's debating team, would more properly call "social democracy," or the redistributive state. This is the Swedish model, which uses massive redistribution through taxation and subsidies to rearrange economic outcomes. The goal is the same as for hot socialism—a fairer allocation of resources—and the animating ideology is economic egalitarianism.

Having spent some time recently in Sweden, I find it hard to imagine that Swedish socialism is creeping anywhere, except possibly under a rock to hide. The Swedish system is in serious trouble. The Swedish economy is no longer creating jobs—private sector employment has been shrinking for decades, and the public sector can no longer absorb more workers. The country is facing a brain drain. A backlash is developing against refugees and immigrants, who once represented Sweden's commitment to human rights and now are increasingly seen as outsiders consuming a fixed welfare pie. Many Swedes are pessimistic about the future, in large measure because they cannot imagine how their system can survive, yet cannot overcome the political obstacles to changing it.

The "social democracy" form of socialism is difficult to maintain because it runs head on into the political pressure of democracy—which replaces abstract issues of "fairness" with the practical calculations of interest-group politics—and the economic pressure of open markets. The Western democracies, Sweden among them, have not been willing to sacrifice their political freedom or their general prosperity to maintain ever-expanding socialism. They haven't, for instance, kept their people from leaving the country or even, in most cases, from sending their money abroad. That freedom has maintained the political legitimacy of social democracies, but it has undermined their ability to stay socialist.

As Hayek noted in *The Road to Serfdom*, "Many kinds of economic planning are indeed practicable only if the planning authority can effectively shut out all extraneous influences; the result of such planning is therefore inevitably the piling-up of restrictions on the movements of men and goods." The flip side of Hayek's observation is that countries that allow the more or less free movement of products, people, and financial capital will find that socialism cannot be sustained. A socialist regime depends on monopoly power that cannot survive the pressures of competition from outside. In the postwar period, a combination of liberal idealism, economic pragmatism, and Cold War calculation led not to Hayek's "piling-up of restrictions" but to increasingly free international markets, greater freedom of movement, and, most recently, ever freer capital flows—all enhanced by advances in communications and transportation.

We are not experiencing "creeping socialism." That is not the challenge we face. If you are used to fighting socialism and have developed your arguments, tactics, and alliances accordingly, it's tempting to define any form of redistribution or regulation as creeping socialism and therefore to declare the expansion of any and all government programs to be socialism. But that sweeping definition leads to political and economic confusion: It destroys the ability to detect threats early, to form alliances and perceive enemies, and to hone arguments.

We must keep in mind what socialism is, and therefore what it is not. Socialism, creeping or galloping, is an ideological concept with a particular sense of what is important. What distinguishes socialism is its appeal to economic fairness. It declares that markets do not allocate wealth and power fairly, and that political processes will do a better job. Socialism is not simply about moving money from the powerless to the powerful—a goal as old as politics—but about flattening the distribution of income and wealth. Pork-barrel spending is not socialism. Farm subsidies are not socialism. "Corporate welfare" is not socialism. These programs are not ideological in nature. They are about competing interest groups.

Socialism is about claims of justice, and it is also about money: about wealth, income, and physical and financial capital. It is an ideology based on allocating economic resources. It may try to achieve that goal by nationalizing assets, by command-and-control regulation, or by taxation and redistribution. But the goal is the same: to rearrange society's wealth, generally from the "haves" to the "have nots." Rearranging wealth (or income) is not the only possible ideological goal of economic regulation. It is merely the goal we have become accustomed to since the late 19th century.

Market processes do more than determine who winds up with which resources. That means that socialism is not the only conceivable ideology that might launch an attack on markets and, conversely, that anti-socialist conservatives are not the only possible allies for classical liberals in defense of economic freedom.

Markets have many characteristics. They serve and express the individual pursuit of happiness. They spread ideas. They foment change in the ways people live and work and in what character traits are valued. They dissolve and recombine existing categories, from artistic genres to occupations. They encourage the constant search for improvements, and they subject new ideas to ruthless, unsentimental testing. Markets evolve through trial and error, experimentation and feedback. They are out of anyone's control, and their results are unpredictable. It is this *dynamism* of markets—their nature as open-ended, decentralized discovery processes—that attracts the greatest ideological opposition today.

The most potent challenge to markets today, and to liberal ideals more generally, is not about fairness. It is about *stability* and *control*—not as choice in our lives as individuals, but as a policy for society as a whole. It is the argument that markets are disruptive and chaotic, that they make the future unpredictable, and that they serve too many diverse values rather than "one best way." The most important challenge to markets today is not the ideology of socialism but the ideology of *stasis*, the notion that the good society is one of stability, predictability, and control. The role of the state, in this view, therefore, is not so much to reallocate wealth as it is to curb, direct, or end unpredictable market evolution.

Stasists object to markets because the decentralized evolution of market processes creates not just change but change of a particular sort. By serving the diverse desires of individuals and by rewarding the innovators who find popular improvements, markets constantly upset unitary notions of what the future should be like. Markets don't build a bridge to the future—a path from point A to point B across a scary abyss; they continually add nodes and pathways in a web of many different futures. Market processes make it impossible to make society as a whole adhere to a static ideal—whether that ideal is a traditional way of life, the status quo, or a planner's notion of the one best future.

As a result, we find stasist enemies of markets arrayed across the old left-right spectrum, which we may define by its relation to socialism. Consider CNN's *Crossfire*, a show whose entire premise is the sparring of left and right. In denouncing the dynamic economy, the show's right-wing host, Pat Buchanan, has joined forces on one occasion with left-wing technology critic Jeremy Rifkin and, more recently, with corporate gadfly Ralph Nader. All agree that international trade, technological innovation, global financial markets, corporate reorganization, the expansion of some industries and the contraction of others—and just about every other manifestation of economic competition or creativity—portend a terrible future. They also agree, in principle at least, that the government should do something to curb market dynamism. This is not a socialist call for regulation. It is a stasist one.

The stasist attack on markets, regardless of what part of the old spectrum it may come from, applies two common tactics that are very different from the old arguments for socialism. First, it argues that we should not let people take chances on new ideas that might have negative consequences. This "precautionary principle" is particularly well developed—and increasingly enshrined in policy—in the environmental arena. But it can crop up anywhere. I recently read an article in *Policy*, the magazine of the Centre for Independent Studies in Australia, in which the author distinguished between conservatives like himself and classical liberals on just these grounds: He criticized the Tory government of London for deregulating the color of buses. "The gain remains potential, and this is the key word," he wrote, while the loss of uniformly red buses is guaranteed.

The precautionary principle counts only the downside of new ideas, not their potential benefits—the potential doesn't count—and it ignores the costs of maintaining the status quo. It puts no value on discovery and learning, either as social processes or as means to individual satisfaction. Market processes simply cannot survive this standard of judgment. It outlaws their inherent uncertainty.

The second stasist attack on markets has equally devastating potential. This is the argument against externalities. Most of us have been willing to grant the problem of externalities in such areas as air pollution and to look for ways of addressing it with minimal disruption of market processes. But it's not that hard to declare that *every* market action has potentially negative spillover effects. The infinitely elastic version of the externality argument turns the language of market-oriented economics against the essential nature of commerce. Indeed, we increasingly see the externality argument aimed not at producers, the traditional target, but at consumers. My choice of which movies to watch creates cultural pollution. My purchase of convenient packaging produces environmental waste. My house color or garage facade does not please the neighbors. My purchase of consumer goods leads to "luxury fever" that hurts everyone. We are all connected in the marketplace, and therefore, in this view, our actions must be tightly regulated to contain spillovers.

Stasists do not just make tactical left-right alliances on specific issues; they share a worldview and similar rhetoric. On the left, stasist critiques of markets are increasingly replacing traditional distributional arguments. Green demands for "sustainability" and a "steady-state economy" have supplanted socialist concerns for fairness. Critics like Juliet Schor and Robert Frank attack markets for encouraging ever-expanding yuppie consumption, not for immiserating the poor. The sociologist Richard Sennett, who was raised on children's books from the Little Lenin Library, attacks today's "flexible capitalism" not for exploiting the workers or paying poorly but for fostering instability and rewarding personal adaptability. Today's jobs, Sennett complains in *The Corrosion of Character*, do not tell workers who they are and thus threaten "the ability of people to form their characters into sustained narratives." Egalitarian bioethicist Daniel Callahan attacks the push for medical progress, which he finds expressed in the dynamic interplay of markets, technological innovation, and individual patients' desires. He calls for "steady state medicine" and "finite health goals." Although socialized medicine might provide a regulatory vehicle for achieving his goals, Callahan is not making a socialist argument.

Turning to the center of the old spectrum, we find stasists who are, if anything, even more upset about market dynamism than their counterparts to the left and the right—because decentralized discovery processes cannot coexist with technocratic, political control. There are many examples of such objections, which are particularly virulent when Europeans start denouncing the "American" openness of the Internet, but one of the best is from Arthur Schlesinger Jr., who defined the postwar "vital center" in the United States. Writing in the 75th anniversary issue of *Foreign Affairs*, Schlesinger condemns the "onrush of capitalism" for its "disruptive consequences." He warns of dire results from the dynamism of global trade and new technologies: "The computer," he writes, "turns the untrammeled market into a global juggernaut crashing across frontiers, enfeebling national powers of taxation and regulation, undercutting national management of interest rates and exchange rates, widening disparities of wealth both within and between nations, dragging down labor standards, degrading the environment, denying nations the shaping of their own economic destiny, accountable to no one, creating a world economy without a world polity."

Meanwhile, over on the right we find two major objections to market dynamism. Like their counterparts on the left, some on the stasist right attack trade, immigration, technology, large-scale retailers like Wal-Mart, and other elements of market dynamism that upset "settled ways." In these attacks, stasist conservatives often make alliances with environmentalists pursuing the same goals. Sometimes it's easy to apply the old left-right distinction—Pat Buchanan is clearly a man of the right—but not always. I would certainly put Prince Charles on the right—he's a hereditary aristocrat, after all—but many people consider his stasist views, especially his views of technology, to be versions of left-wing environmentalism.

At least in the United States, however, the more common right-wing objection is that by serving diverse individual desires, markets undermine a central notion of the good. Thus some conservatives, notably David Brooks and Bill Kristol of the *Weekly Standard,* have called for federal programs to serve the ideal of a "national purpose." More often, we hear markets subjected to conservative attack when they produce goods or institutions—from violent movies to domestic-partner benefits to in vitro fertilization—that do not fit conservative goals.

Even on education policy, where the conservative "line" is support for school choice, there are signs of disquiet. Choice is a useful political tool against the teachers unions tied to the Democratic Party and against secular public schools, but its premises of variety, competition, and tolerance cut against many conservatives' views of good education. When California conservative Ron Unz editorialized against vouchers in the left-wing *Nation,* he shocked many on both the left and the right. But he was only expressing a worldview he absorbed over years of reading neoconservative publications: We know the right answer already; there is no need for a discovery process in education.

The good news is that just as the breakdown of socialism has created new alliances against markets, it has also created new alliances in support of them. The idea that markets produce not chaos and disruption but positive, emergent order has become common in the same circles where a generation ago socialism, or at least technocratic planning, was all the rage. Some of you may have seen, for instance, this endorsement of market dynamism from a noted economist: "What's the single most important thing to learn from an economics course today? What I tried to leave my students with is the view that the invisible hand is more powerful than the hidden hand. Things will happen in well-organized efforts without direction, controls, plans. That's the consensus among economists. That's the Hayek legacy." The source of that upbeat assessment of markets was Larry Summers, now U.S.

secretary of the treasury and the epitome of a Cambridge economist.

If Schlesinger's hysteria exemplifies the attitudes of centrist stasists, Summers' optimism represents a new centrist coalition on the side of dynamism. That does not mean that Summers is a classical liberal, of course. It simply makes him, and other centrist dynamists, the sort of ally on behalf of markets that anti-socialist conservatives were in an earlier time. The American center (and, I suspect, Britain's New Labour) is full of chastened technocrats who have come to accept the practical limitations of state action and the practical advantages of economic freedom.

There are also many political "moderates"—journalists, scholars, technologists, scientists, artists, and business people, all far less famous than Summers—whose intellectual appreciation for self-organizing systems has come from outside economics: from complexity theory, from the decentralized evolution of the Internet, from the process of scientific discovery, from ecological science, from cross-cultural exchange, from organization theory. These centrist dynamists share an appreciation for dispersed knowledge and trial-and-error evolution that spills over into their attitudes toward markets. They do not always prefer markets to government, but they usually do. They lack the reflex that says a single, government-imposed approach is the best solution to public problems. They are more concerned with finding mechanisms to encourage innovation, competition, choice, and feedback. One thing that makes our political discourse confusing is that the term *moderate* does not distinguish between those whose moderation implies an appreciation for market processes and those whose moderation suggests just the opposite—a long list of schemes for small-scale government tinkering.

Even more striking is a profound split on what used to be the left. While leftists like Sennett are attacking economic dynamism, their erstwhile allies are finding in markets the values of innovation, openness, and choice. The counterculture has morphed into the business culture—to the consternation of both commerce-hating leftists and cultural conservatives. The left that gave us socialism is not the left that gave us personal computers and *Fast Company* magazine. Yet both the PC and America's hot new business magazine were unquestionably created by people who, by both personal history and political agenda, saw themselves as left-wing critics of establishment institutions. Individuals who would have no great love of "markets" if that concept implied static, hierarchical, bureaucratic corporate structures have embraced the idea of markets as open systems that foster diversity and self-expression. The very characteristics that make stasists wary of markets lead an emerging coalition of dynamists to defend them.

On the old political spectrum, socialism defined the left. That meant that the more you opposed socialism, for whatever reason, the further right you were. On the old spectrum, therefore, classical liberals were on the right, which makes us the right wing of the dynamist coalition.

It matters a lot whether we define our central challenge today as opposing socialism or as protecting dynamism. If we declare "the left" our enemies and "the right" our allies, based on anti-socialist assumptions, we will ignore the emerging left-right alliance against markets. We will miss the symbolic and practical importance of such cutting-edge issues as biotechnology, popular culture, international trade, and Internet governance. We will sacrifice whole areas of research and innovation to stay friendly with people who'll agree to cut taxes just a little bit, and only for families with children. We will miss the chance to deepen the appreciation for market processes among people who lack the proper political pedigree. We will sacrifice the future of freedom in order to preserve the habits of the past.

So, yes, I am an optimist about creeping socialism. We must always be vigilant, of course, and we still have many socialist legacies with which to deal—legacies that can provide powerful tools for the partisans of stasis. But socialism is dead as an ideal and dying as a policy. The challenges of the 21st century will be different: They will be to defend the virtues of dynamism and to rally a new coalition on its behalf. How we rise to those challenges will determine whether the next century will mark a new flourishing of liberalism, or yet another long era of twilight struggle.

November 1999

All Culture, All the Time

It's easier than ever to make and buy culture. No wonder some people are so upset.

Nick Gillespie

WHATEVER HAPPENED TO THE TELEVISION TEST PATTERN? No more than 20 years ago, most TV stations routinely signed off the air for at least a few hours a day. At the end of their broadcast period, stations would slap a test pattern up on the screen until the next morning's programming began. The test pattern—occasionally an absurd drawing of a Native American but more often a simple geometric shape adorned with call letters—was a great symbol of cultural dead space, of a moment when nothing was happening, when nothing was being transmitted, save perhaps for a monotonous electronic hum.

While some stations still do sign off, they are increasingly rare in a hyperkinetic, always-open America that has shifted fully into 24-7 mode (indeed, one promise of much-hyped digital TV is that it will allow an individual channel to subdivide itself four or more times). If the test pattern symbolized a moment of silence in the cultural process, then it's only fitting that its long run has effectively been canceled.

Similar developments range far beyond the small screen. During the past few decades, we have been experiencing what can aptly be called a "culture boom": a massive and prolonged increase in art, music, literature, video, and other forms of creative expression. Everywhere we look, the cultural marketplace is open and ready for business: The number of places where you can buy books has more than doubled during the past 20 years, while the number of libraries has increased by about 17 percent (to a total of almost 37,000). More than 25,000 video rental stores are scattered across the United States, effectively functioning as second-run theaters and art houses even in the most remote backwaters (a few years back, I was able to rent the 1930 Marlene Dietrich film *The Blue Angel* while visiting friends who lived five miles outside a town of 3,000 people in rural Ohio).

More than 110 symphony orchestras have been founded since 1980, reports the *Wall Street Journal*, which also notes that the national 1997-98 theatrical season "raked in a record $1.3 billion in ticket sales." About 3,500 commercial radio stations and 670 commercial television stations have come on the air since 1970; during the same period, cable viewership has quadrupled, while niche channels such as American Movie Classics and the Independent Film Channel have become more and more common.

The increasingly important World Wide Web has provided space for all sorts of commercial and noncommercial culture, ranging from authorized sites for the Louvre (featuring a virtual tour) to a reader-compiled database of more than 180,000 movies to translations of Dante's sonnets to fan-generated art about the cartoon *Josie and the Pussycats*. Especially in video and music production, where equipment costs were once prohibitive enough to seriously limit access, there is a flourishing, self-conscious "do-it-yourself" movement that has taken great advantage of cheaper technology and distribution methods.

In an important sense, such cultural proliferation is nothing new. It's part of a broad-based, centuries-old trend that also includes generally longer lives, increased wealth, and the greater personal autonomy that accompanies such developments. But there's also a sense that we've reached a tipping point, or at least turned a corner, in the past few years. More and more, people are not merely consuming culture but creating it as well.

In fact, in a world of $100 VCRs, bargain-basement PCs, CD-rewritable drives, and other technologies that allow users to copy and manipulate images, words, and sound in ever-new and seamless ways, even the sharp distinction between producer and consumer seems increasingly blurred. In economic terms, the opportunity costs of both making and enjoying culture have dropped through the floor; it keeps getting cheaper and cheaper both to produce and to consume culture under increasingly diverse circumstances. One predictable—and positive—result: more and more of everything.

Here's another: Gone for good are the days when serious cultural critics, whether on the right or the left (and whether rightly or wrongly), could nod toward Tocqueville and Mrs. Trollope and bemoan a scarcity of "culture" in America. Instead, the contemporary descendants of such folks are more likely to make the sort of claim *Slate*'s Jacob Weisberg did recently in a review of economist Tyler Cowen's *In Praise of Commercial Culture*. After granting that the United States does in fact offer a dizzying array of cultural opportunities, Weisberg complains: "What we lack is a flourishing common, or national, culture. Contemporary classical music goes unperformed, foreign films have no audience, and hardly anyone reads contemporary poetry. Meanwhile, pap abounds."

Though such an argument is not particularly convincing—there are, in fact, healthy, if small, markets for the fare Weisberg prefers—the shift in emphasis is noteworthy. It underscores a recognition that the problem isn't a lack of choice in cultural matters: You want Mozart, Mingus, and Marilyn Manson? No problem—they're all available (and probably at a discount). Rather, the issue is precisely a *profusion* of choice in cultural matters: You want Mozart, Mingus—*and Marilyn Manson?*

The difference in inflection is no small matter. In an increasingly wealthy and educated society where the overwhelming majority of people have concerns about food, clothing, and shelter pretty well covered, culture takes on more and more meaning as the medium through which we articulate our identities, dreams, fears, aspirations, and values. Little wonder, then, that stories about the "culture wars" have been burning up the pages of newspapers, magazines, and intellectual journals for the past few years: There's so much more to fight about these days.

While such battles are typically waged in apocalyptic—and apoplectic—terms, we should be clear about one thing: The very fact that there are culture wars is cause for celebration. They're a flashing neon sign that more and more people are able to express and enjoy themselves on something like their own terms: One man's "pap," after all, is another man's Proust—and we've entered a phase where people are increasingly willing to argue the point. Proclamations of artistic or social value can no longer be issued ex cathedra but must now be submitted before a skeptical audience.

The same decentralization of the cultural process that lets more and more people participate also allows them to opt out of someone else's cultural value system, whether they prefer *Ally McBeal* or *À la recherche du temps perdu.* In essence, the culture boom grants individuals what economists Albert O. Hirschman and Nobel laureate James Buchanan would recognize as a right of "exit" from a given cultural system: People are freer now to look elsewhere, to pursue their own interests to their own ends. Such a development hardly means that cultural standards have been obliterated, any more than freedom of religion means that theological standards have disappeared. Rather, in both instances standards have been vastly multiplied and, as a result, are more likely to clash. In this sense, the culture wars, like competition in economics or politics, are a marker of a healthy, diverse, engaged society.

To be sure, the culture boom is bad news for a "common" or "national" culture, if one conceives of such a thing as a set of relatively fixed artifacts and received interpretations that should not change over time; it certainly spells trouble for commissars, whether conservative or progressive, who argue that culture should be didactic and instructive toward a single set of desired ends, and it similarly makes things more competitive for producers and aesthetic movements alike, who must work harder than ever to gain and hold an audience.

But the effective deregulation of cultural markets is very good news for both individuals and the society comprising them. The most vibrant cultures, like the most vibrant economies and political systems, are ones in which people are as free as possible to define and choose what is valuable and meaningful to them. Ironically, such a viewpoint is hardly controversial when applied to most aspects of American life. Indeed, it is even seen as the embodiment of America's mythic national identity, which is paradoxically predicated upon the pursuit and fulfillment of individual desire. If we recognize heated political debates and loud marketplace haggling as quintessentially American, then we should do the same for cultural proliferation—and the contentious culture wars it inspires.

Cultural Abundance

By virtually any measure, cultural activity has been enjoying an expansion that stacks up to Wall Street's long-running bull market. Far more books and records are being sold these days. In 1985, according the National Endowment for the Arts (NEA), 3 percent of adults reported seeing an opera within the previous year, 22 percent reported going to an art museum, and 56 percent reported reading literature. In 1997, those figures had risen to 5 percent for operas, 35 percent for art museums, and 63 percent for literature. 1997 also saw record levels reported on the activity side, with 16 percent of adults drawing, 17 percent taking art photos, 35 percent buying art work, and 12 percent doing creative writing.

Interestingly, the culture boom has, for the most part, seen older art forms supplemented and preserved, rather than paved over, as might happen in a building boom. Hence, even as classical music sales as a percentage of all prerecorded music sales have been sloping downward in the 1990s (2.8 percent in 1997, down from 3.1 percent in 1990), it has nonetheless remained easy to find an ever-wider variety of classical music recordings. It's also become easier to see an orchestra perform: The total number of concerts increased by about 50 percent between 1990 and 1996, to a total of roughly 29,000 (combined private and public funding for orchestras is also way up in recent years).

To get a firmer grip on the magnitude of change that has been occurring, consider in greater detail two representative areas: TV-related culture and publishing. By 1970, television had saturated U.S. households: 95 percent had at least one set, compared to 98 percent in 1997. The past 30 years, however, have seen a number of developments that have greatly increased the amount and variety of TV-related culture available. The average home now has 2.3 sets, compared to 1.4 sets in 1970. Beyond growth in the number of individual stations, there are now four full-fledged networks and two "mini-networks" (WB and UPN).

Cable, the growth of which was long hampered by the Federal Communications Commission's restrictive, broadcast network-influenced definition of the "public interest," is now in 65.3 percent of all households with TVs (compared to 6.7 percent in 1970). The average subscriber receives 30 to 60 channels, typically including several devoted not merely to shopping but to new and old feature films, reruns of old shows, documentaries, and other sorts of specialized programming (a predictable response to increased competition in any area is, after all, product differentiation and specialization).

Television remains a favorite punching bag of moral crusaders and cultural critics, who tend to view an increase in channels or programs simply as proof of the multiplicative identity of zero: Any number times zero is still zero. But most informed analysts who actually watch TV would almost certainly agree with David Bianculli's assessment in *Teleliteracy* that "TV is better now than it was in the 'Golden Age' of TV, and the best of television compares favorably with the best Hollywood films, and TV deserves more respect than it's getting." Viewers have responded to more varied fare by increasing the amount of time they watch television. During the past decade or so, the average viewer increased his TV consumption by a half an hour, up to a total of 4.5 hours a day.

The variety available on TV is multiplied exponentially when one throws VCRs into the equation. Following one of the quickest possible adoptions of a new technology, about 80 percent of all households with TVs have at least one VCR. In 1990, the average viewer rented the equivalent of about 19 movies a year, a figure that is projected by *Communications Industry Report* to climb to 30 by 2001. Omnipresent video rental stores give virtually everyone access to a film library that a few decades ago even a millionaire wouldn't have been able to afford.

One gets a sense of this by considering the offerings of the typical Blockbuster store. Not only is Blockbuster the country's biggest chain (with about 4,500 stores nationwide), it's arguably one of the blandest and most restrictive in terms of aesthetic judgment. Blockbuster leans heavily toward the highly commercial fare alluded to in its name. And yet it's still got a huge and generally impressive selection of films—the typical franchise rents between 7,000 and 10,000 titles—even as its family-oriented policy creates a niche for stores that carry edgier fare, including pornography. According to the *New York Times*, most Blockbuster franchises have at least two competitors within a couple of miles, suggesting that cultural markets are often not zero-sum games, in which growth for one vendor is loss for another—or, more important, for the consumer.

But VCRs do more than simply allow viewers to watch more TV or film. They profoundly alter the terms of production and consumption. On the production side, movie studios now make roughly as much money from video sales as they do from box office receipts. By providing an after-market, VCRs allow producers—whether large or small, major-studio or independent—to take more risks by giving them a second chance to recoup their investment (that's one reason why there were 139 U.S.-produced independent films released in 1997, 100 more than a decade ago). Additionally, there's a robust market for old TV shows, documentaries, and the like, as well as for direct-to-video materials, ranging from porn to children's series starring the Olsen twins (themselves perhaps a form of porn).

On the consumption side, VCRs allow viewers to watch programs at their leisure, or to effectively watch several shows at once. That inverts what George Gilder has called the "totalitarian" framework of traditional broadcasting, in which the producer of a central signal set the times and terms of reception. Taping further allows individuals to more completely edit what they watch—skipping commercials, fast-forwarding through material they find uninteresting—as well as to "repurpose" material to suit their own desires.

Read All About It

The culture boom is similarly reshaping book publishing. While an enormous amount of ink has been spilled over the demise of print culture, the death of so-called mid-list authors and the threat to diversity posed by mega-mergers among publishers, actual book sales, and related figures suggest a very different picture. Between 1975 and 1996, the number of books sold increased by 817 million units annually. Fifty years ago, Tyler Cowen points out in *In Praise of Commercial Culture*, there were only 85,000 titles in print in the United States. Today, that figure stands at about 1.3 million.

During the same time frame, the number of American publishers increased from only 357 to around 49,000. "Most of these presses are independent small presses or university presses, rather than corporate giants" and are often dedicated specifically to publishing arcane, non-market-driven products, writes Cowen, who chalks up the explosive growth to a "modern commercial world [that] decentralizes editorial decisions and financial support." He also notes that "best-sellers ac-

count for no more than 3 percent of sales" in most big stores and pro-
vocatively argues that "the relevant question is not how many more
copies Grisham sells than Faulkner, but whether notable works of
high quality find their appropriate publishing outlets and readers."

Industry figures suggest they do. During the 1990s, even as publishers ostensibly became obsessed with bottom lines, they responded by
publishing and importing more titles. In 1996, for instance, publishers
brought out 2,800 more new works of fiction than they did in 1990,
770 more art titles, and 690 more volumes of poetry and drama.

The increase in the number of books available has been matched
by an increase in places to get books. Between 1985 and 1993, for
instance, the number of "ultimate companies"—outlets selling books
in some form or another—rose from 9,200 to almost 20,000. As important, the emergence of superstores such as Borders and Barnes &
Noble has redefined bookselling by putting a premium on vastness of
selection. Both chains claim to stock around 150,000 book titles (and
50,000 music titles) at most stores.

Such staggering numbers have, of course, been eclipsed by Web
sellers such as Amazon.com and Barnes & Noble's online outfit
(barnesandnoble.com). Boasting sites that include several million titles,
Amazon and Barnes & Noble have been joined in cyberspace by used-
book sites such as Bibliofind.com and Abebooks.com that combine
lists from hundreds of used-book stores nationwide. The Web retailers
are also leading the way in increasing access to foreign titles that have
traditionally been very difficult to find in the States: Amazon already
has sites specifically for the United Kingdom and Germany; Barnes
& Noble is working with European juggernaut Bertelsmann (which is
merging with Random House) for a multi-language site.

Informal Relations

While statistics about television, video, and publishing suggest the dimensions of the culture boom when it comes to relatively conventional forms of culture, the real hotbed of action may well be in what can
be called "informal culture." Reliable numbers on informal culture
are hard to come by because much of it is either noncommercial or
exists on a scale where there isn't a strong need for such information.

Informal culture includes the thousands of zines that are published
in any given year; self-produced and distributed music, movies, and

books; "taper" culture, which trades in illegal or gray-market copies of copyrighted materials as well as in versions that are doctored for comedic or dramatic effect; micro-broadcasting; fan communities; and Internet-based culture ranging from informal discussion lists to Web sites featuring streaming audio and video outputs. Certainly, it is in informal culture that the empowering aspects of the culture boom are most clearly on display: Much of it is steeped in conscious reaction to or rejection of "mass culture."

How does informal culture foster proliferation? Consider the Internet, which, because of its global reach and increasingly sophisticated and user-friendly multimedia capabilities, is particularly emblematic of cultural proliferation. Undergirding the Internet is the logic of the culture boom. Perhaps most important, it acts as what *Wired*'s Kevin Kelly has called a "supplemental" space. It generally adds to cultural options, rather than simply replacing existing ones—just as television in the end supplemented radio, rather than killing it. Relatively recent (read: already outdated) estimates say the typical Web page has about 500 words on it and put the total number of Web pages at somewhere between 200 million and 1 billion. Using the low estimate, that means the Web has put an extra 10 billion words in circulation, many of which are directed at commenting on and critiquing more-traditional cultural activities.

At the same time, the Web creates opportunities to circumvent traditional cultural gatekeepers by providing additional sites of production and consumption that are difficult, if not impossible, to police and regulate, whether one is talking about content restrictions, copyright infringement, or "responsible" interpretation of a novel. *Cyber Rights* author Mike Godwin has said that the Internet is "best understood . . . as a global collection of copying machines that allows people to duplicate and broadcast all sorts of information." As cheap, movable printing presses did, such a technology empowers individuals precisely by undercutting centralized authorities of all kinds.

While such tendencies are most clearly visible when looking at the Internet, the same forces are at work in other areas of cultural proliferation. If, for instance, you don't like what's on TV, you can change channels (there are, of course, many more of those than before). If you find nothing of interest, you can rent a video. If you're still dissatisfied, you can splice together found footage, perhaps dubbing your own sound. If that doesn't work for you, then you can grab a camera and make your own program. While relatively few people follow such a progression all the way through, the number of options and escapes—and the sense they are worth pursuing—has certainly grown during the past few decades.

In fact, because the culture boom gluts people with choices and opportunities both to make and to consume, it pushes them toward active behavior. Simply to filter out noise from their cultural systems, they must become active agents. As the range of materials to choose from increases, even passive receivers must actively construct the cultural world around them.

Fueling the Explosion

In a pair of articles last year, *Reason* Senior Editor Charles Paul Freund recalled a time in European history when culture was largely the preserve of aristocrats and the leisure class. Understanding that background helps to explain why the culture boom is happening now—and why it will likely continue for a long time to come. Relatively speaking, we're all aristocrats now.

The culture boom is in large part a function of general increases in wealth and related benefits, especially education and increased leisure time. While wealth, education, and leisure do not necessarily create a flourishing culture, they are almost certainly preconditions for a cultural proliferation. If nothing else, NEA data show that increased wealth and education correlate strongly with increased interest in traditionally defined cultural activity.

Americans have in fact been getting substantially richer. Between 1953 and 1993, say W. Michael Cox and Richard Alm in *Myths of Rich and Poor: Why We're Better Off Than We Think*, inflation-adjusted per capita personal income—a comprehensive measure that includes wages and other compensation such as health insurance and retirement plans—rose by about 1.85 percent annually. The boost in income has been very broad-based and cuts across all economic strata.

For instance, an ongoing University of Michigan longitudinal study of several thousand representative individuals found that between 1975 and 1991, people starting in the lowest income bracket on average gained about $28,000 in real income. Such widespread class mobility helps to explain shifting and divergent tastes. Cox and

Alm have also documented the ways in which the increase in income has been greatly magnified by a decrease in the real cost of many consumer goods. Calculating goods in terms of the hours an average industrial laborer would need to work to buy a given product, Cox and Alm find, for instance, that the work time required to purchase a movie ticket is only two-thirds of what it was in 1970; that VCRs today cost only 9 percent of what they did 20 years ago; and that camcorders cost only 28 percent of what they did 10 years ago.

Generally rising wealth has been matched by large-scale increases in education and leisure time. In 1970, for instance, only 52 percent of the population over 25 years of age had a high school diploma and only 11 percent had earned a bachelor's degree or more. By 1995, those totals looked very different: 82 percent had graduated high school and 23 percent had graduated college. Like wealth, more education correlates with more interest in both producing and consuming culture. According to the NEA, for instance, a college graduate is twice as likely as a high school graduate to read literature and three times as likely to attend a jazz concert or visit an art museum. Similarly, college graduates are four times as likely as high school graduates to play classical music, three times as likely to do creative writing, and twice as likely to take art photos.

Twenty-five years ago, Americans spent roughly 64 percent of what's called "waking hours" at "leisure"—that is, not working for pay or doing chores at home. By 1990, that figure had climbed to 70 percent. Although the portrait of "overworked Americans" painted by researchers such as Juliet Schor has been widely embraced by the media, it relies heavily on impressionistic methods such as polls and recollections. In *Time for Life: The Surprising Ways Americans Use Their Time,* John P. Robinson of the University of Maryland and Geoffrey Godbey of Penn State convincingly counter such claims through the use of detailed time diaries. They've found that Americans average about 40 hours of free time per week, a total that represents a gain of about an hour of leisure per day since 1965.

While wealth and related increases in education and leisure are doubtless central to the culture boom, we should not scant the contribution of technology, which economic historian Joel Mokyr dubbed the "lever of riches" in a 1990 book of that title. If Mokyr is correct that "technological creativity" has been one of the "key ingredient[s] of economic growth," it has similarly been a major factor in cultural proliferation. There are obvious examples of this, such as printing processes that have not only enabled books and literature to flourish but have also allowed sheet music and reproductions of artwork to find huge audiences. There are not-so-obvious examples as well, such as how relatively inexpensive musical instruments allowed rock music to develop among lower-class youths and how low-cost stereo equipment essentially made rap music possible: Both are forms that gave voice to people shut out from dominant modes of expression.

Indeed, in a cultural context the most important effect of cheap technology is that it fundamentally reconfigures what Marxists would term an individual's relationship to the means of production. In a world of ubiquitous video and audio cassette recorders—and a world in which personal computer ownership grew by more than 50 percent during the past four years alone—we are well on our way to a society in which everyone, regardless of class, owns multiple means of cultural production.

Exit Strategies

Though today's culture boom is brimming over with unparalleled opportunities, it's hardly unprecedented. The situation is in some ways reminiscent of 17th-century Britain, where the Church of England lost its theological monopoly partly because of rising literacy rates and new printing techniques that allowed more voices to enter into religious debate. England was flooded both with competing translations of the Bible and with tracts written by dissenters arguing about everything from atheism to—even more scandalous—a return to Catholicism.

Religious practice, like cultural activity, is a mix of private belief and public display; both are ways in which individuals explore what they hold true and announce who they are; both often involve intensely held values and evangelical activity that causes conflict with nonbelievers. In England, the breakdown of a central religious authority led to a flourishing of different, competing sects that duked it out in the marketplace of ideas for adherents and status. That struggle had a happy ending: By the end of the 17th century, freedom of "conscience"—that is, of religion—had been recognized as a fundamental right of the individual. That didn't mean, of course, that people believed all faiths to be equally valid or equally worthwhile, or that theological arguments no longer mattered. If anything, official recognition of a right of conscience enriched religious life by allowing people to argue their points more openly and to give fuller public voice to their individual and affiliative identities.

In our own time, the culture boom is similarly deregulating cultural markets by making it easier for people to walk away from offerings they find uninteresting, irrelevant, or objectionable. As James Buchanan has argued, when such an option is introduced in the political sphere, power devolves toward "competing units" of governance, right down to the individual. "Potential mobility among competing political units," says Buchanan, "may offer protection against . . . exploitation in any of several dimensions, including attempts to impose community values. The potential for exit allows at least some matching of personal loyalties and politically promoted common values."

Transposed into the cultural sphere, this suggests at least a couple of things. First, the potential for exit—to go elsewhere—heavily conditions the terms of exchange between producers and consumers; in effect, it forces the producer to provide better terms for the consumer and hence disperses power throughout a system. One reflection of this is the relatively recent and increasingly widespread practice of discounting books. Another is the way that producers must adapt to survive changing tastes. Consider a culture industry giant such as Disney, which rebounded from near-bankruptcy in the late 1970s and early '80s. Disney had to start once again making films that audiences actually wanted to see (out with *The Black Hole* and *Tron*; in with *The Little Mermaid* and *The Lion King*). But it has also flourished by expanding the range of material it is willing to finance. Hence, through its subsidiary Miramax, it has seen fit to help produce and release such quintessentially non-Disney films as *Priest*, *Kids*, and *Pulp Fiction*.

Second, and more important, an increase in the possible sites for cultural production and consumption does allow people to go elsewhere. The effective breakdown of the state church in England did not *cause* the differences among sects, some of which were so deeply held that dissenters shipped out to the New World. Rather, it created a society in which differences could be given voice and debated. Today, it has become increasingly easy for individuals to "make" their own culture, either through actual production or increasingly differentiated patterns of consumption.

The upshot of such a situation is that it is and will continue to be increasingly difficult to enforce any single standard of cultural value or practice, whether the enforcer is a government seeking to regulate material it deems indecent, a corporation trying to protect its franchise, or a group of artists or critics interested in cornering the market with its own aesthetic ideology. In this sense, the increased contests for power, prominence, and prestige that are often lamented in discussions of the "culture wars" are simply signs that all is as it should be in a free society. Indeed, more-serious problems will only be beginning if, as some participants in a recent *Chronicle of Higher Education* symposium suggested, those wars are in fact over.

April 1999

No Fruits, No Shirts, No Service

The real-world consequences
of closed borders

Glenn Garvin

THE LAST PICKUP TRUCK PULLED AWAY from the parking lot, and the men settled back onto the folding chairs of the little cottage in central San Jose where they wait for offers of day labor. The morning rush was over; nothing to do now but wait until after lunch, when a few more contractors and landscapers might stop by looking for a couple of strong backs for the afternoon.

It was a crisp autumn morning, just three weeks before Californians were to vote on Proposition 187, a measure that some hoped—and others feared—might call a halt to the nightly march of undocumented immigrants across the border from Mexico. Even so, the dozen or so men in the cottage—*mojados*, wets, illegals, every single one—were surprised that a visitor wanted to talk about 187.

"It doesn't have much to do with us," said Jose Guadalupe, who at 64 years old has crossed the border more times than he can count over the past four decades. "The immigrants have always been here, and they always will be, come what may. We'll come by water, or land, or whatever." The other men nodded in agreement.

But suppose, the visitor said, suppose the Americans built a fence all along the border that was 50 feet tall.

"Not high enough," interjected Guadalupe.

OK, OK, 100 feet high, or 200 feet, or a thousand—however tall it would have to be to really plug that border. What would happen then?

The men contemplated this idea in bemused silence. "Well," Guadalupe finally replied in a grave voice, "probably then the Americans would have to put black people back into slavery. Because we're the ones who work in all the fields here, picking lettuce and tomatoes and avocados. Americans don't do it. Unless you guys get people from Japan and Russia, who else is going to do it?"

So far, no American politician has been willing to say that if stopping illegal immigration requires repealing the 13th Amendment, then by God that's what we need to do. But just about anything else goes. National ID cards, computerized federal databases, doctors arresting their patients on the operating table, requiring teachers to rat on their students and encouraging the students to rat on their parents, pitching newborn babies back across the border: The Cold War had nothing on this new battle against immigration.

In fact, Bill Clinton last August officially declared that pulling up the national gangplanks now takes precedence over the final skirmishes of the Cold War. He asked Fidel Castro (in return for what under-the-table promises, we still don't know) to put Cuba's secret police to work stopping Cuban refugees from coming to the United States on rafts. It is as if West Germany, as the Berlin Wall was collapsing, had offered a bounty to East German border guards for every fleeing refugee they could gun down.

Although Proposition 187 and Clinton's creation of prison camps for Haitian and Cuban refugees have put the battle against illegal immigrants in the spotlight, legal immigrants are scarcely more popular. Sen. Alan Simpson of Wyoming, the newly triumphant Republican Party's most influential voice on immigration, has promised to introduce a bill slashing the number of legal immigrants by 25 percent. And that makes him an immigration *dove*. Last year a House bill that would cut the number of legal immigrants by 65 percent immediately and 85 percent in the long run attracted 73 co-sponsors from both parties, the single most popular immigration measure introduced during the past Congress. Said Pat Buchanan, the bill's principal champion: "If Republican leaders are frightened by political correctness from doing this, then it is a sign of what is endemic in the Republican Party; it won't touch an issue that somebody may say is evil and hard-hearted."

The most peculiar thing about Buchanan's comment is the implication that it's "politically correct" to support immigration. Quite the contrary: The fashion across the political spectrum, from the tree-huggers at the Sierra Club to Rush Limbaugh's pugnacious "ditto-heads," is to hammer away at immigrants. They steal our jobs. They use up our national resources. They dilute our culture. The timid few who demur are almost universally scorned as ivory-tower knuckleheads who mistake poetry for policy. They aren't out there in the *real world.* They don't "focus on the immigration influx in practice, as opposed to libertarian theory," as *National Review* acidly puts it.

But if there's anyone who's neglecting the real world, it's the people who want to cut immigration. Because they don't answer Jose Guadalupe's question. Once we've gotten rid of the immigrants, who *is* going to pick the lettuce and tomatoes?

A little agricultural math exercise: Of the million or so people who make up the full-time farm work force in the United States—those who work 100 days or more a year—the U.S. Department of Labor estimates that 60 percent are foreign-born. (Some labor specialists say as many as half a million may be illegal aliens, the scourge of the scourge to anti-immigrationists.)

Their average wage is around $6.00 an hour. How much would it cost to find native-born Americans to replace them in the fields? Let's say $12 an hour, which most agriculture experts think is a very conservative estimate. That means wages will jump 100 percent.

Multiply the doubling of wages times 20 percent, since economists say labor costs represent about one-fifth of food prices. Assuming that demand holds constant, what it all adds up to is a 40 percent increase in the cost of farm produce. If America's 68 million households spend an average of $10 a week on fruits and vegetables, that's $272 million a week (or, if you prefer, $14.1 billion a year) as the price we pay for running immigrants out of just one small sector of the U.S. economy.

Not that it would work.

"It's not just money that keeps Americans out of those fields," argues Libby Whitley, an agricultural labor consultant who until recently was a labor specialist with the American Farm Bureau Federation. "I don't know what journalists make. But let's say it's $100,000 a year. OK, I'll give you a nice raise. I'll pay you $110,000 a year to be a migrant farm worker.

"But you'll leave your friends and family. You'll live in a house trailer in an orchard, do your cooking in a group kitchen. And the job will only last for three months. Will you do it? . . .

"It's not just the pay, it's the nature of the work. It's outdoors, it's often in unpleasant weather, it's physical, it's hard. It hurts your back. It's short term. And you can't even guarantee tenure of work. If there's a bad freeze or a hailstorm just as a crop is ready to be picked, you're not guaranteed anything. You go home empty-handed. That's the nature of nature. And that's the nature of farm work."

Throughout most of American history, there's only been one group willing to consistently take on that kind of labor: recent immigrants. People with little education, few skills, and only a smattering of English, but who bring broad backs and the conviction that they're building a better life for their families. (There was, of course, one group of people who kept working in fields for generations after they arrived in America. The people Jose Guadalupe made reference to: slaves.)

Whitley has seen them on farms all over the country: the Mexicans toiling in the avocado and watermelon fields in California, the Jamaicans cutting cane and picking apples in the South, Haitians roaming Florida's citrus orchards, the Hmong tribesmen from Laos working in Minnesota dairy farms. "I even visited one county in upstate New York—I'm not going to tell you which one, because they don't need any trouble with INS—where the work force was predominantly illegal Polish immigrants," she says. "They didn't have much education and they didn't speak much English. So they did what immigrants have always done—they went and picked cabbage."

The crops and the skin tones of the people picking them may change from region to region, but Whitley says one thing is always constant: The immigrants are hard workers.

"You will not find many of the farmers *I* know bashing the foreign worker population," she says. "They will tell you quite honestly that they're excellent workers and decent people. Most farmers will tell you immigrants have a strong commitment to the work ethic. In fact, I'm always trying to hush farmers because they talk about how much better the immigrants are than U.S. workers. I'm always afraid they're going to get charged with some kind of discrimination."

Oh, one other thing: Getting rid of immigrant farm workers, no matter how much it cost American consumers, might not save any jobs for U.S. workers anyway.

"The more expensive labor gets, the more practical it becomes to mechanize," says Dalton Yancey of the Florida Sugar Cane League. His own industry is in the process of shedding the last of 10,000 foreign cane-cutters, in part because the bureaucratic hassles of getting them into the country were becoming too much of a headache. Their work will be turned over to machines. That's the way much of U.S. agriculture is headed.

"Corn and all the feed grains, they can be done mechanically," Yancey notes. "Potatoes, carrots, radishes, red beets, too. Cotton. Pecans can be shaken out of trees, and so can almonds."

Of course, there are some things—mostly fruits, which have to maintain a pretty appearance for the consumer—that can be harvested only by hand. But Yancey doubts that those crops will ever be picked by Americans, either.

"I suppose there's some level of pay at which Americans would be willing to do that work," he says. "The problem is you could fly fruit in from Chile cheaper. I suspect that we'd just do away with those crops in the United States if we somehow lost access to immigrant labor."

To put it another way, immigrant farm workers don't *take* jobs from anyone. Many of them do work that, if they didn't exist, simply wouldn't be done, at least not in the United States. And agriculture is not the only sector of the economy where it happens.

Some of the work is, arguably, trivial. In Miami, for instance, a lot of recent immigrants set up shop at gas stations, washing cars for $10 apiece and splitting the take with the station owner. Nothing high-tech about it—just a guy with a bucket, a sponge, and a willingness to stand around in wet clothes all day wiping down other people's cars. And if he wasn't there, offering his labor so cheaply, most of his customers would simply wash their own cars in their driveways at home.

"Whenever people voluntarily hire someone to do something, the benefit they receive is called consumer surplus," says Timothy Taylor, managing editor of the American Economic Association's *Journal of*

Economic Perspectives, who is fascinated by the economic reverbera-
tions of immigration. "This is one of the reasons so many people
in California have gardeners, because immigrants are there to offer
the service inexpensively. If the immigrants didn't exist, maybe you
wouldn't have had your yard done or your car washed, because it just
wouldn't be worth it."

Western civilization could undoubtedly withstand the dirty autos
and unkempt lawns that would result if all the immigrant car washers
and yard men were eliminated. But there are some consumer-sur-
plus-generated jobs that have more impact on American lives.

"I've had four nannies for my kids, and every single one has been
an illegal alien," says Amy, a Washington architect. "The first one
was British. The second was from Sierra Leone. There was one from
Peru, and the one we have now is a Salvadoran. Every time, I've put
an ad in the paper, but I've never interviewed a single American for
the job. I'm not sure I've even gotten a *response* from an American."

Amy pays $6.00 an hour to her nanny, well over minimum wage.
"But I'm not terribly surprised that Americans aren't interested in the
job," she says. "Taking care of children is hard work. There's no harder work in the world. It's physically difficult and emotionally tough.
Children are demanding. You have to keep them clean. Changing
diapers is not too much fun. And children can be real bratty. I know
my 3-and-a-half-year-old daughter can be a terrible brat. And that's
very difficult when you have no blood relationship with them. Also,
you've got to keep an eye on them at all times, and if there's more
than one, you have to be in more than one place at all times."

As hard as the work is, Amy says that paying significantly more
than $6.00 an hour wouldn't make economic sense to her. "I'd prob-
ably just quit and stay home, taking care of them myself," she says.

Across the country in San Francisco, her words are echoed by journalist Sharon Noguchi, who recently went back to work after having
a baby. She went to a resource center where babysitters register and
took down 50 names. All but one turned out to be immigrants. She
eventually hired a Salvadoran.

"It's the same for all my friends," Noguchi says. "I'm not sure that
wages are the whole story, either. I'm paying $7.00 an hour plus tax-
es and Social Security, and some of my friends are even paying for
health insurance. But Americans just don't apply for the jobs. I think

it also has to do with the nature of the work. The hours are odd and somewhat irregular, and there's no future in it—you work a couple of years and then get laid off when the children are older. That's just not desirable work."

Like Amy, Noguchi says that if there were no immigrants working in child care, she would probably have to quit her job and stay home with her baby. "So would a lot of other mothers like me," she declares. "There are a lot of women like me, women who work not because they have to, but because they like to. We're the people who will be the losers."

So will a lot of Americans who work in the garment industry. Perhaps no other U.S. industry is more intimately linked to immigrants than the rag trade. The ready-to-wear industry was founded in New York in the 1880s, when Jewish immigrants from Russia and Eastern Europe provided most of the labor. As they moved out of production and into management and ownership, they were succeeded by a wave of new Italian immigrants. As European immigration dried up in the 1930s, Puerto Ricans and southern blacks took over the production floors. In the 1960s, Chinese and other Asians poured into the garment factories. These days the jobs are done by new Chinese arrivals along with recent immigrants from Latin America and the Caribbean.

"The second generation never stays," says Muzaffar Chisti, the director of the Immigration Project of the International Ladies' Garment Workers' Union. (Though Indian-born, he's a U.S. citizen.) "We have clearly seen a recurring phenomenon, the replacement of one set of workers by another. But it's a *re*placement, not a *dis*placement. . . . One group of immigrants moves up and out, and another takes its place. That's the whole promise of America.

"That's the whole interesting thing about this immigration debate. Immigration is such a great bargain for this country. Immigrants come to work in what economists call the secondary sectors of the market. The primary sector is the prized jobs, the ones with good wages and upward mobility. The secondary sector is the jobs with low wages, harsh discipline, low mobility. Those are the ones the immigrants take. They do it with the clear promise that it's going to be a better deal for their kids. And it is. The kids of our Chinese immigrants go to Ivy League schools in prodigious numbers."

In some cases it doesn't take a full generation for immigrants to succeed in their new life. Many of the Chinese who arrived in the garment factories in the mid-1960s have already worked their way in the managerial and entrepreneurial classes. "There are 500 to 600 Chinese-owned garment companies in New York," notes Chisti. "In 1960, there were just five. They employ 30,000 workers." Their payroll is more than $200 million.

Anti-immigrant activists would retort, no doubt, that most of those 30,000 jobs go to other immigrants rather than Americans. That's undoubtedly true. But many jobs generated by the garment industry are held by native-born Americans. Packagers, truckers, mid-level managers, and wholesale workers are mostly natives. So are people in countless other jobs that were created by the garment industry, from the assembly-line workers in the plants where sewing machines are built to the pink-collar staffs of the designers who cluster near the garment factories. A 1985 Urban Institute study of the garment industry in Los Angeles, the country's second-biggest, concluded that without Mexican immigrants, the city would have lost 50,000 production jobs, 12,000 management jobs, and 25,000 incidental jobs.

"Immigration not only works for the immigrants, it works for the competitiveness of our country," Chisti says with conviction. "Apparel is still New York's largest industry. New York is still the apparel capital of the world. And it couldn't have been without immigrant labor. The garment industry—collapse may be too strong a word—but the garment industry simply could not continue at anything like its present level. It would lose its principal source of workers. Much of it would move off-shore."

Chisti scoffs at the idea that Americans could take over those jobs, even if the pay could be raised without destroying the industry's competitiveness. "People have the idea garment work is unskilled," he notes. "But if anyone thinks sewing a shirt in less than 20 minutes without cutting off your fingers is unskilled, let him try it. This is a skill, and it's a skill these workers have learned abroad. We don't have programs here to teach people how to sew. Immigrants learn it in informal or family networks. How are you going to replace that?"

And yet the notion persists that immigrants come here and steal jobs, consigning hard-working Americans to the unemployment lines. It is a view that the immigrants find bewildering.

"Listen, señor, what American would want my job?" politely inquires Carlos, an illegal immigrant from Mexico's troubled Chiapas state. Using false documents, he has worked for the past five years in a furniture workshop in downtown Houston. All day long he totes heavy lumber from one side of the room to another for $5.00 an hour. "It's not terrible work, but it's very hard, for very little money," Carlos says. "Americans wouldn't want such a hard job." He's not complaining—in Chiapas there was no work at all—but simply stating the facts. All the other unskilled laborers in the workshop are Mexican immigrants, too.

"People stop by here to offer jobs," says Louise Zwick, who with her husband Mark operates Houston's Casa Juan Diego, a temporary residence for new immigrants. "And you should see the kind of work it is: heavy, distasteful labor. Pouring tar for roofers in the middle of the summer in 100-degree heat. Or, last fall, after we had terrible floods northwest of Houston, people came around looking for help cleaning that dirty water and stinking mud out of their homes. And the whole reason they came here is that they couldn't find Americans to do that work, but they knew immigrants would."

Luis Moreno learned about dirty jobs the hard way. He arrived in Miami in 1989 with CIA help after spending eight years as a commander in the contras, the American-backed rebels who fought Nicaragua's Marxist Sandinista regime. Moreno had a distinguished combat record—after a mortar accident blew off his right arm, he learned to fire a rifle with his left and continued to lead contra troops inside Nicaragua—but he found that setting ambushes and blowing up bridges were relatively undervalued skills in the U.S. economy. And although popular legend has it that the CIA set up ex-contras with luxury condos and country-club memberships, all Moreno got was a work permit and a brisk shake of his left hand.

"I was a man with no way out," he recalls. "I had one arm. I didn't speak English. But I couldn't go back to my country because the communists were still in control. And I had two children to support. So I had to do whatever was necessary." He took a job as a guard at a security company.

"Lots of Nicaraguans were coming to Miami then—that was when it looked like the Sandinistas would stay forever—and I would say that 90 percent of the guards at my company were Nicaraguans like me," he remembers. "And the rest were from other countries in Central America. We were all immigrants. Why? Because we were people who didn't speak English. And people who don't speak English in America don't get treated very well."

The company sent him to various sites during the three years Moreno worked as a guard. But they were all pretty much the same: warehouses in seedy neighborhoods near the city's crime-riddled ghettos. "The places were all difficult assignments," he says. "There was never a toilet, never a place to get a drink of water. I was always outside, in the rain, in the mosquitoes." But that wasn't the worst of it. The worst was standing around unarmed in the dark at 2 a.m., waiting for a crackhead with a 9mm Glock to show up to break into the place.

"Really, we weren't much more than human burglar alarms, there to call for help on the walkie-talkie if something went wrong," Moreno says. "I remember one night when I was guarding a clothing warehouse. And I saw someone breaking in. So I called my supervisor, and he called the owner. If the owner called the police, and it turned out I was wrong, and there was no burglar, then he would have to pay some kind of a fee to the police department. So the owner said, 'Well, there's nothing too valuable inside there. Don't call the police. Just tell the guard to try to catch the guy when he comes out.' So I stayed there all night, with no gun, waiting for this guy—maybe he had a machine gun, for all I know—to come back out. I had plenty of combat experience, so I wasn't scared, exactly. But I thought about my children. What would happen to them if I were killed? Who would take care of them?

"I was getting paid $4.25 an hour for that. And you ask me why there were no Americans working at my company? What American would risk his life to save another man's shirts for $4.25 an hour? Only an immigrant would do that, because he can't do anything else. Once in a while an American came in to apply for a job. And they always got hired on the spot to be a supervisor, because they could speak English, and the supervisors had to speak English to deal with clients and police and insurance companies. The boss loved it when Americans came in, but that didn't happen very often."

Even so, Moreno never complained to his family about his job. Who would have listened? His wife came home squinting and sore from a garment factory where she sewed sleeves on shirts for five cents apiece. His arthritic 57-year-old father wheezed from the perpetual cold he got working at a warehouse, unloading 50-pound boxes of frozen chicken from trucks under Miami's tropical sun, then carting them inside to a meat freezer. One brother could barely drag himself into the house at the end of the day after lugging cement blocks around construction sites in the 90-degree, 90-percent humidity heat. And still another brother was rarely seen.

"Ahhh, he had the worst job of all," Moreno chuckles. "He worked for $100 a week guarding a pigpen on the edge of the Everglades. Have you ever been out there? He had to protect those pigs from all the crazy people who run around in the Everglades. Every night the mosquitoes fell onto him like a cloud. And the snakes. You don't want to know about the snakes. . . .

"It was hard work, his job. My wife's job too. All of us did hard work. But people do it all around the world. That's the kind of job people who don't have education get."

Moreno is getting an education. In between his guard shifts, he took junior-college English classes. His language skills improved to the point where he was able to get a job as a courier shuttling documents between downtown law firms. He has 90 hours of credit toward an accounting degree, and someday he hopes to open a bookkeeping service.

Meanwhile, he stops by the security company every once in a while to say hello. "All the Nicaraguans are gone," he observes. "They've gotten better jobs. All the guards now are Haitians."

When Luis Moreno and Carlos say they didn't take their jobs from Americans, they won't get any argument from the vast majority of economists. Study after study shows that immigrants are at worst a break-even proposition in terms of creating jobs and paying for the government services they consume.

Perhaps the most dramatic was a study by Princeton economist David Card, who looked at the impact of the 1980 Mariel boatlift on Miami employment. That was the year Castro, in an ill-considered fit of pique, briefly opened Cuba's doors to permit free emigration. In just a couple of months, 125,000 refugees flooded into Miami, boosting the city's work force 7 percent overnight.

Card tracked Miami's unemployment statistics for six years after the boatlift, comparing them with those of half a dozen Sunbelt cities with similar economies. What he found was—nothing. Miami's economy swallowed the newcomers without a trace, like a boa constrictor gulping down a pig.

"You couldn't find any effect of the boatlift on employment in any part of the economy," Card says. "Because most of the people who came during Mariel were unskilled workers with little education, even the most optimistic person might have expected some impact at the lower end of the economy. But when I checked on the statistics for unskilled black or non-Hispanics, you couldn't find anything at all." Some workers were undoubtedly displaced, of course, but they apparently were able to find other jobs very quickly.

Although Card admits to some wonder at the speed and totality with which the Mariel refugees were absorbed, he wasn't surprised by the general principle that economies expand to accommodate newcomers.

"When I read letters to the editor, it's plain that most people seem to think that the number of jobs is fixed," he says. "So, in their view, if you add one more worker to the population of a city, it just means that that guy will have to fight with somebody else for an existing job. It's an extremely narrow and very non-economic view of the world. . . . If you look across cities, the number of jobs is proportional to the number of people in the city. The fact that more people have moved to New York than to Atlanta does not mean that a lot of people have been thrown out of work in New York. What it means is that there are 10 times more jobs in New York than there are in Atlanta."

What happens is that every new person who comes to New York—or to the United States—looking for work is also a consumer. He wants a job, but he also has to buy shoes, eat breakfast, and rent an apartment. The more consumer demand for goods and services, the more jobs are created to fill it. As British writer John Toland noted during an influx of foreign Jews in 1714: "We deny not that there will be more tailors and shoemakers; but there will also be more suits and shoes made than before." Were Toland around today, he might point out that Florida's unemployment rate is lower than the national average, even though it has the third-largest immigrant population of all the states.

Who is going to pick the lettuce and tomatoes? has a companion question. It is, *Who is going to design the computers?*

"The United States would not be remotely dominant in high-technology industries without immigrants," flatly declares writer George Gilder, who chronicles international competition along the information superhighway. "We are now utterly dominant in all key information technology domains. And at every important high-tech company in America, the crucial players, half of them or more, are immigrants.

"I've spent 15 years now going from one of these companies to another. And always, when you get past the sales people and the public-relations people, in the back you meet the guy who actually invented the product. And he's always from India or Vietnam or someplace like that.

"You exclude immigrants from our high-tech industries and what you get is Europe, where they have no important computer or semiconductor company now after 20 years of focusing on information technologies. There's been a steady stream of heavily funded European economic community industrial policies focused on semiconductors and computers, and Europe has ended this period without a single important computer or semiconductor company. . . . In fact, many of the key contributors to the U.S. industry came here from Europe: Eastern Europe, Italy, Belgium, Britain, France. Where would we be if we hadn't welcomed them?"

Does Gilder exaggerate? Consider the history of a single company: Intel, the $10-billion Silicon Valley company that is the world's largest producer of semiconductors. It offers a striking example of the creative forces unleashed by bringing together talented, ambitious people from all over the world (including the United States) and allowing them to share ideas in an open, entrepreneurial economy.

1968: The company is founded by two Americans who are quickly joined by Andrew Grove, a 31-year-old Hungarian engineer who fled his country 12 years earlier as Soviet tanks poured in. Grove, who left Hungary with $20 in his pocket, will eventually rise to be Intel's CEO.

1969: Intel scores its first big success with the MOS chip, which becomes the semiconductor industry's favorite technology. The team that develops the chip is spearheaded by Les Vadasz, a Hungarian who will eventually become an Intel vice president.

1970: Intel introduces the DRAM chip, which will soon be one of the fundamental building blocks of virtually all computers. Les Vadasz plays a key role on the development team.

1971: Dov Frohman, an Intel engineer from Israel, invents the EPROM chip, which retains its memory even when the power is turned off. It quickly becomes indispensable in everything from telecommunications equipment to automobiles.

1974: Intel unveils the 8080, the first general-purpose microprocessor. Of the three top people on the development team, one (Federico Faggin) is Italian and one (Masatoshi Shima) is Japanese.

1979: The company produces the 8086 chip, which, with slight modification, will become the brains of the first IBM personal computer. The team that engineers the chip is headed by Jean-Claude Cornet, a French immigrant.

1993: Intel introduces the state-of-the-art Pentium chip. The Pentium project is managed by Vinod Dham of India. And one of the chip's two principal architects is another Indian, Avtar Saini.

So where would Intel be without immigrants? The company's communications director, Howard High, just shakes his head at the question; he can't imagine. But he does know one thing: Intel will continue to profit from imported brainpower. If U.S. law prohibits it from arriving on boats or planes, it will slip in through telephone modems.

"This talk about changing immigration law is not going to impact where the jobs go in high-tech industries," he says. "You can live where you want to live, or have to live, and if you're good, we're going to hire you. There aren't a lot of people who specialize in the kinds of skills we need. So if you live in Tel Aviv, or Manila, or Beijing, or Albuquerque, we're going to hire you and move the necessary facilities to you. . . .

"For $4,000, we can put 150 million instructions per second on the desktop of anybody in the world. If people don't want to live here, or can't live here, they don't have to. With computers and telephones, the border issue just kind of goes away."

Not everyone is quite so sanguine about the possible effect of immigration restrictions on America's high-tech industries. "It's true that a lot of computer programming can be done anywhere in the world," says Nathan Rosenberg, a Stanford economist who studies the history of technology. "They do that now. A number of American firms, Motorola and some others, have large networks of computer programmers in India and elsewhere.

"But if we're talking about more highly engineered and creative work—design work, sophisticated research, the bright big ideas—it's a more synergistic situation involving face-to-face interaction among people. The point is that people need to talk to one another, react directly to one another, and communicate in ways that don't seem to work nearly as productively when you're communicating through a wire or a fiber-optic line. The key word is *synergy*, a creative response to other people's ideas or statements, an energy that results when people are in the same room looking at one another." That synergy enriches not only U.S. companies but, by sparking innovations, the entire world.

Rosenberg is frankly worried about what will happen if Congress passes draconian anti-immigration laws.

"About 60 percent of all students earning advanced degrees in American universities in engineering today are foreign," he observes. "We have benefited—and we continue to benefit immensely—from this flow of foreign talent. For example, Indian immigrants have played a remarkable role in exploiting higher mathematics for purposes of industrial innovation.

"A very large fraction of the foreigners who come to America to study and take advanced degrees in engineering and science stay here. When you combine that with the fact that, for whatever reason, American students are simply not going into many areas of engineering that are relevant to industrial innovation, it's obvious we need these foreigners. We need them very badly. . . .

"It seems to me that the American high-tech industry will suffer, will suffer tremendously, if these anti-immigration measures go into effect."

The prominence of immigrants at Intel is no fluke. Some 15,000 Asian immigrants are employed in Silicon Valley, roughly a quarter of the work force. And the phenomenon is not limited to California. At IBM's facility in Yorktown Heights, New York, a quarter of the researchers are Asians. At AT&T's Bell Labs in New Jersey, 40 percent of the researchers in the Communications Sciences Research Wing were born outside the United States.

In Hawthorne, New York, 60 percent of International Paper Company's engineering department is composed of immigrants. Du Pont Merck Pharmaceutical in Wilmington, Delaware, regularly brings out new products developed by immigrants. One example: the anti-hypertensive drug Losartan, created by a team of scientists that included two Chinese and a Lithuanian. At Phoenix Laser Systems in San Jose, California, founder Alfred Sklar, a Cuban refugee, is pioneering laser technologies that could eventually cure several forms of blindness.

High-tech is not the only expertise that immigrants bring with them. They also bring along knowledge of the way businesses organize and market themselves in other parts of the world, which can be an invaluable source of innovation.

There are few hotter companies in America than Kingston Technology, which designs and manufactures memory upgrades for virtually every kind of computer. Located in Fountain Valley, just south of Los Angeles, Kingston regularly hosts awestruck reporters from the nation's financial press. *Fortune* labeled it "the paradigmatic growth machine," and it was at the top of *Inc.* magazine's 1992 list of the country's fastest-growing privately held companies. No wonder: From its founding in 1987 through 1992, Kingston's sales increased a sizzling 368 percent. Last year they hit $800 million.

And who is behind this classic American success story? Well . . . two Taiwanese immigrants, David Sun and John Tu. And a stroll through the company's semi-chaotic two-story headquarters ("management by shout and grab," Kingston people call it) is like a visit to a real-life version of Disneyland's "It's A Small World" ride. American salesmen consult with Chinese engineers who chatter at Vietnamese testers who banter with Hispanic assemblers. Kingston's 1,300 employees are divided roughly equally among the four groups.

"Southern California is at the forefront of today's immigration," says marketing director Ron Seide. "The same thing that made the United States strong at the turn of the century—the flow of immigrants that built the east and the industrial midwest—is part and parcel of Southern California's success. Without immigrant influence, their ideas, their intellectual capital, the high-tech industry—which is the best thing California has going for it—wouldn't exist."

Seide (who hails from Cleveland and is sometimes referred to as "the Anglo interface" by his polyglot colleagues) recalls that he was stunned by the sheer energy radiating from Kingston's work floor on his first day in the job. He has no doubt that it is generated by the immigrants.

"You've got to have a lot of gumption, get-up-and-go, guts, whatever you want to call it, to pack up your belongings, jump into steerage, and start a new life 5,000 miles away in a country where you don't speak the language," he observes. "It's a self-selecting process. And then they bring it into the workplace. It's infectious."

Kingston works at the center of a tightly knit cluster of independent companies, sharing capital, know-how, and markets. Kingston designs memory boards, which are manufactured by a partner in Taiwan, assembled by another partner down the road in Orange County, and sold by distributors all over the world.

"We operate as a virtual corporation," Seide says. "That's very central to the way Asian companies are structured. And no American could have imagined it. This company is literally an immigrant's dream."

So: Who is going to pick the lettuce and tomatoes? Who is going to design the computers? And, of course, the questions don't stop there. Without Ethiopians, who will be the parking attendants in San Jose? Without Haitians, who will drive Miami's taxis? Without Filipino nurses and Pakistani doctors, who will care for the ill in inner-city and rural hospitals? Without Mexicans, who will build houses in North Carolina? Yes, North Carolina.

"If it were not for the Latin American population here, we'd be in a terrible fix," says the vice president of a large Raleigh construction company. "Unemployment is down under 3 percent here and has been for several years. And when we advertise for workers, we don't get Americans, we get Mexicans. I don't know where they come from. But I do know they believe in a day's work for a day's pay, and we like that."

In a sad indication of today's political climate, the construction man doesn't want his name used: "I don't care to get caught up in any political backlash over anything. There are some things that are politically sensitive, and one of them is immigration. I saw what happened in California with that proposition." In the United States these days, it is potentially controversial to say that you like your workers, if they happen to have been born in the wrong place.

And in the United States soon, it may become more expensive to buy a shirt or build a home, more difficult to hire a babysitter, next to impossible to operate a vegetable farm. Office rents will rise along with janitors' wages; so will the cost of a dinner out, as bus boys, waitresses, and cooks get more expensive. Maids and gardeners may become a thing of the past, along with career women. High-tech research and development will stagnate. Who could have guessed that "pragmatism" would be so extravagant?

April 1995

All I Think Is That It's Stupid

Dave Barry on laughing
at very big government

Interview by Glenn Garvin

A *NEW YORK TIMES* PROFILE once said that *Miami Herald* humor columnist Dave Barry "makes his living by taking prosaic ideas to incongruous extremes." He is the only Pulitzer Prize winner to have a sitcom— CBS's *Dave's World*—based, very loosely, on his life. (They turned his one son and two dogs into just the opposite, but he enjoys cashing the checks.)

The Pulitzer Prize judges gave Barry the award for commentary in 1988 "for his consistently effective use of humor as a device for presenting fresh insights into serious concerns." His concerns include beer, Barbie, a "worldwide epidemic of snakes in toilets," exploding Pop-Tarts, and, perhaps most famously, "the worst songs ever recorded."

To be fair to the Pulitzer committee, the real Dave does devote more column inches than the average pundit to making Very Big Government look silly and obnoxious. This is a fresh insight in New York and Washington, and wildly popular with readers, who have bought more than a million copies of his books.

Taking prosaic ideas to incongruous extremes, he writes things like: "With the federal deficit running at several hundred billion dollars per year, Congress passed a transportation bill that, according to news reports, includes $30 million for a 'hightech' moving sidewalk in Altoona, which happens to be in the district of Rep. 'Bud' Shuster, the ranking Republican on the surface transportation subcommittee.

"I don't know about you, but as a taxpayer, I am outraged to discover that, in this day and age, Altoona residents are still being forced to walk around on regular low-tech stationary sidewalks. I'm thinking of maybe organizing a group of us to go there and carry Altoonans on our backs until they get their new sidewalk. I'm also thinking that maybe we should donate an additional $10 million or so to build them a high-tech computerized Spit Launcher that will fire laser-guided gobs onto the moving sidewalk, so the Altoonans won't have to do this manually. 'What have I done today to help keep 'Bud' Shuster in Congress?' is a question we all need to ask ourselves more often."

Reason: You were in Washington recently to do a story. What was it like there?

Barry: It's like going to Mars. When you come back out no one is talking about any of the things the people in Washington are talking about.

If we're spending $853 trillion on some program now, and next year we spend any less, that's "budget-cutting" to them. For them, the question is always, "What kind of government intervention should we impose on the world?" They never think that maybe we shouldn't.

It gives me a real advantage as a humorist because I get credit for having insight and understanding—and I don't. I don't have any insight or understanding on anything about the government. All I think is that it's stupid—which is the one perspective that's almost completely lacking in Washington.

Reason: Did people there find your perspective peculiar?

Barry: They know this is what I do. Reporters aren't stupid. We were standing around talking about which of the 900 health care proposals that nobody's going to accept is that day's hot news. They know how silly that is. But that's what they do. And if they don't do it, they'll get fired and someone else will do it. There's tremendous pressure, if you're in that system, to be involved and be interested and to care about it. There's no room to say, "This is stupid."

(One of the two tape recorders goes down. The reporter fiddles with it.)

Reason: I see why they wanted me to bring two. I'm totally humiliated. Virginia will be able to say, "Good thing I told you to bring two."

Barry: You know, if we had strict government standards about tape recorders, this kind of thing wouldn't happen. The consumer would be protected.

Reason: Was there anything surprising or unexpected about Washington?

Barry: I've been to Washington many times over the years for stories, and it always seems remarkably the same. More the same than the rest of the country. It's almost like they dress the same as they did 20 years ago. The same old guys are sitting outside the same dirty, dingy secret offices in the Capitol that you're not allowed to go in. But there's always this endless crowd of young, enthusiastic people who are in their Junior Achievement club or whatever, and someday they're going to be assistant to an aide to somebody. But they're making important contacts now that will serve them well the rest of their lives.

Reason: You're not sounding like a guy who has the fire in his belly for the '96 presidential race.

Barry: Oh, I never stop running. I'm not one of the weenies who drop out just because the electoral college votes. I'm still in the race. I'm an extremely corrupt candidate and I stress that in case anybody in our reading audience is interested in sending me money. You can have a naval base, is what I'm saying.

Reason: I would think that Washington would strain one's sense of humor. Sitting there listening to some imbecile like Paul Simon—the imbecile senator, not the folk singer—did you want to leap over his desk and cut his throat?

Barry: I'm a humorist. A guy like Paul Simon just makes my life so much simpler. When I was there, he had a hearing against hate. Steven Spielberg came and testified against hate. Paul Simon said hate was bad. Orrin Hatch was there, and he was against hate too. Everyone was opposed to hate. Is this really a wonderful way to spend our tax dollars, to have these men drone away about how against hate they are?

Reason: Did they make a token attempt to represent the pro-hate position?

Barry: No. But if the pro-hate lobby were to set up a PAC, I'm sure they'd be heard. It's not like they're not fair up there.

Reason: You've written in your columns about the strategic helium reserve the government keeps in case we have a sudden need for a fleet of dirigibles.

Barry: What bugs me when I write that is that I suspect 90 percent of my readers think I made it up.

Reason: What's something about the government that really pisses you off?

Barry: Well, that helium thing does. That's real money. All the tax money that I've ever, ever paid—and I've paid a lot of taxes—will not even begin to pay for one year of the strategic helium reserve. So when I sit and write a check out to the government, I can take it quite personally.

Reason: You don't sound like one of the people who fills out the IRS forms and then sends in voluntary contributions to alleviate the national debt.

Barry: No. Every year I write a tax advice column and I used to always make fun of that. One year, one of my favorite IRS commissioners, I think his name was Roscoe somebody, wrote that one of the most often-asked questions by taxpayers was, "How can I contribute more?" Well, I tell ya, ol' Roscoe's really been doing situps under parked cars again. I've heard a lot of people ask a lot of questions about taxes, but I never heard anybody say, "How can I, the ordinary person, send more money for no reason?"

Reason: Whatever happened to your $8.95 tax plan?

Barry: Oh, the $8.95 tax plan. Well, it was really popular with the average reader. It definitely reduced his taxes significantly. This was years ago, I think during the early Reagan years. I came up with a plan that everybody just pay $8.95 in taxes. Cheating would be allowed. But the incentive to cheat wouldn't be nearly as great if you only had to pay the $8.95. There were a few people who would have to pay hundreds of millions of dollars under this plan. I think it was Mark Goodson and Bill Todman, the guys who do the quiz shows. But almost everybody else would be off really cheap.

Reason: Do you ever get complaints that you're making people cynical?

Barry: Every now and then, when I write my annual tax column, some ex-IRS agent will complain, "There you go IRS bashing again." They're always saying that they're just doing their job. Someone I know once said, "You could get another job."

Reason: In your column I detect a certain skepticism at the notion that congressional spending creates jobs.

Barry: Of all the wonderful things government says, that's always been just about my favorite. As opposed to if you get to keep the money. Because what you'll do is go out and bury it in your yard, anything to prevent that money from creating jobs. They never stop saying it. They say it with a straight face and we in the press will write that down. We will say, "This is expected to create x number of jobs." On the other hand, we never say that the money we removed from another part of the economy will kill some jobs.

Reason: Have you ever had a government job?

Barry: No. I'm trying to think of what government job I would want. Maybe a disgruntled postal worker.

Reason: What's the most ridiculous government program you've ever written about or heard of?

Barry: I would really have a hard time just picking one. Anything at all in West Virginia is a good place to start. My favorite ones are when our own Defense Department says, "No, we really don't want you to build these weapons systems." Where do we stand now with the BI Bomber? We're going to build them but not put wings on them? We call it defense spending, but I wonder why we don't just hand the money to Lockheed and let them go out and spend it and not build a plane that might crash and kill somebody.

I don't think the press has done a very good job dealing with government spending. The Defense Department with the $9,500 toilet seat, that's not the problem anymore. Medicare and Medicaid and Social Security are the problem. That's us. That's our generation. There the press never says a word.

We certainly never require politicians to ever address those issues except really briefly sometimes during the New Hampshire primary, and then everybody falls asleep.

Reason: Have you noticed that baby boomers are showing alarming tendencies toward becoming safety Nazis?

Barry: I hate to speak for the whole society, but I will. I'm a journalist, it's my job. The real repressive, smug part of it seems to have passed. There's been something of a reaction against political correctness. Needless to say, the government hasn't caught up yet.

But when the boomers started to have kids reach adolescence, there was suddenly this feeling that they needed to protect their kids from all the same things they did when they were kids. Which I guess is a natural tendency, but it makes for a less fun society.

Reason: It strikes me as bizarre that a prospective Supreme Court justice has to get up there, in his 40s, and say, "No, I never smoked pot."

Barry: The whole thing about whether you smoke marijuana or not is so ridiculous. That and whether you protested the Vietnam War. Give me a break. Especially the marijuana thing. I'm inclined to think that anybody who never tried it should not be allowed in public office. But to make them get up there and lie, or at least be incredibly disingenuous, is just embarrassing.

After a while, the way this country deals with drugs is just not funny. What a waste of everyone's time and effort. What a waste of a lot of people's lives. The way we deal with drugs and sex. I saw one of these real-life cop drama shows, and they mounted a camera in this undercover agent's pick-up truck, right under the gear shift, and they sent him out to pick up prostitutes.

So the whole show consisted of this guy, who's quite a good actor, driving to this one street, and young prostitutes come up to him and solicit him. He says OK. They get in. They're trying real hard to be nice. He's going to pay $23, that's all he's got and they said that's OK. Meanwhile, behind him the other cops, these fat men with walkie-talkies, are laughing and chuckling because here they are about to enforce the law and protect society. They take her to some street and then of course they come up and arrest her. This poor woman—I don't know whether she's feeding her drug habit or feeding her kids or whatever. And the cops are so proud of themselves, these big strapping guys.

It just made me sick to see this. To treat these people who are trying to make a living, one way or another, this way, and to be proud of it. It's on television and we're all supposed to watch this and feel good about it. It's just disgusting.

It's like when cops sell drugs to people and then arrest them. And then we reach the point where I think it was Sheriff Nick Navarro in Broward County [Florida] had his lab making crack so they could sell it. They couldn't get enough in south Florida, so they had to actually produce it themselves.

What politician would say, "This is really a waste of money to be doing what we're doing? It's ridiculous sending cops out to arrest prostitutes when we're supposed to be concerned about crime in this country." What politician would ever say that? What newspaper person would ever say that without getting stomped all over by all the other hypocrites?

Reason: (Reporter fiddles with broken tape recorder, trying to fix it. It still doesn't work.) I feel guilty sitting here knowing I don't have two tape recorders running like Virginia wanted. No one has ever crossed Virginia Postrel and lived to tell about it.

Barry: I can't help but notice that the Japanese product is the one working.

Reason: Didn't you once get a letter from someone on the Supreme Court?

Barry: I got a letter from [Justice] John Paul Stevens. I won't call it a serious letter. It was on his official John Paul Stevens stationery, though. He brought to my attention a product that I already knew about called Beano, which is an anti-flatulence product. I was very pleased to get a Supreme Court justice suggesting a column, so I went and did a column about Beano. I went with my wife and another guy to a Mexican restaurant which we thought would be the ultimate test for an anti-flatulence product. There's a reason most of Mexico is located out of doors. And it worked. Several newspapers refused to run that column. But they did run advertisements for Beano.

Reason: You write about Miami as a place filled with people from many different lands, cultures, backgrounds, walks of life, all of whom want to kill each other. When they were going bring a pro-basketball team, you suggested we call it the "Giant Blood-Sucking Insects." So why do you live here?

Barry: Well, for one thing the *Herald* is here. If the *Herald* was in Minneapolis, I'd probably be in Minneapolis.

That isn't the main reason. I actually like south Florida. I never lived in a more interesting place than this. I've never met such a wide range of people. I guess when I came here I thought there were Cubans and then there were people from New York and that was Miami. Now I know that it's Cubans, people from New York, and some people from New Jersey.

Actually, there are people from all over—not just Latin America, certainly not just Cuba, but all over Europe, all over the United States. A lot of them just got here and have interesting stories to tell about where they are from. I like that. I like knowing a lot of different types of people. And I can afford to live in a relatively safe part of Miami.

Reason: Do you go along with the conventional Miami opinion that we should invade Haiti since they've sent all these dangerous rafts to our shores?

Barry: I guess like every other American I feel very threatened by the situation in Haiti. I know our own lifestyle here is hanging by a thread because of what's going on down there.

Reason: What about Cuba? What's the solution to this Cuban business?

Barry: Let them in! Look what they did for Miami. This was a pathetic little town and now it's a big city. It's just so silly. Let people come in and work, but come in and work. If we let them come in for the purpose of signing them up for government programs, I'm not too enthused about that.

Reason: One of the planks in your presidential campaign is the Department of Two Guys Named Victor.

Barry: This is one of those times I wasn't kidding. At the time, we were mad at Moammar Gadhafi, which resulted in us bombing all over Libya and killing a bunch of people, but not him. Then Ronald Reagan gets up and says we're not trying to kill him, we're just dropping bombs. You can kill all the Libyans you want, but legally you can't try to kill the leader.

The other one was Manuel Noriega. Here we have a problem with just one person, and we send all these troops down to deal with it. All these people get killed and hurt, but not Noriega.

So instead of messing around with armies, get a couple of guys named Victor. The president meets with them and has breakfast, or he goes to dinner with them at the restaurant of their choice, and suggests that he's having a problem. Then the next thing you know, you read in the paper that Saddam Hussein has suffered an unfortunate shaving accident resulting in the loss of his head. We don't involve a lot of 22-year-old kids in this dispute between George Bush and Saddam Hussein.

Reason: Let's talk about Vietnam. Did you think the war was evil, that we were fighting the wrong guys, or was it like, to paraphrase Muhammad Ali, "You didn't have any quarrel with no Vietcong"?

Barry: First of all I thought that was the best argument anybody ever gave against going to Vietnam. The most articulate, clear-cut, understandable, accurate, rational argument ever. To me, it showed a lot more wisdom than a lot of stuff I heard from anti-war people. There was a lot of talk about why we should be opposed to the war that was pro-totalitarian.

I felt ashamed at the time to say I didn't want to go. I didn't have any stake in that war. I didn't want to get killed; I didn't know anybody over there that I wanted to go over and kill on behalf of. I think the real gut-level reason was what Ali said. But at the time I felt that you had to have a moral justification. It didn't occur to me then that the moral justification is that other people can't tell you who to kill.

If they come for my kid, I'd say, "Go, if you want to go fight a war. If you don't, you don't. Nobody's got the right to tell you." I see that more clearly now than I did then. But in the climate of the times I believed the government did have the right to tell us all what to do, but that in this case they were just making a terrible mistake. I admire more the people who just said, "I'm not going because I don't want to."

But I had conscientious objector status. I got it because my dad was a C.O. in World War II. My dad was a Presbyterian minister. And I went to a Quaker college. Neither of those things had anything to do with me. But to my draft board—a bunch of plumbers in Peekskill, New York, making decisions about who should go and who shouldn't—that looked good.

I was really against that war, but to be a C.O., you had to believe that there was no circumstance under which you would ever kill anybody. And I can't say I honestly felt that. I would definitely kill people. I would have liked to have killed my draft board at the time.

This was in 1969 and it was getting harder to find jobs that were acceptable because they were all getting filled up with C.O.s. I ended up working for the Episcopal Church national headquarters in New York City as a bookkeeper. That's what I did for two years. But I was happy, because I knew guys who were getting shot. Sometimes I can't believe this actually happened in this country.

Reason: Let's play a little game.

Barry: You're not gonna ask me what kind of tree I would be?

Reason: That's the last question. Let's do a little word association.

I'll give you the name of a political figure and you say the first thing that comes to mind.

Barry: Oh, I hate this.

Reason: Oliver Stone.

Barry: Am I only allowed to say one word? Shithead. Oliver Stone—did you mean Oliver North or Oliver Stone?

Reason: Oliver Stone.

Barry: Oh, Oliver Stone. Shithead.

Reason: Janet Reno.

Barry: Out of her depth. I actually kind of like Janet Reno. She seems like a nice enough lady. But when you're basically going through the entire phone book trying to find women lawyers who don't have maids to pick the attorney general of the United States, how well can you do?

Reno taking responsibility for the Waco thing made me crazy. I was enraged. Seemingly nobody wants to know what actually happened. There were some gun violations and we end up in a situation where we are surrounding them. I kept saying, "Why don't they just walk away? Just walk away. Nobody has to die. Walk away. Later on, arrest them when they come out. But walk away."

But no, we can't do it. So we order these tanks to attack this building full of crazy people with kids, and lo and behold, bad things happen. Ha! Knock me down with a feather. It got me when Janet said, "I'll take responsibility." No. You can't say that. And if you mean it, then you have to resign your job right away.

Maybe what she meant was "I'll take political responsibility for it," which turns out to be a big plus. But if you're going to take real moral responsibility for those deaths, then take it. But don't take it and say you're still going to be the chief law enforcement officer of the United States.

That's not what you wanted. You wanted a one-word answer.

Reason: That's OK. Bill Clinton.

Barry: He's such a putz. He's basically my age; I knew a lot of people like him in college. It starts to really come home to you how inadequately prepared anybody is to be in charge of your life from a distance and to be given a lot of power when that person is basically your age and background. He strikes me as a pathetic figure. Because you can be the smartest person in the world—which he is, and if he's not, his wife is—and care more than anybody else in the world—which he does, I don't doubt that for a minute. And you can care so much that you're willing to be dishonest—you can tell people one thing but do another because you really know it's for their own good. And you'll still screw it all up. Because the whole premise of what you're doing's wrong!

Reason: I was talking to one of your editors as I did my lengthy—lengthy, Virginia!—preparation for this interview.

Barry: And it cost a lot, too!

Reason: One of your editors said, "Well, Dave's a libertarian, that's true. But he's not an irresponsible libertarian." Doesn't that kind of take the fun out of it?

Barry: I'm not sure what they mean by that. If you tell most people what libertarians think, they immediately assume that you cannot mean it all the way, that you're really just taking a position for argument's sake. When you say you don't think we should have public schools, they can't believe you mean that. You must mean that they should be smaller. But you can't really mean no public schools. Therefore, if I don't argue too much, they probably think I'm responsible. I don't think I'm particularly responsible. I resent that!

Reason: Last fall you wrote a piece in the *Tropic* and explicitly acknowledged being a libertarian. . . .

Barry: John Dorschner, one of our staff writers here at *Tropic* magazine at the *Miami Herald*, who is a good friend of mine and an excellent journalist, but a raving liberal, wrote a story about a group that periodically pops up saying that they're going to start their own country or start their own planet or go back to their original planet, or whatever. They were going to "create a libertarian society" on a floating platform in the Caribbean somewhere. You know and I know there's never going to be a country on a floating anything, but if they want to talk about it, that's great.

John wrote about it and he got into the usual thing where he immediately got to the question of whether or not you can have sex with dogs. The argument was that if it wasn't illegal to have sex with dogs, naturally people would have sex with dogs. That argument always sets my teeth right on edge.

And I always want to retort with, "You want a horrible system, because you think the people should be able to vote for laws they want, and if more than half of them voted for some law, everyone would have to do what they said. Then they could pass a law so that you had to have sex with dogs."

I was ranting and raving about this here in the office. So my editor, Tom Shroder, said "Why don't you write a counterpoint to it?"

So I wrote about why I didn't think libertarians are really doing this kind of thing so that they can have sex with dogs. I discussed some of the reasons that a person might want to live out of the control of our federal, state, local, and every other form of government. Actually, I don't think I even called myself a libertarian in the article. I think Tom Shroder identified me as one.

Reason: Did that give you pause, coming out of the closet on this?

Barry: I guess libertarianism is always considered so weird and fringe that people assume that you're in the closet if you don't go around talking about it. Usually in interviews we're talking about humor writing and they don't bring it up. Because I don't write an overly political column, people just assume I'm not. I guess nobody assumes anybody is a libertarian. It's a more complex political discussion than most people are used to, to explain why you think the way you do about public education or drug laws, and why it's not as simple as being for or against something.

Reason: Did you get any mail about being a libertarian after that article?

Barry: I got a few letters, mostly pretty nice. One or two letters saying, "Here's why it wouldn't work to be a libertarian, because people will have sex with dogs." Arguments like, "Nobody would educate the kids." People say, "Of course you have to have public education because otherwise nobody would send their kids to school." And you'd have to say, "Would you not send your kids to school? Would you not educate them?" "Well, no. I would. But all those other people would be having sex with dogs."

Reason: How did you become a libertarian?

Barry: I can tell you the person responsible. His name is Sheldon Richman and he is still something of a wheel in libertarian circles. He's at the Cato Institute now. Sheldon and I were working for competing newspapers when we met in suburban Philadelphia in the early '70s. We were at municipal meetings, which were hell for Sheldon. He was a libertarian way, way back. I don't know what I was. I came out of college with lots of trappings of '60s radicalism which had been tempered somewhat by the fact that almost all the real radicals I knew were assholes. You know, the guys who were "for the people," but really just seemed to hate people. And guys who wanted to be in Weatherman mainly so they could get into fights.

Sheldon and I would argue. I mean, really argue. Well, what if a baby is born with no arms and no legs and his parents both die? Huh? Doesn't society have a obligation? Sheldon was wonderfully patient and had a excellent sense of humor and never lost his temper, which is not true of me. I'd yell at Sheldon and get furious at Sheldon, but we were still friends.

I left journalism for a while and I was working for a consulting company where I taught effective writing seminars and by my recommendation we hired Sheldon. We argued more. I was a middle-of-the-road Democrat more than anything else. I know I voted for Carter. Watergate taught me how bad the Republicans were. Then in the late '70s, I began to see. I think the gas crisis had something to do with it. I began to realize, this is all happening because of the government. And I began to think about all the government people I knew, all the times I'd sat in meetings with Sheldon, watching people who were theoretically for the common good. Then I realized not one of them was and none of them ever have been. All these things Sheldon had said to me: There is no such thing as the common good, there is no such thing as society. He was right.

So I wrote him a letter. "Sheldon, I just wanted to let you know that in all the arguments you were right."

Reason: Here you are a libertarian and you work for the *Miami Herald*, conceivably the most anti-libertarian newspaper in North America.

Barry: You mean our editorial board. The eight or 10 people who nobody knows here who speak for this paper.

I don't like anything unsigned in a newspaper that purports to be the opinion of some group if we don't know who the group is. It's laughable to say that the *Miami Herald's* editorials or any newspaper's editorials represent any views other than those of the people writing them, so why don't we tell everybody who they are?

It bothers me greatly that we have this system of opinion pages that dates back to when you knew who the owner of the paper was and his editorial told you what he thought. We should call editorials what they are: columns written by committees. If you want to agree with the committee, that's great. But they don't speak for me and they don't speak for a lot of people who work at the paper. I want to gag sometimes when I see who "we" are recommending that people vote for, and not just as a libertarian.

Reason: Is this a reference to the First Lady's brother?

Barry: Yeah. We are recommending that people vote for Hugh Rodham for the Senate of the United States!

Reason: You write a lot about rock 'n' roll. From a philosophical standpoint, what's the worst rock 'n' roll song of all time?

Barry: My nomination right off the top my head is a song that was a hit in the '70s—"Signs, signs, everywhere signs. blocking up the scenery, breaking my mind, do this, don't do that, can't you read the signs?" Basically a diatribe against property rights.

Reason: That was by The Five Man Electrical Band.

Barry: It's a real smug self-righteous punk kid saying nobody has the right to tell him what to do and how dare you put a sign up saying that I can't go on your property? Hey, kid! Stick this sign up your ass.

Reason: You wrote a serious column about your son's bicycle accident, in which you concluded that he should wear a helmet even though he looks like a dork. Now a lot of states are considering mandatory bicycle helmet laws. What do you think about that?

Barry: I got a lot of mail about that column, which is the only serious column I've ever written that went out as a regular column. It was the only time I ever had anything to say, which is, "Make a kid wear a helmet."

I got a lot of mail from organizations concerned with bike safety. Then I got a couple from people who wanted my support for mandatory helmet laws. I can't support that. If you pass a law like that you'll do more harm than good, because you'll make people think they've done something about the problem when they haven't.

There's only one way kids will wear helmets, and that's if their parents are nagging them to. They will never wear helmets because some state passes a law requiring it.

I genuinely think in this case—just 'cause I know my son and I know his friends—that kind of legislation would focus responsibility in the wrong place. It's not up to the cops, for God's sake. So I know that all over America there's probably politicians sending out pictures of themselves signing that mandatory helmet bill, but it's bullshit. I say that as a parent.

Reason: As your son grew up and began getting into activities where he had the potential to break things and kill himself, did that cause you to rethink your views?

Barry: No. He does hurl that back in my face sometimes. I said, "Rob, as soon as you are paying your own way in life, I'll stop telling you what to do. But you're not. You're taking money from me, living in my house." I try really hard to make him a responsible person.

Reason: What if the 7-Eleven down the street put in a vending machine where you could get heroin for a quarter?

Barry: And then have sex with a dog? Meaning what? My son wouldn't go get heroin. If he did or didn't, it wouldn't have anything to do with whether it was legal or illegal. I did all this stuff that was illegal when I was a kid. I drank beer when I was 15. I smoked cigarettes when I was 13. I drove to New York City when I was 14—don't tell my son. Those things were against the law, but I did them anyway. I didn't become a heroin addict, although I probably could have gotten heroin somehow. I don't think my son would buy heroin at any price. He knows what it is, and he knows how stupid it is. Any parent that relies on any law to help him parent is an idiot.

Reason: Why did you leave Coral Gables, the Miami suburb that's the libertarian paradise?

Barry: God, you talk about a libertarian nightmare! We got a ticket for painting our own living room white. And they came to the door, a guy in a uniform.

Reason: This is inside the house?

Barry: The interior living room. It turned out you had to have a permit if the job cost more than $50. I don't know what you can possibly do for less than $50 to have somebody come in your house. I had to pay the painter to go down to the city hall. This is after I called up city hall and ended up actually screaming. The painter spent a day getting a permit to do a job that took about half a day to actually do.

Then I wrote a column about that and discovered that there were people in Coral Gables who would wait until 2 o'clock in the morning to replace a sink because to do it during the daytime you'd see the trucks outside. Two trucks. That's a carpenter and a plumber. So that's two different permits. People were not fixing their houses because they didn't know how to get the permits. It was crazy.

Reason: If you have a cat out of the house, it's supposed to be on a leash there.

Barry: Yeah, and you're not allowed to park a truck in your driveway. You're not allowed to work on your house on Sunday. The people who enforce these laws are nuts. After I wrote a column on this, I got I don't know how many letters from Coral Gables homeowners, story after story after story, wonderfully horrible stories. And the venom they felt for their own government! You cannot paint the exterior of your house. You have to take the paint chip down to show the paintchip Nazis. It goes on all the time and it's hilarious. People are afraid to own their own homes. People are afraid their own government will catch them fixing their houses.

December 1994

The Battle for Your Brain

Science is developing ways to boost intelligence, expand memory, and more. But will you be allowed to change your own mind?

Ronald Bailey

"WE'RE ON THE VERGE OF profound changes in our ability to manipulate the brain," says Paul Root Wolpe, a bioethicist at the University of Pennsylvania. He isn't kidding. The dawning age of neuroscience promises not just new treatments for Alzheimer's and other brain diseases but enhancements to improve memory, boost intellectual acumen, and fine-tune our emotional responses. "The next two decades will be the golden age of neuroscience," declares Jonathan Moreno, a bioethicist at the University of Virginia. "We're on the threshold of the kind of rapid growth of information in neuroscience that was true of genetics 15 years ago."

One man's golden age is another man's dystopia. One of the more vociferous critics of such research is Francis Fukuyama, who warns in his book *Our Posthuman Future* that "we are already in the midst of this revolution" and "we should use the power of the state to regulate it." In May a cover story in the usually pro-technology *Economist* worried that "neuroscientists may soon be able to screen people's brains to assess their mental health, to distribute that information, possibly accidentally, to employers or insurers, and to 'fix' faulty personality traits with drugs or implants on demand."

There are good reasons to consider the ethics of tinkering directly with the organ from which all ethical reflection arises. Most of those reasons boil down to the need to respect the rights of the people who would use the new technologies. Some of the field's moral issues are common to all biomedical research: how to design clinical trials ethically, how to ensure subjects' privacy, and so on. Others are peculiar to neurology. It's not clear, for example, whether people suffering from neurodegenerative disease can give informed consent to be experimented on.

Last May the Dana Foundation sponsored an entire conference at Stanford on "neuroethics." Conferees deliberated over issues like the moral questions raised by new brain scanning techniques, which some believe will lead to the creation of truly effective lie detectors. Participants noted that scanners might also be able to pinpoint brain abnormalities in those accused of breaking the law, thus changing our perceptions of guilt and innocence. Most nightmarishly, some worried that governments could one day use brain implants to monitor and perhaps even control citizens' behavior.

But most of the debate over neuroethics has not centered around patients' or citizens' autonomy, perhaps because so many of the field's critics themselves hope to restrict that autonomy in various ways. The issue that most vexes them is the possibility that neuroscience might enhance previously "normal" human brains.

The tidiest summation of their complaint comes from the conservative columnist William Safire. "Just as we have anti-depressants today to elevate mood," he wrote after the Dana conference, "tomorrow we can expect a kind of Botox for the brain to smooth out wrinkled temperaments, to turn shy people into extroverts, or to bestow a sense of humor on a born grouch. But what price will human nature pay for these nonhuman artifices?"

Truly effective neuropharmaceuticals that improve moods and sharpen mental focus are already widely available and taken by millions. While there is some controversy about the effectiveness of Prozac, Paxil, and Zoloft, nearly 30 million Americans have taken them, with mostly positive results. In his famous 1993 book *Listening to Prozac*, the psychiatrist Peter Kramer describes patients taking the drug as feeling "better than well." One Prozac user, called Tess, told him that when she isn't taking the medication, "I am not myself."

One Pill Makes You Smarter . . .
That's exactly what worries Fukuyama, who thinks Prozac looks a

lot like *Brave New World*'s soma. The pharmaceutical industry, he declares, is producing drugs that "provide self-esteem in the bottle by elevating serotonin in the brain." If you need a drug to be your "self," these critics ask, do you really have a self at all?

Another popular neuropharmaceutical is Ritalin, a drug widely prescribed to remedy attention deficit hyperactivity disorder (ADHD), which is characterized by agitated behavior and an inability to focus on tasks. Around 1.5 million schoolchildren take Ritalin, which recent research suggests boosts the activity of the neurotransmitter dopamine in the brain. Like all psychoactive drugs, it is not without controversy. Perennial psychiatric critic Peter Breggin argues that millions of children are being "drugged into more compliant or submissive state[s]" to satisfy the needs of harried parents and school officials. For Fukuyama, Ritalin is prescribed to control rambunctious children because "parents and teachers . . . do not want to spend the time and energy necessary to discipline, divert, entertain, or train difficult children the old-fashioned way."

Unlike the more radical Breggin, Fukuyama acknowledges that drugs such as Prozac and Ritalin have helped millions when other treatments have failed. Still, he worries about their larger social consequences. "There is a disconcerting symmetry between Prozac and Ritalin," he writes. "The former is prescribed heavily for depressed women lacking in self-esteem; it gives them more the alpha-male feeling that comes with high serotonin levels. Ritalin, on the other hand, is prescribed largely for young boys who do not want to sit still in class because nature never designed them to behave that way. Together, the two sexes are gently nudged toward that androgynous median personality, self-satisfied and socially compliant, that is the current politically correct outcome in American society."

Although there are legitimate questions here, they're related not to the chemicals themselves but to who makes the decision to use them. Even if Prozac and Ritalin can help millions of people, that doesn't mean schools should be able to force them on any student who is unruly or bored. But by the same token, even if you accept the most radical critique of the drug—that ADHD is not a real disorder to begin with—that doesn't mean Americans who exhibit the symptoms that add up to an ADHD diagnosis should not be allowed to alter their mental state chemically, if that's an outcome they want and a path to it they're willing to take.

Consider Nick Megibow, a senior majoring in philosophy at Gettysburg College. "Ritalin made my life a lot better," he reports. "Before I started taking Ritalin as a high school freshman, I was doing really badly in my classes. I had really bad grades, Cs and Ds mostly. By sophomore year, I started taking Ritalin, and it really worked amazingly. My grades improved dramatically to mostly As and Bs. It allows me to focus and get things done rather than take three times the amount of time that it should take to finish something." If people like Megibow don't share Fukuyama's concerns about the wider social consequences of their medication, it's because they're more interested, quite reasonably, in feeling better and living a successful life.

What really worries critics like Safire and Fukuyama is that Prozac and Ritalin may be the neuropharmacological equivalent of bearskins and stone axes compared to the new drugs that are coming. Probably the most critical mental function to be enhanced is memory. And this, it turns out, is where the most promising work is being done. At Princeton, biologist Joe Tsien's laboratory famously created smart mice by genetically modifying them to produce more NMDA brain receptors, which are critical for the formation and maintenance of memories. Tsien's mice were much faster learners than their unmodified counterparts. "By enhancing learning, that is, memory acquisition, animals seem to be able to solve problems faster," notes Tsien. He believes his work has identified an important target that will lead other researchers to develop drugs that enhance memory.

A number of companies are already hard at work developing memory drugs. Cortex Pharmaceuticals has developed a class of compounds called AMPA receptor modulators, which enhance the glutamate-based transmission between brain cells. Preliminary results indicate that the compounds do enhance memory and cognition in human beings. Memory Pharmaceuticals, co-founded by Nobel laureate Eric Kandel, is developing a calcium channel receptor modulator that increases the sensitivity of neurons and allows them to transmit information more speedily and a nicotine receptor modulator that plays a role in synaptic plasticity. Both modulators apparently improve memory. Another company, Targacept, is working on the nicotinic receptors as well.

All these companies hope to cure the memory deficits that some

30 million baby boomers will suffer as they age. If these compounds can fix deficient memories, it is likely that they can enhance normal memories as well. Tsien points out that a century ago the encroaching senility of Alzheimer's disease might have been considered part of the "normal" progression of aging. "So it depends on how you define normal," he says. "Today we know that most people have less good memories after age 40, and I don't believe that's a normal process."

Eight Objections

And so we face the prospect of pills to improve our mood, our memory, our intelligence, and perhaps more. Why would anyone object to that?

Eight objections to such enhancements recur in neuroethicists' arguments. None of them is really convincing.

• *Neurological enhancements permanently change the brain.* Erik Parens of the Hastings Center, a bioethics think tank, argues that it's better to enhance a child's performance by changing his environment than by changing his brain—that it's better to, say, reduce his class size than to give him Ritalin. But this is a false dichotomy. Reducing class size is aimed at changing the child's biology too, albeit indirectly. Activities like teaching are supposed to induce biological changes in a child's brain, through a process called learning.

Fukuyama falls into this same error when he suggests that even if there is some biological basis for their condition, people with ADHD "clearly . . . can do things that would affect their final degree of attentiveness or hyperactivity. Training, character, determination, and environment more generally would all play important roles." So can Ritalin, and much more expeditiously, too. "What is the difference between Ritalin and the Kaplan SAT review?" asks the Dartmouth neuroscientist Michael Gazzaniga. "It's six of one and a half dozen of the other. If both can boost SAT scores by, say, 120 points, I think it's immaterial which way it's done."

• *Neurological enhancements are anti-egalitarian.* A perennial objection to new medical technologies is the one Parens calls "unfairness in the distribution of resources." In other words, the rich and their children will get access to brain enhancements first, and will thus acquire more competitive advantages over the poor.

This objection rests on the same false dichotomy as the first. As the

University of Virginia's Moreno puts it, "We don't stop people from giving their kids tennis lessons." If anything, the new enhancements might increase social equality. Moreno notes that neuropharmaceuticals are likely to be more equitably distributed than genetic enhancements, because "after all, a pill is easier to deliver than DNA."

• *Neurological enhancements are self-defeating.* Not content to argue that the distribution of brain enhancements won't be egalitarian enough, some critics turn around and argue that it will be too egalitarian. Parens has summarized this objection succinctly: "If everyone achieved the same relative advantage with a given enhancement, then ultimately no one's position would change; the 'enhancement' would have failed if its purpose was to increase competitive advantage."

This is a flagrant example of the zero-sum approach that afflicts so much bioethical thought. Let's assume, for the sake of argument, that everyone in society will take a beneficial brain-enhancing drug. Their relative positions may not change, but the overall productivity and wealth of society would increase considerably, making everyone better off. Surely that is a social good.

• *Neurological enhancements are difficult to refuse.* Why exactly would everyone in the country take the same drug? Because, the argument goes, competitive pressures in our go-go society will be so strong that a person will be forced to take a memory-enhancing drug just to keep up with everyone else. Even if the law protects freedom of choice, social pressures will draw us in.

For one thing, this misunderstands the nature of the technology. It's not simply a matter of popping a pill and suddenly zooming ahead. "I know a lot of smart people who don't amount to a row of beans," says Gazzaniga. "They're just happy underachieving, living life below their potential. So a pill that pumps up your intellectual processing power won't necessarily give you the drive and ambition to use it."

Beyond that, it's not as though we don't all face competitive pressures anyway—to get into and graduate from good universities, to constantly upgrade skills, to buy better computers and more productive software, whatever. Some people choose to enhance themselves by getting a Ph.D. in English; others are happy to stop their formal education after high school. It's not clear why a pill should be more irresistible than higher education, or why one should raise special ethical concerns while the other does not.

- *Neurological enhancements undermine good character.* For some critics, the comparison to higher education suggests a different problem. We should strive for what we get, they suggest; taking a pill to enhance cognitive functioning is just too easy. As Fukuyama puts it: "The normal, and morally acceptable, way of overcoming low self-esteem was to struggle with oneself and with others, to work hard, to endure painful sacrifices, and finally to rise and be seen as having done so."

"By denying access to brain-enhancing drugs, people like Fukuyama are advocating an exaggerated stoicism," counters Moreno. "I don't see the benefit or advantage of that kind of tough love." Especially since there will still be many different ways to achieve things and many difficult challenges in life. Brain-enhancing drugs might ease some of our labors, but as Moreno notes, "there are still lots of hills to climb, and they are pretty steep." Cars, computers, and washing machines have tremendously enhanced our ability to deal with formerly formidable tasks. That doesn't mean life's struggles have disappeared—just that we can now tackle the next ones.

- *Neurological enhancements undermine personal responsibility.* Carol Freedman, a philosopher at Williams College, argues that what is at stake "is a conception of ourselves as responsible agents, not machines." Fukuyama extends the point, claiming that "ordinary people" are eager to "medicalize as much of their behavior as possible and thereby reduce their responsibility for their own actions." As an example, he suggests that people who claim to suffer from ADHD "want to absolve themselves of personal responsibility."

But we are not debating people who might use an ADHD diagnosis as an excuse to behave irresponsibly. We are speaking of people who use Ritalin to change their behavior. Wouldn't it be more irresponsible of them not to take corrective action?

- *Neurological enhancements enforce dubious norms.* There are those who assert that corrective action might be irresponsible after all, depending on just what it is that you're trying to correct. People might take neuropharmaceuticals, some warn, to conform to a harmful social conception of normality. Many bioethicists—Georgetown University's Margaret Little, for example—argue that we can already see this process in action among women who resort to expensive and painful cosmetic surgery to conform to a social ideal of feminine beauty.

Never mind for the moment that beauty norms for both men and women have never been so diverse. Providing and choosing to avail oneself of that surgery makes one complicit in norms that are morally wrong, the critics argue. After all, people should be judged not by their physical appearances but by the content of their characters.

That may be so, but why should someone suffer from society's slights if she can overcome them with a nip here and a tuck there? The norms may indeed be suspect, but the suffering is experienced by real people whose lives are consequently diminished. Little acknowledges this point, but argues that those who benefit from using a technology to conform have a moral obligation to fight against the suspect norm. Does this mean people should be given access to technologies they regard as beneficial only if they agree to sign on to a bioethical fatwa?

Of course, we should admire people who challenge norms they disagree with and live as they wish, but why should others be denied relief just because some bioethical commissars decree that society's misdirected values must change? Change may come, but real people should not be sacrificed to some restrictive bioethical utopia in the meantime. Similarly, we should no doubt value depressed people or people with bad memories just as highly as we do happy geniuses, but until that glad day comes people should be allowed to take advantage of technologies that improve their lives in the society in which they actually live.

Furthermore, it's far from clear that everyone will use these enhancements in the same ways. There are people who alter their bodies via cosmetic surgery to bring them closer to the norm, and there are people who alter their bodies via piercings and tattoos to make them more individually expressive. It doesn't take much imagination to think of unusual or unexpected ways that Americans might use mind-enhancing technologies. Indeed, the war on drugs is being waged, in part, against a small but significant minority of people who prefer to alter their consciousness in socially disapproved ways.

• *Neurological enhancements make us inauthentic.* Parens and others worry that the users of brain-altering chemicals are less authentically themselves when they're on the drug. Some of them would reply that the exact opposite is the case. In *Listening to Prozac,* Kramer chronicles some dramatic transformations in the personalities and attitudes of his patients once they're on the drug. The aforementioned Tess tells him it was "as if I had been in a drugged state all those years and now I'm clearheaded."

Again, the question takes a different shape when one considers the false dichotomy between biological and "nonbiological" enhancements. Consider a person who undergoes a religious conversion and emerges from the experience with a more upbeat and attractive personality. Is he no longer his "real" self? Must every religious convert be deprogrammed?

Even if there were such a thing as a "real" personality, why should you stick with it if you don't like it? If you're socially withdrawn and a pill can give you a more vivacious and outgoing manner, why not go with it? After all, you're choosing to take responsibility for being the "new" person the drug helps you to be.

Authenticity and Responsibility

"Is it a drug-induced personality or has the drug cleared away barriers to the real personality?" asks the University of Pennsylvania's Wolpe. Surely the person who is choosing to use the drug is in a better position to answer that question than some bioethical busybody.

This argument over authenticity lies at the heart of the neuroethicists' objections. If there is a single line that divides the supporters of neurological freedom from those who would restrict the new treatments, it is the debate over whether a natural state of human being exists and, if so, how appropriate it is to modify it. Wolpe makes the point that in one sense cognitive enhancement resembles its opposite, Alzheimer's disease. A person with Alzheimer's loses her personality. Similarly, an enhanced individual's personality may become unrecognizable to those who knew her before.

Not that this is unusual. Many people experience a version of this process when they go away from their homes to college or the military. They return as changed people with new capacities, likes, dislikes, and social styles, and they often find that their families and friends no longer relate to them in the old ways. Their brains have been changed by those experiences, and they are not the same people they were before they went away. Change makes most people uncomfortable, probably never more so than when it happens to a loved one. Much of the neuro-Luddites' case rests on a belief in an unvarying, static personality, something that simply doesn't exist.

It isn't just personality that changes over time. Consciousness itself is far less static than we've previously assumed, a fact that raises contentious questions of free will and determinism. Neuroscientists are finding more and more of the underlying automatic processes operating in the brain, allowing us to take a sometimes disturbing look under our own hoods. "We're finding out that by the time we're conscious of doing something, the brain's already done it," explains Gazzaniga. Consciousness, rather than being the director of our activities, seems instead to be a way for the brain to explain to itself why it did something.

Haunting the whole debate over neuroscientific research and neuroenhancements is the fear that neuroscience will undercut notions of responsibility and free will. Very preliminary research has suggested that many violent criminals do have altered brains. At the Stanford conference, *Science* editor Donald Kennedy suggested that once we know more about brains, our legal system will have to make adjustments in how we punish those who break the law. A murderer or rapist might one day plead innocence on the grounds that "my amygdala made me do it." There is precedent for this: The legal system already mitigates criminal punishment when an offender can convince a jury he's so mentally ill that he cannot distinguish right from wrong.

Of course, there are other ways such discoveries might pan out in the legal system, with results less damaging to social order but still troubling for notions of personal autonomy. One possibility is that an offender's punishment might be reduced if he agrees to take a pill that corrects the brain defect he blames for his crime. We already hold people responsible when their drug use causes harm to others—most notably, with laws against drunk driving. Perhaps in the future we will hold people responsible if they fail to take drugs that would help prevent them from behaving in harmful ways. After all, which is more damaging to personal autonomy, a life confined to a jail cell or roaming free while taking a medication?

The philosopher Patricia Churchland examines these conundrums in her forthcoming book, *Brainwise: Studies in Neurophilosophy.* "Much of human social life depends on the expectation that agents have control over their actions and are responsible for their choices," she writes. "In daily life it is commonly assumed that it is sensible to punish and reward behavior so long as the person was in control and chose knowingly and intentionally." And that's the way it should remain, even as we learn more about how our brains work and how they sometimes break down.

Churchland points out that neuroscientific research by scientists like the University of Iowa's Antonio Damasio strongly shows that emotions are an essential component of viable practical reasoning about what a person should do. In other words, neuroscience is bolstering philosopher David Hume's insight that "reason is and ought only to be the slave of the passions." Patients whose affects are depressed or lacking due to brain injury are incapable of judging or evaluating between courses of action. Emotion is what prompts and guides our choices.

Churchland further argues that moral agents come to be morally and practically wise not through pure cognition but by developing moral beliefs and habits through life experiences. Our moral reflexes are honed through watching and hearing about which actions are rewarded and which are punished; we learn to be moral the same way we learn language. Consequently, Churchland concludes "the default presumption that agents are responsible for their actions is empirically necessary to an agent's learning, both emotionally and cognitively, how to evaluate the consequences of certain events and the price of taking risks."

It's always risky to try to derive an "ought" from an "is," but neuroscience seems to be implying that liberty—i.e., letting people make choices and then suffer or enjoy the consequences—is essential for inculcating virtue and maintaining social cooperation. Far from undermining personal responsibility, neuroscience may end up strengthening it.

For Neurological Liberty

Fukuyama wants to "draw red lines" to distinguish between therapy and enhancement, "directing research toward the former while putting restrictions on the latter." He adds that "the original purpose of medicine is, after all, to heal the sick, not turn healthy people into gods." He imagines a federal agency that would oversee neurological research, prohibiting anything that aims at enhancing our capacities beyond some notion of the human norm.

"For us to flourish as human beings, we have to live according to our nature, satisfying the deepest longings that we as natural beings have," Fukuyama told the Christian review *Books & Culture* last summer. "For example, our nature gives us tremendous cognitive capabilities, capability for reason, capability to learn, to teach ourselves things, to change our opinions, and so forth. What follows from that? A way of life that permits such growth is better than a life in which this capacity is shriveled and stunted in various ways." This is absolutely correct. The trouble is that Fukuyama has a shriveled, stunted vision of human nature, leading him and others to stand athwart neuroscientific advances that will make it possible for more people to take fuller advantage of their reasoning and learning capabilities.

Like any technology, neurological enhancements can be abused, especially if they're doled out—or imposed—by an unchecked authority. But Fukuyama and other critics have not made a strong case for why individuals, in consultation with their doctors, should not be allowed to take advantage of new neuroscientific breakthroughs to enhance the functioning of their brains. And it is those individuals that the critics will have to convince if they seriously expect to restrict this research.

It's difficult to believe that they'll manage that. In the 1960s many states outlawed the birth control pill on the grounds that it would be too disruptive to society. Yet Americans, eager to take control of their reproductive lives, managed to roll back those laws, and no one believes that the pill could be re-outlawed today.

Moreno thinks the same will be true of the neurological advances to come. "My hunch," he says, "is that in the United States, medications that enhance our performance are not going to be prohibited." When you consider the sometimes despairing tone that Fukuyama and others like him adopt, it's hard not to conclude that on that much, at least, they agree.

February 2003

Observations From a
Reluctant Anti-Warrior

Peter Bagge

What do any of these pet issues have to do with a WAR in IRAQ, anyway? What are all these "PIGGIE-BACKERS" DOING HERE? (BESIDES GETTING ON MY NERVES, THAT IS)? SHOULDN'T WE BE STICKING TO THE MATTER AT HAND"?!?

PALESTINE INFORMATION PROJECT

VOT COMMU

CITIZENS IN SOLIDARITY WITH THE PEOPLE OF EL SALVADOR

EAS TIMO ACTIO NETWO

VEGAN OUT-REACH

I ASKED AN ORGANIZER FROM THE "NOT IN OUR NAME" COMMITTEE THIS VERY QUESTION. HE REPLIED THAT "JOB ONE" WAS GETTING PEOPLE TO SHOW UP AT ALL, AND THAT HE'S NOT GOING TO SPURN ANYONE WHO SHOWS UP WITH A SEPARATE CAUSE IN TOW.

HE ALSO MADE THE FOLLOWING SUGGESTION:

YOU SHOULD ATTEND A "S.N.O.W." MEETING. THEY'RE ALL OLDER, CHURCH-Y TYPES...

THEY'RE ALSO THE REAL ORGANIZING FORCE BEHIND THE LOCAL ANTI-WAR MOVEMENT...

HUH. SOUNDS BORING, BUT OKAY.

*"SOUND NATIVES OPPOSED TO WAR"

I SOON FOUND MYSELF IN A CHURCH BASEMENT SURROUNDED BY GRAYING PETER PAUL + MARY FANS. AND I WAS RIGHT: IT WAS BORING! STILL, I WAS IMPRESSED WITH THE WAY THOSE FOLKS HAD THIS WHOLE "PROTEST" ROUTINE DOWN PAT...

...A FEW OF OUR OLDER FRIENDS HAVE REQUESTED FOLDING CHAIRS FOR NEXT WEEK'S SIT-IN...

INSTRUCTIONS ON WHAT TO DO IN CASE YOU GET ARRESTED CAN BE FOUND NEXT TO THE COFFEE MAKER...

AGENDA
7:00: INTRODUC
7:15: REVIEW OP
:30   OS
:09

IT'S NOT SURPRISING, THEN, THAT THESE PROTESTS USUALLY FEEL RATHER SCRIPTED — LIKE THIS ONE MARCH THROUGH DOWNTOWN STAGED BY A GROUP OF HOOKY-PLAYING COLLEGE AND HIGH SCHOOL STUDENTS...

NO BLOOD FOR OIL!

OH, LOOK! HOW CUTE!

DON'T TRASH THE STARBUCKS, KIDS! HA HA!

RIDE A BIKE INSTEAD

I HOPE I DON'T GET GROUNDED FOR THIS!

ALL THE PASSERS-BYE SEEMED TO BE GIVING THEM THE THUMBS-UP FOR THEIR CUTENESS FACTOR ALONE. IT WAS LIKE A LI'L HIPPIE CHRISTMAS PAGENT!

THESE PROTESTS ATTRACT A WIDE VARIETY OF HARMLESS NUTS AS WELL — LIKE THE "CLOWNS AND WIZARDS FOR PEACE," WHO INCLUDED AN ELDER-LY CLOWN IN A WHEELCHAIR WHO KEPT INSISTING THAT SHE WAS A BABY...

I'M A BABY CLOWN! CAN YOU TELL ME HOW TO BE A GROWN UP CLOWN ONE DAY?

I, UH, H VE NO IDEA...

CAN YOU DESIGN A WEB SITE FOR US?

LIVE WITH A KIND HEART

THEIR MOTTO

SUCH DISPLAYS OF WILLFUL NAIVETÉ ARE VERY TYPICAL AMONG PACIFISTS, SADLY.

IN FACT, EVERY ARCHETYPE IMAGIN-ABLE COMES OUT OF THE WOODWORK AT THESE EVENTS, EACH ONE PLAY-ING THEIR "ROLE" TO THE HILT — LIKE THIS ONE MULLETHEAD, WHO RIGHT ON CUE CONFRONTED A GROUP OF MARCHERS TO DECLARE:

HEY, I'M FOR PEACE, TOO...

NUKE SADDAM!

THESE COLORS

DON'T BLEED

Native Son

Why a black supreme court justice has no rights a white man need respect

Edith Efron

FOR YEARS, DR. ALVIN POUSSAINT, associate professor of psychiatry at Harvard Medical School, has been faced with the thankless, if well-rewarded, task of explaining to "enlightened" white script writers—including those for *The Cosby Show*—that their heads are stuffed with offensive racist stereotypes.

"It's a problem," Poussaint said in a speech several years ago at Stanford. "What you get in the scripts is their perception of blackness."

One of the major reasons for the persistent problem is that millions of white adult Americans define "racism" as its most pathological manifestations: wearing white gowns and hoods, burning crosses, tarring and feathering blacks, hunting them down with dogs. Because those same millions of white Americans would not dream of committing such atrocities; because they vote for political representatives who pass civil-rights bills; because they applauded Martin Luther King and Thurgood Marshall; because they respect the changing nomenclature by which certain blacks wish to be addressed, they imagine themselves to be free of racism.

What they have never learned is that racism is an idea, a very old and intransigent idea. That idea exists on an unbroken continuum—all the way from a form that is fully conscious to a form that is unconscious. Its manifestations can range from the most grossly offensive and scornful invective to a compulsive noblesse oblige that cannot permit itself to make any criticisms at all. But whatever the degree or kind of racism, it invariably contains a double standard: The racist simply does not treat black individuals the same way he treats whites.

The effect of stereotypes on blacks is a sense of being unseen, as in Ralph Ellison's *Invisible Man*. The effect on whites is the corollary: They do not perceive blacks as real or make the same fine discriminations among blacks that they habitually make among whites. In the last analysis, they do not perceive black individuals; they perceive black skins. And this remains true at every step of the continuum.

It should not, therefore, come as an insuperable shock that the Senate Judiciary Committee hearings on the nomination of Judge Clarence Thomas to the Supreme Court were a racist phenomenon. The "nice" kind; no Simon Legrees or fiery crosses here. But racist nonetheless. Setting aside old segregationist Strom Thurmond, who conscientiously counterfeited a dead man and may, for all I know, actually have been dead, the other senators participated, singly and collectively—and unwittingly—in a process that ceaselessly generated negative stereotypes about Thomas.

So unaware were these men of their own racist stereotyping that when, at the 11th hour, they were forced consciously to deal with a negative stereotype, they didn't recognize it and had no principles with which to assess it or with which to differentiate between the black individuals involved. The press commentators generally revealed the same incapacities. All eventually ended up mired in an unspeakable crudity that would never have occurred had the protagonists been white.

Stereotypes

The original hearings generated at least five negative racist stereotypes, all in one way or another springing from acts of omission, defaults of thinking, rather than conscious racism. The senators blinded themselves profoundly to what they were doing, and that self-blinding led to the ultimate explosion, the meaning of which they and the agitated white press do not understand to this day. I present those initial stereotypes roughly in order of ascending gravity:

1. **The Nomination.** Much has been made of the fact that President George H. W. Bush lied when he said, in nominating Clarence Thomas to the Supreme Court, that Thomas was the "best" candidate

and that Thomas had not been chosen because he is black. Of course that was a lie, and so happy were Bush's critics to have caught him in a lie that they gave no thought to the implications of that particular lie for Thomas, and neither, of course, did Bush.

To omit the serious intellectual reasons for wanting a black nominee, and for wanting this particular black nominee, was to leave a vacuum. And the vacuum was implicitly filled by a negative stereotype. What Bush's lie implied, without his knowing or intending it, was: "I'm naming an empty suit with a black body inside it and with nothing worthy of presidential note in that black body's head." From Day One, thanks to the president, Clarence Thomas was *an empty-headed black in an empty suit*. That's Stereotype 1. Start counting.

2. The Strategy of Evasion. The second, and reinforcing, stereotype emerged as a byproduct—again unintended—of the Republican strategy of evasion, the tactic that had worked with David Souter in contrast with the opinion-laden Robert Bork and with which Thomas had agreed to cooperate. Whatever objections can be raised to that tactic—and there are dozens—the one that was not raised was the effect on Clarence Thomas. Thomas was not, as some historical revisionists are now claiming, an incompetent candidate. His legal writings and his opinions on one of the most prestigious appellate courts of the land had been carefully read by 1,000 members of and consultants to the American Bar Association, including "reading committees" from some of the most distinguished law schools in the country. Thomas' work was found to be well researched and economically and lucidly written; he was adjudged competent to sit on the Supreme Court.

The Republican strategy of evasion had the cumulative effect of destroying most of the evidence of Thomas' competence. As he gradually realized, he could only smuggle in a few of his own ideas and correct a few misinterpretations of his writings. And while Souter had been able to dance theoretical pirouettes around constitutional issues while landing nicely on his feet, having said absolutely nothing, Thomas lacked such balletic skills. He had crammed for months just to learn what he might be required to say—and then he had crammed all over again to learn how not to say it. When the time came to evade, he could perform no theoretical arabesques; he just plain, lumberingly, evaded—monotonously, over and over again. He wasn't used to it. To his credit, he was an abysmally bad evader.

The result was yet another offensive stereotype. *The empty-headed black in an empty suit became, in addition, a dumb, shifty, and evasive black.*

3. Senatorial Etiquette. An ostensibly simpler piece of advice from Thomas' "handlers" pertained to the etiquette deemed obligatory when addressing senators. And again, this boomeranged against Clarence Thomas. For various reasons, our senators engage in incessant mutual flattery and proclamations of collegial devotion. The more they despise each other, the more they do it. When they are at the point of mutually induced nausea, the air around them resonates with "My distinguished colleague from Dubuque," "My good old friend from Peoria, whom I hold in the highest esteem." The participants understand that such fawning formulations are riddled with dark jokes, cynicism, and arrant hypocrisy and are not to be believed for an instant.

But to coach Thomas in such heavily deferential courtesies, when the mutual mockery and cynicism were absent, was to inflict damage on him yet again—above all because he was already intellectually muzzled. Had Thomas been able to perform theoretical legal pirouettes around the senators, had he simply been free to talk eloquently and extensively about the issues of greatest concern to him, then the formulae of excessive and humorless deference might not have mattered so much. But in this case, they mattered dreadfully.

The empty-headed black in an empty suit; the dumb, shifty, evasive black now turned into (in George Will's words) a "cringing and groveling" black—a black tugging his forelock before Massa, a black who knows his place.

4. The "Character Issue." A more complex, and a more complexly stupid, enterprise—and this one allegedly dedicated to the *protection* of Thomas—was the attempt to establish the nominee as a paragon of virtue.

The original lies about Thomas' nomination, namely that he was the "best" person for the Court and that he had not been chosen because he is black, bore bizarre fruits. Absent a forthright statement of intellectual and political purposes, the goal became to defend both Bush and Thomas against the liberal interpretation of the nomination. George Bush knew, as did the entire political universe, that his use of the Willie Horton ad and his stated opposition to quotas had generated unceasing charges from liberals that he was a "racist" and that Clarence Thomas would be tagged as yet another black exploited by Bush for political purposes—a Willie Horton in reverse.

So a defensive solution designed to outfox liberals in what Republicans thought were liberal terms was devised. According to the *New Republic*'s Sidney Blumenthal—a forthright critic of both Bush and Thomas—Bush asked whether Sen. John Danforth, a known and loyal friend of Clarence Thomas, would "go to the mat" for his protégé if Thomas were nominated to the Court. Danforth said yes, and that, reports Blumenthal, was Bush's "decisive moment." It meant to Bush that his nominee would be protected "by a figure of moral stature," one widely respected by U.S. senators. Blumenthal elaborates: "Part of the reason it has been difficult to associate Thomas with Bush's racial tactics, and thus isolate him, is that the leading critic of such gambits happens to be Jack Danforth."

It became Danforth's appointed mission to orchestrate a chorus of witnesses, all proclaiming Thomas the embodiment of two particular virtues, chosen, obviously, because they are crucial virtues for a justice of the Supreme Court: "fierce independence" and "integrity." Patiently, endearingly, Danforth marshaled his little legion of personal witnesses from different periods of Thomas' life to attest fervently, all in the same language, that Clarence Thomas, as child, as boy, as youth, as young man, and as grown man, revealed "fierce independence" and "integrity." And for all I know it may have been true. The reason I don't know, and that nobody could know from this extended photo op and mass recitative, is that "independence" and "integrity"—"fierce" is lovely but unnecessary—*are virtues of mind, virtues of intellect.* Eviscerated of ideas, those words meant exactly nothing. The famous character issue was an attempt to assert character without intellectual content.

These testimonials certainly meant nothing to the Judiciary Committee liberals who were the objects of the anti-intellectual charade; who never for a moment forgot that they were fighting the ideas that Clarence Thomas might or would bring to the Court; who knew full well that Thomas had been chosen because he is black; and who knew, finally, that Thomas had opposed affirmative action's double standards and preferential quotas. And since, to conventional liberals, such views are racist, not a liberal brain cell was budged by this two-week long photo op, which boiled down to a constant loving cry that Thomas was "good."

By the time the parade of devoted witnesses shepherded by Danforth was over, irretrievable damage had once again been done to Clarence Thomas. *Thomas was not only the emptyheaded black in an empty suit. . . . He was not only a dumb, shifty, evasive black. . . . He was not only a cringing and groveling black who knew his place. . . . But he was a good black, a willing pawn in the hands of conservative white masters.*

Did the Republicans do this on purpose? No. This came, yet again, from the belief that *ideas* were dangerous, and that defensive tactics, as opposed to a bold hoisting of one's own flag, were safer. Of course, that is about as safe as a Lynching, but I anticipate myself.

5. The Abortion Issue. Customarily, this is simply classified as one manifestation of the evasion strategy. But it had a status of its own. It played a unique role at the hearings, and it produced two particularly damaging stereotypes of Thomas.

Legalized abortion was, for the Democrats, a substitute for the problem they were most frightened to discuss, one of the problems that could destroy their future as a party—the mounting animosity of white workers and middle-class citizens toward double-standard affirmative action, which gives preferential treatment to blacks over whites in hiring and in school admissions. While it was continually discussed at Democratic party councils, and while a major campaign was being planned to regain the votes of the fleeing working- and middle-class whites, this was not an issue the Democrats wanted to discuss at the televised hearings. And they certainly did not want Americans to see a strong and thoughtful black man—a black Republican—advocating equality of access for the disadvantaged and colorblind, meritocratic solutions. So the Democrats evaded the issue.

As Juan Williams wrote in the *Washington Post*, "For all the verbiage, the hearings before the Senate Judiciary Committee on Clarence Thomas were much more interesting for what wasn't said than for what was. . . . Affirmative action is the dog that hardly barked."

To fill the resulting intellectual vacuum, the Democratic senators organized a furor over legalized abortion. It consisted of two things. First, they asked Thomas almost 100 times to explain, in advance, what his legal and political opinions would be in any upcoming abortion case, when he had a right to decline to answer such questions. The only contribution of the Republicans to the out-of-control Democrat batterings was . . . to count the questions!

Next, the Democrats put on an array of witnesses who foresaw only legions of butchered women if Thomas were confirmed. On that charge, the Republicans strangled. The effect on Thomas, the advocate of fair, colorblind solutions, was appalling.

He was not only the empty-headed black in an empty suit. . . . He was not only a dumb, shifty, evasive black. . . . He was not only a cringing and groveling black who knew his place. . . . He was not only a good black, a willing pawn in the hands of his conservative white masters. . . .

But he had been cast in the role of a black criminal taking the Fifth, 100 times, and a would-be butcher of women.

With this last, as any cop on the beat could have told the senators, Thomas had been smacked on the equivalent of a "Most Wanted" list, with the annotation "black—43 years old—reputed mass murderer—armed—dangerous." Thomas had been set up for a kill.

"Roots"
Why didn't the senators grasp the dangerous stereotypes they had generated? Why didn't they recognize what they were doing? Because the stereotyping was camouflaged for them by their enormous hypocrisy, a hypocrisy that took two forms—the first, a counterfeit reverence for Clarence Thomas' achievements and "roots"; the second, a counterfeit concern with his intellectual history and ideas.

Nothing could have been more proudly offered by committee Republicans and more flatteringly received by Democrats than the tale of the black boy from Pin Point, Georgia, and the saga of his studies at Holy Cross, his law degree from Yale, and his eventual rise to prominence. It was a Horatio Alger story that tugged at every American's heartstrings, and even when it didn't, it was supposed to.

The tale that Thomas himself told was accurate, and he told it with justified pride. It was the compulsive and wide-eyed gushing over it by the senators that was counterfeit and tacitly offensive to blacks. Thomas was scarcely the first small-town boy from the South to have achieved an important measure of success in the United States, and it was both patronizing and hypocritical to celebrate him as though he were. But that was just a symptom of a deeper hypocrisy: Few, if anyone at all, on the Senate committee, plus its legions of staff "researchers," actually cared a fig about Thomas' background or "roots."

The roots of an American black are not to be found in the town in which he was born or reared. They are plunged deep in the dark loam of slavery and its ongoing and unfinished business of institution-alized racism. No senator, and apparently no staffer, even considered for a moment investigating Thomas' real roots or his real struggle with American racism.

They should have done so, for the same reasons they should not have evaded one of their major political problems and buried it in legalized abortion. Because they all knew that white racism, both of the deeply entrenched kind and of a reactive, defensive kind, was ex-ploding all about them in workplaces, in schools, and in police depart-ments in response to double-standard affirmative action; because it was an issue that in one form or another might come before the Court; because it was an issue about which the nominee had thought deeply for most of his life—and because it was an issue that was affecting, must be affecting, the real black man sitting before them.

Except . . . the subject for the Democrats was taboo. And Clar-ence Thomas wasn't real to the Senate Judiciary Committee: He was a black pawn in their evasive political chess game; he was a collection of stereotypes. So no one, apparently, thought of doing some research on what really lay behind all the mutually congratulatory, intensely "caring" backslapping about Clarence Thomas' roots.

Here are just a few things someone might have dug up about those roots by grabbing an old copy of *The Black Bourgeoisie* by E. Frank-lin Frazier, professor of sociology at Howard University and former president of the American Sociological Association. Here are a few of the events that were still living memories transmitted to those who reared Thomas:

• Thomas' great-grandfather was alive in 1857 when the question of whether the Negro was or was not only property and therefore had or had no rights as a human being was raised. This question was ad-dressed in the Dred Scott case, which was taken to the Supreme Court where Chief Justice Taney inscribed the famous answer: "A Negro has no rights which a white man need respect."

- In 1898, close to the date of birth of Clarence Thomas' grandparents, Rep. A. Dearmond of Missouri described Negroes as "almost too ignorant to eat, scarcely wise enough to breathe, mere existing human machines."
- In 1900, perhaps within Thomas' grandfather's memory, the American Book and Bible House published *The Negro, A Beast*, which depicted God as an idealized white man, along with a white man made in his image and a caricature of a Negro intended to show that the Negro was "simply a beast without a soul."
- At the same time, says Frazier, the Negro was ceaselessly portrayed as "a gorilla dressed up as a man." The newspapers described him as "burly or apelike." Even the white-skinned products of intensive racial mixing were cartooned as "black with gorilla features." This stereotyping, says Frazier, was "constantly representing the Negro as subhuman, a beast, without any human qualities."
- In 1915, an army surgeon informed people that "many animals below man manifest a far greater amount of real affection in their love-making than do Negroes."
- In the early 1920s, a doctoral dissertation in Columbia University's Department of Studies in History, Economics, and Public Law presented as "scientific" fact that the Negro was "as destitute of morals as any of the lower animals."

Such facts are integral to an understanding of Thomas' "roots." If anyone on the Judiciary Committee had shown the slightest interest in such matters, he might have speculated on the degree to which the worst stereotyped hatreds entangled in those roots were still alive. He might have remembered the recent videotaped beating of a black man by out-of-control Los Angeles cops and the investigation that had brought to life the voices on the police radio crackling with jokes about "gorillas in the mist." He might have realized that those white cops were not joking about their night school courses in zoology. He might have wondered if Clarence Thomas were still subjected to such dangers and to such assumptions of bestiality. He might have wondered how Thomas might feel about it. And what Thomas might do if such a thing happened.

But these are questions, or speculations, one raises about a *man—* and Thomas was not a man to the Senate Judiciary Committee. Both the men on the committee who were hurled into panic by new ideas and the men on the committee who were hurled into panic by all ideas asked no such questions and gained no such insights. They had lost all contact with the human being they were "judging."

They didn't even know that he was judging *them.* They didn't notice that his eyes, once twinkling, had become dark and impenetrable, that his once spontaneous laugh had vanished, and that he now smiled through tightly clenched teeth, with the muscles in his jaws working tensely beneath the surface of his skin. They didn't even realize that Clarence Thomas was terribly, terribly angry.

They didn't observe that as each day passed, Thomas' body had grown more rigid, that he was being held upright now only by a few powerful ideas, which he repeated like a mantra—by the ideas of "the nuns," the first teachers to instruct him explicitly that he was the metaphysical equal of whites . . . by the idea of "my grandfather," the first to teach him that whatever legal and constitutional victories had been achieved for his racial group, his personal efforts, his personal achievements, his personal pride, were his own to forge . . . by the idea of his lifelong "dilemma" over the "fundamental contradiction" in the U.S. Constitution, which he wove, over and over again, into his answers—the "contradiction" that had, historically, refused him membership in the human race.

The ideas that held him upright helped him mask his terrible anger. But even to the power of these ideas to sustain him there were limits—limits to what he could or would tolerate.

Limits? The concept never entered the heads of the senators who recognized no limits on themselves. A black who sets limits? That did not conform to the stereotyped creature they had created. Blinded by "caring" hypocrisy, no one thought to investigate what those limits might be, or to consider that they were precariously close to those limits.

Books
And then there was the second major source of self-blinding, which reinforced the first—the senators' counterfeit interest in Thomas' intellectual history. It kept them from discovering that right under the senatorial noses, there was clear-cut information about the limits to what Clarence Thomas could and would tolerate.

Throughout the hearing the Democrats in particular pretended that they were deeply interested in, indeed determined to discover, the nature of Thomas' ideas. The Republicans were not in the idea business; they had left that up to the Democrats. But the Democrats had compiled all the papers and speeches Thomas had written and the interviews he had given. They knew, they said, the books he had read, the authors who had influenced him. All, they said, they had carefully examined and thought about. But they hadn't.

They had simply been searching for fragments of sentences with which to indict Thomas as politically extreme or politically unreliable or politically unrespectable. Had they been authentically interested in Thomas' ideas, they would have read, and read carefully, one of the first documents brandished by Sen. Joseph Biden on the air, complete with references. It was an interview given by Thomas to *Reason* four years ago. One passage in that interview should have sounded a red alert to the men who professed to be interested in Thomas' ideas. It went as follows:

> **Reason:** Are there any writers who were really influential to you when you were young, and still are?
>
> **Thomas:** Richard Wright. I would have to put him number one, numero uno. Both *Native Son* and *Black Boy* really woke me up. He captures a lot of the feelings that I had inside that you learn how to repress.

Richard Wright, "number one, numero uno"—until this very day? Richard Wright, one of the most powerful black writers ever to have appeared in America? How could that have been overlooked by men who were trying, as his interrogators claimed to be trying, to understand this particular man? How could they have overlooked the observation that Wright "captures a lot of the feelings that I had inside that you learn how to repress." How could they have missed the switch to the present tense?

But his interrogators missed this. Had they not missed it, it is conceivable, just barely conceivable, that the hearings might have run a different course.

Wanting very much to understand this man who had been stereotyped out of existence and who was controlling a violent anger at what was happening to him, I reread *Native Son.* It had been published in 1940, and I had not read it for 50 years. One finds many things relevant to Thomas and to his roots and his lifelong concerns in this book. But in this particular context, one finds one crucial thing—his limits. The one thing Thomas would not, could not, permit, whatever else might be at stake, the one stereotype that it would be downright dangerous to paste on him, leaps out from those pages.

Native Son is the story of Bigger Thomas, a defiant, terrified, sensitive black tough, a chronic delinquent trapped for life in a white world where he dreams of experiencing connectedness to others but cannot. He gets a job as a chauffeur for a rich white family. Entirely by accident—there is nothing equivocal about this—he suffocates their daughter with a pillow when she is dead drunk. In terror that he will be charged with murdering her, he burns her body in a furnace. It does not occur to him that he will automatically be charged with raping her and that he has burned the evidence that he did not. One lie leads to another, one crime to another, and eventually the young Bigger Thomas becomes the object of a 5,000-man police hunt that combs every inch of the segregated slum in which he is trapped. Eventually he is caught; he is defended by two white communists; their efforts fail, and Bigger is found guilty—guilty, above all, of the two crimes he has not committed, the rape and the murder of the white girl.

Here are four passages from the book:

***

It was all over. He had to save himself. But it was familiar, this running away. All his life he had been knowing that sooner or later something like this would come to him. And now, here it was. He had always felt outside of this white world, and now it was true. It made things simple. He felt in his shirt, yes, the gun was still there. He might have to use it. He would shoot before he would let them take him; it meant death either way, and he would die shooting every shot he had.

***

He looked down and read, REPORTERS FIND DALTON GIRL'S BONES IN FURNACE. NEGRO CHAUFFEUR DISAPPEARS. FIVE THOUSAND POLICE SURROUND BLACK BELT. AUTHORITIES HINT SEX CRIME. . . .

He paused and reread the line, AUTHORITIES HINT SEX CRIME. These words excluded him utterly from the world. To hint that he had committed a sex crime was to pronounce a death sentence. It meant a wiping out of his life even before he was captured; it meant death before death came, for the white men who read those words would at once kill him in their hearts.

***

"Come on, now, boy. We've treated you pretty nice, but we can get tough if we have to, see? It's up to you! Get over there by that bed and show us how you raped and murdered that girl."

"I didn't rape her," Bigger said through stiff lips.

"Aw, come on. What you got to lose now? Show us what you did."

"I don't want to."

"You have to!"

"I don't have to."

"Well, we'll make you!"

"You can't make me do nothing but die!"

And as he said it, he wished that they would shoot him he could be free of them forever.

***

He did not turn to the papers until after the man had left the room. Then he spread out the Tribune and saw: NEGRO RAPIST FAINTS AT INQUEST. He understood now; it was the inquest he had been taken to. He had fainted as they had brought him here. He read:

Overwhelmed by the sight of his accusers, Bigger Thomas, Negro sex-slayer, fainted dramatically this morning at the inquest of Mary Dalton, millionaire Chicago heiress.

Emerging from a stupor for the first time since his capture last Monday night, the black killer sat cowed and fearful as hundreds sought to get a glimpse of him.

"He looks exactly like an ape!" exclaimed a terrified young white girl. . . .

The moment the killer made his appearance at the inquest, there were shouts of "Lynch 'im! Kill 'im!"

But the brutish Negro seemed indifferent to his fate. . . . He acted like an earlier missing link in the human species. He seemed out of place in a white man's civilization.

***

One of these paragraphs above all contains Clarence Thomas' limits—the charge, the very intimation of a charge, that he could not, would not be able to permit:

"He paused and reread the line AUTHORITIES HINT SEX CRIME. These words excluded him utterly from the world. To hint he had committed a sex crime was to pronounce a death sentence. . . . It meant death before death came, for the white men who read these words would at once kill him in their hearts."

The men on the Judiciary Committee, and their staffers, had not read this. Or if a few of the oldest ones had ever read the book, they had long since forgotten it. By climaxing the hearings with an 11th-hour charge of a "sex crime," the ingenious staffers were only seeking to disseminate what they conceived of as "dirt." They did not know that to Clarence Thomas, given his background, his roots, and his intellectual history, such a charge meant: *Death.*

Rarely has there been so poignant an example of life imitating art. But the senators and their "researchers" were not imitating art; there was no one on the Judiciary Committee or its staff with the literary imagination, let alone the vicious literary imagination, to do so. They were simplehearted souls, party hacks, whose only aspiration was to disgrace a political enemy. They didn't understand this political enemy. They didn't know that Thomas carried Richard Wright engraved upon his heart, that he had carried Richard Wright right into that hearing room.

"The Sex Crimes"

When Clarence Thomas learned he was going to be charged with a pack of "sex crimes," lumped together under the heading of "sexual harassment," and that they were to be discussed at a mock trial, he reacted with the swiftness of lightning. He fired his Republican handlers, who had not only dressed him in a dumb clown suit but had not known how to protect him from being portrayed as a criminal taking the Fifth and as a would-be butcher of women. If he had once believed that the men at the peak of the power establishment knew what they were doing, he believed it no more. He took his life out of their hands and back into his own.

Certainly, no one knew better than Thomas what "sexual harassment" had become over the years—a cultural phenomenon beyond his or, apparently, anyone's control. Once an objective description of the use of male employers' power to subjugate and exploit female subordinates, this new and ever-expanding legal offense, first defined in 1986, had turned into pure feminist dementia. Now "sexual harassment" meant anything or everything said or not said, done or not done, to a woman by a male superior, by a male co-worker, by any male in the vicinity, which upset, angered, or offended her—in the woman's judgment. Men's judgments had become legally irrelevant. The subjectivity and dubious First Amendment implications of the New Harassment are well-known. Thomas was charged by Anita Hill with crimes of "verbal conduct"—"speech crimes," which, of course, implies thought crimes.

Thomas' legal analysis of his alleged speech crimes was that of a trained Yale lawyer, a judge of a Court of Appeals, and the former head of the EEOC. But his decisions about what to do and say were pure Richard Wright. The two roles were different, but both were functions of the "evidence."

The charges against him, Thomas saw quickly, were legal junk. One aspect of that junk was dangerous legal junk—a set of charges that he had boasted of his "sexual prowess," of the "larger than normal" size of his own penis, accompanied by a drumbeat of other references to the mythic dimensions of black men's genitals.

"Legal junk," of course, means evidentiary junk, and that means something in addition to the fact that the charges were unprovable and there were no witnesses to attest to them. It means that, save for the *dangerous* allegations, the speech crimes as presented at the hearings had little or no significance to begin with. Anita Hill simply made a group of empty generalizations or recited a list of subjects that one can find in library card catalogs, in dictionaries, in encyclopedias, in articles, in monographs, and in books. How, in what words, in what style, Thomas had discussed those subjects, at all, were the crucial missing factors. Most of Hill's charges were an invitation to mass projection.

There was also corroborative junk. Three witnesses—all lawyers— testified that Hill had told them 10 years ago that she was depressed and was blaming her depression on unspecified verbal behavior, by implication of a sexual nature, by her boss. Hill did not even offer her subject list or her generalizations to those lawyers. She gave them no information at all. The lawyers were preternaturally incurious, asked no questions, requested no evidence, and, according to their testimony, all said the equivalent of, "Poor dear." A fourth lawyer testified that some years later Hill had told him that she left the EEOC because she had been "sexually harassed" by her boss. But still this famous list of speech crimes did not surface.

All that was established by her friends' testimony was that 10 years ago Anita Hill had been depressed and had attributed her depression to Thomas. This total absence of legal evidence was no doubt the reason that Hill's lawyers gave her a polygraph test, which is further evidentiary junk not accepted by our courts. It was an act of legal desperation to help a client who had been blowing evidentiary smoke.

Finally, there may have been outright psychological junk. Hill's strangely passive legal witnesses were aware of her depression but did not check her competence. One witness tried to establish Hill's competence by saying, "I have never known Anita to express anger," a bizarre comment, since repressed anger is a common characteristic of depression. Another witness sought to strengthen the claim that Hill is stable by testifying that to Hill fictional characters are not "real." Apart from the implication that people who read novels suffer from instability, the fact is that fictional characters are more intensely real than everyday people—that is the purpose of art. Hill's inability to accept fictional beings as "real" and her inability to express anger may have reflected an emotional disorder—one that could prevent her from correctly interpreting the style, mood, and intent of any discourse dependent on affect. To say any consideration of Hill's psychological or emotional states is "blaming the victim" is to beg the question.

In summary, evidentiary junk, corroborative junk, and possibly psychological junk, had all been dragged out at the last minute to destroy a Supreme Court nominee.

Danger

But all this junk Thomas denied, then swept aside. What he took seriously was the dangerous junk interwoven throughout. He immediately saw that he had been hit by the oldest and most murderous racist stereotype directed at the black male: the black male as sexual beast; the subhuman, predatory ape without sensibilities and without morals; the stereotype amply documented by Franklin Frazier in the

1950s (his 10th edition still being read in 1968) and exemplified by the crackling radio jokes about "gorillas in the mist" from the white Los Angeles cops in 1991. That stereotype was hundreds of years old, it was still alive, and Thomas accurately understood that it had been aimed at him.

He also knew its origins, its vicious hypocrisy, and its social uses. For all the constitutional talk forbidding blacks human status, our Founding Fathers—like the French, Spanish, and Portuguese aristocrats who imported black slaves into the New World—were fully aware that blacks were human beings. Such men happily slept with black women, fell in love with them, protected the children they fathered by them, freed those children, adopted them. They safeguarded their own black sons, often by sending them abroad for higher education. But they reserved a different and frightful fate for the unprotected black boy—not for the girl, only for the boy. As soon as he reached puberty, as soon as he was sexually mature, he turned, magically and abruptly, into the Mythic Black Beast who became sexually taboo for white women. Thus did the white men control their paternity and property lines. Any alleged breach of the sexual taboo could, and often did, mean death—for the black male.

That is what the dangerous legal junk meant to Thomas. He knew that, regardless of the lack of legal evidence, the humanity of his female accuser would be assumed, as indeed it was. He knew he would have to establish his own humanity, and to do so at a mock trial.

The Thomas who reentered the hearing room was the "real" Clarence Thomas, the man without Republican handlers, with only two people at his side: his old and trusted friend Danforth, who was shaking with volcanic rage, and Virginia Lamp Thomas, his white wife, who sat motionless, tears rolling down her cheeks. From the depths of his Richard Wright–infused subconscious, Thomas made statements and leveled his own charges, charges that totally disoriented the Senate Judiciary Committee. The senators, like children who had played too long with matches, suddenly grasped that they had set the whole house afire and had no idea what to do about it.

Thomas said, "I died. The person you knew—whether you voted for me or against me—died." He said, "I've been harmed, my family has been harmed. I've been harmed worse than I've ever been harmed in my life. I wasn't harmed by the Klan. I wasn't harmed by the Knights of Camelia. I wasn't harmed by the Aryan Race. I wasn't harmed by any racist group. I was harmed by this process—this process, which accommodated these attacks on me. . . . I would have preferred an assassin's bullet." He described what had occurred as a "high-tech lynching" and informed the Judiciary Committee grimly: "I will not provide the rope for my own lynching."

Even when he talked quietly and calmly, he was clearly in a state of uncontrollable mutiny. When asked whether he wanted to withdraw his name from nomination, he replied, "I'd rather die than withdraw. If they're gonna kill me, they're gonna kill me. . . . I'd rather die than withdraw from the process—not for the purpose of serving on the Supreme Court but for the purpose of not withdrawing from this process." Somewhere inside Clarence Thomas was the unmistakable voice of Bigger Thomas, refusing in extremis to submit to the white man's power: "You can't make me do nothing but die!" And whatever these white senators understood, they knew that to be true. Their power had become entirely destructive; they could make him do nothing but die.

It was mainly from Sen. Orrin Hatch, who by means sensible and not had consistently conveyed his sympathy for Thomas, that Thomas consented to hear Anita Hill's charges. He had refused to attend or to listen to the session at which she herself had testified. In this exchange, Hatch became the only man on the committee to admit, honestly, that he did not understand the phenomenon of the stereotyped racist attack:

> **Hatch:** You said some of this is stereotyped language. What does that mean?
>
> **Thomas:** Senator, language throughout the history of this country, and certainly throughout my life, language about the sexual prowess of black men, language about the sex organs of black men, and the sizes, etc., that kind of language has been used about black men as long as I've been on the face of the earth, and these are the kind of charges it is impossible to wash off. . . .
>
> If you want to track through this country in the 19th and 20th century, the lynching of black men, you will see that there is invariably—or in many instances—a relationship with sex, and an accusation that that person cannot shake off.

That's the point I am trying to make, and that is the point that I was making last night, that this is a high-tech lynching. I cannot shake off these accusations because they play to the worst stereotypes we have about black men in this country.

Many other things happened, but there is no need to recapitulate. The real end of the hearings, where racism is concerned, occurred in this exchange. The hearings, which had woven a web of progressively destructive racist stereotypes around Thomas, had culminated in the worst conceivable stereotype of all—the black male as mythic sexual beast. And most of the nation—80 percent of it—found itself watching a black nominee to the Supreme Court discussing, before a Senate committee of white men, the subject of black men's genitals.

The vast majority of watching Americans, white and black, "believed" Clarence Thomas; the vast majority, white and black, "disbelieved" Anita Hill. Even many people who believed Hill's story, or parts of it, were deeply shocked by the episode.

Some whites are baffled by the question, Why would a black woman seek to destroy a black man by means of a deadly racist stereotype? How can it possibly be "racist" if it comes out of a black woman's mouth? That, too, is racism. It rests on the assumption that blacks are an undifferentiated mob with a "leadership" in the place of a brain. A black does not crack up in incomprehension at the idea of a black seeking to hurt another black.

I address this question only because it is so commonly asked, not because it is important or because one needs the answer to know whom to "believe" or "disbelieve." Indeed, too much attention has been focused on whom we should "believe" or "disbelieve." Most significant is the fact that we were asked to function as "believers" or "disbelievers" at all.

Examine the role that we, as witnesses to the execrable spectacle, were all asked to play. We ourselves were asked to serve as jurors at a mock trial. We ourselves were asked to believe or disbelieve in matters pertaining to "the sexual prowess of black men, the sex organs of black men, the sizes. . . ." We ourselves were asked to relive Richard Wright's *Native Son.* We ourselves were asked to play the role of the "terrified young white girl" at the inquest, gawking at the Beast.

That is sufficient reason to reject those who organized and orchestrated this spectacle.

It is not sufficient reason to reject Clarence Thomas. There may be, as he himself has said, constitutional reasons for opposing him, or reasons pertaining to his qualifications, or reasons pertaining to the desire for a more politically balanced Court. But I myself am willing to take a chance on Thomas, and I am heartily glad he is now wearing his justice's robes.

I hope that as the advocate of a colorblind society arranges his new offices, he puts two huge pictures on his walls—one of Chief Justice Taney and one of Richard Wright. For it is because of them that he endured so much and fought so hard and because of them, ultimately, that he is on that Court.

And it would be salutary for all of us to realize that every single day that this particular justice sits on that Court will be a silent requiem for Bigger Thomas, the fictional slum boy of 50 years ago who is engraved on Clarence Thomas' heart and whose real-life descendants, trapped in America's slums, are still hit at puberty by the potent remnants of the dehumanizing myth. This country can only benefit from the presence on the U.S. Supreme Court of a man who authentically understands that deadly myth and has the ego strength to talk about it and to fight it.

February 1992

Rage On

The strange politics of millionaire rock stars

Brian Doherty

"A GOOD SONG SHOULD MAKE YOU wanna tap your feet and get with your girl. A *great* song should destroy cops and set fire to the suburbs. I'm only interested in writing great songs."

So says Tom Morello, guitarist for the Los Angeles–based band Rage Against the Machine. He and his bandmates are not simply against cops and the suburbs, of course. They also stand for the Zapatistas and the Shining Path, for freeing Mumia Abu-Jamal and Leonard Peltier, for giving California back to Mexico, and for destroying stores where rich people like themselves shop.

That's pretty strong stuff coming from work-for-hire employees of one of the great cogs in the global capitalist machine, the megaconglomerate Sony, which wholly owns and distributes Rage's music and even is a co-owner of the group's publishing. Since 1992, Rage has sold nearly 7 million records, and it's safe to say that nobody has benefitted more from that commerce than the band's unabashedly capitalist paymaster.

In the world of high-profile popular music, Rage Against the Machine is far from alone in advocating a radical leftism, even one that shades into old-style, let's-nationalize-everything-but-the-music-industry communism. Indeed, Rage has plenty of fellow travelers, most of whom are equally unironic about being fabulously wealthy rock stars.

Comrades in the struggle to overthrow "late capitalism" include Chumbawamba, a collective of British anarchists who hit major pop stardom with their rousing 1997 sing-along drinking anthem "Tubthumping." Chumba (as their fans call the group) declares on its Web site that it wants "to destroy the moral code that says you can only have what you can afford to pay for." And it wants a social order where nothing happens without everyone—*everyone!*—agreeing to it. Folk-rocker Ani DiFranco is best known for refusing to be part of a "corporate" machine, saying that the record business is "dehumanizing and exploitative, not much different from any other big business." Thus, refusing to work on Maggie's Farm no more, she operates her *own* corporate machine, Righteous Babe Records (and pockets far more per record as a result).

Then there's Patti Smith, the over-the-hill punk poetess who once wowed Madison Square Garden audiences with songs about adolescent alienation and all-night sex. Smith includes a 10-minute-plus tribute to Ho Chi Minh and a snappy pop tune against the World Trade Organization on her latest album, *Gung Ho*. The members of the British band Primal Scream, who originally gained fame as drug-addled hedonists, have taken a page from Rage Against the Machine's little red playbook, lately recasting themselves as born-again followers of Noam Chomsky, the tenured MIT professor and favorite "dissident" intellectual of politicized rock bands everywhere.

If pop stars' politics aren't hard left, they can at least be counted on to be firmly liberal, as evidenced by the anti-nuke, pro-green activism of the likes of Jackson Browne, Bonnie Raitt, Sting, and Bono (who has also met with the pope and Bill Clinton to help forge policy on debt forgiveness for the Third World). Oddly, this even holds true for ostensibly redneck bands. When *George* magazine, that self-styled arbiter of what's important in politics and popular culture, devoted a 14-page spread to rock and politics in March, it found notable such glorious rockin' moments as the Allman Brothers' endorsement of Jimmy Carter. The *George*ists suffered no mental strain reconciling support for Jimmy Carter with their declaration that "rock is the music of rebellion and freedom of expression. [It] pushes limits and challenges the established order." Jimmy Carter, the ultimate Ramblin' Man.

To be sure, fighting The Man has its rewards: Rage Against the Machine has landed on the covers of both *Rolling Stone* and *Spin* to promote its capitalist products. There's no social capital to be lost, and much to be gained, by being a socialist.

Despite such occasional freakish and unrespected outliers as that pro-gun and anti-immigrant Motor City Madman Ted Nugent (whose music is mostly a distant memory as his stage pronouncements against non–English speakers still get negative press attention), and the Ayn Rand–grokking band Rush (which produced a screed about trees who end up getting hacked with axes when they try to enforce equality among themselves—"that song about the trees who join a labor union," as *Village Voice* music editor Chuck Eddy once put it), leftism in one form or another is the backbeat of much modern pop. If a political message is an integral part of any pop band's image or music, it's bound to be leftist. If otherwise nonpolitical bands make public comments, those comments are almost inevitably left-leaning.

This nearly ubiquitous connection is, to put it mildly, rather strange. Pop music—especially that expansive, vague subcategory known as rock—is universally recognized as the soundtrack of rebellion, whether the authority in question is Daddy taking the T-bird away or the Soviet Union. (The former Czechoslovakia's Velvet Revolution was so named in part because its participants drew inspiration from those poster children of bourgeois decadence, the Velvet Underground.) While rock hugely, hilariously upset right-wing record burners in the '50s and '60s, it was also officially outlawed in all the great Worker's Republics of the same era—indeed, it was seen as the very apotheosis of capitalist hedonism. (But then if only Richard Nixon, that notable Elvis fan, could go to China, then perhaps only Rage Against the Machine, those millionaire communists, could bring Mao back across the Pacific.)

As important, rock and the larger pop music scene are so clearly a function of the wealth, innovation, and leisure time thrown off by capitalism that it should be nothing less than mind-boggling that pop stars themselves mutter incessantly about toppling the very system that pays them so well. But to most rock stars and rock critics, the link between the music and left-wing politics is so natural and so expected that it is simply assumed.

The connection, however, is a matter of attitude and style, not logic. In truth there isn't even any necessary connection among the varied elements of most "progressive" causes: Rage Against the Machine tries to jerry-rig such a link, but it doesn't really argue it so much as assert it. Of course, the band's members assume, someone who doesn't want women raped also hates the rich, wants to return California to the Mexicans, and craves the utter abolition of private property—but there is no logical link between those attitudes.

As impossible as such givens may be to justify intellectually, they are of great importance culturally. By insisting on a connection between a set of logically unconnected propositions, people can forge powerful coalitions that make these fake categories real. For examples of this sort of group building, look no further than the Democratic and Republican parties, neither of which is particularly philosophically consistent—try to find the logical link between socializing medicine and expressing support for free speech, say, or between prayer in school and lowering the capital gains tax.

Or consider the inchoate American gang identified as "Bohemian" in *New York Times* rock critic Ann Powers' new book, *Weird Like Me: My Bohemian America.* Powers casually links rock music with her version of bohemia, that world of young and not-so-young hipsters living and behaving in nontraditional ways. Rock, she writes, "inspires fans to dye their hair green and wear thigh-high leather boots; to defy their parents, skip school, and tell off the boss; or even, sometimes, to take a new turn and change their lives completely." Her bohemia is inexorably linked with progressive politics, not holding down a decent job, being kind to gays and minorities, and all else that's "cool."

Powers fails to recognize that her bohemia is predicated upon a market liberalism that throws off so much wealth that you can live like a Pharaoh just by scavenging what other people throw out—as she and her slacker buddies did in San Francisco in the '80s and early '90s. Her bohemian lifestyle is part of the same system that underwrites free markets, consumerism, and tolerance for all sorts of offensive speech and alternative lifestyles. In other words, the liberty to be bohemian is a glorious result of the very capitalist reality that Powers says a real bohemian must be against.

In a slightly different vein, well-known rock critic Dave Marsh asserts a necessary connection between the progressive left and rock music. Marsh, a former *Rolling Stone* mainstay, brings it all back home to race and class in *Rock and Rap Confidential,* the monthly newsletter he's edited since 1983. Rock, he says, was the result of breaking down traditional race and class barriers. It represents, Marsh writes, "a chance to communicate across all the gaps in our society—gaps of class, race, region, gender, generation, education, you name it. Used this way rock 'n' roll became not just a 'way out' of impoverished working class or straight-jacketed middle class existence but a method of absolutely transforming yourself, a means of becoming who you'd always dreamed of being. . . . Of such things is freedom constructed."

A certain poetic internal freedom, yes. But about more mundane freedoms—to earn money, say, and spend it how you see fit, or to not have decisions made for you by a nanny state—Marsh is as quiet as audiences at a Canned Heat reunion.

Unlike many leftists, Marsh understands the oppressive potential of government clearly enough to tell me this in an interview: "The difference between a left-progressive-socialist or communist, or whatever the fuck anyone wants to call me, and a liberal is precisely the degree to which you trust the government. And the difference on gun control is precisely the degree to which you trust the government. The First Amendment is first for a reason, and the Second Amendment is second for a reason."

But Marsh can't sensibly reconcile the liberty whose praises he sings with the kind of state necessary to forge the classless egalitarianism that he wants. "I'm trying to find a way to develop a society where people work cooperatively most of the time in order to act on individuality some of the time," he tells me.

But Marsh's conflation of rock as class-and-race mixer with rock as progressive force foists a narrow, partisan political agenda on a more general form of pre-political expression. Certainly such fathers of rock as Chuck Berry, Jerry Lee Lewis, Little Richard, and Elvis Presley shattered race and class taboos: Crossing such lines explains in large part why they were loved and hated by so many.

More than that, though, such figures helped craft the legend of being young and being American as very heaven. Their foot-tapping, ass-shaking rhythms communicate Dionysian excess, a liberating, often frenzied release from *all* sorts of restraint and control. It is precisely this aspect that cultural conservatives on both the right and the left have always found suspicious about rock 'n' roll. Rock inspires a devil-may-care sense of fun in both individuals and groups, one that doesn't crave any social purpose higher than making the listener feel a particularly energetic and lively brand of good.

Elvis, Chuck Berry, and the rest did this as artists, not proselytizers. If they were the voice of those suffering social injustice and prejudice, they broke free by standing up for a joyous liberty of pleasure and expression, not by campaigning for *campesinos* and a ban on nuclear power. They were about flamboyance and excitement—especially their own highly individualized visions of such things—not dour attempts to institute Chumbawamba's dream of endless town meetings.

It's easy, of course, simply to accuse stinking rich entertainment celebs who talk about overthrowing the system that pays them so well of being hypocrites. Easy, perhaps, and necessary, since of course they are. It's a pose that, however stylish, is just that. But there's something more interesting going on than either conscious or naive hypocrisy.

What rockin' leftists have the hardest time facing up to is rock's reality as a product of capitalism. Chumbawamba claims it is playing the game of "exist[ing] within [the capitalist system] and at the same time trying to find ways to bring the bastard down." The members also admit that, thanks to their deal with a major label, they have "a decent standard of living for the first time in their lives." (These quotes all from the FAQ on their official Web site, www.chumba.com. On the site, they also fend off accusations from young fans who complain that Chumba should never suggest that it's all right to get drunk if you enjoy it—that beer money, after all, could have been spent helping the downtrodden.)

To justify its compromised position, Rage Against the Machine drags Noam Chomsky into the debate, making the twisted analogy that Chomsky wouldn't object to Barnes & Noble—a big, bad company—selling his books, because that's where people buy books. That analogy might explain why Rage would allow its records to be sold at Tower megastores, but not why its members would become employees of and sell ownership of their music to Sony, which makes far more money selling Rage records than Rage itself does.

Leftists desperately want to avoid real discussion of such contradictions. That's because such contradictions suggest that if it's impossible to escape acting like capitalists, maybe there isn't anything wrong with openly being one.

In a curious way, left-leaning rockers and critics are abetted in their cognitive dissonance by right-wingers, who are similarly uncomfortable with the liberating and wild aspects of capitalist culture, especially its willingness to give people whatever they want regardless of the "morality" of the desire. Right-wingers, every bit as much as their left-wing counterparts, are fundamentally troubled by the cultural implications of capitalism.

As Bill Bennett's periodic jeremiads against advertising that exhort consumers "to break the rules" and "to peel off inhibitions" suggest, ostensibly pro-market conservatives are among the last ones to sell capitalism for what it is: a realm of groovy freedom filled with a dizzying and ever-expanding panoply of strange and wonderful and disturbing lifestyles and identities in which even the lousiest jobs can buy enormous amounts of leisure and the coolest movies, music, video games, and whatever else you want.

Both the right and the left are fully invested in a Puritan-work-ethic version of capitalism, no matter how at odds with reality such an approach is. For the right, Max Weber's world of long hours and forgone pleasure is precisely what is good about the system: It creates a society of God-fearing, hard-working, well-behaved individuals. For the left, capitalism not only immiserates all but the top 1 percent of income earners, it crushes difference, breeds racism, and regiments free expression; hence the need for revolution. (Precisely how Ho's Vietnam, say, or Mao's China, two alternatives invoked by rockers as preferable to contemporary America, provide models for a freer world is left unspecified.)

It's not clear who is listening to Bennett and his ilk's worries that record companies and others are "exploiting the youth rebellion instinct." Nor is it clear that music fans either understand or pay much heed to their favorite performers' anti-capitalist rants. Beyond the question of whether the lyrics are actually intelligible, one great truth of capitalism is that the consumer is king and often, perhaps typically, uses products in unintended ways. (Just ask manufacturers of model airplane glue.)

This is certainly the case with music, often with comical results. During his 1984 re-election run, for instance, Ronald Reagan—dubbed Ronnie Ray-Gun by punk wags—co-opted Bruce Springsteen's anguished vet's lament "Born in the U.S.A." as a feel-good campaign anthem. Springsteen and his leftish admirers cried foul and asked Mr. Ray-Gun—*if he could read*—to read the lyrics, for God's sake. The song's lyrics are about a shell-shocked vet with "no place to run, nowhere to go." But who's to say Reagan wasn't right to insist the song was an upper? When I hear those notes and that drumbeat, and the Boss' best arena-stentorian, shout-groan vocals come over the speakers, I feel like I'm hearing the national anthem.

For its part, Rage Against the Machine performs music that eloquently conveys anger and the desire to tear things up; indeed, that inchoate destructive energy may be the real draw for the band's largely adolescent male fan base. But what the lyrics actually convey is another matter. Not only are they frequently impossible to decipher, they are frequently incomprehensible even on paper. Try figuring out the specific call to action embedded in lines such as: "Merge on the networks, slangin' nerve gas/Up jump the boogie then bang, let 'em hang/While the paranoid try to stuff the void/Let's capture this AM mayhem/Undressed, and blessed by the Lord/The power pendulum swings by the umbilical cord/Shock around the clock from noon til noon/Men grabbing they mics and stuff em into the womb."

Politically engaged pop artists don't like to think about the fact that most people don't get what they're trying to say. Nirvana's Kurt Cobain, arising from a punk rock bohemia that saw intolerant, stupid mainstream dudes and dudettes as the enemy, killed himself at least partially because of this dilemma. Tom Morello of Rage Against the Machine believes he doesn't have to worry about fan misunderstanding (a much hardier type than Cobain, Morello presumably would just picket that Guess? Jeans store with an extra ounce of determination if his fans weren't quite getting his band's message). Morello doesn't see Rage as educating its fans. He says, "It's not at all the case where our audiences are empty glasses that we pour knowledge in . . . a lot of them are pretty pissed off and have got their own ideas."

Do they ever. If you surf Rage Against the Machine fan Web boards, you find kids shouting things like, "Spring break! Woooo!" On one board, an earnest Rage fan gives a long definition and defense of democratic socialism, while another, not clearly trying to be a wise-ass, replies, "Sweden is run by social democrats—All it really is is super high taxes."

The medium is resolutely not the message when it comes to rock songs and rock style. Aping their favorite performers, fans may dress like Che, sport a stylish, pre-Monica beret, or even get a tattoo of him. But that doesn't mean they're signing on to Guevara's economic plan, which helped sink the Cuban economy during the '60s.

On another popular Rage message board, a fan told of spotting a fellow high school student wearing a Rage T-shirt. The fan engaged the shirt wearer in a discussion of Rage's socialism. But the shirt wearer didn't believe it: How could his rockin' rebels be socialists, since "socialists were fascists who stifle freedom"? The wounded reporter of this exchange noted, "I hope people will actually find out what a shirt stands for before they wear it."

But the other kid knew what he knew. And in the market system that pays Rage so handsomely for its anti-capitalist songs, he's the one who imposes value on the objects that he uses to create his public personality. No matter what Rage's members might think, he knows they stand for freedom when he listens to them.

October 2000

Risky Journalism

ABC's John Stossel bucks
a fearful establishment.

Interviewed by Jacob Sullum

WHILE PREPARING A 20/20 SEGMENT on multiple chemical sensitivity that aired in January, John Stossel sent ABC associate producer Deborah Stone and her sister-in-law, Julie, to Dr. Grace Ziem, an MCS specialist in Baltimore. Prior to the visit, Ziem sent the two healthy women a 16-page questionnaire that included items such as "Do you crave sweets?" and "Do you ever forget what you read?" as well as queries about headaches, chest pains, and other symptoms. They answered the questions honestly and brought the completed forms to Ziem's office, where a physician's assistant gave them brief physical exams. After looking at their answers, Ziem told them they were chemically sensitive. She warned Julie not to get pregnant. She recommended that Deborah move out of New York City and enlist a "smelling buddy" to walk around with her, steering her away from dangerous odors. She charged each woman $925 and prescribed $3,300 in lab tests.

Later Ziem heard through the grapevine that the patients were ABC confederates and that Stossel, who had requested an interview, planned to discuss MCS in the context of "junk science." She also read a transcript of Stossel's 1994 special, "Are We Scaring Ourselves to Death?," in which he took a hard look at overhyped hazards such as dioxin, asbestos, and pesticide residues. Surmising that Stossel would not portray her in a positive light, Ziem not only backed out of the interview, she filed criminal charges against him, Deborah Stone, Julie Stone, and two other producers, accusing them of surreptitiously recording the conversation at her office. In Maryland, that's a felony. ABC said no such recording was made, and the charges were dropped about a month and a half later for lack of evidence. A disappointed Ziem promised further, unspecified legal action, and her bewilderment at the prospect of a journalist's skeptical treatment was almost touching. According to the Associated Press, "she had always considered the news media 'a friend' but now wonders who she can trust."

Many of Stossel's critics exhibit a similar sense of betrayal. As a consumer reporter at WCBS-TV in New York and, beginning in 1981, at ABC's *Good Morning America* and *20/20*, he acquired a reputation as an enemy of greedy capitalists, a champion of government regulation, and a protector of the public from the insidious hazards lurking in everyday life. Gradually, however, he came to see that businesses are not always evil, regulation can be harmful, and the risks that get the most publicity are usually trivial, if not non-existent.

As this new perspective began to shape Stossel's TV reports, his erstwhile allies in the consumer movement were not pleased. Ralph Nader, who came across as a paternalistic worrywart (imagine that!) in "Are We Scaring Ourselves to Death?," told *TV Guide* that Stossel "used to be on the cutting edge—now he's gotten lazy and dishonest." Sidney Wolfe, executive director of the Public Citizen Health Research Group, told the *Washington Post*, "I think he's really a menace. This guy is doing a massive amount of damage."

Nader and Wolfe probably were not thinking about Stossel's special on "The Mystery of Happiness" or his stories about relationships and child rearing. A psychology major at Princeton, Stossel has long shown an interest in topics that have little to do with public policy. No doubt Nader and Wolfe would prefer that he stick with those, instead of mucking about with their cherished assumptions. This Stossel does both on *20/20* and in his one-hour, prime-time specials, which air four times a year—a privilege he won from ABC when Fox tried to lure him away in 1993. His first special, "Are We Scaring Ourselves to Death?," featured themes that are rarely explored on TV, including the hidden costs of regulation and the exaggeration (or invention) of risks by interest groups and the news media. Subsequent specials examined the flight from responsibility toward victimhood, the durability of sex differences, the chilling effects of litigation, and the perversion of science by lawyers, activists, and politicians. Watching Stossel confront an EPA bureaucrat or a plaintiff's lawyer in his deceptively low-key manner, you get a surreal feeling: The techniques are familiar to anyone who has seen *60 Minutes*, but the targets are not.

Contrary to the impression you might get from the Naderites, Stossel's villains are not limited to public officials and pro-government activists. In his recent special on dubious science, for instance, he scored tobacco companies and promoters of vitamin C along with the EPA and the federal government's anti-salt crusaders. Last year he testified in a defamation case involving a 1991 *20/20* story that accused Ft. Lauderdale banker Alan Levan of cheating real estate investors. "The primary motive was to inform people about deals where they could lose millions," he told the court. Although another jury had awarded the investors $8 million in damages, concluding that Levan had defrauded them, the jurors in the libel case never heard about that verdict, which was vacated as part of a settlement. In December they ordered ABC and the segment's producer to pay Levan and his bank $10 million. ABC is appealing.

Stossel, who turned 50 in March, has won 19 Emmys, the George Polk Award, and the George Foster Peabody Award. The National Press Club has recognized him five times for excellence in consumer reporting. He is still proud of stories he did a decade ago, but concedes that he sometimes was guilty of the alarmism he now decries—a point confirmed by the titles of some of his *20/20* segments from the '80s, which included "Danger in the Grass" (about pesticides) and "Brewing Disaster" (about exploding coffee pots). On the other hand, exposing scams has been a persistent theme in Stossel's career as a consumer reporter, and he continues to go after hucksters, swindlers, and charlatans, even when they happen to work for the government or serve a fashionable cause.

Reason: Let's talk about your political views while you were in college and how they changed over time.

John Stossel: I bought into what was trendy—trendy is harsh—what was prevailing wisdom at the time, which was that capitalism is useful but evil. But I wasn't particularly political.

Reason: Did you work on the school paper?

Stossel: I was the business manager. I once tried to write an article about something in the editorial column, but the editorial staff snickered at me. And, in fact, writing has never been my strength.

Reason: In retrospect, would you say you were a left-liberal? Is that how you started out in journalism?

Stossel: I always had an interest in economics, so I was less knee-jerk anti-capitalist than my colleagues. But I certainly had a basic [feeling] that markets are cruel and that we need aggressive consumer regulation by lawyers and government to protect the consumer from being victimized.

Reason: How did your views begin to change? Through experience or reading?

Stossel: A combination. I saw that regulation rarely worked on even the most obvious of crooks, that the people selling breast enlargers and penis enlargers—all those people would get away with it. They would hold off attorneys general for a couple of years, and then when the law enforcement machine finally came after them they would hire their own slick defense lawyers, who would hold the regulators off for another few years. And then they would just change the name of the product or sign a consent order (which is like saying, "I don't admit doing anything wrong, but I won't do it anymore"). Then they would do it again in a different state or under a different name. The rules didn't hurt the obvious bad guys, but the good companies would have to spend vast sums hiring squads of bureaucrats to obey the OSHA rules or equal opportunity rules, the FDA, EPA, CPSC—and [paying for] the PACs. All the energy that used to be poured into making the product better and getting it to the customer sooner is now put into massaging the leviathan.

Reason: When did you start reading economics and political philosophy?

Stossel: It's embarrassing as a Princeton graduate how little serious economics reading I had done. As this was happening, when I was in New York City—I started in Portland, Oregon—I felt very alone. I would read the *New York Times, Time, Newsweek,* and nobody was saying any of these things. But then I found *Reason,* and read *In Pursuit,* by Charles Murray. I realized there were other people who were talking about these things, and there was an intellectual basis for what I was feeling.

Reason: You've said that you look back at some of your early work with regret. Give me some examples.

Stossel: I did a lot of alarmist reporting. I did an Alar story on *Good Morning America*. I did a story on exploding coffee pots that was probably alarmist. I did a story, because of a very passionate producer who dragged me in despite my reluctance, on a subject that is dear to your heart, passive smoke. I took a quote from [anti-smoking activist] Stanton Glantz, which if I looked at now would make me cringe a bit.

Reason: With your Alar story, was it full-blown hysteria, or did you say there were questions about the evidence?

Stossel: I felt I was reporting on breaking news. The EPA had just made an announcement. I think I was less hysterical than others, but I basically said the EPA said this chemical, daminozide, which is used to keep the apples fresh longer, has been shown to cause cancer in rats—and just saying that will terrify some people. I wish I had the knowledge at the time to say the new testing mechanisms are finding possible carcinogens in most anything these days, and I certainly intend to keep eating apples. But at the time I just reported the breaking news.

Reason: Have you done anything on breast implants?

Stossel: I did a lot of stories on breast implants—at WCBS, when I worked there, just on the cosmetic procedure, interviewing women while they were having it done. Taking the feminist point of view that it's a tragedy that people aren't comfortable with their own bodies, that women would do this even when the men in their lives didn't want them to do this, go through all this risk and pain just to look better. And yet they said they were happier because of it. A lot of them turned out to be doing it because their mothers used to make fun of them for being flat-chested.

But I'm not answering your question, because I guess you're asking about safety issues. I have a special on bad science, which is scheduled to be broadcast soon [it aired on January 9], which talks about breast implants in the light of what is known today. I did not do the alarmist number on breast implants.

Reason: In coming to see that health hazards were often exaggerated, what writers were influential?

Stossel: Aaron Wildavsky [the late political scientist and risk specialist]. Bernard Cohen, a physicist who was writing an obscure physics journal, came to my attention. Unfortunately, that was about it at the time. There may be others.

Reason: How have the ratings been for your specials?

Stossel: Most of them were top-20 programs, which even surprised ABC.

Reason: What about the reviews?

Stossel: I can give you some summaries. There have been some very good, some very nasty. One said I was sucking up to the Republicans, so I could eat giraffe tartar at Newt's house. That was Tom Shales in the *Washington Post.*

Reason: What reactions to the specials have you found most gratifying?

Stossel: The first [special] was the most difficult and interesting. It's a good example of the market working, in that I had been talking to ABC about a risk program for several years. They had basically stared at me blankly, said they would get to it, but never did. Rupert Murdoch offered me a job, and to keep me ABC gave me four specials a year. I insisted the first one be "Are We Scaring Ourselves to Death?" Some executives argued that I shouldn't make that my first one because no one would watch, [that I should] do something on diet, body image, or raising children, which we know the audience likes. But I insisted on doing "Are We Scaring Ourselves to Death?"

In the course of doing the hour, two freelance producers quit, saying this was not journalism. It was OK to say that regulatory money was being misspent, that less should be spent on Superfund, perhaps, but more must be spent on self-extinguishing cigarettes or fire-proof furniture. To simply say that regulation itself might be damaging to health and the economy was something no respectable journalist should be allowed to do. There was a meeting at ABC. I laid out what I wanted to do, and they laid out what they thought should be done. ABC's news management, to their credit, said, "Well, I don't agree with you about all of this, but it's a valid intellectual argument, and you deserve to have this on." So those two producers quit, and the program, to a lot of people's surprise, was, I think, the number 15 program for that week. We got a thousand or more letters, 99 percent positive—people saying, "Thank God, somebody's finally saying these things."

Reason: Is that a lot of letters for this kind of show?

Stossel: That's a lot of letters. And I think it got the record number of requests for videotapes ABC has received for a news program, with the exception of one news special on Pearl Harbor.

Reason: What reactions to that special or other specials have you found upsetting, disappointing, or irritating?

Stossel: Sometimes it's disappointing how little impact a program seems to have. I fought so hard to get my risk analysis chart on "Are We Scaring Ourselves to Death?," which I believe helps the public understand relative risk. It's one thing to say smoking is much more likely to hurt you than flying in an airplane, or pesticide residues, or living in Love Canal. It's another thing to see the huge disparity and to see the damage that poverty causes. I hoped that these bar graphs would be picked up by other media and used as a foundation for debating risk intelligently. And of course, none of that has happened.

The other funny thing is that, in the midst of "Are We Scaring Ourselves to Death?," there was an alarmist ad for an upcoming news program, on pharmacists mixing things up badly and injuring their customers. All these are stories that deserve to be done, but the issue is how breathlessly we do them.

Reason: Do you think people would be more receptive to you if you seemed to be basically like them—a liberal, but with idiosyncratic views on certain topics?

Stossel: It's an interesting question. Gregg Easterbrook was vilified for the book he wrote [*A Moment on the Earth*], which was quite middle-of-the-road, I thought. There is a sense that he stepped off the curb, he betrayed his community. I think there is the same sense about me. I was a consumer reporter for 20 years, and to now criticize the consumer movement on regulation—I have betrayed my religion.

Reason: When someone like Sidney Wolfe calls you "a menace" and says you're "doing a massive amount of damage," how do you feel? Annoyed? Amused? Proud?

Stossel: I'm developing thicker skin. When I first read these things, it was awful. I crashed; I wanted everyone to love me. And when I was a consumer reporter, everyone did. I wasn't used to criticism. That [1994 *Washington Post* story quoting Wolfe] was one of the first major articles. I think it's a great example of how the press works. After I did "Are We Scaring Ourselves to Death?," I was promoting it on some talk radio program, and someone called and said, "Watch out for Howard Kurtz. He's the enforcer for the liberal interest groups." And months after the broadcast, the same day I received a phone call from a liberal interest group wanting to write a newsletter [article] about my heresy, the call came from Howard Kurtz of the *Washington Post.* I think Kurtz is a pretty fair writer, in that he makes an effort to talk to a lot of people and get the story right. But in the story with the quotes from Ralph Nader and Sidney Wolfe and others—[even though] this program had 20 million viewers, most of whom thought it was a good thing—he could only find critics to quote.

Reason: What does it signify to you when Ralph Nader says you are "the most dishonest journalist I've ever encountered," that you "used to be on the cutting edge," but now you've "gotten lazy and dishonest"?

Stossel: It's hard to speculate on what other people are thinking. I assume Ralph was upset that I, a consumer reporter, would criticize him. In the course of the interview [for "Are We Scaring Ourselves to Death?"], I asked him about many of the things he says we should worry about. And he gave endless, detailed answers about hot dogs, coffee, flying, and carpets, which we in TV cut down to their essence. I guess he felt that was unfair. I suspect, in terms of him calling me names, it's the tendency of these groups to demonize people who criticize them.

Reason: What about Nader's argument that it's hard attacking corporations, and now you're taking the easy way out by parroting the free market line?

Stossel: In the culture where I work—in network TV, living on the Upper West Side of Manhattan—it was much easier to go after the corporate bad guys. Then all my colleagues were on my side. To talk about abstractions such as how freedom and voluntary transactions can benefit people in ways that central planning can't even approach—that is much more difficult to do on TV. So I think he is totally wrong about that.

Reason: How do you respond to the criticism that giving speeches to business or free market groups creates a conflict of interest?

Stossel: I think it's good it's being brought up. It's interesting that when I was speaking to consumer groups no one ever complained. It is true that I now speak for absurdly high honoraria. That raises eyebrows. All the money goes directly to charity. I did this before ABC's ban [on honoraria from businesses and trade associations] went into effect, but consumer activists still write articles implying that I am keeping the money, not mentioning that it at all goes to charity. I think what happens is that once you start saying on TV that markets work, that business is not evil, then more businesses want to invite you to speak, because people like to be told they are good guys.

Reason: How have your colleagues at ABC reacted to your political views? Would it be easier if you were, say, a Marxist or an animal rights activist?

Stossel: It hasn't been hostile here. People just give me blank stares. There has been very little criticism to my face.

Reason: ABC News officially urges its employees to avoid taking "a public position on any significant issue of controversy," but that rule does not seem to be enforced. Hugh Downs condemns the war on drugs, for example. What does the policy actually require?

Stossel: It's a mushy line that forbids us to participate in a political campaign, to be outspoken on topics that are hot current political debates.

Reason: Even if you're not covering them as a reporter?

Stossel: It depends on the debate. To speak forcefully about who should win the election, to take a clear, vocal position on abortion during an abortion debate, to take a position while something is being voted on in Congress—that is forbidden. To discuss things in the context of programming we're doing is OK. And when I take a point of view on air, it's not kept secret from the audience. I declare it at the beginning of the program usually: "Here's what my point of view is. I'm laying this out for you to make your own judgment about it." I always put the other side on, and I always ask tough questions of the people who might agree with my point of view.

Reason: What is the rationale behind ABC's policy against taking sides on controversial issues?

Stossel: All we have in news is our reputation. People have a hundred choices for news now, and if we are perceived as closed-minded, people will not watch us or trust us. To me, that's a precious commodity, and to ABC News, too.

Reason: I already don't watch the network news because I perceive them as closed-minded. Is it just that you don't perceive biases when they are the same as yours? Is this notion of unbiased coverage a fiction?

Stossel: I think that's best commented on by people not working for a network. It is true that the hometown paper for most everyone in my business is the *New York Times*. People have grown up with the *New York Times*, and people here believe that it's a middle-of-the-road newspaper. Dan Rather says even the editorial page is middle-of-the-road. So talking about a liberal slant to my business is a little like talking to a fish about water. The fish says, "Water? What's water?" It's just what we swim in.

Reason: I notice that you use a lot of rhetorical questions in your TV reports and articles. Is that just a matter of style, or is it a way to avoid stating your opinions directly?

Stossel: I would have preferred to have called "Are We Scaring Ourselves to Death?" just "Scaring Ourselves to Death." I don't know if it began as my style or a way of being slightly less opinionated in presenting these issues, but clearly Dick Wald [senior vice president in charge of ABC's Standards and Practices] prefers it as a question mark.

Reason: Have you been told by producers or other people at the network to tone down your scripts or your articles?

Stossel: When I started at ABC, often the lawyer who vets each piece would say, "You can't say that as a statement, but you can ask it as a question."

Reason: Was the lawyer vetting your material for libel or for compliance with ABC's policy on strong opinions?

Stossel: That's a mushy line. Supposedly for libel—that's what their job starts as—but no one knows what a lawyer will define as libel, so their mandate is broad.

Reason: So a lawyer would say, "You really have to qualify this," or, "Make it into a question"?

Stossel: He would say, "You can't say that." You say, "What if I say it this way, that way, how 'bout if I make it a question?" "OK, you can do that."

Reason: Does that happen much anymore?

Stossel: Now, I just make it a question.

Reason: You've been criticized for crossing the line into advocacy. In your view, have you blazed a new trail in TV journalism, or is it just a matter of using the same techniques from a different perspective?

Stossel: I think two things are happening. One is that I have always avoided professional news-speak. Maybe I have been successful in television because I was never a very good literature student. I didn't go to journalism school. I learned out of fear of failure. I had to figure out how to write for television. And I learned to write conversationally. Then, as a consumer reporter, I would clearly come down on one side of an issue: This product is better than that product. This company is ripping people off—it's a bad thing. As I ventured into more political areas, I continued that style of speaking plainly, saying, "I'm a human being who's investigated this. Here's what I think." And people who disagree with what I think now say I shouldn't be doing it.

Reason: What about the idea that reporters should be objective? Is that a reasonable goal? Would the public be better served if reporters dropped the pretense, if they said, "Here are my biases, and here is my story," rather than pretending to be objective?

Stossel: I wouldn't go as far as you do there, because we're all trying to be objective, but we all have points of view, and we'd probably do better acknowledging that. People who think that every time someone dies there must be a new government agency to prevent the next death ought to acknowledge that they have a bias in that direction. But they are not aware that they have that bias—they just think they are being compassionate.

There are all shades of gray here. My most opinionated work falls between an op-ed piece and a news article. When I get too opinionated, they make me superimpose the word *commentary* over what I am saying.

Reason: When does that happen?

Stossel: On *20/20*, it's assumed that the chats with Hugh [Downs] and Barbara [Walters] are commentary. But on "Are We Scaring Ourselves to Death?," for example, when I made the argument that regulation, by increasing poverty, was killing people, they made me superimpose the word *commentary*.

Reason: Can you give some examples of stories people have pitched to you that you refused to do?

Stossel: Sure. Dozens. They are always trying to get me to do stories on airline safety—the most dangerous airport; where you should sit on the plane so you can get out more quickly if it fills with smoke; how you are supposed to count the seats to the exit row so if it's filled with smoke you can get out—and I refuse, because I just think the more we make people frightened about flying, the more people will drive, and that's more dangerous, so we're killing people by scaring them. I think it's irresponsible.

One clear turning point was the Bic lighter story. Our producer rushed in breathlessly [talking] about how four people over four years have been killed by Bic lighters catching fire in people's pockets. By then, I had my death list that we compiled [based on] data from scientific and government agencies as to what kills people. I said, "I'll do Bic lighters if we first do plastic bags, which kill 11 people a year; or garage door openers, which kill six; or buckets, which kill 50 people a year." He then staggered out of my office, calling me insensitive. And they got another correspondent to do the story.

Reason: Can you give some examples of stories you wanted to do that were shot down?

Stossel: I have wanted to do privatization of Social Security, which I still hope to have success at. I have wanted to do decriminalization of prostitution, which I appear to be having success with. [The report aired January 31.]

Reason: These would be stories on *20/20?*

Stossel: Yes. I must say that the stories I most want to do are stories that show how freedom works and how privatization works. Frankly, these are not very exciting television. I'm most proud of stories that I did years ago on the benefits of deregulation or on the entitlements crisis, which I did 10 years ago. They were very hard stories to get on the air. The same thing [is true] in the case of the story of how FDA regulation may be killing people as well as saving people. It took 10 years of pushing to get that on the air—not so much because there is overt political opposition but because television is a collaborative business, and to get anything done you need to have at least one producer who is enthusiastic and an executive producer who is at least tolerant. It's a little bit like pushing string. There was no blatant resistance, but there wasn't enthusiasm. I finally got the FDA story on the air after we came across the story about a breast self-examination device that wasn't being approved. "Breasts" helped me get the story on the air.

I want to do more stories on free markets. And I hope to do them, but I am aware I have to intersperse them with stories about raising children, and peeping toms, and diseases of the week.

Reason: Do you find people are resistant because they perceive you as pushing an agenda, or is it just that they think it won't play well on TV?

Stossel: Producers think the audience isn't interested, but they'd go along if they thought it would play well on TV. In the case of Social Security, they don't understand. It would be a difficult story to produce. It's much easier in TV to cover the fire, or the presidential election, or O.J. You know you'll get ratings and interest. It's much harder to cover abstract issues.

Reason: What tricks do you use to get complex or subtle ideas, such as the unseen costs of litigation or regulation, across on TV? Do you find the medium's limitations frustrating?

Stossel: Yes, it is frustrating. The temptation is to do a survey, because you do the research on the issue and you find, in the case of lawsuit abuse, a thousand examples. And you want to tell them all. The best TV stories, and I found this from watching *60 Minutes*, may have only three characters in them. My bad tendency is to have 10 characters in the story, and I'm distressed to still have to cut it down. The editing process helps, because we will shoot 10 hours of tape, and the producer will cut it down to an hour of the best material. Then I will cut it down further, and we will cut it down again and again and again. And each time you look at it, you see new ways to make it clearer as you make it shorter.

Reason: Are there scholars or public policy experts whose work you admire but whom you wouldn't want to put on camera because they don't play well on TV?

Stossel: "Play well" is a tough phrase. There are plenty who would play OK, but I would be reluctant to use them because they are not bombastic enough to make abstract issues come alive on TV. In the case of "The Trouble with Lawyers," we searched through many critics of the system who were wise and articulate, but none were as clear as John Langbein, a [Yale] law professor, simply because he spoke explosively. People like Virginia Postrel, Ed Crane, Jim Bovard, Richard Epstein all speak well. I would use them, but they aren't John Langbein. They are too intellectual. Peter Huber is another brilliant individual and speaker. But not dramatic, not explosive.

Reason: Aside from what you've mentioned, are there other topics you'd like to cover?

Stossel: There is always an endless list. I would like to do a story on how licensing hurts entrepreneurs starting off. I would like to do some lawsuits the Institute for Justice is pushing. I might want to do one of your smoking topics.

Reason: Have you done any stories about the war on drugs?

Stossel: I did one [five years ago]. It was about the pro-legalization argument, for *20/20.* We focused on [Baltimore Mayor] Kurt Schmoke.

Reason: Have you seen any sign that the big media mergers have had an impact on news coverage?

Stossel: Not yet. The big fear within the journalistic pack is that the evil conglomerates, which were eating us, would censor the news. There was a lot of vigilance and wailing when GE bought NBC. I think there is so much vigilance, and we reporters are so naturally prickly about businesses censoring us, that there is very little danger that Disney will have me doing puff pieces on Mickey Mouse or GE would have NBC squelching pieces on GE engines. I don't think that'll happen. And Disney, to its credit, so far has made it clear that ABC News has been doing quite well on its own.

In terms of squelching stories, I think the underreported story is the self-censorship that takes place because of lawsuits, because of the rich bullies who are willing to use lawyers to get special treatment. A libel suit is so viciously expensive even if you win. That's what scares reporters.

Reason: What kinds of stories do the networks cover well?

Stossel: Breaking stories. The fire that happened today, the crisis elsewhere in the world. I love getting up and watching *Good Morning America* to see what's happened in my world last night, yesterday, and to know my world is still safe. I think that's what we do the best.

Reason: What do the networks do worst?

Stossel: We do the worst on the slower stories. Most of the important things that happen—Virginia Postrel has written brilliantly about this in her editorials—are, I think, the slow developments: the development of the computer chip, the way Hewlett-Packard was run, the invention of the birth-control pill, the sexual revolution, changing attitudes. Those things don't happen today; they happen this month, this year. We do a bad job covering that.

Reason: How would you describe your politics now?

Stossel: I believe, just as Jefferson did, that less government is good government, and as George Washington did, that government is not reason or persuasion, government is force. I think the issue of the day is how big should government be. Ours has grown over 100 years from 1 or 2 percent of the GDP to about 36 percent of the GDP. I think the debate should be about what percentage is [optimal]. I think it's somewhere around 18 percent, and that's my main political issue. I don't think that makes me a Republican or Democrat, liberal or conservative.

Reason: Are people confused by the mix of your interests? On the one hand, you are doing something they perceive as conservative, saying that environmental regulation can be harmful. On the other hand, you're doing this story on the decriminalization of prostitution, which is seen as a liberal issue.

Stossel: I hope it's good I do those things. I receive letters from all sorts of different people on different stories—those who are provoked and those who are grateful. I certainly enrage conservative viewers, who write dismayed that I, who they thought was the one voice of reason on ABC News, would do a story on, for example, kids cursing, and conclude by saying we have bigger problems to worry about.

April 1997

Child-Proofing the World

By every measure, children are doing better than ever. Why all the anxiety? And where will it end?

Nick Gillespie

ABOUT A YEAR AGO, early on a Saturday morning, I walked out into the courtyard of my apartment building in Los Angeles to pick up the newspaper and received an impromptu education about contemporary childhood. My 11-year-old neighbor was getting set to embark on a quintessential kid activity: riding his bike. I waved hello and stared transfixed at the boy's elaborate preparations. First, he shimmied a set of hard-plastic and soft-cushion pads over his sneakers. He worked them up his shins and positioned them carefully over his knees for maximum protection. He did the same with a pair of elbow pads, flexing his arms to make sure the fit was right. Then came the gloves, thickly padded on the palms and across the knuckles. Finally, he picked up the helmet, adjusted it on his head, strapped it down across his chin, and rapped on it once (for luck, I suppose).

As he peddled off in his body armor, his father appeared, coffee mug in one hand. "You be careful," he called after his son. And then the father, who like me is in his 30s, turned my way and added, somewhat sheepishly, "I remember riding my bike barefoot in the rain. Things sure are different nowadays with the kids."

About six months ago, I received another unscheduled lesson in contemporary childhood (or, more precisely, contemporary parenting). My wife and I had moved to a small town in southeast Texas, and I was dropping our 3-year-old son off for the first time at his new day care center. As I started out of the U-shaped driveway, I saw some-thing that made me hit the brakes so hard I almost cracked my head against the windshield: A car pulled into the driveway with a toddler jumping up and down in the passenger seat of the automobile; in the back seat, I saw another unbelted child climbing the upholstery. *What the hell kind of parent would allow such a thing?* I wondered for a second before the answer came to me: my mother, my father, and every other parent I knew growing up during the '60s, '70s, and early '80s.

Things sure are different nowadays with the kids, and in a most puzzling way. By most standards, the vast, overwhelming majority of American children are doing better than ever. With some notable, in-sistent, and tragic exceptions, indicators such as mortality and accident rates, life expectancy, and educational attainment all suggest that the kids are more than all right. In fact, they are flourishing, brimming over with the potential to live longer, to live better, and to be smarter than their parents (just as their parents outstripped *their* parents).

And yet, the national discourse on children—the way we talk about "the kids" and their future—describes a tableau of unremitting fear and trembling, a landscape marked by relentless risk and deprivation. Although apocalyptic rhetoric in general has diminished in recent years—overpopulation, nuclear war, global warming, and the like just don't pack the same wallop they did in years past—the air remains thick with stories of how children must be protected from a world that is conceived largely as a malevolent presence that seeks only to hurt them, a sort of Mad Max environment for the younger set.

While not exactly new, this trend has been intensifying over the past two decades or so, lurching from isolated scares about poisoned Hal-loween candy in the 1970s and child abduction in the 1980s to a gen-eralized calculus that places perceived harm to children at the center of seemingly every discussion. The tendency is ubiquitous enough to be fair game for parody. On *The Simpsons,* for instance, one character routinely asks at any public gathering, "What about the *children?*" It is not coincidental that the rise of such attitudes to cultural dominance occurred as the baby boom generation—that gargantuan cohort born between 1946 and 1964—shifted into parenting mode and started to grapple with the most unfamiliar role of authority figure. While it is unclear what effect this may have on the kids themselves—will they respond to doomsday scenarios by shrinking from the world or by becoming what-the-fuck nihilists?—one result has been a gradual shifting of the costs of raising children onto wider and wider swatches of society, and not merely in dollars: If kids have access to TV, for instance, then all programs must be made child-safe.

The threats are everywhere, we are told: If children are not hounded by ritual satanic child abusers at day care or by perverts on the Internet, then they're sucking in too much asbestos at school, or chewing on too much lead at home; if television, purportedly the babysitter of choice in the overwhelming majority of American homes, hasn't transformed kids into underperforming, slackjawed dullards, it has overstimulated them into feral children who must be tamed with Ritalin and Prozac; if we haven't failed the kids by not spending unlimited amounts of tax money on them, then we have transformed them into shallow consumers who can only measure affection in terms of dollars spent; if they're not at elevated risks of brain cancer from eating hot dogs, then they're likely to become punch-drunk from heading soccer balls; and on and on.

Interestingly, such stories tend not to focus on the kids who may truly be most at risk, such as impoverished children in the inner city or rural outposts. Instead, the tendency is to paint with a broad brush, to talk about that great hypothetical abstraction, "middle-class America." As Hillary Clinton put it in last year's *It Takes A Village and Other Lessons Children Teach Us*, "Like many parents, I feel there is much to worry about when it comes to raising children in America today. . . . Against this bleak backdrop, the struggle to raise strong children and to support families, emotionally as well as practically, has become more fierce." It doesn't matter if you're in the first income quintile or the fifth: We're all in this bleak backdrop together.

This is hardly a hobby horse the First Lady rides alone. Judging from national polls and random conversations, her feelings are widely shared. "Yeah, I'm really worried about raising my kids," a college friend with two pre-teen girls tells me. "Everything's out of control: drugs, schools, college costs." I try reminding him that he himself first smoked dope at age 15 and that his and his wife's combined income—somewhere around the $100,000 mark—should let them be good providers, but he cuts me off: "No way, it's totally different now. Do you know how *much* college costs? Have you *seen* the kids today? Do you hear the music? They're out of control," he says, forgetting for the moment his early-'80s penchant for humming Sex Pistols lyrics such as, "I am an anti-Christ, I am an anarchist, don't know what I want, but I know how to get it" and "God save the Queen, she ain't no human being. . . . No future for *you!*"

We are suckers for tales of decline. Most of the fears and worries regarding children, however, are less based on shared experience and more the result of relative affluence, indiscriminate risk assessment, and a generational solipsism that seems particularly acute in baby boomers. The first generation to "discover" alienation, rebellion, sex, and drugs has been painfully slow to recognize recurrent truths: that parenting is an awesome and fearsome experience, that your children grow up speaking a foreign language, that youth culture is always precisely calculated to maximize disgust in parents.

It is, of course, always worth paying attention to the particular ways in which children and childhood are discussed. That's because on one level, children simultaneously incarnate both vulnerability and the future—they are, in that most threadbare of clichés, the "leaders of tomorrow." More than that, they are relatively clean slates that must be etched in properly. As such, they are the repository of parental and societal aspirations and anxieties; they function as a sort of communal ink-blot test upon which adults project their own hopes and fears. On another level, kids represent the cutting edge of public policy. As concerns about children get translated into policy, the tendency almost invariably is to centralize and to consolidate power in fewer hands in hopes of eliminating all risk, of sweeping away broken glass from any place where small feet might tread: If something can hurt (or help) one child, it makes sense to ban (or extend) it to all children. A parallel impulse is to expand the reach of policy (how else to child-proof the world?), even while trying to place it beyond the scrutiny of reasoned analysis. Invoking "the children" is the rhetorical equivalent of zipping yourself into a Kevlar suit: Only a heartless bastard would dare question the efficacy or efficiency of programs for the kids.

Welcome to what might be called the Buddhafication of American children. Not long after the birth of my son a few years back, I realized that the legend of the Buddha was, in a very real way, about parental anxiety. Siddartha—the Buddha—is born to a wealthy, doting king who seeks to keep his son from experiencing the world as it actually is in it all its variety, its richness, and its poverty. To that end, the father builds a huge, extravagant walled palace around the child and never lets him leave the grounds. "The king was anxious to see his son happy," goes one telling of the tale. "All sorrowful sights, all misery, and all knowledge of misery were kept away from Siddartha, for the king desired that no troubles should come nigh to him."

One doesn't need to be a parent to sympathize with the king and understand his motivation: He only wants his child to be untroubled by the harshness, the difficulties, the indifference of the wide, wide world. As a society, we are following his lead. We, too, are wealthy and, we, too, desperately (and understandably) try to wall our children off from everything that is harsh and ugly in life. We, too, are raising little Buddhas whom we believe face unprecedented and ubiquitous threats.

Risks that were once taken for granted have now become plainly intolerable and have fueled any number of "common-sense" policies passed during the past decade or so. Hence, the removal of asbestos from school buildings (more than $10 billion spent over the past decade, with $20 billion more already in the pipeline); more and more efforts to educate school kids about drugs; mandatory bicycle helmet laws for kids (adopted by more than a dozen states); the V-Chip and television ratings; increasingly elaborate sports safety equipment; proposed Federal Aviation Agency guidelines requiring separate seats for children under 2 (who can currently share an adult's seat); and government plans for a "universal" child's car-seat attachment harness that, as White House spokesman Mike McCurry put it, will at last ensure that parents can "get the little thingy in through the back and get it stuck into the little deal that goes in the side."

Such policies are of a piece with discussions that see environmental, sociological, and even neurophysiological dangers everywhere. *Redbook* warns about "Bullies: The Big New Problem You Must Know About." "There have always been tough boys and girls who pick on other kids," reads the story. "But it's the '90s, and the bullies have become more dangerous." (Despite the threat-filled language, the piece is pointedly not about gun- or knife-wielding teens; rather, it focuses on a child taunted about his ears.) The subtitle of Barbara Dafoe Whitehead's *The Divorce Culture,* a book based on her widely discussed 1993 *Atlantic* article, "Dan Quayle Was Right," indicates "how divorce became an entitlement and how it is blighting the lives of our children." In a "special report" on "How a Child's Brain Develops," *Time* frets,

"Too many children today live in conditions that threaten their brain development. What can we do?"

As the *Time* reference suggests, the endpoint of these discussions is often an implicit call to public action: What can *we* do? "Is your playground safe?" asks *Parents* magazine in a recent article that notes, "More than 267,000 children will sustain playground-equipment-related injuries this year. . . . A number of children will even die as a result." Later, the story suggests that "one reason for the safety problem is that there are no federally mandated playground-safety standards."

Other times, the call to arms is explicit. In 1995, the Environmental Protection Agency and the Department of Health and Human Services proclaimed lead the top "environmental disease of children, affecting at least 10 percent of preschoolers" and responsible for behavioral problems ranging from attention deficit disorder to juvenile delinquency. The Centers for Disease Control, which has called lead poisoning the "most common and societally devastating environmental disease of young children," has issued guidelines supporting universal lead testing of all children, regardless of risk factors. (The threat from lead was a truly unprecedented risk. As Ellen Ruppel Shell pointed out in *The Atlantic*, "To get to the 'one out of ten preschoolers' figure, regulatory agencies now deem as 'poisoned' children whose lead-to-blood ratios fall between 10 and 25 micrograms per deciliter"—levels considered acceptable in 1990. Children in the 1960s, Shell notes, averaged more than 20 micrograms.)

Less-journalistic analyses are no less hyperbolic and wide-ranging. "The present state of children and families in the United States represents the greatest domestic problem our nation has faced since the founding of the Republic," warns Cornell University psychologist Urie Bronfenbrenner. "Childhood is beginning to seem downright grim," write Joanne Barbara Koch and Dr. Linda Nancy Freeman in *Good Parents for Hard Times: Raising Responsible Kids in the Age of Drug Use and Early Sexual Activity.* "In the back of every parent's mind is the realization that one mistake made by their children can be fatal. . . . One impulsive sexual encounter with a person with AIDS can lead to death. One 'experiment' with highly addictive crack can suddenly pull a young person into committing desperate crimes—a way of life that is a living death. One vehicle accident under the influence of alcohol. . . . "

There is, of course, some truth in such statements: One mistake can end a child's life—a thought that is indeed ever-present in parents' minds. But, in a common move, Koch and Freeman discover potential mortality as an ominous new development. What actually is different today is the decreasing likelihood of such an event, as the author's own examples suggest. Between 1980 and 1989, for instance, arrests for 16- and 17-year-olds for driving under the influence dropped 24.7 percent. It is extremely rare for kids to "experiment" with crack at all, much less become regular users. Indeed, according to government statistics, in 1995, only 0.8 percent of kids between 12 and 17 reported past-month use of the far-larger category of cocaine (compared with 1.5 percent in 1985). The rate of increase of AIDS cases among children has been slowing; as important, unlike child-killing diseases of the past, AIDS can be largely prevented through relatively simple behavior modification.

Such trends might be cause for celebration, or at least a brief sigh of relief. But reductions in risks to children seem only to fire the imaginations of those who see ruin as imminent. In the 1992 revised edition of Dr. Spock's *Baby and Child Care*, by far the most influential child-rearing manual over the past 50 years, Spock and co-author Michael B. Rothenberg see the unprecedented sadness and malaise they claim is affecting children as part of a larger assault on civilization itself. The roots of this assault are only hinted at, but seem to encompass almost every social trend since the Industrial Revolution allowed people the luxury of worrying about their quality of life.

In a section called "Raising Children in a Troubled Society," they write, "American society in the 1990s is extraordinarily stressful. Normal family tensions are heightened in many ways: Our society is excessively competitive and materialistic; many working parents find less satisfaction and pleasure at their jobs while the good day care they depend on becomes harder to find; there is less spiritual and moral direction compared to the past; the traditional supports of the extended family and community are breaking up; and a growing number of people are concerned about the deterioration of the environment and international relations." This vague jeremiad (what does it mean to be "excessively" competitive or materialistic?) has a timeless air about it: When hasn't the world been running down, becoming more secular, less traditional, or been anything other than "extraordinarily stress-ful" compared to an implied golden age? "We live in a disenchanted, disillusioned age," they write elsewhere, rounding out a list of griev-ances that have been perennial since the dawn of history by invoking an ostensibly contemporary trend that dates back to 1960s-era "black humor": "Even greeting cards, instead of wishing invalids and relatives well, jeer at them."

Not surprisingly, such sentiments get even more overheated when expressed by lobbyists and policy makers. The introduction to *Baby and Child Care*, for instance, contains a plug for the Children's De-fense Fund, perhaps the most influential child advocacy group in the country. In *Guide My Feet: Prayers and Meditations on Loving and Working for Children*, CDF head Marian Wright Edelman speaks the language of crisis and emergency—and, by implication, ever-greater collective action—to salvage that ultimate public good: children. She invokes a biblical king remembered for his proclivity toward infanti-cide: "Herod is searching for and destroying our children, pillaging their houses, corrupting their minds, killing and imprisoning the sons, orphaning the daughters, widowing the mothers," writes Edelman. "Herod's soldiers are everywhere, in government, on Wall Street, in the church house, schoolhouse, and moviehouse. Lead us and our children to safety." Drastic times call for drastic measures.

Although Edelman has reportedly had a falling out with the Clinton administration over last year's welfare bill, it's clear that at least one resident of the White House still thinks along similar lines. In argu-ing that "everywhere we look, children are under assault," Hillary Clinton outlines the culprits: "from violence and neglect, from the breakup of families, from the temptations of alcohol, tobacco, and sex, and drug abuse, from greed, materialism, and spiritual emptiness." These problems, the First Lady suggests, "are not new, but in our time they have skyrocketed." It is an interesting progression—from conceivably measurable social facts to long-standing human urges to unprovable commentary on contemporary mores. Given that the end of the century looms large, we can perhaps forgive such millenarian fervor—problems are *skyrocketing!*—but we need not embrace it as a basis of public policy.

Indeed, such notions are wrong on two very basic counts: First, de-spite a nod to historical context, they ignore the tremendous progress in child well-being over the past 100 years. Second, they generalize risks for specific subgroups to children writ large.

Consider a fairly representative family history: When my grandparents were born in Europe near the end of the 19th century, a fair question was whether they would survive their first few years of life. By the time my parents were born in America a quarter-century later, the question was whether (or when) they would contract polio or some other life-threatening, debilitating disease. When my siblings and I were born toward the end of the baby boom, the question was whether we'd have our own bedrooms. When my own child was born a few years ago, the question was which college he would attend.

Encoded in the sharply diminishing seriousness of such questions is one of the century's great self-erasing success stories. In 1900, about 186 out of 1,000 children died before their 15th birthday. In 1950, that figure had been cut to about 35 per 1,000. By 1990, the number had dropped to about 10 per 1,000. Life expectancy at birth has risen from 47 years in 1900 to 68 years in 1950 to 75 years in 1990 (to a projected 77 years in 2000).

Educational attainment—which correlates strongly with income and other living-standard measures—has similarly booted upward. In 1970, about 52 percent of the population had completed four years of high school or more; in 1993, the figure was about 80 percent. In 1970, about 11 percent of the population had a bachelor's degree or more. Twenty-three years later, 14.5 percent had at least a B.A. The rate is higher still for younger age ranges—18.6 percent of people ages 25 to 34 had a college diploma.

These indicators track consistently across all racial and ethnic groups as well. In fact, despite lower absolute percentages, the rate of increase in life expectancy and educational attainment for black children—who are disproportionately poor—actually outstrips that of whites. In these very important ways, things are, on the whole, getting better for the overwhelming majority of children.

Even the one apparent major counter-trend of the past few decades—the percentage of children living below the poverty level—appears to have more or less stabilized during the past 15 years. In 1970, roughly 15 percent of children under 18 lived below the official poverty line. By the early 1980s, the rate had increased to about 20 percent, where it has remained, within a relatively narrow band of fluctuation. Of course, having one in five kids in poverty—or 1970's one in six—is nothing short of tragic. But there are also reasons to believe that the official statistics overstate the extent of poverty in the country. As Bruce Bartlett of the National Center for Policy Analysis has suggested, official poverty statistics tend to "obscure the true condition" of the poor not only by excluding non-cash benefits such as food stamps, school-meal programs, and housing allowances, but by failing to account for the poor's consumption levels, which are more than double their reported income.

Perhaps more important, the Consumer Price Index's overstatement of inflation has a huge effect on official poverty statistics. As the editors of *The American Enterprise* have pointed out, if the CPI has overstated inflation by 1.5 percentage points annually since 1967 (within the variance suggested by the recent Boskin Commission), there were 15 million poor—about 6 million of them children—in 1996, rather than the 38 million counted in official statistics. While poverty exists, it has at least been heavily mitigated and is not indicative of the typical child's lot.

Similarly, risks for children are in no way distributed evenly across the population. For instance, lead poisoning—rarer than ever today—is confined almost exclusively to poor children living in old housing stock. For all the talk of a crime wave perpetrated by and against juveniles, most of the increase in criminal behavior is focused on a relatively small section of the youth population: black males between the ages of 12 and 19. As Boston University's Glenn Loury has documented, black males are at least 25 percent more likely to be victims of crime than white males of the same age. The murder rate for black youths, already three times that of whites, doubled between 1986 and 1991. That such disturbing trends affect relatively few children is not a reason for us to breathe easy, but neither is it a reason to generalize or exaggerate risk.

By implying that the typical child is understimulated—and, hence, at risk of underdeveloped brain functions—*Time* suggests a widespread problem where there is none, says Jerome Kagan, a psychology professor at Harvard University who has done groundbreaking work on developmental issues. "If babies are not played with at all, if no one talks to them at all, they will not develop well. If they just lie in their cribs, with a bottle propped up, they will not develop well. That's a fact. Everybody knows that and no one denies it," says Kagan. "However, most infants—certainly most middle-class infants—get plenty of stimulation." Lack of interaction, according to Kagan, to the extent it is a problem at all, is generally concentrated among "poor women and adolescents who are having infants, the mother who doesn't read *Time*."

Talking about specific matters as broad-based trends compounds the often tragic nature of such problems by diverting attention, time, and resources from where they are most needed. Such "democratization of risk," however, is a common rhetorical strategy when it comes to competing for attention in the "social problems marketplace," says sociologist Joel Best of Southern Illinois University. In *Threatened Children: Rhetoric and Concern About Child-Victims*, Best documents how advocates for missing-children groups promoted broader and broader definitions of child abduction, despite weaker and weaker evidence for the phenomenon. That's a tendency shared by most activists, regardless of issue or political persuasion. "Social problems claims-making is rarely static," writes Best. "Claims-makers are likely to offer a new definition, extending the problem's domain or boundaries, and find new examples to typify just what is at issue."

Perhaps the one trend that has significant negative effects on children is divorce. Divorce, like marriage, is an evolving institution. In the late 1960s and early '70s, many states liberalized their divorce laws, making it easier to dissolve marriages. There is a growing consensus that such legislation has failed to adequately protect the interests of the children involved, and it is likely divorce laws, at least where children are concerned, will be toughened.

Between 1970 and 1992, the divorce rate per 1,000 people climbed from 3.5 to 4.8, where it has roughly stabilized. About 60 percent of divorces involve children. The economic effects of divorce are unambiguous, especially when the mother becomes the primary caretaker: somewhere between a 30 percent and 50 percent drop in income in the first year of divorce. It takes most divorced women and children at least five years to regain their predivorce standard of living (if they ever do), often through remarriage. Such divorce-driven dislocation ripples throughout children's lives: Compared with kids in two-parent marriages, they are one-third more likely to move (and they tend to move more often), they are three times as likely to be in poverty, and their mothers are likely to have increased their work hours significantly.

Depending on the level of animosity between parents, the psychological impact of divorce may well outstrip economic issues, especially in the short run. Adjustment patterns vary widely for both parents and children; not surprisingly, problems tend to be worse in ugly divorces. Problems are most intense for parents and children alike during the first two years following separation (psychologists speak of a "crisis period"). In response to divorce, children often become anti-social, disruptive, depressed, or withdrawn. "You lose a lot more than money when your parents split up," says a friend whose parents went through a particularly rancorous divorce when she was a teenager. "You lose a sense of connection, of security, of stability. It isn't easy to get that back. It sets you back years. That's what you lose ultimately: years of your childhood."

But, says the friend, "you end up working through it or moving on, more out of necessity than anything else." Most research confirms that, after the "crisis period," once routines are re-established, children from divorced parents tend to return to more or less normal development. It is hard to gauge the effects of divorce on children partly because it's virtually impossible to identify and study an appropriate control group of conflicted but intact families (some research indicates that children in highly conflicted but intact two-parent families fare worst of all children).

"Divorce, or the conflict that is usually a prelude to it, increases the risk to children of encountering problems later in life: dropping out of school, marrying and having children in the teenage years, and becoming divorced themselves. And whether or not they avoid long-term effects, children are likely to endure a wrenching period of upset and adjustment," write sociologists Frank F. Furstenberg Jr. and Andrew J. Cherlin in *Divided Families: What Happens to Children When Parents Part.* Some solace can be taken from the fact that, despite heightened risks, "Studies based on nationally representative samples . . . suggest that the long-term harmful effects of divorce . . . occur only to a minority."

If things are not so bad for so many children, where do the stories come from? Harvard's Kagan sees the impulse as part of human nature. Today, he says, "there's less stress in a real, serious sense. But every generation of parents is anxious about their children. Every single one. And you always think yours is the most stressed."

Kagan is at least partly right. Parenting is inherently anxiety inducing: Children are impossibly soft, the world indifferently hard. And, despite knowledge transmitted from generation to generation, parenting is always learned anew. It's different when it's *your* child, and the urge is to emphasize both the softness of the child and the hardness of the world. It is hard to strike a balance between protection and isolation, to clear a play space of sharp edges for your charges without sliding into the excesses of the Buddha's father. The tendency is to compare the responsibilities of being a parent to your own experience as a child—a misleading comparison. Things were different when you were a kid. First and foremost, *you were a child,* not an adult. Similarly, it is easy to forget that being a child and especially an adolescent is often intrinsically a difficult, frustrating experience.

But there are also a number of reasons why attitudes toward "the kids" have been intensifying over the past 15 years or so. These break down into three basic categories—economic, demographic, and psychological—all of which are related to developments in postwar America and all of which incline us to heightened concerns and fears about children.

In any generally wealthy society, it is common for each generation to tolerate less risk than the one before it. Hence, the progression from automobile safety belts to three-point harnesses, which are supplemented by driver-side airbags, then passenger-side airbags, then side-panel airbags, and so on. (The example of airbags underscores that it is no simple march from absolute risk to absolute safety.) Economist W. Kip Viscusi and others have suggested that safety is essentially a "good" that we purchase. In general, the more money we have, the more safety we can buy. In this sense, the overall rise in income, compensation, and wealth over the past half-century allows and perhaps even predisposes us to buy more safety: We worry more about our children because we can afford to.

But it is not simply that we can buy more safety for our children. Not to put too fine a point on it, or to slip into unnuanced nostalgia for the good old days of nickel sodas and whooping cough epidemics, but kids cost more these days. Or, more precisely, we spend more on them—and not simply in terms of CD players, designer clothing, and sports equipment. Consider education, the importance of which has never been greater. As *U.S. News & World Report* noted in its 1996 college guide, "nearly two out of three of June's 2.5 million high school graduates are enrolling in some form of post-secondary education." To paraphrase Bacon, knowledge is opportunity, but in what *U.S. News* calls "The K-16 Era," such opportunities do not come cheap.

Kids have become more expensive in another way, too: There are fewer of them. The rate of births per 1,000 people was 24.1 in 1950 and 23.7 in 1960. By 1970, it had dropped to 18.4, reaching a low of 14.6 in 1975 and 1976. Throughout the 1980s, the rate crept up, averaging 15.8 and peaking at 16.7 in 1990 before subsiding once again (it was 16.0 in 1992). The trend toward fewer children—another correlate of increased wealth—will apparently be a long-term one. In 1995, children 17 years and under made up 26 percent of the overall U.S. population. The Census Bureau projects that figure to be 24.6 percent in 2010 and 23.9 percent in 2025 (the downward trend holds true at different levels for whites, blacks, Hispanics, and all other minority groups). Almost literally, we are putting fewer eggs in our basket. Psychologically and economically, we expect more from fewer children. And at the same time, we guard them all the more closely.

The trend toward fewer children intersects with baby boom demographics in an interesting way. What has led to "all these fears about kids was the aging of the baby boomers," says Gary Alan Fine, a sociologist at the University of Georgia who has studied risk attitudes toward children. As the boomers started becoming parents in force, their attention naturally focused on child-related issues. "Because it is such a large generation," says Fine, "the problems of the boomers have been taken to be *the* problems of society."

The boomers are anomalous for a number of reasons besides their sheer numbers: They tend to be better-educated and wealthier than their parents, predisposing them to greater interest in safety issues. Even more important, says Fine, the boomers grew up with an ideal of home life they found themselves hard-pressed to replicate as they became parents. The 1950s and '60s, he argues, represent a "unique" period in American cultural history because the model—if not necessarily the lived reality—was a relatively isolated suburban household in which the mother was a near-constant presence during childhood. A generation later, he notes, not simply dual-worker but dual-*career* households had become the new model. Because our parenting ideals come largely from our own childhood experiences, the difference in circumstances leads to heightened anxieties; we are uncomfortable with what we don't know. As parents choose to devote themselves to careers, at the expense of their ideals of childhood, the urge to child-proof the world makes more and more sense.

Another element of the boomers' upbringing that predisposes them to be particularly anxious about their children is what psychiatrist E. Fuller Torrey has called the "malignant effect" of Freudian psychoanalytic theory, particularly its emphasis on how early childhood experiences irrevocably shape (or warp) an individual. "I doubt there's been a time in history where there has been the obsession with child rearing that we have now," says Torrey. "Especially from the World War II era on, parents have had an inordinate fear that any little thing they do may permanently misshape their child's psyche." This fear is particularly intense in the boomers, the first generation fully raised under such a supposition.

In his 1992 book, *Freudian Fraud: The Malignant Effect of Freud's Theory on American Thought and Culture,* Torrey attributes this fear in large part to Benjamin Spock's *Baby and Child Care.* Spock, writes Torrey, "did more than any single individual to disseminate the theory of Sigmund Freud in America." Through the sale of over 40 million copies of his baby book and his writings in popular magazines, says Torrey, "Spock persuaded two generations of American mothers that nursing, weaning, tickling, playing, toilet training, and other activities inherent in childhood are not the innocuous behaviors they appear to be on first glance. Such activities, according to Spock, are psychic minefields that determine a child's lifelong personality traits, and maternal missteps on such terrain can result in disabling and irrevocable oral, anal, or Oedipal scars. Throughout his career Spock was deeply imbued with Freudian doctrine and in a 1989 interview he acknowledged, 'I'm still basically a Freudian.'"

Spock's vision of parenting, says Torrey, sends a disabling double message. Even as *Baby and Child Care* famously exhorts the parent to "Trust yourself—you know more than you think," it suggests that any parental misstep will have long-lasting, disastrous effects. The rise of such Freudian-inflected thought has, says Torrey, "made parenting much more difficult because of the generally accepted theory that—to exaggerate it a little bit—if you look at your child cross-eyed, your child will never be the same again."

Where Freudian-inflected thought stresses how "fragile" the psyche is, Torrey argues for its resiliency. Where Freudian-inflected thought stresses the parental role in personality development, Torrey makes a case for inborn temperament and a wider-ranging array of influences. An appendix to *Freudian Fraud* summarizes more than two dozen studies that attempt to substantiate a link between toilet training and personality traits and finds none (Freud hypothesized that botched toilet training leads to a number of possible "problems," ranging from homosexual orientation to paranoia to a fixation with order). Twin and adoption studies, says Torrey, suggest that "parents have much less effect on their children than we have been led to believe—or would like to believe."

Despite their lack of descriptive or predictive powers—Torrey notes that "except for grossly aberrant events, there is no evidence that the normal developmental events of childhood shape personality traits to any significant degree"—Freudian ideas have become deeply embedded into our culture, "integrated in a very general way." Indeed, we can read much of contemporary popular discourse on children as a sort of mass merchandising of Freudian theory: Since one incident—a bike accident, smoking a joint, a violent TV show—can have such deleterious effects on long-term development, we must be ever-vigilant. As with the young Buddha, "all sorrowful sights, all misery, and all knowledge of misery" must be avoided: The stakes are simply too high.

So, what if the concern for children today is less the product of actual threats and dangers and more an artifact of various unarticulated social forces? What if we are mistaking the inherent difficulties of parenting and childhood for an unprecedented assault upon all that is good, decent, and optimistic in the world? Where's the harm in waging total war on every possible risk facing children, real or imagined? After all, as a society, we are relatively rich, with the time and the energy to devote to making life safer for our charges.

One thing to recognize is that the law of unintended consequences is not repealed when it comes to kids; there is often a huge chasm yawning between stated goals and actual effects. Perhaps, then, it is not at all surprising that most experts agree that removing asbestos exposes students to higher risks than simply covering the stuff up. Or that past-month drug use among adolescents, still well below levels of 20 years ago, began its increase only after a decade of DARE and "Just Say No!" Or that the added cost of a plane ticket for an infant—representing a 50 percent fare increase for a family of three—might cause some parents to travel by car, a far riskier alternative to flying. Or that "soft" baseballs recommended by the Consumer Product Safety Commission actually weigh more than traditional hardballs, and according to sports doctors, apparently increase injuries.

Children—perhaps more than any other group—represent the no man's land where the private sphere blurs into the public, with all the attendant problems centralized decision making brings. Examples such as car seats and bike helmets suggest that what may be a good idea in the former is likely to become a mandate in the latter. Examples such as airbags and separate seats for infants on airplanes suggest that this is not always such a good thing. When it comes to setting policy, activists routinely use children as hostages, figuratively holding a gun to their temples and proclaiming that if some demand is not met, the kids will get it. It is hard to see how the shifting of more and more parental responsibilities—and costs—onto society at large will increase responsible behavior at any level.

At some point, the rate of return runs into the negatives in cultural terms, as well. What sort of message, we might ask, borrowing a favorite phrase of child advocates, does it send to paint the world in the most horrific terms possible, to see danger and disorder lurking everywhere? Do we best prepare our children for responsible, engaged lives by seeking to child-proof the world? What are the costs (to adults and minors alike) of thinking of our children as little Buddhas who must at all costs be prevented from living in the world they will one day inherit? Will kids imbibe such an ethos and respond by shrinking from the world in all its dangers and opportunities alike, seeking first and foremost to avoid the confrontations, negotiations, and possibilities entailed by a robust life? Or will they rebel against overprotection and take more and more unmeasured risks? Perhaps a harbinger of the second response is the rising popularity of extreme sports and increases in teen smoking (still far below 1980 levels). Whatever happens, it seems likely that extremity will breed extremity.

The Buddha's story may be instructive here, too: Despite his father's desires, he insists on seeing the world beyond the palace walls. The king finally relents, but secretly orders his servants and subjects to spruce up the tour route, to hide poor people, sick people, and old people, to create a scene bereft of physical decay or human misery. The attempt fails and the Buddha forsakes his father's world, first overindulging in all the pleasures of the flesh and then renouncing the body altogether and embracing rigorous asceticism. The legend has it, of course, that the Buddha found enlightenment through the latter route, but there is little reason to believe that the way we talk about our own children will lead to a similarly happy ending.

October 1994

St. Martha

Why Martha Stewart should go to heaven and the SEC should go to hell

Michael McMenamin

JUNE DID NOT BRING MUCH SUNSHINE FOR NEW YORK CITY or good news for Martha Stewart. After twisting in the wind for nearly a year and a half, the Diva of Domesticity was sued for insider trading by the Securities and Exchange Commission (SEC) and indicted for securities fraud and obstruction of justice by the Department of Justice.

Those who are salivating over Stewart's demise should put down their forks. In early 2002, when she was first questioned by the feds, all the news outlets reported speculation, based on anonymous government sources, that she had sold the last remnant of her ImClone stock on December 27, 2001, because her buddy, ImClone founder and CEO Sam Waksal, had told her that the Food and Drug Administration was about to reject an application for Erbitux, the company's highly touted cancer drug. The news reports also suggested that she had lied to the feds about Waksal's tip. But as the government now tacitly admits, neither of these allegations is true. That fact helps explain why the feds waited until June 2003 to bring charges: They had trouble finding anything to pin on Stewart.

The most serious criminal charge against her is not perjury or insider trading but securities fraud, based on the fact that she denied to the press, personally and through her lawyers, that she had engaged in insider trading. This was done, the feds say, not for the purpose of clearing her name, but only to prop up the stock price of her own publicly traded company, Martha Stewart Living Omnimedia. In other words, her crime is claiming to be innocent of a crime with which she was never charged.

As for the SEC's civil case, it hinges on an elastic understanding of insider trading, an offense Congress has never defined. The justification for the ban on insider trading, which makes little economic or legal sense, is just as murky as the behavior covered by it. Given the difficulty of figuring out exactly what constitutes insider trading (let alone why it's illegal), it is entirely possible that Stewart and her lawyers weren't sure whether she had broken the rules. In any event, under existing case law, it's clear that she didn't.

What Did She Know?

All Stewart knew when she ordered the sale of her 3,928 ImClone shares was that, according to her broker, the price of the company's stock had dropped from $64 at opening to $58 under heavy selling (7.7 million shares vs. the daily average of 1.1 million), and that his clients, Sam Waksal and his daughter, Aliza, also had been selling. The SEC charged Stewart with insider trading because her broker told her the Waksals were selling, and the Department of Justice indicted her because she denied any culpability for insider trading.

Stewart was not the only investor connected to Waksal who joined the selling mob that day. She just received the most scrutiny. There was Martha's friend, Mariana Pasternak, who was on vacation with her when all this happened and whose ex-husband coincidentally sold more than 10,000 shares of ImClone that day. He wasn't charged with insider trading. Then there were the two unnamed friends of Waksal described by the *New York Times*: One sold $600,000 of ImClone stock on December 27, while another sold ImClone stock worth $30 million on December 27 and 28. Phone records show the sales took place "almost immediately" after contact between Waksal and the sellers. The government has refused to identify these anonymous investors and so far has declined to indict or sue them for insider trading.

Finally, there were Waksal's daughter, Aliza Waksal, a 29-year-old actress, and his octogenarian father, Jack Waksal. On December 27, Sam Waksal telephoned Aliza at the ski resort where she was vacationing and told her to sell all her ImClone shares (40,000 for $2.5 million). Before government investigators questioned Aliza, Waksal told her to conceal their conversations, using the cover story that she needed the proceeds to buy an apartment (which she didn't do until seven months later, spending $1.4 million to buy it from her daddy's development company). After talking to his son, Jack Waksal sold more than 136,000 shares on December 27 and 28 for more than $8 million. Jack Waksal also lied to the government, denying that he spoke to Sam Waksal prior to selling his ImClone stock. This was before prosecutors produced phone records showing that calls between them all had taken place before the trades were made. Neither Aliza Waksal nor her grandfather has been indicted or sued for insider trading or lying to the government.

The disparate treatment of Stewart and the other ImClone investors is especially troubling when you consider the government's definition of insider trading and rationale for prohibiting it. The government says insider trading occurs when someone buys or sells stock based on material, nonpublic information received from an insider. While Aliza Waksal spoke directly with her father prior to her sale, Stewart knew the Waksals were selling (arguably not material information, since insider sales are not always reliable predictors of a stock's movements) only because her broker (not a true corporate insider) told her so. Although Martha tried to speak to Waksal, she was unable to get hold of him before selling her stock.

Likewise, the government says insider trading is illegal because it does "economic harm" to the market. Therefore the size of the trade must matter. Aliza Waksal avoided $630,295 in losses and her grandfather three times that, while Stewart saved only $45,000. By this measure, Aliza Waksal's sale and her grandfather's did more "economic harm."

Suppose we stretch the definition of insider trading beyond economic harm caused by the use of material, nonpublic information, and instead use the SEC's long discredited "fairness" or "level playing field" theory. According to this view, it was not fair that Martha knew the Waksals were selling before the rest of the market knew. That standard still wouldn't explain why Aliza Waksal's trade was legitimate. Stewart's excuse was that she had already told her broker she wanted to sell when the ImClone share price fell below $60, which is what happened on December 27. Aliza Waksal's excuse was that although she's an adult, she is still financially dependent on her father, so she had no choice but to do as he instructed, which included selling the stock and lying to government investigators. Which explanation sounds more plausible?

When Waksal worked out a settlement with the government, it reworded the language regarding Aliza Waksal's sale. The settlement now says Waksal "directed Aliza to sell all of her ImClone shares," and Waksal "benefited because he was her entire means of financial support." Thus Sam Waksal is guilty of his adult daughter's insider trading because if she hadn't sold, he would have ended up paying more of her bills. She didn't benefit from the trade, according to the government; he did.

Birth of a Crime

As the treatment of Aliza Waksal and other lucky ImClone investors suggests, the prosecution of insider trading has nothing to do with supposed economic harm or even "unfair" tips, let alone lying to the government. Instead it's about bringing down the biggest and best-known targets to make it look like the laws against insider trading are accomplishing something.

Such publicity stunts are necessary because the insider trading ban is bad economics and worse law. Although there's a broad consensus, among Wall Street executives as well as Washington policy makers that trading on inside information is harmful to investors and the market, this consensus has never been supported by solid evidence. Yet during the last four decades the SEC has waged a campaign to maintain and expand the scope of the insider trading ban, perpetuating the myth that scores of insiders are secretly enriching themselves at the expense of the investing public.

It has been, in many respects, a successful campaign. In a June survey by the Sienna Research Institute, 60 percent of those polled thought Martha Stewart was guilty of insider trading, and 51 percent thought she was guilty of obstruction of justice. Many people think Stewart "should have known better" because she used to be a stockbroker. But when it comes to insider trading, the SEC and the Justice Department don't want anyone to know better. If they did, they would have long since asked Congress to clearly define the offense. Instead, as *Barron's* Editor Thomas G. Donlan wrote in June, "The government prefers to define [insider trading] case by case. 'He did what? Oh, that should be illegal.' So it is."

Insider trading was not a crime until passage of the Securities and Exchange Act of 1934, Section 10(b), which prohibits "fraud" in the sale of securities. This offense was intended by Congress to cover stock trades by a corporate officer, director, or major shareholder—someone with a fiduciary responsibility to a company's stockholders—based on nonpublic, material, "inside" information. In 1961 the SEC for the first time claimed that Section 10(b) and its SEC-promulgated companion, Rule 10(b)(5), extended beyond people traditionally considered to be corporate insiders. The case involved a Cady, Roberts & Co. broker who learned from a director of Curtis-Wright Corp. that the company was going to reduce its dividend. Before the reduction became public knowledge, the broker sold Curtis-Wright shares owned by his wife and clients.

Although the broker was not a traditional insider and did not have a fiduciary duty to Curtis-Wright or its stockholders, the SEC charged Cady, Roberts & Co with insider trading. It argued that Section 10(b) was "designed to encompass the infinite variety of devices by which undue advantage may be taken of investors and others." The SEC thought it was inherently "unfair" for the broker to sell shares when he knew that the people buying them did not have the same information he had. The SEC ignored the fact that all trades on impersonal stock exchanges involve the potential for asymmetric information; one party frequently will know something the other does not. That is how markets work. It's why two people can simultaneously think XYZ stock is a buy *and* a sell at $2.

Yet the SEC is still using the same "fairness" rationale today. Commenting on the insider trading case against Martha Stewart, SEC enforcement director Stephen M. Cutler told the *Washington Post*, "It is fundamentally unfair for someone to have an edge on the market just because she has a stockbroker who is willing to break the rules."

Bad Economics

That position makes no economic sense. In his classic 1966 book *Insider Trading and the Stock Market*, Henry Manne of George Mason University Law School demonstrated that inside information makes stock markets more efficient. Stock market efficiency depends on the speed and the accuracy with which new information is assessed by the market and reflected in share prices. When insiders trade on their knowledge, that information is immediately reflected in stock prices, thereby conveying this "inside" information to the market. The more information available, the more accurate the stock prices and the more efficient the allocation of capital.

What's more, there is no evidence that insider trading harms the market. The SEC says insider trading has to be prevented because it would cause the public to lose confidence in the market and abandon it. Yet such flight does not seem to have occurred in the years before 1934, when insider trading was still legal, and scholars such as Manne point out that the 1929 stock market crash was not caused by insider trading.

A 1987 study by the SEC's own economists casts further doubt on the commission's view of insider trading. The study, which looked at the effect of corporate takeovers on stock prices during the 1980s, determined that, on average, nearly 40 percent of the increase in a target company's stock price occurred before the takeover announcement. Yet the economists found that insider trading did not cause the pre-bid rise, which was entirely the result of speculation in the media, how much stock the acquirer bought before announcing the takeover bid, and whether the bid was hostile or friendly.

A footnote to the report questioned the assumption that inside traders profit at the expense of less-informed investors. "Those selling into the market when the better informed are buying probably would not have sold had they possessed the same valuable information," the economists noted. "However, they still would have sold if the information specialist had refrained from buying, especially if the trading of the specialist did not affect significantly the stock price. This holds true whether the trading is based on insider information or on careful analysis and successful anticipation of the event."

An insider, by definition, has better information than an outsider. So does a market professional. Market professionals sometimes track insiders' buying and selling of their company's positions, which are available through public filings. Whether the trader with better information acquired it from an inside tip or simply through diligence and hard work, the SEC economists reasoned, does not change the effect on either the market or the other party to the trade.

Bad Law

Not only is the SEC's "level playing field" theory bad economics, the U.S. Supreme Court has held that it is bad law. The Court first rejected the theory in a 1980 case involving Vincent Chiarella, who worked in the composing room of a financial printing company, Pandrick Press. Chiarella handled the announcements of five corporate takeover offers. Despite Pandrick's use of code names for the companies, Chiarella was able to deduce their identities. Armed with this knowledge, he bought modest amounts of the target companies' stock before the takeover announcements and sold it immediately afterward. The SEC investigated, confronted Chiarella, and not only made him give up his profits (about $30,000) but referred the case to the U.S. attorney for criminal prosecution. Based on the SEC's level playing field theory, Chiarella was indicted for securities fraud, brought to trial before a jury, and convicted. The always SEC-friendly U.S. Court of Appeals for the 2nd Circuit rubber-stamped the verdict.

On appeal, however, the Supreme Court ruled that Chiarella could not have been guilty of securities fraud. His employer worked for the corporate raider, not the target. Chiarella therefore had no duty to shareholders of the target corporation. "Section 10(b) is aptly described as a catchall provision," Justice Lewis Powell wrote for the majority, "but what it catches must be fraud. When an allegation of fraud is based upon nondisclosure, there can be no fraud absent a duty to speak." Chiarella had no such duty, unless the law required *all* market participants to disclose what they know or to refrain from trading on such information. As Powell noted, "Neither the Congress nor the Commission ever has adopted a parity-of-information rule."

The second defeat for the SEC's level playing field theory involved an investment analyst, Ray Dirks, who specialized in the insurance industry. Two employees of Equity Funding Corp. of America gave Dirks information that enabled him to uncover a shocking and pervasive insurance scandal. Dirks learned that Equity Funding had invented records of policies that never existed to bolster sales figures, intimidated employees who threatened to expose the fraud, and falsified other corporate records to paint a picture of fiscal health. The corporation's executives knew all this was taking place.

Upon learning the extent of the scandal, Dirks told his clients, who promptly sold their Equity Funding stock. Then he told the SEC and the *Wall Street Journal.* Instead of praising Dirks for uncovering the scandal, the SEC hauled him into court. As punishment for giving his clients the "inside information" on Equity Funding, Dirks was prohibited for six months from trading or associating with a registered broker/dealer.

The U.S. Court of Appeals for the District of Columbia Circuit upheld the SEC's action. In a decision that can charitably be described as confused, the D.C. Circuit ruled that the Supreme Court really did not mean what it said in *Chiarella.* Even though Dirks had no fiduciary responsibility to Equity Funding, the appeals court said, he had an overriding obligation to the SEC and the trading public to disclose the fraud or to refrain from trading.

The Supreme Court, which ruled on Dirks' appeal in 1983, was not pleased. In unusually blunt language, Justice Powell wrote: "We were explicit in *Chiarella* in saying that there can be no duty to disclose where the person who had traded on inside information was not [the corporation's] agent . . . was not a fiduciary, [and] was not a person in whom the sellers [of the securities] had placed their trust and confidence."

The Supreme Court's message to the SEC in *Dirks* was as clear as it was in *Chiarella*: If you want a level playing field, go see Congress, not us. Section 10(b) is about fraud, not fairness. The Court also went out of its way to chastise the SEC for its inconsistency in insider trading enforcement. Suggesting that it was "hazardous" to deal with the SEC, the Court accused the commission of bringing "test cases" that contradicted its stated enforcement policies. In his opinion, Powell quoted from a speech by a former SEC chairman who said the commission "does not contemplate suing everyone who may have come across inside information" and specifically listed as people who would not be sued "persons outside the company such as the analyst or reporter who learns of inside information"—in other words, people like Ray Dirks.

Misappropriated Logic

When Powell retired from the Supreme Court, the SEC got the opportunity to try out a new version of the level playing field theory based on the concept of "misappropriation." It's best illustrated by *Wall Street Journal* reporter Foster Winans, who was one of the writers of the *Journal*'s "Heard on the Street" columns, which frequently affected stock prices. Perhaps comforted by that SEC chairman's assurances that reporters wouldn't be sued, Winans agreed to disclose the subject of the next day's column to a broker who sometimes traded on that information, giving Winans a small portion of his profit.

Like Chiarella, Winans was hit with both civil and criminal charges even though he had no fiduciary obligations to either the buyers or the sellers of the stocks traded. The only party he defrauded was his employer, the *Wall Street Journal* (which fired him but did not pursue criminal charges). The only basis for the insider trading charges against Winans was the level playing field theory, i.e., the idea that selling advance information about the column wasn't "fair" to the market. Yet the SEC argued that because he had committed a fraud on his employer, the *Wall Street Journal*, by "misappropriating" information that belonged to it, Winans was guilty of securities fraud under Section 10(b), even though the entity he defrauded, the *Wall Street Journal*, had no connection with any securities trade. Winans was convicted of insider trading as well as federal mail and wire fraud, and the 2nd Circuit upheld his conviction. The Supreme Court affirmed Winans' mail and wire fraud conviction but split 4–4 on the insider trading conviction and issued no opinion. Powell, who had retired a few months earlier, would have been the deciding vote.

It wasn't until 1997, in *United States v. O'Hagan*, that the Supreme Court approved the misappropriation theory. O'Hagan was a lawyer whose firm represented a company that intended to make a tender offer for Pillsbury. O'Hagan "misappropriated" this information without his client's knowledge or consent by buying call options in Pillsbury stock, which became very valuable when the tender offer was announced. O'Hagan took home a tidy $4.3 million in profits. As with Chiarella, Dirks, and Winans, no one in the market was hurt by this action, not even O'Hagan's client. The government, under the same misappropriation theory it had used with Winans, secured a conviction. The U.S. Court of Appeals for the 8th Circuit reversed on the grounds that the misappropriation theory was beyond the scope of Rule 10(b)(5) and did not involve fraud directed toward a buyer or seller of securities. The 8th Circuit also reversed O'Hagan's mail fraud and money laundering convictions, concluding that they rested on violations of the securities laws that had not been proven.

There was no way the Supreme Court could let a lawyer get away with making millions of dollars by stealing confidential client information, so it reinstated the conviction and approved the misappropriation theory. But the Court said its decision was not based on fairness or protecting the trading public. The Court in its decision and the government in oral argument agreed that it would have been perfectly legal for O'Hagan or Foster Winans to trade on their inside information had they privately disclosed to their client and employer, respectively, what they were doing, notwithstanding the "unfairness" to the market. No deception, no foul.

Although the misappropriation theory narrows the definition of insider trading, the SEC continues to believe in the level playing field and to look for ways to broaden its approach. In *O'Hagan* the government argued that "the very aim of [section 10(b)(5)] was to pick up unforeseen, cunning, deceptive devices that people might cleverly use in the securities markets." Justice Clarence Thomas quoted this claim in his dissent, along with the dry response of one of his colleagues: "That's rather unusual for a criminal statute to be that open-ended, isn't it?" Yes, it is. But open-endedness has its advantages. It allows the SEC to ignore, condone, or even facilitate insider trading when it chooses and then go after a juicy target like Martha Stewart, whose alleged insider trading is well outside anything recognized as such by the Supreme Court.

Ivan the Not-So-Terrible

In its heart of hearts, even the SEC knows insider trading doesn't hurt the market. Remember the financier Ivan Boesky? Back in the 1980s, Boesky agreed to pay a record $100 million in penalties for trading on inside information purchased from the Drexel Burnham Lambert investment banker Dennis Levine. the *Wall Street Journal* estimated that Boesky had made more than $200 million in profit from Levine's information. By cutting a deal, the SEC let Boesky keep half of his illicit profits.

But wait, it gets better. Before the SEC announced the settlement, it allowed Boesky to cut his trading partnership's liabilities by $1.3 billion through a series of government-sanctioned insider trades. SEC Chairman John Shad later told a House committee that the market wasn't hurt by those trades because it bounced back after a one-day loss. So keeping $100 million in ill-gotten gains and executing insider trades totaling more than $1 billion are both OK if the SEC says so.

Yet Martha Stewart got nailed for saving $45,000 without breaching a fiduciary duty to anyone. The initial trading case against her centered on whether she knew that Sam Waksal was selling his Im-Clone stock because of the FDA's impending rejection of the company's anti-cancer drug. The feds interviewed Stewart about the sale and claim that during the interview she lied to cover up her wrongdoing and then issued false claims of innocence when anonymous government sources leaked these unproven accusations against her, allegedly doing so to support her own company's stock price.

The government now admits Stewart never had inside information from Waksal. Here are the facts patched together from various pleadings and other public accounts:

On December 27, Stewart and her friend, Mariana Pasternak, were flying in Stewart's private jet to San Jose del Cabo, Mexico, for a vacation at a resort. The plane stopped to refuel in San Antonio, where Stewart called her office on her cell phone and learned that her Merrill Lynch broker (and friend), Peter Bacanovic, had telephoned. Bacanovic, who was also a broker for Waksal and his daughter, Aliza, was in Miami at the time and didn't connect with Stewart when she returned his call at Merrill.

According to the SEC, Douglas Faneuil, Bacanovic's assistant, who copped a plea in exchange for a misdemeanor slap on the wrist, advised Stewart, at the behest of Bacanovic, that the Waksals were selling their ImClone stock. In doing so, Faneuil (and allegedly Bacanovic) broke Merrill Lynch's customer confidentiality rule. Stewart asked Faneuil where the stock was trading. Faneuil said $58, and Stewart told Faneuil to sell her remaining ImClone shares (3,928 shares for close to $230,000). Stewart then left a message for Waksal at his office, subsequently summarized in a note from Waksal's secretary: "Martha Stewart. Something is going on with ImClone and she wants to know what."

The SEC started investigating ImClone within days of the FDA announcement on December 28, 2001. It first interviewed Bacanovic on January 7, 2002, and Stewart on February 4. Stewart and Bacanovic each told investigators that she unloaded her shares because of an oral arrangement they had to sell her ImClone shares at $60. Faneuil initially backed them up but later recanted, telling prosecutors there was no agreement. He said Bacanovic pressured and bribed him (with extra vacation and free airline tickets) to lie. As further proof of this cover-up, the Justice Department's indictment cites the fact that Bacanovic marked "@60" near the listing for Stewart's ImClone holdings in a blue ink different from the blue ink he used on a spreadsheet where he wrote down portfolio decisions for Martha's various holdings on December 20. The feds claim the different ink proves that he made the notation after December 27. Forensic experts say there is no way to tell when the "@60" notation was made.

The SEC also charges that prior to the initial February interview, Stewart temporarily changed an entry in her telephone log from "Peter Bacanovic thinks ImClone is going to start trading downward" to "Peter Bacanovic re: ImClone." Then she had second thoughts and changed the log back to its original form. This aborted tampering with evidence does not prove Stewart was guilty, but it does illustrate the uncertainty created by the government's murky insider trading rules.

The Real Insiders

A better approach would focus on actual wrongdoing rather than the perceived unfairness of unevenly distributed information. Insider trading should be regulated by existing criminal laws that prohibit industrial espionage and the theft of trade secrets and sensitive commercial information. Dennis Levine, for instance, could have been prosecuted for stealing proprietary information from his employer and selling it to Boesky. Ditto O'Hagan. At most, Foster Winans and Peter Bacanovic should have been fired for violating their employers' internal policies, not prosecuted or sued for insider trading.

Anything more should be left to the public companies and the stock exchanges on which their shares are traded. If companies want to permit or prohibit insider trading by their executives, let them say so publicly and let investors decide if they want to buy shares based on that policy. If a stock exchange believes insider trading damages investor confidence, it should require companies whose shares trade on the exchange to have rules against it.

The SEC does not want this to happen. Its prosecution of Ray Dirks for saving his clients from the Equity Funding fraud and its failure to sue Sam Waksal's daughter, father, and anonymous friends for their insider trading suggest why. The SEC does not care about protecting individual investors; insider trading has no effect on them anyway. It does not care about the integrity of the market or capital formation; insider trading has no effect on them either. The only people protected by SEC prosecution of the nebulous "crime" of insider trading are SEC lawyers and their allies, who can keep on inventing new definitions of the offense as they go along. Before suing Stewart, the SEC had *never* gone after the customer of a broker who offered his knowledge of what another customer had done as a reason to make a trade.

The Justice Department and the SEC don't care about the "fairness, efficiency, and integrity" of our capital markets. Letting Aliza Waksal keep her profits from insider trades proves that. The government lawyers want to enhance their own power and prestige. They don't care who they hurt in the process, such as the shareholders of Martha Stewart Living Omnimedia, who saw the company's value drop by over $400 million between December 2002 and August 2003.

What's worse, these government lawyers don't seriously expect to prevail at trial. Without a credible claim of insider trading against Stewart, the securities fraud charge based on her public (and truthful) denials of the government-leaked claims that she was guilty of insider trading will collapse. Martha will walk, and it will be a good thing. But she and her shareholders will have paid an unnecessary price. That's not a good thing. It's a disgrace. And a damn shame.

October 2003

No Relief in Sight

Torture, despair, agony, and death are the
symptoms of "opiophobia," a well-documented
medical syndrome fed by fear, superstition, and
the war on drugs. Doctors suffer the syndrome.
Patients suffer the consequences.

Jacob Sullum

DAVID COVILLION FINALLY GOT RELIEF FROM HIS PAIN with the help of
Jack Kevorkian. The pain came from neck and back injuries Covillion
had suffered in April 1987 when his station wagon was broadsided
by a school bus at an intersection in Hillside, New Jersey. The crash
compounded damage already caused by an on-the-job injury and a
bicycle accident. Covillion, a former police officer living in upstate
New York, underwent surgery that fall, but it only made the pain
worse. Along with a muscle relaxant and an anti-inflammatory drug,
his doctor prescribed Percocet, a combination of acetaminophen and
the narcotic oxycodone, for the pain.

The doctor was uneasy about the Percocet prescriptions. In New
York, as in eight other states, physicians have to write prescriptions
for Schedule II drugs—a category that includes most narcotics—on
special multiple-copy forms. The doctor keeps one copy, the patient
takes the original to the pharmacy, and another copy goes to the state.
After a year or so, Covillion recalled in an interview, his doctor started saying, "I've got to get you off these drugs. It's raising red flags."
Covillion continued to demand painkiller, and eventually the doctor
accused him of harassment and terminated their relationship.

"Then the nightmare really began," Covillion said. "As I ran out of medication, I was confined to my bed totally, because it hurt to move. . . . At times I'd have liked to just take an ax and chop my arm right off, because the pain got so bad, but I would have had to take half of my neck with it." He started going from doctor to doctor. Many said they did not write narcotic prescriptions. Others would initially prescribe pain medication for him, but soon they would get nervous. "I'd find a doctor who would treat me for a little while," he said. "Then he'd make up an excuse to get rid of me." Eventually, Covillion went through all the doctors in the phone book. That's when he decided to call Kevorkian.

The retired Michigan pathologist, who has helped more than 40 patients end their lives, was reluctant to add Covillion to the list. At Kevorkian's insistence, Covillion sought help from various pain treatment centers, without success. He called Kevorkian back and told him: "I'm done. I have no more energy now. I just don't have the fight. If you don't want to help me, then I'll do it here myself." Kevorkian urged him to try one more possibility: the National Chronic Pain Outreach Association, which referred him to Dr. William E. Hurwitz, an internist in Washington, D.C., who serves as the group's president.

The day he called Hurwitz, Covillion was planning his death. "I had everything laid out," he said. "I got a few hoses and made it so it would be a tight fit around the exhaust pipe of my car. I taped them up to one of those giant leaf bags, and I put a little hole in the end of the bag. All I had to do was start the car up, and it would have filled the bag right up, pushed whatever air was in there out, and it would have filled the bag up with carbon monoxide. Same thing as what Dr. Kevorkian uses. And then I had a snorkel, and I made it so I could run a hose from the bag full of gas and hook it up to that snorkel, and all I had to do was put it in my mouth, close my eyes, and go to sleep. And that would have been it. I would have been gone that Friday."

But on Thursday afternoon, Covillion talked to Hurwitz, who promised to help and asked him to send his medical records by Federal Express. After reviewing the records, Hurwitz saw Covillion at his office in Washington and began treating him. "The last three years I've been all right," he said in a July interview. "I have a life." Yet Covillion was worried that his life would be taken away once again. On May 14 the Virginia Board of Medicine had suspended Hurwitz's license, charging him with excessive prescribing and inadequate supervision of his patients. At the time Hurwitz was treating about 220 people for chronic pain. Some had been injured in accidents, failed surgery, or both; others had degenerative conditions or severe headaches. Most lived outside the Washington area and had come to Hurwitz because, like Covillion, they could not find anyone nearby to help them.

In July, after the case was covered by the *Washington Post* and CBS News, the Pennsylvania pharmaceutical warehouse that had been supplying Covillion with painkillers stopped filling Hurwitz's prescriptions, even though he was still licensed to practice in D.C. The pharmacist who informed Covillion of this decision (in a telephone conversation that Covillion recorded) suggested that Hurwitz had prescribed "excessively high amounts." At the same time, he recommended that Covillion "find another doctor" to continue the prescriptions. Covillion's reply was angry and anguished: "There is no other doctor!"

Hurwitz may not be the only physician in the country who is willing to prescribe narcotics for chronic pain, but there are few enough that patients travel hundreds of miles to see them. "I call it the Painful Underground Railroad," says Dr. Harvey L. Rose, a Carmichael, California, family practitioner who, like Hurwitz, once battled state regulators who accused him of excessive prescribing. "These are people who are hurting, who have to go out of state in order to find a doctor. We still get calls from all over the country: 'My doctor won't give me any pain medicine.' Or, 'My doctor died, and the new doctor won't touch me.' These people are desperate."

So desperate that, like Covillion, many contemplate or attempt suicide. In an unpublished paper, Rose tells the stories of several such patients. A 28-year-old man who underwent lumbar disk surgery after an accident at work left him with persistent pain in one leg. His doctor refused to prescribe a strong painkiller, giving him an antidepressant instead. After seeking relief from alcohol and street drugs, the man hanged himself in his garage. A 37-year-old woman who suffered from severe migraines and muscle pain unsuccessfully sought Percocet, the only drug that seemed to work, from several physicians. At one point the pain was so bad that she put a gun to her head and pulled the trigger, unaware that her husband had recently removed the bullets. A 78-year-old woman with degenerative cervical disk disease suffered from chronic back pain after undergoing surgery. A series of physicians gave her small amounts of narcotics, but not enough to relieve her pain. She tried to kill herself four times—slashing her wrists, taking overdoses of Valium and heart medication, and getting into a bathtub with an electric mixer—before she became one of Rose's patients and started getting sufficient doses of painkiller.

Patients who cannot manage suicide on their own often turn to others for help. "We frequently see patients referred to our Pain Clinic who have considered suicide as an option, or who request physician-assisted suicide because of uncontrolled pain," writes Dr. Kathleen M. Foley, chief of the pain service at Memorial Sloan-Kettering Cancer Center, in the *Journal of Pain and Symptom Management*. But as she recently told the *New York Times Magazine*, "those asking for assisted suicide almost always change their mind once we have their pain under control."

One thing that supporters and opponents of assisted suicide seem to agree on is the need for better pain management. Concern about pain was an important motivation for two 1996 decisions by federal appeals courts that overturned laws against assisted suicide in New York and Washington. In the New York case, the U.S. Court of Appeals for the Second Circuit asked, "What business is it of the state to require the continuation of agony when the result is imminent and inevitable?" With the U.S. Supreme Court scheduled to hear a combined appeal of those decisions during its current term, the persistent problem of inadequate pain treatment is sure to be cited once again.

In medical journals and textbooks, the cause of this misery has a name: opiophobia. Doctors are leery of the drugs derived from opium and the synthetics that resemble them, substances like morphine and codeine, hydromorphone (Dilaudid) and meperidine (Demerol). They are leery despite the fact that, compared to other pharmaceuticals, opioids are remarkably safe: The most serious side effect of long-term use is usually constipation, whereas over-the-counter analgesics can cause stomach, kidney, and liver damage. They are leery because opioids have a double identity: They can be used to get relief or to get high, to ease physical pain or to soothe emotional distress.

Doctors are afraid of the drugs themselves, of their potency and addictiveness. And they are afraid of what might happen if they prescribe opioids to the wrong people, for the wrong reasons, or in the wrong quantities. Attracting the attention of state regulators or the Drug Enforcement Administration (DEA) could mean anything from inconvenience and embarrassment to loss of their licenses and livelihoods. In the legal and cultural climate created by the eight-decade war on drugs, these two fears reinforce each other: Beliefs about the hazards of narcotics justify efforts to prevent diversion of opioids, while those efforts help sustain the beliefs. The result is untold suffering. Dr. Sidney Schnoll, a pain and addiction specialist who chairs the Division of Substance Abuse Medicine at the Medical College of Virginia, observes: "We will go to great lengths to stop addiction—which, though certainly a problem, is dwarfed by the number of people who do not get adequate pain relief. So we will cause countless people to suffer in an effort to stop a few cases of addiction. I find that appalling."

Because pain is hard to verify objectively, the conflict between drug control and pain relief is inevitable. It can be alleviated through regulatory reform, but it can never be eliminated. A system that completely prevented nonmedical use of prescription drugs would also leave millions of patients in agony. Conversely, a system that enabled every patient with treatable pain to get relief would also allow some fakers to obtain narcotics for their own use or for sale to others. In deciding how to resolve this dilemma, it's important to keep in mind that people who use prescription drugs to get high do so voluntarily, while patients who suffer because of inadequate pain treatment have no choice in the matter.

A woman who recently served as a chaplain at a New York City hospital encountered many patients in severe pain. "You let them squeeze your hand as hard as they want to, and cry, scream, express their frustration," she says. "It's horrible being in pain. It's really debilitating. It kills the spirit." She found that nurses were reluctant to give patients more medication. "If a patient seemed to really be in agony, I would go to a nurse," she says. "They were concerned about giving them too much." She recalls one patient who was in "terrible pain" following surgery. "They only had him on Tylenol," she says. "He complained about it, but then he said, 'Well I suppose they know best. They don't want me to get addicted to anything.'"

Clinicians and researchers have long remarked on the link between opiophobia and undertreatment of pain. In a 1966 pharmacology textbook, the psychiatrist Jerome H. Jaffe, who later became Richard

Nixon's drug czar, noted that patients who take narcotics long enough develop tolerance (a need for larger doses to achieve the same effect) and physical dependence (resulting in withdrawal symptoms). But he cautioned that "such considerations should not in any way prevent the physician from fulfilling his primary obligation to ease the patient's discomfort. The physician should not wait until the pain becomes agonizing; *no patient should ever wish for death because of his physician's reluctance to use adequate amounts of potent narcotics.*"

Jaffe's admonition suggests that undertreatment of pain was common, an impression confirmed in the early 1970s by two psychiatrists at Montefiore Hospital and Medical Center in New York. Assigned to handle "difficult" patients, Richard M. Marks and Edward J. Sachar discovered a very good reason why so many continued to complain even after being treated with narcotics: They were still in pain. "To our surprise," they wrote in the February 1973 *Annals of Internal Medicine*, "instead of the primary issue being personality problems in the patient, in virtually every case it was found that the patient was not being adequately treated with analgesics and, further, the house staff for various reasons was hesitant to prescribe more."

Marks and Sachar's surveys of patients and doctors found "a general pattern of undertreatment of pain with narcotic analgesics, leading to widespread and significant distress." In part they blamed "excessive and unrealistic concern about the danger of addiction," which doctors erroneously equated with tolerance and physical dependence. Marks and Sachar emphasized the distinction between a patient who seeks a drug for pain relief and an addict who seeks a drug for its euphoric effects: The patient can readily give up the drug once the pain is gone, whereas the addict depends on it to deal with daily life. (The definition of addiction is fraught with social and political implications, but this distinction suffices for the purposes of this article.) Marks and Sachar estimated that less than 1 percent of patients treated with narcotics in a hospital become addicts. Although they urged better training in pain treatment, they concluded with a prescient warning: "For many physicians these drugs may have a special emotional significance that interferes with their rational use."

Subsequent studies confirmed that patients treated with narcotics rarely become addicts. In 1980 researchers at Boston University

Medical Center reported that they had reviewed the records of 11,882 hospital patients treated with narcotics and found "only four cases of reasonably well documented addiction in patients who had no history of addiction." A 1982 study of 10,000 burn victims who had received narcotic injections, most of them for weeks or months, found no cases of drug abuse that could be attributed to pain treatment. In a 1986 study of 38 chronic pain patients who were treated with opioids for years, only two became addicted, and both had histories of drug abuse.

Despite such reassuring findings, many patients continued to suffer because of their doctors' opiophobia. In December 1987 the *New York Times* ran a story with the headline, "Physicians Said to Persist in Undertreating Pain and Ignoring the Evidence." Russell Portenoy, director of analgesic studies at Memorial Sloan-Kettering Cancer Center, told the *Times*, "The undertreatment of pain in hospitals is absolutely medieval. . . . The problem persists because physicians share the widespread social attitudes that these drugs are unacceptable." He added that "many physicians fear sanctions against themselves if they prescribe the drugs more liberally." The article cited a recent survey in which 203 out of 353 patients at a Chicago hospital said they had experienced "unbearable" pain during their stay. More than half were in pain at the time of the survey, and 8 percent called the pain "excruciating" or "horrible." Most of the patients said nurses had not even asked them about their pain. The same study found that nurses were dispensing, on average, just one-fourth the amount of painkiller authorized by physicians.

The ordeal of Henry James, which began and ended the same year the *New York Times* article appeared, illustrates this stingier-than-thou tendency. James, a 74-year-old with prostate cancer that had spread to his leg and spine, was admitted to Guardian Care of Ahoskie, a North Carolina nursing home, in February 1987. Like many patients in the late stages of cancer, James was in severe pain, and his doctor had prescribed 150 milligrams of morphine every three or four hours, "as needed." The nursing staff thought that was far too much. They started cutting back his doses, substituting headache medicine and placebos. He received 240 doses in January but only 41 in February. The nursing supervisor, Rebecca Carter, told James and his family that she didn't want him to become an addict. She also said that if he took too much pain medication early on, it wouldn't work anymore when he really needed it.

James died after four months of agony. His family sued Guardian Care, and at the trial pain experts testified that the amount of medication Carter and her staff dispensed was grossly inadequate. They also noted that narcotic doses can be increased indefinitely to compensate for tolerance, so Carter's concern that the medicine would stop working was "ridiculous." In November 1990 the jury ordered the nursing home to pay James's estate $15 million, including $7.5 million in punitive damages. After the verdict, an unrepentant Carter told the *Los Angeles Times* "nothing whatsoever has changed. . . . We still give drugs the way we always have."

Outside of Guardian Care, however, things were starting to change by the mid-'80s. As critics drew attention to the torture inflicted by undertreatment, the use of painkillers began rising substantially. Between 1979 and 1985, for example, consumption of oxycodone and hydromorphone rose 40 percent and 67 percent, respectively, according to DEA figures. The National Institute on Drug Abuse (NIDA) acknowledged the problem of opiophobia. In 1989 NIDA Director Charles Schuster confessed, "We have been so effective in warning the medical establishment and the public in general about the inappropriate use of opiates that we have endowed these drugs with a mysterious power to enslave that is overrated." A 1993 article in NIDA's newsletter said "these drugs are rarely abused when used for medical purposes" and lamented that "thousands of patients suffer needlessly." In 1992 and 1994 the U.S. Department of Health and Human Services (HHS) issued guidelines urging more aggressive treatment of postoperative pain and cancer pain, respectively. The 1994 guidelines said 90 percent of cancer pain could be controlled with available methods. On the same day that HHS released the guidelines, the *New England Journal of Medicine* published a national study estimating that 42 percent of cancer outpatients do not receive adequate pain treatment.

It is startling to realize, as the end of the 20th century approaches, that the idea of giving patients enough medication to relieve their pain is just catching on. One reason for the slow progress is that advocates of better pain treatment have been fighting deeply rooted prejudices. Americans have always had mixed feelings about psychoactive substances. To deal with our ambivalence, we tend to divide drugs into neat categories: good and bad, legal and illegal, therapeutic and recreational. We are not comfortable with drugs that straddle categories, as the opioids do. The discomfort is strengthened by historical experience, ranging from Civil War veterans hooked on morphine to middle-class housewives hooked on over-the-counter remedies in the years before the Harrison Narcotics Act of 1914. The nexus between medical treatment and opiate addiction was vividly portrayed in Eugene O'Neill's *Long Day's Journey into Night*, written in 1940 and set in 1912. Mary Tyrone, the wife of a stage actor, is a shaky, nervous woman who uses morphine to escape her troubles. She became addicted as a result of injections she received following the birth of her son. "I was so sick afterwards," she says, "and that ignorant quack of a cheap hotel doctor—all he knew was I was in pain. It was easy for him to stop the pain."

Patients still worry about getting hooked on painkillers. Schnoll, the Virginia pain and addiction specialist, cites the impact of anti-drug propaganda "telling us that there's an addict on every corner, under every stone. So of course people are fearful. I find that my own patients are often unwilling. I have to convince them to take the medications I'm prescribing them." Foley, the Sloan-Kettering pain specialist, says the problem is especially vexing in the case of children. "Parents are so afraid of addicting their kids that they do not want to treat them," she says. "They say, 'The pain's not so bad,' or, 'We don't want him to be sleepy,' or, 'We don't want to make him an addict.' They say to the kid, 'Be tough.' But they're very torn and confused. They're afraid of the drugs, because every parent has heard Nancy Reagan say, 'Say no to drugs.' So they're saying, 'My God! Drug addiction could be worse than my child's cancer.'"

By perpetuating such attitudes, the war on drugs obstructs pain relief. Through efforts to prevent narcotics from falling into the wrong hands, it has a more direct effect. A 1987 DEA report cites declines of 30 percent to 55 percent in the use of Schedule II drugs within two years after the adoption of multiple-copy prescription programs in various states during the 1960s and '70s. "I think it's a testament to the percentage of misprescribing and criminal prescribing that goes on," says Gene Haislip, the DEA's director of diversion control. "I don't think there's any evidence that they're discouraging appropriate medical use. We think there's some evidence to suggest they're discouraging *in*appropriate prescribing, but I don't have any reason to think they really have an impact on legitimate practitioners." Haislip likens compliance with a multiple-copy prescription program to filing an income tax return. "We don't decide not to make money because we have to report it," he says. "And I don't think doctors are deciding, 'Well, this patient isn't going to get medical treatment that's appropriate because somewhere somebody may read something and ask me some questions.'"

The tax code, of course, has a big impact on the way people make (or don't make) money. And despite Haislip's reassurances, there is substantial evidence that prescription monitoring has a chilling effect on the practice of medicine. To begin with, a large percentage of doctors in multiple-copy states—in California, almost half—do not even request the special forms, which suggests that "legitimate practitioners" are deterred by the hassle and scrutiny involved. "When I was in Illinois," says Sidney Schnoll, "there were physicians who just didn't want to carry triplicate forms. Sometimes they would call me up and say, 'You have triplicates, don't you? Can you write a prescription for so-and-so?' That's not good medicine."

Furthermore, it hardly seems plausible that frivolous or fraudulent prescriptions could account for a third to a half of a state's licit narcotic use, as Haislip suggests. The limited research on this question does not support that view. A 1984 study reported in the *American Journal of Hospital Pharmacy* found that Schedule II prescriptions at a major Texas hospital dropped more than 60 percent the year after the state began requiring triplicate forms for such drugs. At the same time, prescriptions of analgesics not covered by the program rose. A 1991 study reported in the *Journal of the American Medical Association* found a similar pattern in New York state, which added benzodiazepines, a class of sedatives that includes Valium, to the drugs covered by its monitoring program in 1989. Prescriptions for benzodiazepines dropped substantially in New York, while use of several other sedatives rose, even as consumption of those drugs fell in the rest of the country. The researchers noted that "[t]he alternative sedative-hypnotic medications are less effective, more likely to be abused, and more dangerous in overdose than benzodiazepines." These studies suggest that multiple-copy prescription programs lead physicians to replace monitored drugs with less appropriate alternatives.

This sort of behavior is reinforced every time a conscientious doctor gets hassled by the authorities because someone thought his prescriptions looked suspicious. In 1987 two state drug agents visited the office of Ronald Blum, associate director of New York University's Kaplan Comprehensive Cancer Center. "They showed me their badges and guns, and read me my rights," he told the *Journal of NIH Research.* It turned out that Blum had filled out some narcotic prescription forms incorrectly. The Department of Health charged him with three administrative violations, including failure to report his cancer patients to the state as habitual drug users. A year and a half later, after Blum had spent $10,000 in legal fees, the state finally dropped the charges. In 1987 the DEA investigated Portland, Oregon, oncologist Albert Brady because he was prescribing high doses of Dilaudid to a cancer patient in a nursing home. Although the DEA concluded that Brady was not supplying drugs to the black market, it notified the state Board of Medical Examiners, which fined him $5,000 for overprescribing and suspended his license for a month. It does not take many incidents like these to "have an impact on legitimate practitioners." Brady told the *Journal of NIH Research* that his two partners "changed their practice overnight and became reluctant to prescribe sufficient doses of painkillers."

As the Brady case illustrates, even in states that do not require special forms for certain drugs, physicians have to worry about attracting the attention of state licensing boards. A 1991 survey of 90 physicians reported in the *Wisconsin Medical Journal* found that most were concerned enough about regulatory scrutiny to prescribe lower doses, indicate smaller amounts, allow fewer refills, or select a different drug than they otherwise would have. Given the attitudes of many regulators, such caution is understandable. In 1992 the University of Wisconsin Pain Research Group surveyed state medical board members throughout the country. The results, as reported in the newsletter of the American Pain Society, were striking: "Only 75% of medical board members were confident that prescribing opioids for chronic cancer pain was both legal and acceptable medical practice. . . . If the patient's chronic pain did not involve a malignancy, only 12% were confident that the practice was both legal and medically acceptable." Since these are the people who define the limits of appropriate medicine, their beliefs are bound to affect the treatment of pain.

Dr. C. Stratton Hill, a professor of medicine at the M.D. Anderson Cancer Center in Houston, became interested in the impact of regulatory expectations on medical practice about a decade and a half ago. "Patients with obvious cancer pain were given doses that were not adequate," he says. "So I began looking at why physicians were reluctant to prescribe opioids in appropriate amounts, and I realized that the bottom line was that they were afraid of sanctions by regulatory agencies."

Hill and other physicians lobbied for what came to be known as the Intractable Pain Treatment Act, which the Texas legislature approved in 1989. Essentially, the law said doctors would not be punished for prescribing narcotics to patients suffering from pain that could not be relieved through other means. But this assurance "did not make any difference in what the doctor did," Hill says, "because there was no commonly understood standard of practice. The doctor could still be charged and have to defend himself, and that cost money. Maybe the doctor would win, but that would be $25,000 later."

In 1995 Hill and his colleagues convinced the state Board of Medical Examiners to adopt rules clarifying the vague provisions of the state Medical Practice Act under which doctors were most commonly charged. Under the new rules, a doctor who prescribes a drug in good faith for a legitimate medical purpose (including pain relief) is not subject to sanctions, provided he observes certain safeguards and keeps careful records. Hill thinks the new policy may be having an impact. The year after the rules were issued, 17 doctors were charged under the relevant sections, compared to 37 the year before.

Hill's work in Texas helped inspire similar efforts in California, where Harvey Rose emerged from his battle with regulators—which took $140,000 in legal fees and five years to resolve—determined to help other doctors avoid similar conflicts. In 1990 the state legislature adopted an Intractable Pain Treatment Act modeled after the Texas statute, and in 1994 the Medical Board of California issued guidelines intended to reassure wary doctors. Although California's current approach is decidedly more enlightened than the policies of other states, Rose says "doctors are still fearful. They just don't want to deal with patients like this, because they're afraid it's too difficult. They're never sure if they're getting enough records and covering their butts enough. It's much easier just to say, 'No, I'm sorry. I don't take care of your kind.'"

That was essentially the response encountered by Cynthia A. Snyder, a nurse who recently described her own search for pain relief in the *Journal of Law, Medicine, and Ethics*. After a cerebral aneurysm and brain surgery in 1983, Snyder suffered from seizures, memory loss, and "terrible, unrelenting pain." But she soon learned that "I lacked the 'proper diagnosis' to control my pain. I did not have terminal cancer." Like many other patients in the same situation, Snyder found that her desperation for relief was viewed with suspicion. "Several times," she writes, "I was openly accused of being an 'addict' and of falsely reporting chronic pain just to obtain prescription drugs. . . . Finally, I found myself begging, as though I were a criminal." After five years of suffering, she found a physician willing to prescribe regular doses of codeine. "Within two weeks, I felt reborn!" she recalls. "I began writing again. My doctorate was completed, and once more I began to teach part-time. *My hope was restored, and my life was no longer crippled by constant severe pain.*"

Eventually, Snyder reports, "the precise neuropathology of the pain was discovered." But that was years after her brain surgery. When she was searching for a doctor to help her, she could not offer any definitive evidence of her pain. There were records of the aneurysm and the operation, but only her complaint testified to her ongoing suffering. This is often the case with intractable pain. How do you prove the existence of migraine headaches or back pain, not to mention poorly understood conditions such as fibromyalgia and chronic fatigue syndrome? A doctor can take a patient's history, inquire about symptoms, and perform an exam. He can consider the patient's character and reputation. But in the end, he is only surmising that the pain is real. Ultimately, he has to take the patient at his word, knowing that misplaced trust could mean professional ruin.

Ask William Hurwitz. The doctor who offered David Covillion an alternative to a Kevorkian-style death lost his license in August, as did Jerome A. Danoff, the pharmacist who filled prescriptions for many of Hurwitz's patients. The investigation began in May 1995, when agents of the DEA and the Virginia Department of Health Professions visited Danoff's store because a wholesaler had reported unusually large orders of narcotics. Hurwitz asked his patients to sign waivers of confidentiality and opened up his records to the investigators. A year later, when relatives of two patients who had died in January 1996 complained to the Virginia Board of Medicine, the board suspended Hurwitz's license, charging him with misprescribing not only for those patients but for 28 others.

It's doubtful that the deaths resulted from Hurwitz's negligence. One patient, a Tennessee man with a head injury that impaired his sense of smell, died after eating rotten chicken fajitas and vomiting all weekend. Hurwitz believes he died of intestinal hemorrhaging caused by food poisoning, but the medical examiner, after finding a lot of empty Dilaudid bottles, concluded that the man had died of an overdose, a theory that was not supported by a blood test. On the other hand, needle tracks indicated that the man had been dissolving his painkiller and injecting it, contrary to Hurwitz's instructions, and his girlfriend said he had been taking excessive doses of a muscle re-laxant. In the other case, which involved a Florida woman suffering from facial pain after failed jaw surgery, toxicology tests showed that she had taken oxycodone and morphine in much higher doses than Hurwitz had prescribed. He believes her death was a suicide, and the patient's mother, who defends him, concurs. Her ex-husband thinks his daughter died of an accidental overdose and blames Hurwitz.

The investigators found one former patient who complained that Hurwitz had given him too many pills and too little information about their side effects. But none of his current patients had anything bad to say about him. Many traveled long distances to show their support at his hearing before the Board of Medicine, and more than 50 testified on his behalf. Hurwitz's motives were not in doubt, and the hearing focused largely on the amounts of medication he had prescribed. His patients were taking anywhere from 10 to 200 pills a day.

Hurwitz explained that some patients are especially resistant to nar-cotics to begin with, and all develop tolerance. He insisted that the number of pills is not the issue, since a patient who would otherwise be incapacitated by pain can function well on doses of narcotics that would kill the average person. In fact, Virginia has an Intractable Pain Treatment Act that allows doctors to prescribe narcotics "in excess of the recommended dosage upon certifying the medical necessity." Dr.

Mitchell Max, director of the Pain Research Clinic at the National Institutes of Health, testified: "I see nothing wrong with the doses, the amount, the number of pills per se. . . . He is just taking regimens that work in cancer patients that everyone agrees on, and using them in people who had life-impairing, or even life-threatening, levels of pain. . . . We routinely give doses up to 10 times that size in patients with cancer."

The state questioned the thoroughness of Hurwitz's examinations, documentation, and monitoring. Hurwitz says most of his pain patients came to him with well-established problems, and "my main purpose in doing the diagnosis was to make sure that the patients were who they said they were. If they said they had back surgery, I wanted to see a back scar. If they said they had no leg, I wanted to look at the stump. So my physical exam was really limited to confirmatory findings that would illustrate the complaints and make sure they weren't conning me." As for monitoring, he saw patients who lived in the area once a month, but those who lived hundreds of miles away might visit his office only once or twice a year. The visits were supplemented by a monthly written report and telephone calls.

"The average practitioner does have reservations about prescribing long-term opiates," testified Dr. Stephen P. Long, director of acute pain services at the Medical College of Virginia Hospitals. "I would have performed a more thorough physical exam. I would like to have seen more detailed documentation." On the other hand, Dr. James Campbell, director of the Blaustein Pain Treatment Center at Johns Hopkins University, said Hurwitz "is doing heroic things for his patients. I think what he is doing involves enormous sacrifice. There are a lot of bad doctors out there, but he is not one of them."

On August 10, after the longest hearing in its history, the Virginia Board of Medicine found Hurwitz guilty of inadequate screening, excessive prescribing, and deficient monitoring. It revoked his license, saying it would be restored after three months if he agreed to take courses in narcotic prescription, pharmacology, psychiatry, addiction, medical record keeping, and pain management. Even then, he would be forbidden to prescribe narcotics for a year. Hurwitz has registered for the courses, but he has also filed an appeal in Arlington Circuit Court. After the Virginia ruling, the D.C. Board of Medicine suspended Hurwitz's license. Unable to practice, he had to give up his office. About the same time, the Virginia Board of Pharmacy revoked

Jerome Danoff's license for two years and fined him $10,000. He also planned to appeal.

Meanwhile, Hurwitz's patients were left high and dry. "I'm flabbergasted," he told the *Washington Post* after his Virginia license was revoked. "The Board of Medicine has told my patients, 'Drop dead.'" Said Laura D. Cooper, a patient with multiple sclerosis: "The board has made no provision for the patients. If I can't get medicine, I'm going to die the next time I get sick, and that's not histrionics. Some of us are candidates for suicide right now." Cooper, an attorney, has filed a federal class-action suit against the Virginia Board of Medicine, the Department of Health Professions, and the DEA on behalf of herself and Hurwitz's other pain patients.

David Covillion is not a party to the suit. He killed himself on September 11.

January 1997

Velvet President

Why Vaclav Havel is our era's George Orwell and more

Matt Welch

LAST FALL, AS THE UNITED STATES RUMBLED TOWARD WAR against Saddam Hussein, literary reviews and higher-brow magazines wrestled with an intriguing if unlikely hypothetical: What would George Orwell say if he were here today?

Christopher Hitchens, the fire-breathing British journalist who kick-started the discussion with his book *Why Orwell Matters*, suggested that a contemporary Eric Blair "would have seen straight through the characters who chant 'No War On Iraq'" and helped the rest of us to "develop the fiber to call Al-Qaeda what it actually is." *Washington Post* book reviewer George Scialabba stated confidently that "Orwell would associate himself with the unsexy democratic left, notably *Dissent* and the *American Prospect*," and that "he might, in particular, have wondered aloud why the heinous terrorist murder of 3,000 Americans was a turning point in history." *Commentary* tried yet again to claim Orwell as a neocon, and the *Weekly Standard*'s David Brooks argued that the great man's mantle and relevance had actually passed onto a new contrarian's shoulders: "At this moment, oddly enough, Hitchens matters more than Orwell."

At exactly the same time, the one man in the world of the living who could justifiably claim to be Orwell's heir was expounding almost daily on Saddam Hussein and international terrorism—even while rushing through one of the most frenetic periods of a famously accomplished life. Vaclav Havel, the 66-year-old former Czech president who was term-limited out of office on February 2, built his reputation in the 1970s by being to eyewitness fact what George Orwell was to dystopian fiction. In other words, he used common sense to deconstruct rhetorical falsehoods, pulling apart the suffocating mesh of collectivist lies one carefully observed thread at a time.

Like Orwell, Havel was a fiction writer whose engagement with the world led him to master the nonfiction political essay. Both men, in self-described sentiment, were of "the left," yet both men infuriated the left with their stinging criticism and ornery independence. Both were haunted by the Death of God, delighted by the idiosyncratic habits of their countrymen, and physically diminished as a direct result of their confrontation with totalitarians (not to mention their love of tobacco). As essentially neurotic men with weak mustaches, both have given generations of normal citizens hope that, with discipline and effort, they too can shake propaganda from everyday language and stand up to the foulest dictatorships.

Unlike Orwell, Havel lived long enough to enjoy a robust third act, and his last six months in office demonstrated the same kind of restless, iconoclastic activism that has made him an enemy of ideologues and ally of freedom lovers for nearly five decades.

Consider:

• Last September he delivered a rousing anti-communist speech over Radio Martí, a much-mocked station funded by Washington and beamed to Cuba. "When the internal crisis of the totalitarian system grows so deep that it becomes clear to everyone," he declared, "and when more and more people learn to speak their own language and reject the hollow, mendacious language of the powers that be, it means that freedom is remarkably close, if not directly within reach." He also nominated Oswald Paya Sardinas—the Cuban spokesman for the Varela Project, an opposition group modeled directly on Havel's 1970s movement Charter 77—for the Nobel Peace Prize. The speech was virtually ignored by the American press.

• In the days preceding, he gave a series of speeches across America that existentially questioned his own fitness for higher office, while still tossing off backbone-stiffening zingers like, "Evil must be confronted in its womb and, if it can't be done otherwise, then it has to be dealt with by the use of force."

• In November he orchestrated and hosted a historic NATO summit in Prague, where the Western alliance formally accepted seven formerly communist countries for membership. Havel, who has long been the most influential advocate for expanding NATO eastward, marked the occasion by installing above the Prague Castle—the Czech presidential residence—a goofy neon heart, of the same design that he draws atop his signature. In his major speech at the event, with George W. Bush looking on, Havel analyzed Iraq through the prism of the 1938 Munich Agreement, when war-shy British Prime Minister Neville Chamberlain notoriously sacrificed western Czechoslovakia to Hitler in the name of "peace with honor" and unknowingly gave generations of American interventionists a go-to example whenever it came time to attack another dictator. But before Paul Wolfowitz could high-five Condoleezza Rice, Havel warned that eerily similar high-sounding rhetoric was used to justify the Warsaw Pact's indefensible 1968 invasion of Prague.

• In January, in one of his last official acts as president, he joined seven other European political leaders in signing an open letter supporting Bush's policy toward Iraq. The act drove a wedge between what Defense Secretary Donald Rumsfeld gleefully called the "Old Europe" and "New Europe," and led French President Jacques Chirac to threaten to bar the Czech Republic and any other war-supporting Central European country from joining the European Union.

Most normal politicians, after nearly 13 years in power (including two and a half years as president of a unified Czechoslovakia), would lament the end of their special treatment and cling to whatever bureaucratic influence they could grasp. But most normal politicians don't make a life's work out of analyzing the inextricable link between personal freedom and a society's overall health. Though the Czech Republic is exponentially more free than it was when Havel first made his fairy tale ascent from gulag to castle, the former playwright has suffered personally under the constraints imposed by official decorum.

"What I really long for is that I shall be free of duties dictated by protocol," he told London's *Sunday Times* earlier this year. "Naturally, I have had to express myself in a more cautious and diplomatic manner and I have not been very happy about it."

The Right to Rock

Like Bill Clinton, Vaclav Havel is a product of the 1960s. Unlike
Clinton, he inhaled. "That was an extraordinarily interesting, fertile,
and inspiring period, not only here, but in the culture of the entire
world," he told interviewer Jiri Lederer in 1975. "Personally, too, it
was a relatively happy time: 1968 [the year of the 'Prague Spring']
was, for me, just a natural climax of that whole period."

From 1964 until August 21, 1968, Bohemia rediscovered bohemia,
producing arguably the most dynamic artistic flowering communism
ever tolerated, highlighted by Milos Forman and the Czech New
Wave of cinema, novelist Bohumil Hrabal's Slavic take on magical
realism, and the madcap theatrical rock band The Plastic People of
the Universe. Havel spent this period at the influential and radical
Theatre of the Balustrade, where he gobbled speed and pushed the
free expression envelope with absurdist topical plays such as *The
Memorandum* and *The Increased Difficulty of Concentration.*

Despite its 1.2 million residents, Prague is a surprisingly small town,
where artists of all disciplines bounce off each other on the street or
in the pub, and eventually on the newspaper page and gallery wall.
Havel, the somewhat shy scion of a bourgeois family (which owned,
among other things, the wonderful Lucerna Theatre on Wenceslas
Square), was particularly drawn to and awed by the "authentic culture" of unbridled rock music, in a way that recalls the rather prim
Orwell's fascination with Henry Miller. He preferred the Stones to
the Beatles (let alone Clinton's favorite, Fleetwood Mac), and took
from rock-influenced '60s culture "a temperament, a nonconformist
state of the spirit, an anti-establishment orientation, an aversion to
philistines, and an interest in the wretched and humiliated," he wrote
in his underrated 1991 reflection on governing, *Summer Meditations.*

During this period of cultural thaw and exploration, Havel began
to explore the political essay, a form he would eventually master with
Orwellian power. "His essays, lectures, and prison letters from the
last quarter century are, taken altogether, among the most vivid, sustained, and searching explorations of the moral and political responsibility of the intellectual produced anywhere in Europe," wrote Timothy Garton Ash, the foremost chronicler of revolutionary Central
Europe, in his 1999 collection *History of the Present.* "Indeed, it is difficult to think of any figure in the contemporary world who has more

cumulative authority to speak on this issue than Vaclav Havel."

The first targets of Havel's considerable wrath and sarcasm were the poor fools making "halfhearted" efforts at creating "Socialism with a human face." One of his first essays, 1965's "On Evasive Thinking" (collected in the English-language volume *Open Letters*) makes cruel sport of a newspaper essayist who—not unlike his modern American counterparts—attempted to assess and then dismiss the broader significance of a temporal tragedy, in this case, a building ledge falling and killing a passerby. "The public," Havel wrote, "again showed more intelligence and humanity than the writer, for it had understood that the so-called prospects of mankind are nothing but an empty platitude if they distract us from our particular worry about who might be killed by [another] window ledge, and what will happen should it fall on a group of nursery-school children out for a walk."

Here, in Havel's earliest essay to be translated into English, you can already find the four main themes that have animated his adult nonfiction writing ever since. One is the responsibility to make the world a better place. Another is that the slightest bit of personal dishonesty warps the soul. ("The minute we begin turning a blind eye to what we don't like in each other's writing, the minute we begin to back away from our own inner norms, to accommodate ourselves to each other, cut deals with each other over poetics, we will in fact set ourselves against each other . . . until one day we will disappear in a general fog of mutual admiration.")

A third theme is that ideology-driven governance is practically doomed to fail. ("It prevents whoever has it in his power to solve the problem of the Prague façades from understanding that he bears responsibility for something and that he can't lie his way out of that responsibility.") Finally, there is his belief in the revolutionary potency of individuals speaking freely and "living in truth."

The last of these phenomena became nearly extinct after the tanks of 1968 rolled in from Russia. The new rulers ushered in the "normalization" period, during which tens of thousands emigrated and most "nonconformist" writers (including Havel) were inconvenienced, banned, or sometimes just locked away. In April 1975, facing an utterly demoralized country and an understandable case of writer's block, Havel committed an act of such sheer ballsiness that the shock waves are still being felt in repressive countries 30 years later. He simply sat down and, knowing that he'd likely be imprisoned for his efforts, wrote an open letter to his dictator, Gustav Husak, explaining in painstaking detail just why and how totalitarianism was ruining Czechoslovakia.

"So far," Havel scolded Husak, "you and your government have chosen the easy way out for yourselves, and the most dangerous road for society: the path of inner decay for the sake of outward appearances; of deadening life for the sake of increasing uniformity; of deepening the spiritual and moral crisis of our society, and ceaselessly degrading human dignity, for the puny sake of protecting your own power."

It was the Big Bang that set off the dissident movement in Central Europe. For those lucky enough to read an illegally retyped copy or hear it broadcast over Radio Free Europe, the effect was not unlike what happened to the 5,000 people who bought the Velvet Underground's first record: After the shock and initial pleasure wore off, many said, "Wait a minute, I can do this too!" By standing up to a system that had forced every citizen to make a thousand daily compromises, Havel was suggesting a novel new tactic: Have the self-respect to tell the truth, never mind the consequences, and maybe you'll put the bastards on the defensive.

"I felt the need to stir things up," he told his interviewer Lederer at the time, "to confront others for a change and force them to deal with a situation that I myself had created."

This act of literary punk rock was followed, logically enough, by a defense of rock music that sparked the Charter 77 movement. Or, as Havel told a startled Lou Reed when he met the Velvet Underground's former frontman in 1990, "Did you know that I am president because of you?"

Defending the Plastic People

In 1968 a rare copy of the Velvet Underground's first record somehow found its way to Prague. It became a sensation in music circles and beyond, eventually inspiring the Czech name for their bloodless 1989 overthrow of Communist rule, "the Velvet Revolution." The Plastic People, then a newly formed troupe that borrowed heavily from Frank Zappa and the Mothers of Invention, quickly added a half-dozen songs from *The Velvet Underground & Nico* to their repertoire. The group was banned not long after the Prague Spring concluded but continued to play at weddings and secret shows.

Then, in 1976, four members were arrested on charges of "disturbing the peace." The Czech dissident movement, newly roused by Havel's open letter, made the trial an international cause. Havel, who intuitively grasped the symbolism of the case, was in the courtroom every day to witness and document the judicial farce. Just as George Orwell saw picking up a gun to shoot fascists in the Spanish Civil War as "the only conceivable thing to do," Havel understood this assault on freedom as one outrage too far. It was a turning point in his life. "Everyone understood," he wrote later, "that an attack on the Czech musical underground was an attack on a most elementary and important thing, something that in fact bound everyone together: it was an attack on the very notion of living within the truth, on the real aims of life."

His essay on the trial has the rushed and liberated tone of someone who has just crossed a personal point of no return, or has just heard the Sex Pistols' *Never Mind the Bollocks* for the first time. It ends with a classic description of Havel bumping into a film director who didn't understand the sudden enthusiasm for defending some derelict rock musicians.

"Perhaps I'm doing him an injustice," Havel wrote, "but at that moment, I was overwhelmed by an intense feeling that this dear man belonged to a world that I no longer wish to have anything to do with—and Mr. Public Prosecutor Kovarik, pay attention, because here comes a vulgar word—I mean the world of cunning shits."

The Plastic People trial spurred Havel and his friends to form Charter 77, a human rights organization built around a petition that asked, simply, that the Czechoslovak government adhere to the Final Act of the 1975 Helsinki Agreement—specifically its covenants on civil, political, and economic rights—to which it had recently become a signatory. Living up to Helsinki would have meant allowing free expression, "freedom from fear," freedom of religious practice, and other rights then quashed by the Communists. This narrow, legalistic tactic, which has since been emulated the world over, allowed the dissidents to claim that they were not, after all, agitating against the regime, but rather asking it to follow its own acknowledged legislation.

The wind now at the anti-Communists' sails, Havel uncorked his most famous and influential essay of all, "The Power of the Powerless." It starts by dissecting exactly why a greengrocer would put a sign in his window saying "Workers of the world, unite," and how this "dictatorship of the ritual" is used as a knowingly false brand of ideological glue to keep the Party in charge.

If shopkeepers and others suddenly stopped observing the rituals, and instead spoke and acted freely, he predicted (with unnerving accuracy), "The entire pyramid of totalitarian power, deprived of the element that binds it together, would collapse in upon itself, as it were, in a kind of material implosion." The essay, which was addressed to 20 prominent dissidents from around the East Bloc, also served as a micro-analysis of the new "dissent." Just 40 months after delivering his bolt out of the blue to Gustav Husak, Havel was now breaking down the finer points of a movement that his own open letter forced into the world. As a direct result, he spent most of the next five years in jail.

After being released, with his health now diminished, Havel could not resist the temptation to bite the hands even of those who would reach out to him, should they be deserving. Perhaps the most remarkable essay in this genre was 1985's "Anatomy of a Reticence," where Havel described the dissidents' suspicion of the "Western peace movement" then lobbying for an end to the nuclear arms race. It foreshadowed his later impatience with reflexive anti-Americanism. Here's a stirring passage on ideology and the Soviet invasion of Afghanistan:

"How much trust or even admiration for the Western peace movement can we expect from a simple yet sensitive citizen of Eastern Europe when he has noticed that this movement has never, at any of its congresses or at demonstrations involving hundreds of thousands of participants, got around to protesting the fact that five years ago, one important European country attacked a small neutral neighbor and since that time has been conducting on its territory a war of extermination which has already claimed a million dead and three million refugees? Seriously, what are we to think of a peace movement, a European peace movement, which is virtually unaware of the only war being conducted today by a European state? As for the argument that the victims of aggression and their defenders enjoy the sympathies of Western establishments and so are not worthy of support from the left, such incredible ideological opportunism can provoke only one reaction—utter disgust and a sense of limitless hopelessness."

The Culture of Markets
The same instincts and habits that made Havel the foremost observer of modern-day Stalinism got him into unexpected trouble not long after he helped engineer one of the most inspiring and bloodless revolutions in history. It is one thing to shoot your mouth off, tell your audience the opposite of what they want to hear, and hang around with beer-swilling "underground" characters. It's quite another to deftly juggle the nuances of presidential behavior in a newly emergent democracy.

In July 1990 *Washington Post* legend Benjamin Bradlee detected "early warnings of threats to the new Czech freedom" after Havel complained to him that the local press "forgets . . . that the freedom is only one side of the coin, where the other side is represented by responsibility." Free traders grimaced at Havel's repeated railings against the "ideology of the market," especially when compared to then Finance Minister Vaclav Klaus and his blunt adulation of Milton Friedman, Margaret Thatcher, and "a market economy without adjectives." Staunch Czech anti-Communists, particularly the generation that fled the country after 1968, begrudged their *samizdat* hero for using his new power to seek reconciliation with, not justice against, the hundreds of thousands of collaborators who made the police state logistically possible.

Political realists had their doubts about Havel as well. In 1990 he emptied Czechoslovakia's prisons and shuttered its national arms factories, acts that smacked of rash hippie idealism—a diagnosis consistent with his disturbingly fuzzy talk of "nonpolitical politics." Klaus, meanwhile, was busying himself with the urgent task of herding antitotalitarians into a professional political party that promptly trounced all comers. Even Havel's admiring former advisers, such as Boston University's Chandler Rosenberger, warned at the time that the utopian Castle longhairs "became prone to fantastic delusions" of "transforming the politics of the planet."

With dissident contemporaries such as Lech Walesa, Adam Michnik, and Alexander Solzhenitsyn dropping out of post-communist politics and into self-parody, it was hardly a stretch to imagine Havel as destined for a position more suited to his talents: editing a Czech literary magazine, say, or running an Open Society think tank funded by George Soros. When Czechoslovakia's June 1992 elections placed Klaus and Slovak nationalist Vladimir Meciar firmly in charge of the increasingly incompatible Czech and Slovak republics, Havel resigned rather than preside over the "Velvet Divorce" he felt was a "fatal error." It seemed logical that the unglamorous, nuts-and-bolts business of "transition" would now be managed by the more technocratically adept Klaus.

But the smart money was wrong. Havel was the only real choice considered when the new Czech Republic needed a president in January 1993. And Havel's entire career and philosophy, like Orwell's, were dedicated to navigating ideological minefields under the extreme duress of personal participation and suffering. This skill, it turns out, had some relevance in the post-Gorbachev world too. Like Orwell's, Havel's words and zesty one-liners can be (and have been) quoted selectively to make him sound conservative, liberal, and otherwise, and his bedrock belief in the transformative power of "calling things by their proper names" virtually ensured that some of his freewheeling opinions would set off alarm bells among those who see the shadow of socialism in such phrases as "civil society" and "new politics."

"I once said that I considered myself a socialist," Havel wrote in *Summer Meditations.* "I merely wanted to suggest that my heart was, as they say, slightly left of center." The words could have come directly out of Orwell's mouth: "In sentiment I am definitely 'left,'" he wrote in 1940, "but I believe that a writer can only remain honest if he keeps free of party labels."

Havel went on to discuss the futility of those who would pin an ideological tag to his lapel. "All my adult life, I was branded by officials as 'an exponent of the right' who wanted to bring capitalism back to our country," he wrote. "Today—at a ripe old age—I am suspected by some of being left-wing, if not of harboring out-and-out socialist tendencies. What, then, is my real position? First and foremost, I have never espoused any ideology, dogma, or doctrine—left-wing, right-wing, or any other closed, ready-made system of presuppositions about the world. On the contrary, I have tried to think independently, using my own powers of reason, and I have always vigorously resisted attempts to pigeonhole me."

No one tried to pigeonhole Havel more than his revolutionary comrade turned rival Vaclav Klaus, and many of the president's comments that were perceived initially to be illiberal were, in fact, thinly veiled rebukes to Klaus, whom Havel suspected of placing his own political ambitions above genuine concern for the country. In a society seeking moral footing after 50 years of totalitarian rot, Havel found Klaus' public manners personally appalling and potentially combustible.

Passing early judgments on Central European politics can be a loser's game, but Havel's warnings about Klaus—and on the dangers of immorality in post-revolution politics—turned out to be prescient. Despite his still-glowing reputation among American conservatives, Klaus has been nobody's Thatcherite since at least 1993, and probably earlier. Reforms that the Hungarian Socialist Party was ramming through in 1995—freeing rent and utility prices, cleaning up and selling off banks, introducing greater capital markets transparency—Klaus never bothered with at all. This despite having a clear mandate from 1989 to late 1997, when a collapsing economy and various corruption scandals forced him to resign. As Thomas Hazlett wrote in the March 1998 issue of *Reason*, Klaus had "all but shelved further efforts at economic liberalization and declared the transformation complete."

The one Czech politician who consistently challenged Klaus to get economic reform rolling again was none other than Vaclav Havel, the same guy suspected in the early '90s of being a Third Way quasi-socialist without the "stomach" for market policies. For those more interested in facts than in stereotypes, Havel's remarkable December 9, 1997, speech to the Czech Parliament took Klaus to the woodshed for dragging his feet on reforms and advocated specific measures far toothier than the shock therapy slogans Klaus had been mouthing since 1990. According to Havel, reforms had resulted in the appearance of a market rather than the real thing.

"I do not share the view held by some of you that the entire transformation started from the wrong foundations, was wrongly devised and wrongly directed," Havel said. "I would rather say that our problem lies in the very opposite: the transformation process stopped halfway, which is possibly the worst thing that could have happened to it.

"Many businesses have been formally privatized, but how many have concrete visible owners who seek increasing effectiveness and who care about the long-term prospects of their companies? . . . [T]hose who represent the owners see their role not as a task, mission or commitment but simply as an opportunity to transfer the entrusted money somewhere else and get out. . . . A rather strange role, to my mind, is often played by our banks: they indirectly own companies that are operating at a loss, and the more the companies lose the more money the banks lend them. . . . The legal framework of privatization, as well as of the capital market, is being perfected only now. Is it not rather late?"

In a region where power has almost always corrupted, Klaus has had more of it, and for longer, than any of his transition peers. (Even when he lost the 1998 elections, he entered a controversial power-sharing agreement with the ruling Socialists.) Havel's hectoring surely served as a restraint on Klaus' ambitions. It is hardly surprising that, after Havel stepped down, Klaus succeeded by the narrowest of margins in replacing his long-time rival at the Castle.

Rumpled Prophet
Havel is a short and rumpled man, even in a sharp presidential suit. He's a disaster at press conferences, wiggling his tube-socked feet under the table and making chewing sounds into the microphone before each response. He nearly died three times in the last eight years from various illnesses, and he reportedly headed to Portugal for a long cure soon after stepping down as president. He describes himself as perpetually nervous, afraid someone's going to wake him from the dream and put him back in jail, where he probably belongs. He may have been the life of the party a time or two, but overall the impression he gives is that of an unspectacular man who probably would rather be drunk.

This is one of his true gifts to the rest of us, and once again recalls Orwell's legacy. As in Orwell's case, Havel's talents seem far more the result of hard work and discipline than any once-in-a-generation gift of talent. If this normal-looking character could shake off the hangover long enough to give an eloquent finger to The Man, well, what were *you* doing with your time?

Once in office, Havel took pains to remain himself. On his first New Year's speech, in 1990, he started by saying "I assume you did not propose me for this office so that I, too, would lie to you," and from that point on tried to give his fellow citizens the feeling that one of *them* was up in the Castle. The same impact can be seen on many of his foreign admirers; when I ask my American or British friends who lived in Prague to tell me their favorite story about Havel, it usually involves them bumming a smoke off the guy, or sharing a urinal, or seeing him with a hot blonde at a rock show. Though he quickly grew out of the blue jeans phase, and was careful about the ceremonial dignities of office, he was forever injecting informality into the serious work of public life. He was trying to practice democracy with a human face.

When Clinton or Boris Yeltsin or Pink Floyd came to town, Havel would take them out to a typical Czech pub. "As for heads of state," he once told the Czech newspaper *Mlada fronta Dnes*, "I haven't met anyone yet whose eyes didn't shine with delight when I suggested that after the official reception we should go get a beer somewhere really quick." For years, he lived in an accessible apartment along the river, and most Praguers can still tell you his favorite pubs.

Three successive United States presidents have fallen under Havel's spell, and he in turn has used his access to cajole them into taking military action against Slobodan Milosevic, expanding NATO, and minding the lessons of Munich. Clinton and George W. Bush in particular seem tongue-tied and awe-struck in the presence of someone who actually fought communism and lived to tell about it; Havel returns the favor by flattering America's role in taking down the Evil Empire. His open, though qualified, flattery of the U.S. is one reason Noam Chomsky considers him "morally repugnant" and on an "intellectual level that is vastly below that of Third World peasants and Stalinist hacks."

Chomsky's insults aside, Havel has enabled Czechs to punch above their weight in international affairs for 13 years; this will likely end as the extraordinary geopolitical circumstances that created him fade and are replaced by more provincial Czech political concerns. Havel himself sees his career as a massive historical accident, even a joke. But as he walks off the global stage, Czechs and the rest of the world can be thankful that someone like him was essentially in the wrong place at the right time. He remains a figure from whom not just insight but inspiration can be drawn.

"The most important thing," Havel said in his final New Year's address as president, "is that new generations are maturing, generations of people who grew up free and are not deformed by life under Communist rule. These are the first Czechs of our times who inherently consider freedom normal and natural. It would be great if the breaking through of these people into various parts of public life leads to our society more factually, thoroughly and impartially examining its past, without whose reflection we cannot be ourselves. I also hope it will lead to our successfully parting with many ill consequences of the work of destruction the Communist regime wreaked upon our souls."

May 2003

Free Radical

Journalist Christopher Hitchens explains why he's no longer a socialist, why moral authoritarianism is on the rise, and what's wrong with anti-globalization protestors.

Interview by Rhys Southan

IN THE ROUGHLY TWO DECADES SINCE British writer Christopher Hitchens arrived in the U.S., he has emerged as a singularly insightful, provocative, and impossible-to-ignore critic of American politics and culture. His regular columns for the left-wing think magazine the *Nation* and the glitzy celebrity sheet *Vanity Fair* stand out in both publications for their clarity of thought and prose. He famously served as one of the models for Peter Fallows, the memorable dissipated Brit journalist in Tom Wolfe's *Bonfire of the Vanities*. His television appearances are legendary, none perhaps more so than his contretemps with Charlton Heston during CNN's live coverage of the Gulf War. Hitchens insisted that Heston list what countries have borders with Iraq. After Heston flubbed the answer, he upbraided the journalist for "taking up valuable network time giving a high-school geography lesson." To which Hitchens replied: "Oh, keep your hairpiece on."

Though the 52-year-old Hitchens clearly enjoys mocking the famous and the powerful—he once derided the House of Windsor for "sucking off [Britain's] national tit"—he's no mere gadfly. In books such as *The Missionary Position, No One Left to Lie To*, and *The Trial of Henry Kissinger*, he has crafted thoughtful and provocative extended indictments of Mother Teresa, Bill Clinton, and the former secretary of state and Nobel Peace Prize winner; his recent collection, *Unacknowledged*

Legislation: Writers in the Public Sphere, was reviewed in the July issue of *Reason.*

Hitchens' willingness to put moral principles before political alliances has earned him the wrath of ideological compatriots. When he signed an affidavit contradicting testimony by Clinton administration aide Sidney Blumenthal that the president had never circulated tales of Monica Lewinsky as a crazed stalker, Hitchens was attacked as a liar and a snitch in the pages of the *Nation* and almost ended his relationship with the magazine.

Hitchens' newest book is *Letters to a Young Contrarian: The Art of Mentoring,* in which he exhorts youth to remain both principled and oppositional, freethinkers in the best Enlightenment tradition. Given such thoughts, it's not surprising that Hitchens' next book will be about George Orwell. Nor is it surprising to find him increasingly interested in alternatives to orthodox left-wing thinking. A regular reader of *Reason*— a few years back, he wrote that he gets "more out of reading . . . *Reason* than I do out of many 'movement' journals"—Hitchens has become increasingly interested in the libertarian critique of state power and its defense of individual liberty. "I am," he says, "much more inclined to stress those issues . . . to see that they do possess, with a capital H and a capital I, Historical Importance."

Reason: How were you different as a young contrarian than you are as an older one?

Christopher Hitchens: The book forces me to ask that question, and yet I don't quite. I must say that I've always found the generational emphasis on the way that my youth was covered to be very annoying. There were a lot of other people born in April 1949, and I just don't feel like I have anything in common with most of them. I forget who it was who said that generation—age group, in other words—is the most debased form of solidarity. The idea of anyone who was born around that time having an automatic ticket to being called "a '60s person," is annoying to me. Especially membership in the specific group that I could claim to have been a part of: not just of "the '60s," but of *1968.* There's even a French term for it: *soixante-huitard.* You can now guess roughly what the political parameters were for me at the time. And you can also guess at least one of the sources of my irritation, which is that by generational analysis, Bill

Clinton and I are of the same kidney and same DNA. I repudiate that with every fiber.

But I'm postponing an answer to your question. In those days, I was very much in rebellion against the state. The state had presented itself to [my fellow protestors and me], particularly through the Vietnam War, in the character of a liar and a murderer. If, at a young age, you are able to see your own government in that character, it powerfully conditions the rest of your life. I was taught very early on that the state can be, and is, a liar and a murderer. Yet I have to concede that I didn't think there was a problem *necessarily* with the state, or government, or collective power.

I had been interested in libertarian ideas when I was younger. I set aside this interest in the '60s simply because all the overwhelming political questions seemed to sideline issues of individual liberty in favor of what seemed then to be grander questions. I suppose what would make me different now is that I am much more inclined to stress those issues of individual liberty than I would have been then. And to see that they do possess, with a capital H and a capital I, Historical Importance, the very things that one thought one was looking for.

Reason: When did your focus change? In *Letters*, you write that you've "learned a good deal from the libertarian critique" of the idea that the individual belongs to the state and you praise a friend who taught you that "the crucial distinction between systems . . . was no longer ideological. The main political difference was between those who did, and those who did not, believe that the citizen could—or should—be the property of the state."

Hitchens: It's hard to assign a date. I threw in my lot with the left because on all manner of pressing topics—the Vietnam atrocity, nuclear weapons, racism, oligarchy—there didn't seem to be any distinctive libertarian view. I must say that this still seems to me to be the case, at least where issues of internationalism are concerned. What is the libertarian take, for example, on Bosnia or Palestine?

There's also something faintly ahistorical about the libertarian worldview. When I became a socialist it was largely the outcome of a study of history, taking sides, so to speak, in the battles over industrialism and war and empire. I can't—and this may be a limit on my own imagination or education—picture a libertarian analysis of 1848 or 1914. I look forward to further discussions on this, but for the moment I guess I'd say that libertarianism often feels like an optional philosophy for citizens in societies or cultures that are already developed or prosperous or stable. I find libertarians more worried about the over-mighty state than the unaccountable corporation. The great thing about the present state of affairs is the way it combines the worst of bureaucracy with the worst of the insurance companies.

What I did was to keep two sets of books in my mind. I was certainly interested in issues that have always interested libertarians—defining what the limits to state power are. The first political issue on which I'd ever decided to take a stand was when I was in my teens and before I'd become a socialist. It was the question of capital punishment. A large part of my outrage toward capital punishment was exactly the feeling that it was arrogating too much power to the government. It was giving life-and-death power to the state, which I didn't think it deserved, even if it could use it wisely. I was convinced it could not and did not.

In the mid-1970s, I first met someone whom I've gotten to know better since, Adam Michnik, one of the more brilliant of the Polish dissidents of the time. Michnik made the luminous remark you quoted about the citizen and his relation to the state. I remember thinking, "Well, that's a remark that's impossible to forget."

Reason: So, do you still consider yourself a socialist?

Hitchens: Brian Lamb of C-SPAN has been interviewing me on and off for about 20 years, since I'd first gone to Washington, which is roughly when his own *Washington Journal* program began. As the years went by, he formed the habit of starting every time by saying: "You haven't been on the show for a bit. Tell me, are you still a socialist?" And I would always say, "Yes, I am." I knew that he hoped that one day I would say, "No, you know what, Brian, I've seen the light, I've seen the error of my ways." And I knew that I didn't want to give him this satisfaction, even if I'd had a complete conversion experience.

The funny thing is that, recently, he stopped asking me. I don't know why. And just about at that point, I had decided that however I would have phrased the answer—I didn't want to phrase it as someone repudiating his old friends or denouncing his old associations—I no longer would have positively replied, "I am a socialist."

I don't like to deny it. But it simply ceased to come up, as a matter of fact. And in my own life there's a reason for that.

There is no longer a general socialist critique of capitalism—certainly not the sort of critique that proposes an alternative or a replacement. There just is not and one has to face the fact, and it seems to me further that it's very unlikely, though not impossible, that it will again be the case in the future. Though I don't think that the contradictions, as we used to say, of the system, are by any means all resolved.

Reason: Many socialists have a radically anti-authoritarian disposition, even though the policies they would enact end up being authoritarian. What causes this divide?

Hitchens: Karl Marx was possibly the consummate anti-statist in his original writings and believed that the state was not the solution to social problems, but the outcome of them, the forcible resolution in favor of one ruling group. He thought that if you could give a name to utopia, it was the withering away of the state. Certainly those words had a big effect on me.

The reason why people tend to forget them, or the left has a tendency to forget them in practice, has something to do with the realm of necessity. If you make your priority—let's call it the 1930s—the end of massive unemployment, which was then defined as one of the leading problems, there seemed no way to do it except by a program of public works. And, indeed, the fascist governments in Europe drew exactly the same conclusion at exactly the same time as Roosevelt did, and as, actually, the British Tories did not. But not because the Tories had a better idea of what to do about it. They actually favored unemployment as a means of disciplining the labor market.

You see what I mean: Right away, one's in an argument, and there's really nothing to do with utopia at all. And then temporary expedients become dogma very quickly—especially if they seem to work.

Then there's the question of whether or not people can be made by government to behave better. They can certainly be made to behave worse; fascism is the proof of that, and so is Stalinism. But a big experience, and this gets us a bit nearer the core of it, a very big influence on a number of people my age was the American civil rights movement, and the moral grandeur of that and also the astonishing speed and exclusiveness of its success. A lot of that did involve asking the government to condition people's behavior, at least in the sense of saying there are certain kinds of private behavior that are now not lawful. And there seemed to be every moral justification for this, and I'm not sure I wouldn't still say that there was.

But it's become too easily extended as an analogy and as a metaphor—and too unthinkingly applied. In my memory, the demand of the student radical was for the university to stop behaving as if it was my parent, *in loco parentis.* They pretend they're your family, which is exactly what we've come here to get away from. We don't want the dean telling us what we can smoke or who we can sleep with or what we can wear, or anything of this sort. That was a very important part of the '60s.

Now you go to campus and student activists are continuously demanding more supervision, of themselves and of others, in order to assure proper behavior and in order to ensure that nobody gets upset. I think that's the measure of what I mean.

Reason: Does that explain Ralph Nader's popularity among students during last year's election? He came across as a contrarian in his campaign, and became a hero to a lot of college students. You supported him, too. But he's essentially a curmudgeon with a conservative disposition who advocated lots of regulation.

Hitchens: If I separate in my mind what it is that people like about Ralph, I'm certain the first thing is this: There are people who support him who don't agree with him politically at all, or have no idea of what his politics are. I would be hard-put to say that I knew what his politics were, but the quality that people admired of him was certainly his probity, his integrity. It's just impossible to imagine Ralph Nader taking an under-the-table campaign donation or a kickback. Or arranging to have someone assassinated, or any of these kinds of things. That's not a small thing to say about somebody.

You're right that his approach to life is in many ways a very conservative one. He leads a very austere, rather traditional mode of life. I met him first about 20 years ago. He contacted me, in fact, as he'd admired something I'd written. We met, and the main outcome of this was a 20-year campaign on his part to get me to stop smoking. In fact, he even offered me a large-ish sum of money once if I would quit. Almost as if he were my father or my uncle. Yes, generally speaking, he is a believer in the idea that government can better people, as well as condition them. But he's not an authoritarian, somehow. The word would be *paternalist,* with the state looking after you, rather than trying to control you. But there's some of us who don't find the state, in its paternal guise, very much more attractive. In fact, it can be at its most sinister when it decides that what it's doing is for your own good.

I certainly wish I wasn't a smoker and wish I could give it up. But I'm damned if I'll be treated how smokers are now being treated by not just the government, but the government ventriloquizing the majority. The majoritarian aspect makes it to me more repellent. And I must say it both startles and depresses me that an authoritarian majoritarianism of that kind can have made such great strides in America, almost unopposed. There's something essentially un-American in the idea that I could not now open a bar in San Francisco that says, "Smokers Welcome."

Reason: The right and the left have joined together in a war against pleasure. What caused this?

Hitchens: The most politically encouraging event on the horizon—which is a very bleak one politically—is the possibility of fusion or synthesis of some of the positions of what is to be called left and some of what is to be called libertarian. The critical junction could be, and in some ways already is, the War on Drugs.

The War on Drugs is an attempt by force, by the state, at mass behavior modification. Among other things, it is a denial of medical rights, and certainly a denial of all civil and political rights. It involves a collusion with the most gruesome possible allies in the Third World. It's very hard for me to say that there's an issue more important than that at the moment. It may sound like a hysterical thing to say, but I really think it's much more important than welfare policy, for example. It's self-evidently a very, very important matter. Important enough, perhaps, to create this synthesis I've been looking for, or help to do that.

Reason: What are the signs that political fusion between some libertarians and some leftists is happening?

Hitchens: One reason the War on Drugs goes on in defiance of all reason is that it has created an enormous clientele of people who in one way or another depend upon it for their careers or for their jobs. That's true of congressmen who can't really get funding for their district unless it's in some way related to anti-drug activity. There's all kinds of funding that can be smuggled through customs as anti-drug money—all the way to the vast squads of people who are paid to try to put the traffic down, and so forth. So what's impressive is how many people whose job it has been to enforce this war are coming out now and saying that it's obviously, at best, a waste of time.

The other encouraging sign is that those in the political-intellectual class who've gone public about it have tended to be on what would conventionally have been called the right. Some of them are fairly mainstream Republicans, like the governor of New Mexico. *National Review*, under the ownership of William Buckley, published a special issue devoted to exposing the fallacies and appalling consequences of the War on Drugs. I thought that should have been *The Nation* that did that. I now wouldn't care so much about the precedence in that. It wouldn't matter to me who was first any longer. I don't have any allegiances like that anymore. I don't ask what people's politics are. I ask what their principles are.

Reason: Has your own shift in principles changed your relationship with the *Nation?*

Hitchens: For a while it did. I thought at one point that I might have to resign from the magazine. That was over, in general, its defense of Bill Clinton in office, which I still think was a historic mistake made by left-liberals in this country. It completely squandered the claim of a magazine like the *Nation* to be a journal of opposition. By supporting Clinton, the *Nation* became a journal more or less of the consensus. And of the rightward moving consensus at that, because I don't think there's any way of describing Bill Clinton as an enemy of conservatism.

I'd been made aware by someone in the Clinton administration of what I thought was criminal activity. At any rate, the administration engaged in extraordinarily reprehensible activity by way of intimidating female witnesses in an important case. I decided that I would be obstructing justice if I'd kept the evidence to myself. That led to me being denounced in the *Nation* as the equivalent of a McCarthyite state invigilator, which I thought was absurd. Where I live, the White House is the government. So if one attacks it, one isn't reporting one's friends to the government, so to speak, by definition.

The controversy shows the amazing persistence of antediluvian categories and habits of thought on the left, and these were applied to

me in a very mendacious and I thought rather thuggish way. I had
to make an issue of it with the magazine, and I was prepared to quit.
But we were able to come to an agreement. They stopped saying this
about me, in other words.

But there is no such thing as a radical left anymore. *Ça n'existe pas.*
The world of Gloria Steinem and Jesse Jackson, let's say, has all been,
though it doesn't realize it, hopelessly compromised by selling out to
Clintonism. It became, under no pressure at all, and with no excuse,
and in no danger, a voluntary apologist for abuse of power.

It couldn't wait to sell out. It didn't even read the small print or
ask how much or act as if it were forced under pressure to do so. I
don't think they've realized how that's changed everything for them.
They're not a left. They're just another self-interested faction with an
attitude toward government and a hope that it can get some of its people in there. That makes it the same as everyone else—only slightly
more hypocritical and slightly more self-righteous.

Reason: In *Letters to a Young Contrarian,* you talk about how it was
libertarians—specifically Milton Friedman and Alan Greenspan—
who did the most to end the draft by persuading President Nixon's
special commission on the matter that mandatory military service represented a form of slavery. Is it the contrarians from unexpected ranks
that enact real change?

Hitchens: Absolutely. Mr. Greenspan and Mr. Friedman used my
mantra correctly by saying the draft would make the citizen the property of the state. To argue against them, however, I'll quote someone
whom neither of them particularly likes, but whom I think they both
respect. John Maynard Keynes said somewhere—I think in *Essays in
Persuasion*—that many revolutions are begun by conservatives because
these are people who tried to make the existing system work and they
know why it does not. Which is quite a profound insight. It used to be
known in Marx's terms as revolution from above.

It would indeed come from enlightened and often self-interested
members of the old regime who perfectly well knew that the assurances being given to the ruler were false. That the system didn't know
what was going on or how to provide for itself, but couldn't bear to
acknowledge that fact and had no means for self-correction. That is
indeed how revolutions often begin.

Reason: What do you think about the anti-globalization movement? Is it contrarian or radical in your sense?

Hitchens: There was a long lapse where it seemed that nobody took to the streets at all, and where the idea of taking to the streets had begun to seem like something really from a bygone era. It came back very suddenly, initially in Seattle. In some kind of promethean way, the idea was passed on and contained, perhaps like fire in a reed, only to break out again.

In a way I should have been pleased to see that, and I suppose in some small way I was, but a lot of this did seem to me to be a protest against modernity, and to have a very conservative twinge, in the sense of being reactionary. It's often forgotten that the Port Huron Statement, the famous Students for a Democratic Society (SDS) document, was in part a protest against mechanization, against bigness, against scale, against industrialization, against the hugeness and impersonality of, as it thought of it, capitalism. There were elements of that that I agreed with at the time, particularly the interface between the military and the industrial [segments of society].

I do remember thinking that it had a sort of archaic character to it, exactly the kind of thing that Marx attacked, in fact, in the early critiques of capitalism. What SDS seemed to want was a sort of organic, more rural-based, traditional society, which probably wouldn't be a good thing if you could have it. But you can't, so it's foolish to demand such a thing. This tendency has come out as the leading one in what I can see of the anti-globalization protesters. I hear the word *globalization* and it sounds to me like a very good idea. I like the sound of it. It sounds innovative and internationalist.

To many people it's a word of almost diabolic significance—as if there could be a non-global response to something.

Reason: This anti-global approach seems especially surprising coming from the left.

Hitchens: The Seattle protesters, I suppose you could say, in some ways came from the left. You couldn't say they came from the right, although a hysterical aversion to world government and internationalism is a very, very American nativist right-wing mentality. It's the sort that is out of fashion now but believe me, if you go on radio stations to talk about Henry Kissinger, as I have recently, you can find it. There are people who don't care about Kissinger massacring people in East Timor, or overthrowing democracy in Chile, or anything of that sort.

But they do believe he's a tool of David Rockefeller, and the Trilateral Commission, and the secret world government. That used to be a big deal in California in the '50s and '60s with the John Birch Society.

There are elements of that kind of thing to be found in the anti-globalization protests, but the sad thing is that practically everything I've just said wouldn't even be understood by most of the people who attend the current protests, because they wouldn't get the references.

Reason: You've called yourself a socialist living in a time when capitalism is more revolutionary.

Hitchens: I said this quite recently. I'm glad you noticed it. Most of the readers of the *Nation* seemed not to have noticed it. That was the first time I'd decided it was time I shared my hand. I forget whether I said I was an ex-socialist, or recovering Marxist, or whatever, but that would have been provisional or stylistic. The thing I've often tried to point out to people from the early days of the Thatcher revolution in Britain was that the political consensus had been broken, and from the right. The revolutionary, radical forces in British life were being led by the conservatives. That was something that almost nobody, with the very slight exception of myself, had foreseen.

I'd realized in 1979, the year she won, that though I was a member of the Labour Party, I wasn't going to vote for it. I couldn't bring myself to vote conservative. That's purely visceral. It was nothing to do with my mind, really. I just couldn't physically do it. I'll never get over that, but that's my private problem.

But I did realize that by subtracting my vote from the Labour Party, I was effectively voting for Thatcher to win. That's how I discovered that that's what I secretly hoped would happen. And I'm very glad I did. I wouldn't have been able to say the same about Reagan, I must say. But I don't think he had her intellectual or moral courage. This would be a very long discussion. You wouldn't conceivably be able to get it into a *Reason* interview.

Marx's original insight about capitalism was that it was the most revolutionary and creative force ever to appear in human history. And though it brought with it enormous attendant dangers, [the revolutionary nature] was the first thing to recognize about it. That is actually what the *Manifesto* is all about. As far as I know, no better summary of the beauty of capital has ever been written. You sort of know it's true, and yet it can't be, because it doesn't compute in the way we're taught to think. Any more than it computes, for example, that Marx and Engels thought that America was the great country of freedom and revolution and Russia was the great country of tyranny and backwardness.

But that's exactly what they did think, and you can still astonish people at dinner parties by saying that. To me it's as true as knowing my own middle name. Imagine what it is to live in a culture where people's first instinct when you say it is to laugh. Or to look bewildered. But that's the nearest I've come to stating not just what I believe, but everything I ever have believed, all in one girth.

November 2001

Kroger Babb's Roadshow

How a long-running movie walked the thin line between exploitation and education

Joe Bob Briggs

"Once in a lifetime comes A Presentation That TRULY PULLS NO PUNCHES! Now YOU Can SEE The Motion Picture That DARES DISCUSS and EXPLAIN SEX AS NEVER BEFORE SEEN and HEARD! THE ONE, THE ONLY, THE ORIGINAL . . . MOM AND DAD . . . Truly The World's Most Amazing Attraction! NO ONE UNDER HIGH SCHOOL AGE Admitted Unless Accompanied By Parents!! EVERYTHING SHOWN! EVERYTHING EXPLAINED!"

If you lived in a small town in the 1940s or '50s, it was virtually impossible *not* to know about a film called *Mom and Dad.* Sooner or later a flamboyant publicity man would drive into town, the ads would appear, and the tempestuous debate would begin. Plastered on every available storefront, barn, bus bench, and shoeshine stand was a poster seducing you with an attractive couple in mid-kiss and black bold-faced ballyhoo exploding all around them. And in a black box in the lower left-hand corner:

"Extra! IN PERSON: ELLIOT FORBES, 'THE SECRETS OF SENSIBLE SEX.'"

Alarmed letters to the editor would appear in the newspaper. Clergymen would express opinions from the pulpit. If you were Catholic, you'd be banned from attending. In some towns the police would send men to check the film for violations of the obscenity statutes.

And as soon as the first women-only matinee was screened, at 2 p.m. on a Friday afternoon, the town would blaze with *Mom and Dad* gossip. Though all but forgotten today, *Mom and Dad* was so heavily promoted that *Time* once remarked that the ad campaign "left only the livestock unaware of the chance to learn the facts of life."

But this was not Hollywood promotion. In fact, Hollywood spent 20 years campaigning to get rid of movies like *Mom and Dad*. This was the last wave of the 19th-century medicine shows—part biology lesson, part sideshow, part morality play, part medical "shock footage"—and to this day many old-timers regard it as the purest and most successful exploitation film in history. It played continuously for 23 years, still booking drive-ins as late as 1977, and grossed an estimated $100 million.

Kroger Babb, who billed himself as "America's Fearless Young Showman," ruled over a vast army of *Mom and Dad* "roadshow units" from his headquarters in Worthington, Ohio. He used a form of exhibition that has all but disappeared today, called "fourwalling." Instead of booking his film into theaters for a percentage of the box office, he would simply rent the theater outright and take it over for the week or, in smaller markets, just one or two days. He would pay for all advertising and promotion, put his own banners and marquees out front, and turn the theater into a midway attraction, complete with lobby curiosities designed to lure customers. But because he was a pariah in Hollywood, he had to use independent mom-and-pop theaters that weren't part of the big chains like Paramount and RKO, and he had to fight censorship boards, police forces, judges, clergy, and outraged newspaper editors everywhere he went. The film was in 400 separate court proceedings during its run.

The Blowoff

Babb was an expert at creating a kind of mob psychosis that peaked at the moment the projector started to roll. Watching the film today, it's all but impossible to recreate the atmosphere of a capacity audience waiting breathlessly to see things they knew were forbidden and probably shocking. It was Babb's peculiar genius that he was able to evoke the emotions of a horror movie using what is actually one of the blandest, most formulaic stories ever concocted.

When the opening titles come up and the lush strings of the orchestra play the *Mom and Dad* theme music, the first thing you see is a type crawl: "Foreword. Our story is a simple one! It happens every night, somewhere. It is the story of Joan Blake—a sweet, innocent girl growing up in this fast moving age. The temptations which she faces are as old as Time itself. But Joan is no better fortified against them than was the girl of yesteryear, because her mother—like many mothers—still thinks that ignorance is a guarantee of virtue. 'IGNORANCE IS A SIN—KNOWLEDGE IS POWER.' In this modern world Youth is entitled to a knowledge of Hygiene—a complete understanding of the Facts of Life. Boys and girls of today aren't bad! But millions of them are becoming sexual delinquents and the victims of venereal disease, simply because they do not know the Full Truth about these subjects. This problem is a challenge to every Mom and Dad. If our story points the way to a commonsense solution . . . and saves one girl from unwed motherhood . . . or one boy from the ravages of social disease . . . it will have been well told! THE PRODUCERS."

This had two functions: to lessen the chance of obscenity prosecutions, and to make the film palatable to women. In fact, women tended to like the film more than men, who were often a little disappointed by the lack of sex and nudity.

The first hour of the movie was devoted to showing how a sweet and pretty young girl like Joan Blake could easily have her life ruined by pregnancy. She goes to a local dance, where she's swept off her feet by a handsome and worldly pilot who steals a kiss as they walk outside. They hold hands and make eyes at each other while watching a jitterbug contest, a torch singer, and a teenage acrobatic act—all the usual padding found in exploitation films of the period. The next night he takes her to a smoky night club in his roadster, overwhelms her with sweet talk on a moonlit lover's lane, and convinces her that two people as much in love as *this* should definitely go all the way with it. Slow fade as the young lovers descend into the front seat.

Shortly thereafter the handsome pilot has to leave town on business, but he continues to write to her. When he mentions in one of his letters that it's been four weeks since he left, Joan suddenly becomes concerned. She checks her calendar and is obviously worried. She goes to her mother and asks if she has any "hygiene books," but her parent is flabbergasted by the request. "You're not married yet," says Mom.

A short time later Joan's father notices an article in the newspaper: A young man named Jack Griffith—the pilot who took her virginity—has been killed in a plane crash. Joan drops a dinner plate when she hears the news, goes to her room, tears up the love letter she's just written, and puts her head down on her desk.

At this point the film would stop entirely and the house lights would come up. Elliot Forbes, an "eminent sexual hygiene commentator," would stride onto the stage and deliver a 20-minute lecture on the need for openness in sex education, the morality of the times, the biology of the body, and what the community can do to avoid the ruination of its youth.

If anyone checked the credentials of Elliot Forbes, he would have discovered that the speaker was the busiest man in the history of the lecture circuit, appearing 78 times a day in cities scattered from Maine to Oregon. There were actually 26 Elliot Forbeses, one for each road-show, and Babb hired most of them from the ranks of retired or un-deremployed vaudeville comedians. They knew how to work crowds with a combination of earnestness, humor, and downhome "just folks" patter that would always crescendo at the moment when they held up two paperback books—one called *Man and Boy*, the other called *Woman and Girl*—and made a spiel for "a set of these vitally important books to be read in the privacy of your own home." Two women in nurse uniforms—supposedly stationed in the theater to take care of people who fainted or had heart attacks—would then pass among the crowd collecting money and distributing the volumes.

The books themselves were rehashes of venereal disease and preg-nancy information that could be obtained at any public health agency. The Elliot Forbes speech was what is known in the carnival world as a "blowoff," long used in 10-in-one freak shows to hustle additional money from people who had already paid an admission price. In any good blowoff, there's the constant implication that the "good stuff" is in the attraction you haven't paid for yet—in this case, the book. Forbes' main job was to sell the books, which frequently augmented the box-office take by as much as 50 percent. In 1957, for example, at a four-week showing of *Mom and Dad* in Baltimore, the box-office gross was $82,000, but 45,000 copies of the books were sold, result-ing—after deducting printing and expenses—in a $31,000 additional profit.

The Busybody Villainess

After Forbes had left the stage and the money had been collected, the film would resume with our heroine sick to her stomach, sleeping late, and discovering that her clothes no longer fit her. (The actors never use the word "pregnant.") After a few scenes of dramatic desperation—including an off-screen suicide attempt—Joan's brother forces her to tell him the truth. Knowing he can't trust their straitlaced parents, he seeks advice from Carl Blackburn, a kindly teacher who was fired from the high school for teaching sex education and now sells insurance. After a night of agonizing, Blackburn calls on Joan's mother and informs her that "your daughter is going to have a baby."

The mother has been the busybody villainess of our story all along. As the member of a women's club that constantly crusades against public lewdness and drinking—the same club that got the science teacher fired—she believes that sex should never be discussed in the home. Her reaction to the news: "Who was the boy? I'll have him arrested."

"They didn't tell me his name," replies the defrocked teacher. "After all, why blame the boy?"

The hysterical mother demand to know who Blackburn *would* blame. "I'd blame you, Mrs. Blake," he replies, "you and every parent who neglects the sacred duty of telling their children the real truth. Why were your children afraid to come to you in their trouble? Why did they have to come to me for advice? Remember this, Mrs. Blake, when your children have to go to someone else for advice, you've fallen down from your job."

In the next scene Joan and Mrs. Blake are riding the train to Boston, where Joan will finish her pregnancy in secret under a doctor's care, but the grim faces of mother and daughter tell us all too plainly that their lives will never be the same.

Pickles and Beaver

At this point the story is, for all practical purposes, over. There's one point of minor suspense—will Joan be OK and what will she do with the baby?—but very little is made of that. In fact, the whole first 90 minutes has been a set-up for three films-within-the-film that everyone will remember long after they've left the theater.

With wife and daughter packed off to Boston, Mr. Blake is suddenly roused out of his blasé attitude and tells Blackburn that he intends to go to the school board and get him rehired. Now more than ever, "They need that class in social hygiene!" Cut to the principal's office where, in one of the more forced segues in screenwriting history, the returning teacher tells the principal, "I was talking with Mrs. Hayworth yesterday. You know, she's the sister of the famous Chicago specialist Dr. Ashley. She tells me he has some wonderful films explaining childbirth. But best of all, she says he's due here for a rest in October!"

"Do you suppose we could get him to talk to a small group like ours?" asks the principal.

"Well, I'll ask her to write to him about it. You never know until you try!"

In the next scene Blackburn is introducing Dr. John D. Ashley, an obstetrician, to a class of high school girls. Dr. Ashley has been kind enough to bring along some films made in his hospital. The first one is called *The Facts of Life: An Explanation of Sex Cycles.* An authoritative narrator begins: "Every girl should know the functions of the female body." Charts are revealed, showing the female menstrual cycle, drawings of the genital organs, how ovulation occurs, how spermatozoa impregnate an ovary, time-lapse depictions of the growing fetus, and then suddenly—almost without warning—graphic footage of a live birth!

The umbilical cord has scarcely been snipped before the second film commences: *Modern American Surgery,* in which a "famous American Surgeon" will perform a Caesarian section on-camera. In an operating theater full of white-masked attendants and spectators, we watch as the incision is made ("from pubis to umbilicus"), as layer after layer of the skin and womb are cut open, as water and other fluids spray wildly, and then as the baby is removed with forceps. The film lingers for the sewing up and a few injections "to relax the mother," followed by an encomium to "one of the great miracles of modern surgery."

But wait! There's more! Two scenes later an expert on venereal disease named Dr. Burrell addresses an all-*male* class. And now comes the *piece de resistance.* The third film-within-the-film is called *Seeing Is Believing,* and it's every teenage boy's nightmare, showing grainy footage of syphilis victims struggling to walk, blinded, horribly scarred, teeth rotting, their bodies oozing with chancres and open sores, and, in one case, a fleeting image of a person whose feet have been eaten away by disease.

Throughout the film there are silent-movie-style caption cards: "Millions learn these facts the hard-way . . . by bitter experience!" "The Price of Ignorance!" "Self-Styled MORALISTS Would Like To Keep These Facts A Secret!!!" "Is The Gamble Worth the Price?" The audience sees crippled and blind crying babies, horrible pox-ridden arms and legs, a festering sore where someone's eye used to be, and the big payoff, introduced by the title card "Doctors and Health Officials Agree—These shocking pictures of infected genital organs will awaken you!" What follows are fully naked bodies, but so bruised and disease-ridden that they're anything but attractive. The film concludes, oddly, with images of track and field athletes, healthy young swimmers, and the U.S. Army marching in formation, as though to say, "This is what Americans *should* look like."

Joan's story has three more brief scenes, concluding with a doctor coming into a waiting room where the nervous Blake family is pacing and praying, to say "It's all over." Joan has a good chance of recovery. And the baby? In the version I saw, the doctor says the baby has just barely survived—presumably to be adopted by a childless couple—but I've also seen accounts by *Mom and Dad* viewers who claim the baby is stillborn. The fact is, there were dozens of versions of *Mom and Dad*, including some that didn't have any films-within-the-film, so that the movie could still play in markets with strict obscenity laws. Babb was not above showing his "cold" version to local authorities and screening the "hot" version in the theater. He also always carried with him a "square-up reel." In cases where he was forced to show the "cold" version, he would sometimes be faced with an angry audience that felt cheated by the absence of what they felt they had been promised by the advertising. To appease them, he would quickly rack an additional reel of what the carnies called "pickles and beaver"—footage of full-frontal nude bodies. Remarkably, it worked. The audience left feeling they had experienced at least a little of the "good stuff."

There's one additional piece of film after the story ends. The final screen image is Kroger Babb himself, sitting at his desk and speaking directly to camera. "And now, friends, you've seen the entire production," he says. "If you agree that these pictures have been bold and shocking enough, that you've learned a very worthwhile lesson from them, I wish you'd show the management your appreciation at this time. By your applause." And of course the theater, so prompted, would erupt in applause, thereby cutting down on the possibility of anyone ever asking for his money back.

Clap Operas

This brief coda is actually the essence of Babb's shell game. He says "if you agree that . . . " and then includes *two* reasons to like the movie—that it was shocking and that it was educational. But he speaks as though they're the same thing. An astute student of human nature, he knew everyone needed both—you bought the ticket because you wanted to be exposed to the forbidden, but you *told* yourself and others that you had no choice but to be educated. It was a movie that could be marketed with a straight exploitation campaign if it played in grindhouses and all-male theaters, or an "educational" campaign that would have entire high schools buying tickets for its students.

Although syphilis and gonorrhea had periodically ravaged America throughout the 19th century, the subject was not addressed on stage or screen until 1913, when Eugene Brieux wrote a play called *Damaged Goods*. In it, a young lawyer gets syphilis from a streetwalker while drunk at his bachelor party. Ignoring the advice of his doctor, he marries his fiancée in order to collect a dowry, thereby infecting his wife and baby. The drama avoided censorship by being sponsored by a medical organization and exploiting a common fear of the time—that the upper classes were in danger of strange diseases brought to America by the hordes of lower-class immigrants. When the play was made into a Mutual Film in 1914, it took in $2 million at the box office, a virtually unheard-of amount at the time.

Damaged Goods marked the birth of the sex-hygiene film. A ripoff called *A Victim of Sin* came out almost immediately, and there were at least 20 more films about VD before 1920. But the real birth of what producers would come to call the "clap opera" occurred at the end of World War I, when a man named Isaac Silverman purchased two films that the armed services had used to train soldiers about the dangers of venereal disease. *Fit to Fight*, the story of five young men in army training camp, and *The End of the Road*, the story of two women in trouble, included explicit medical footage showing the ravages of gonorrhea and syphilis, complete with pus-filled open sores.

What could be better for a film-hungry public constantly in search of new sensations? Silverman booked the films all over the country, where they played to capacity audiences, including 12 weeks (!) at the Grand Opera House in Brooklyn. They also attracted the attention of local morals crusaders, who managed to get them banned in many cities. The Catholic Church, upset by the films' advocacy of "chemical prophylaxis," organized a pamphlet campaign to stop the films.

The Outlaw Studio

From that time forward, a new kind of film exhibition would arise. Silverman showed his films to "adults only" (no one under 16), a phrase that would become code for titillating subject matter, and he also segregated the screenings by gender. Babb would later codify this tradition in every contract he ever signed, specifying that the words "Adults Only" must be on all advertising and barring any distributor from showing *Mom and Dad* to mixed audiences. Women would be too embarrassed to watch a sex hygiene film in the company of men, so he would have two women's-only screenings per day, one at 2 and one at 7. The men wouldn't be allowed to see the film until 9, and by that time they were so overwhelmed with curiosity, wanting to know WHAT THE WOMEN WERE TALKING ABOUT, that his late-night males-only screenings came to be called "The Thundering Herd."

The sex hygiene film contributed greatly to the notorious Production Code that would muzzle Hollywood studios for decades to come. The first motion picture censorship law had been passed in Chicago in 1907, and by 1921 seven states had censorship boards, with new ones sprouting all the time. In an effort to head off government control of movies, Hollywood adopted "Thirteen Points or Standards," forbidding such things as the on-screen exploitation of sex, white slavery, nakedness, "illicit love and vice," narcotics use, vulgarity, ridicule of authority, miscegenation, profanity, and disrespect for religion. This list evolved into the "Don'ts and Be Carefuls" of 1927, which specifically added sex hygiene and venereal disease, childbirth scenes, and children's sex organs. And all of this was consolidated into the Production Code of 1930, after which 98 percent of all movies released were judged and censored.

But there was still that 2 percent of movies made outside the Hollywood system. They not only defied the Production Code, but used it as a sort of manual for subjects that *could* be exploited. There was a boom in exploitation films dealing with crime, white slavery, and drug addiction—not to mention nudist-camp movies. Mainstream Hollywood despised these films, mainly because they feared they would lead to more censorship, but in their efforts to run the exploitation producers out of business they had to argue against what were always presented as *educational* films. Remarkably, the Production Code Administration eventually issued policy statements saying that the purpose of motion pictures should be pure entertainment, and that education has no place in theaters!

The carnies on the exploitation circuit—guys with flashy names like S.S. "Steamship" Millard and Howard "Pappy" Golden—eventually banded into a sort of informal trade association. Calling themselves the Forty Thieves, they essentially became a vertically integrated outlaw studio, using something called the "states rights" system. In the 1890s, licensing for the Kinetoscope and Vitascope had resulted in the United States being carved up into 32 exhibition territories, and this system of sub-distribution lasted well into the '80s. Hence a producer could sell his film territory by territory, allowing the local "thief" to market it any way he knew how. He could re-edit the film, shoot additional scenes, design his own ad campaign, and create any kind of come-on. (Lobby displays of drug paraphernalia were common in the '30s.) One of the most foolproof gimmicks in the business was live birth footage. No one knows exactly where the footage came from—some say medical training films, some say it was paid for overseas—but within the world of the Forty Thieves, it was constantly recycled into movie after movie.

In 1936 Surgeon General Thomas Parran initiated a public information campaign to stamp out venereal disease, making Hollywood look more and more silly as it tried to ban the films. The studios were especially incensed in 1937 when a film called *Sex Madness* showed up as the second feature with Shirley Temple's *Wee Willie Winkie*, but by the following year the government had filed an antitrust suit against them—the famous Paramount case—and they pretty much abandoned their crusade against the exploitation films because it made them look like monopolists.

Vices for Squares

By the time Kroger Babb came along, the formula for a sex hygiene movie was so well established that all he did was incorporate every element of every sex hygiene movie in history into a single film. But in search of even better profits, he changed the rules slightly. Many of the old sex-hygiene films had played in grindhouses or marginal theaters or even bars and restaurants. He wanted to break through to the biggest theaters in the country.

Howard W. Babb had gotten the nickname "Kroger" from the name of the grocery store where he worked as a boy growing up in Lees Creek, Ohio. Born in 1906, he was a sportswriter, a newspaper reporter, an ad manager, and, by his late 20s, publicity manager for the Chakeres-Warners theater chain, where he distinguished himself with publicity stunts such as having a man buried alive in front of a theater. He got the exploitation roadshow bug when he hooked up with an outfit called Cox and Underwood, which was peddling an aging sex hygiene film called *Dust to Dust* that was actually a 1935 film called *High School Girl* with a live-birth reel slapped onto the end. Proving that he was born to be in the business, it's the same plot Babb would use in *Mom and Dad*. (The Forty Thieves frequently quarreled over territories, but they never sued for copyright infringement. Of course, many of them were carnival men, who regarded all cons as ancient and passed down from generation to generation, but they may also have simply *sold* stories the same way they occasionally sold sideshow acts.)

Anxious to go out on his own, Babb got 20 investors to put up the money to make *Mom and Dad*. The script was written by Mildred Horn, who would later become his wife, and who would also write *Man and Woman* and *Boy and Girl*. To direct he hired William "One Shot" Beaudine (so named because he never did a second take), who dated back to the Bowery Boys serials and had made over 200 B movies. He made the whole film in six days in 1944.

Perhaps the most revolutionary thing Babb did was to give his film such a bland and praiseworthy title. Who could object to a movie called *Mom and Dad*? This wasn't a movie about crazed sex maniacs or loose women or pregnant girls or the vice rackets. It was a movie about the education of all the moms and dads in the world, and, in fact, he wanted every mom and every dad to see it. His principal weapon, when he came under attack, was the very ordinariness of his story.

End of the Hygiene Era

Babb was not just prepared for the inevitable censorship battles he would face. He egged them on. He stirred up the Catholics at every opportunity, capitalizing on the church's "C" rating (for "condemned") of his film. He wrote fake letters to the editor in advance of the film's arrival in town, hoping there would be controversy. His most successful letter was supposedly written by the anonymous mayor of a small town. The "mayor" explained that he had opposed the showing of *Mom and Dad* in his town, too, but then the 17-year-old daughter of a local churchgoing couple found herself "in trouble." He saw *Mom and Dad* with a friend, and as a result had the courage to tell her parents about her predicament. They were shocked, but forgave her. The girl gave birth to a healthy boy, which was adopted by a childless couple. The girl then completed high school and is now engaged to a fine young man. The mayor goes on to thank Babb for having the courage "to tell young people what their parents didn't." And the letter ends: "P.S. That girl was my daughter."

Babb's company, Hygienic Productions, sent out an advance man to place letters like this, buy advertising, do mailings, and hold screenings for town fathers and religious leaders. (If the town's leaders liked the film, a "soft" campaign would be used. If they didn't like it, a "hard" campaign, advertising it as "the movie self-styled moralists don't want you to see," would be used. Both campaigns worked.) The advance man would be followed a week later by a crew of four—including "Elliot Forbes" and two "nurses"—to actually manage the film during its run. The crews would stay on the road for 20 weeks at a time. Babb even had one all-black crew for black theaters, with Olympic champion Jesse Owens substituting for Elliot Forbes.

As the *Mom and Dad* exploitation scheme evolved over time, it attracted imitators. By 1950 there were so many sex-hygiene roadshows that they were starting to get in each other's way, and after a town was "scorched" by a promotional campaign, it would be spoiled for any film arriving later. So four of the films—*Mom and Dad, Street Corner, Because of Eve,* and *The Story of Bob and Sally*—banded together to form Modern Film Distributors, carving out territories and agreeing not to steal markets.

But the genre's days were numbered. The irony of the sex-hygiene explosion is that it depicted a world that didn't exist. The communities in the films had more in common with turn-of-the-century towns than with anything more modern. Millions of young men had already been exposed to venereal disease films during World War II, and millions of women had been touched by out-of-wedlock births, abortions, or abandonment. Perhaps the films succeeded because they gave a comforting message to panicked moms and dads, promising that, with just a little more education, these things could be eradicated. But many of the problems already *were* being eradicated, first by penicillin, which had made new syphilis cases virtually unheard of by the time *Mom and Dad* came out, and then by more sophisticated forms of birth control that gave young girls more control of their sex lives.

The biggest irony of all is that the public schools actually *did* follow Kroger Babb's example and start showing sex-education films not unlike *The Facts of Life: An Explanation of Sex Cycles.* And once the information was available in schools, Babb was out of business.

The immediate cause of Babb's declining box office, though, was the burlesque film, which showed up in the early '50s. Crudely made movies filmed in aging burlesque halls, featuring strippers and comedians doing what they'd been doing for decades, these offered titillation and a hint of nudity without any of the scarifying disease subtext. By the time the second wave of nudist films came along, in 1959, it was all over for sex hygiene.

Kroger Babb died January 28, 1980, in Palm Springs, California, at the age of 73. And now, friends, you've seen the entire production. If you have been shocked and educated, please show the management your appreciation. By your applause.

November 2003

Battlefield Conversions

Reason talks with three ex-warriors who now fight against the War on Drugs.

Interviews by Mike Lynch

LIKE ANY WAR, THE WAR ON DRUGS HAS ITS GOOD SOLDIERS—a varied bunch, coming from all walks of life and filling all ranks. They include eager volunteers, from the drug czars at the top of the command chain to the beat cops, Drug Enforcement Administration and Customs Service agents out in the field. The war also has reluctant conscripts, such as state and federal judges compelled by mandatory minimum sentencing rules to enforce laws that many see as counterproductive and unjust.

Increasingly, the War on Drugs also has what its partisans might consider traitors—former soldiers who have become convinced that U.S. drug policy is ineffective, immoral, or some combination of the two. *Reason* recently spoke with three such figures who were once integral cogs in the drug war machine.

The Cop: Joseph D. McNamara

Joseph D. McNamara started out as a grunt in America's battle against drugs. "It was sort of like the body count in Vietnam," says McNamara about the petty arrests for heroin he made as a Harlem beat cop in the late 1950s. "The department loved to count these drug arrests and release statistics to show we were winning the war." In 1969, he spent a year as a criminal justice fellow at Harvard Law School. Eventually, he ended up earning a Ph.D. in public administration. "I wrote my dissertation in 1973 and predicted the escalation and failure of the drug war—and the vast corruption and violence that would follow," recalls McNamara. "I never published it because I wanted a police career and not an academic career."

That's exactly what he got. He served as chief of police in Kansas City from 1973 to 1976. In the bicentennial year, he moved on to become the top cop in San Jose, California, a post he held until he retired in 1991. He currently hangs his hat at the Hoover Institution at Stanford, where he conducts seminars on the War on Drugs for law enforcement officials. The author of six books, including the drug war detective novel *Code 211 Blue*, the 66-year-old McNamara is working on a new book titled *Gangster Cops: The Hidden Cost of America's War on Drugs.*

Reason: How did you get involved in what is now called the War on Drugs?

Joseph D. McNamara: I got involved as a foot patrolman in Harlem way back in 1957. A few years later the heroin epidemic swept through Harlem and was devastating. And so the police did what the police do: We arrested everyone in sight. It soon became apparent that it wasn't reducing drug use or drug selling. My eyes were really opened one day when my partner and I arrested a heroin addict. The addicts gathered on the top floor landings of buildings, which we referred to as shooting galleries. We used to routinely bust them for possession of hypodermic needles and also for the big crime of having cookers with residues of heroin.

One day an addict asked if we could give him a break. He said, "I'll give you a pusher if you let me go." We followed him down Lenox Avenue in uniform and in a marked police car. As he talked to one man after another, it struck me how little impact the police had on the drug problem. If we hadn't known what he was talking about, we would've thought they were just two men talking sports or the weather or whatever.

Reason: Is this why police rely on informants and sting operations?

McNamara: Since the police can't do their job the way they do it with other crimes, they resort to informants and to illegal searches. This is a major problem underlying police integrity throughout the United States.

Last year, state and local police made somewhere around 1.4 million drug arrests. Almost none of those arrests had search warrants. Sometimes the guy says, "Sure, officer, go ahead and open the trunk of my car. I have a kilo of cocaine back there but I don't want you to think I don't cooperate with the local police." Or the suspect conveniently leaves the dope on the desk or throws it at the feet of the police officer as he approaches. But often nothing like that happens.

The fact is that sometimes the officer reaches inside the suspect's pocket for the drugs and testifies that the suspect "dropped" it as the officer approached. It's so common that it's called "dropsy testimony." The lying is called "white perjury." Otherwise honest cops think it's legitimate to commit these illegal searches and to perjure themselves because they are fighting an evil. In New York it's called "testilying," and in Los Angeles it's called joining the "Liar's Club." It has lead some people to say L.A.P.D. stands for Los Angeles Perjury Department. It has undermined one of the most precious cornerstones of the whole criminal justice process: the integrity of the police officer on the witness stand.

Reason: What role do institutional interests play in the drug war?

McNamara: One year when I was police chief in San Jose, the city manager sent me a budget that contained no money for equipment. I politely told him that when you have a police department, you have to buy police cars, uniforms, and other equipment for the cops. He laughed, waved his hand, and said, "Last year you guys seized $4 million dollars. I expect you to do even better this year. In fact, you will be evaluated on that and you can use that money for equipment." So law enforcement becomes a revenue-raising agency and that takes, in too many cases, precedence over law enforcement.

Reason: From the perspective of the working police officer, how has the War on Drugs changed over the years?

McNamara: It has become the priority of police agencies. It's bizarre. We make 700,000 arrests for marijuana a year. The public is not terrified of marijuana. People are terrified of molesters, school shootings, and people stalking women and children. The police are not putting the resources into those crimes where they could be effective if they gave them top priority.

Reason: There's some controversy over whether the arrests for possession are really for possession or if they are for dealing but prosecuted as possession. Do you have any thoughts on that?

McNamara: It's both true and false. Most low-level dealers are users, like the guy that we finally did bust after we let the addict go. He was an addict, too, and he was no better or worse than the guy we let go. But what we had actually done, which is standard operating procedure in the drug war, is let someone go who had committed a crime because they enticed someone else to commit a more serious crime.

Reason: What role does race play in the War on Drugs?

McNamara: The drug war is an assault on the African-American community. Any police chief that used the tactics used in the inner city against minorities in a white middle-class neighborhood would be fired within a couple of weeks.

It was a very radical change in public policy for the federal government to criminalize drugs in the early 20th century. Congress was reluctant to pass it because you had a very small federal government in 1914 and to interfere with the state police powers was a big deal. They couldn't get this legislation passed until they played the race card: They introduced letters and testimony that blacks were murdering white families; the police in the South were having trouble with "Negroes" because of these drugs; there were white women in "yellow" opium dens. The same prejudice popped up in 1937 when they outlawed marijuana.

If anyone tried to pass laws on those same bases today, they'd be condemned. Yet the laws that we have are the last vestiges of Jim Crow. You don't have to identify yourself as a bigot anymore—you can be for the drug war and you really are getting "them."

Reason: Do you think there's a greater risk in just questioning the operation of the War on Drugs than there is to testilying and going along with it in unethical ways?

McNamara: For police chiefs, there is some wiggle room. They can support sterile needle exchanges, medical marijuana treatment, and education diversion instead of incarceration. But it's asking an awful lot for them to come out and say, "Look, this drug prohibition is a stupid thing we shouldn't have started in 1914 and it gets worse and worse every year." That's a big step for a police chief. That's asking them to commit career suicide.

Reason: Were you frustrated as a police chief with the constraints of the law?

McNamara: Enormously. Police chiefs are sitting on kegs of dynamite. Many of them are really decent, progressive guys. They are worried about the disproportionate racial impact and the corruption. But there's nothing they can do. There's just too much money in it. You don't have the ability, regardless of the propaganda, to eliminate the code of silence. You don't have unlimited power. You have lots of constraints on how the police can discipline themselves, even for chiefs who are legitimately interested in doing so.

The Fed: Michael Levine

Michael Levine was born to fight the War on Drugs. He grew up tough in the Bronx during the 1950s and was an accomplished brawler by junior high school. Though Jewish, he identified with the Puerto Ricans moving into the neighborhood and he picked up fluent Spanish, a skill that came in handy later when he started doing undercover work in Latin America. He was personally motivated to fight drugs: His kid brother was addicted to heroin. "I saw it killing my brother," says Levine, 60. In 1965, Levine started a 25-year career in federal law enforcement that included stints in the Customs Service, the Drug Enforcement Administration (DEA), and the Bureau of Alcohol, Tobacco, and Firearms. He traveled the world and arrested some 3,000 people.

Yet it wasn't long before Levine noticed a gap between the rhetoric and reality of the drug war. Says Levine, "Among DEA agents, the notion of really winning the drug war is so far out of the question that anyone who even mentions it is considered some kind of nut." Today, he serves as an expert witness on all things drug-related and hosts a radio show, *Expert Witness*, on WBAI, Pacifica Radio, in New York. He's authored and co-authored numerous books, including *Deep Cover: The Inside Story of How DEA Infighting, Incompetence, and Subterfuge Lost Us the Biggest Battle of the Drug War* and the novel *Triangle of Death: Deep Cover II.*

Reason: Why did you want to become a drug agent?

Michael Levine: I believed that it was the number one national security threat. I saw heroin killing my brother. I saw people around me dying. I saw the crime rate skyrocketing. I fell into the same trap that we are in right now. I blamed everything on those evil drug dealers.

Reason: After a quarter-century as an agent, how have you seen the drug war change at the agent level?

Levine: It has become murderous. I remember back to the beginning of the DEA, which was founded in 1973 by President Richard Nixon. At that time, three agents went into the wrong premises in Collinsville, Illinois. They were prosecuted for breaking down the wrong door.

I was involved as an expert witness in the Donald Carlson case, which was on *60 Minutes.* In that case, a multi-agency task force, outfitted in high-tech guerrilla gear, crashed into the home of a Fortune 500 executive and shot him down in his own living room on the basis of the word of an uncorroborated informant. Nobody was penalized for it. In fact, the people who did it were eventually promoted.

As the expert witness, I had access to all the reports and I recommended that these people be prosecuted. They paid no attention to the man's civil rights. He had no record or reputation for drugs. They did nothing but crash through his door on the basis of an informant's say-so. The drug war has succeeded in militarizing police against their own people.

Reason: At what point did you start to question the War on Drugs?

Levine: I was sent undercover to Bangkok during the Vietnam War. I was hanging with Chinese drug dealers in Bangkok. They were smuggling heroin into the U.S. in the dead bodies of GIs who were trans-shipped through Thailand. The Chinese drug dealers invited me to go to the factory up in the Golden Triangle area in northern Thailand, where much of the heroin sent to the United States originated.

All of a sudden I was cut off from logistical support. I was given no money to pay my hotel bills. There were these snafus going on with administrative stuff. They were so strange and inopportune that the dealers were starting to suspect me. It started to get really dangerous. A CIA agent informed me that I wasn't going undercover to the factory. I asked why. First he told me it was dangerous, that we had lost people up there. But I insisted. Finally, he said, "Levine, our country has other priorities." That was the first time I heard that phrase. That was the beginning of me doubting the intentions of our leaders in the drug war.

Reason: What year was that?

Levine: That was 1971.

Reason: And yet you continued on.

Levine: I was a good soldier. I had come out of the military. My brother was still a heroin addict. At that point, I thought my experience in Thailand was an isolated incident here in Southeast Asia. I couldn't conceive of my country lying to me.

Reason: In the chapter you contributed to *After Prohibition: An Adult Approach to Drug Policies in the 21st Century,* you argue that drug agents have come to recognize that their efforts ultimately have no impact on the drug trade. What's the mindset of agents in this war?

Levine: Before you become an agent, you're bombarded with stories of drug war victories. It's painted as heroic—guys in guerrilla outfits and jungle gear fighting the drugs everywhere. You want to do something for your country. Then when you get in, the first thing you discover is that you can't touch some of the biggest drug dealers in the world because they're protected by the CIA or they're protected by the State Department. Everyone from Carlos Salinas de Gortari of Mexico to Manuel Noriega to the contras in Nicaragua to the Mujahedin in Afghanistan. Those of us who work overseas realize that this whole thing is a three-card monte game, that it's a lie.

Reason: You say the cartel responsible for much of the cocaine in the U.S. during the '80s not only didn't fear the drug war but that they counted on it to increase the price and to weed out smaller dealers. What is your evidence for that?

Levine: It's 1987 and I'm posing as Luis Miguel-Garcia, an undercover Mafia don who's half Sicilian and half Puerto Rican. I'm in a meeting at a restaurant outside of Panama with another undercover customs agent and the ruling faction of La Corporacion, the Bolivian cocaine cartel. They invited us to Bolivia to look at their production facilities. At that time, the U.S. had begun its paramilitary operations in Bolivia, which are now in Colombia.

So as a pretext, I told the man that we can't go down there because we read in the newspapers that the U.S. military is down there. He laughed and said, "That's just for the gringos. That's not real." And his hand slid up and down above the table. He said, "They have helicopters that go up and that go down. We know what they are doing before they do." That's the reality of the drug war. It's completely fictitious. It's only for the American people.

Reason: You think that's still the case?

Levine: It's absolutely still the case.

Reason: You say, in your experience, that 90 percent of drug users are white. What do you base this on?

Levine: That's DEA statistics. I've spent much of my life in these ghetto neighborhoods watching drug dealers. I would say 95 percent of the customers are white.

Reason: If this is the case, why are the statistics almost reversed when it comes to drug arrests?

Levine: Because you go after the dealer. You have a lot of these think tanks, such as The Lindesmith Center, saying that it's a racist drug war and that the cops go after users. That mistaken theory is based on the statistic of arrests for possession. I have made 3,000 arrests myself and, as a supervisor of squads of agents for 17 years, have probably been involved in 8,000 arrests. A huge amount of them are for possession. But none is for using drugs. Not one. We didn't go after users. We went after a dealer, street-level or whatever, and charged them with possession because it's easy to prove.

Reason: You said that when you were stationed in New York, news directors would call up the DEA for a drug story on a slow news week and ask if they could go along with a bust. Did you have personal experience with that?

Levine: I've been on video with my face blacked out. Dan Rather, *20/20*, ABC News.

Reason: You actually had personal experience with news directors calling up and then raids being hurried up or fabricated?

Levine: Here's what happens. A news director needs a story. The special agent in charge of New York, who we called Captain Video, because he was very media conscious, would call our squad and say so-and-so is on the phone from ABC. Do you have anything going? Do you got anything you can make an arrest on?

Is that manufacturing news? I don't know. You tell me. That's what would happen.

Reason: You claim to have witnessed numerous constitutional abuses. Can you give me some examples?

Levine: The Carlson case is the best. The man was a Fortune 500 executive and had no reputation whatsoever. He didn't know coke from garden mulch. A criminal informant pointed out his house and two other houses. Agents, without any investigation whatsoever, just crashed into his house and shot the man down. That is now typical. *60 Minutes* did a wonderful piece on it in 1993 called "The Informers." There is no U.S. Constitution any more when it comes to the drug war.

Reason: What is the relationship between informants, drug agents, and arrests?

Levine: Informants run the drug war. Ninety-nine percent of all drug cases start off with a criminal informant. These informants are criminals and liars and they will create crimes to make money and, at the same time, get the protection of the people they are working for.

Reason: For all this, you're against complete drug legalization. Why?

Levine: You can't do it because certain drugs are just so addictive. I grew up in a bad neighborhood in South Bronx. Like I said, my brother became a heroin addict. I didn't touch drugs because of the stigma. You weren't a victim in those days; you were a scumbag lowlife and you were a felon. That worked on me. It was no surprise to hear from a poll taken during the first Bush administration that of the 99 percent of kids in ghettos who don't touch drugs, the main reason they give is because they are illegal.

What do you do when you legalize it? You are the government crack dealer and a 14-year-old kid comes up to you. Do you sell it to him? If you say no, then you're already talking about another prohibition, another market. So what do you do when you sell legal crack to a guy who's 30 and he turns around and sells it to 15-year-old kids? That's illegal! It doesn't work. And, then you get into other drugs like Angel Dust, methamphetamines, LSD. What do you do with that stuff? Is it legal? You are talking about stuff that directly affects the public safety.

Reason: Do you think people can use these drugs recreationally, like alcohol?

Levine: Some drugs, yes, and some drugs, no. The blanket prohibition of drugs, I think, is wrong.

The Judge: James P. Gray

Most individuals arrested by a cop eventually appear before a judge. These days, they won't be appearing in Judge James P. Gray's Southern California courtroom. Since publicly questioning the U.S. drug strategy, the Orange County Superior Court judge has kept himself off the criminal calendar. But, like Levine and McNamara, he has witnessed the reality of the U.S. drug war—as a defense attorney in the Navy, as a prosecutor in Los Angeles, and as a judge. Says the 56-year-old Gray, "We're flooding our courts with these cases that aren't making any difference whatsoever."

In 1998, Gray ran unsuccessfully against then Rep. Bob "B-1" Dornan in the Republican congressional primary for the 46th District in Orange County, California. Gray is particularly frustrated with what he says is a major pillar supporting the drug war: the informal prohibition of discussing options other than, well, prohibition. "The World Affairs Council in Orange County invited then drug czar Gen. Barry McCaffrey to come here and debate me on drug policy," says Gray. "His answer was, 'No, I don't have time to give a debate, but I do have time to give a speech.'" Gray never booked a debate with McCaffrey, but he put his side of the debate in a new book, *Why Our Drug Laws Failed and What We Can Do About It.*

Reason: What has been your involvement with the War on Drugs?

James P. Gray: I go way back. I am a former drug warrior. I believed in it and I did it with a bold heart. I was a criminal defense attorney in the Navy and handled drug cases. I was a federal prosecutor in Los Angeles in the U.S. Attorney's Office. For a short time, I held the record for the largest drug prosecution in the Central District in California. Having been a judge since 1983, I've seen in my own court that we just churn these people through the system and we seldom get the real top bananas.

Reason: Did any specific event prompt you to question your involvement with the drug war?

Gray: It just really evolved. I've been clipping newspaper articles now for about 20 years. It's just the lights go on, and then the lights go on a little stronger. I can't say there was an epiphany. It just was kind of a Chinese water torture. It just kept going and kept going, where eventually I just had to say something publicly about it.

Reason: What is the typical drug case that comes before your court?

Gray: The typical drug case is a small amount of drugs that is being sold by somebody to support his or her habit. You get into some larger ones. A couple of weeks ago we had a 12-ton shipment of cocaine coming towards San Diego. But mostly it's just the low-level users and the low-level drug sellers. And we fill our prisons with them.

Reason: How do you adjudicate those typically? Does the law force you to adjudicate them in ways you think are counterproductive?

Gray: The answer to the second question is certainly yes. There are documented situations in which very conservative federal judges are literally in tears because they are required by the law to sentence a particular offender to a draconian sentence.

Reason: What's the worst drug case you've had come before you?

Gray: I was on Juvenile Court for Abused and Neglected Children. I can't get these cases out of my mind. It was common that a single mother—say she has two children—would hook up with the wrong boyfriend, who would be a drug dealer. One fine day he would tell her, "Look, Maria, I'll pay you $500 to take this package across town to Charlie." She basically knows it has narcotics in it. She gets arrested and gets five years in prison.

What happens to her children? They come into my court as abused and neglected children. There's the mother in a prison jumpsuit and handcuffs and I tell her the truth. "You know, ma'am, you're not going to be a functional part of your children's lives for the next five years." She starts to well up with tears. Then I tell her that unless she's fortunate and has either a close personal friend or family member who is both willing and able to take custody of her children, they are very likely going to be adopted by somebody else by the time she gets out of prison. She dissolves into tears.

Taxpayers can start to dissolve in tears, also. Because for the next year they're going to spend $25,000 of taxpayer money to keep this mother of two in prison. We're going to spend upwards of $5,000 a month to keep each child in a group home until they are finally adopted by somebody else. So that's $60,000 a year per child, plus $25,000 for the mother. We are spending $145,000 of taxpayer money to physically separate a mother from her children. It just doesn't make any sense.

Reason: You write about a drug exception to the Bill of Rights.

Gray: When I graduated from law school in 1971, it was illegal for a police officer, even after arresting you, to search anything that was outside of your grasp. If you can reach over to something, then you could search it. But if a suitcase you were carrying was locked, the police could not go in there unless they got a search warrant first. They couldn't go into the trunk of your car, they couldn't go into the glove compartment, and they couldn't go into the backseat.

That has totally been reversed. The police not only can search you and everything in your car, but they can also search your passengers. They can search your mobile home, which is in effect a home on wheels. They can go through and search everything.

Reason: There's a debate over whether the arrests for drug crimes are casual users for possession or dealers who are charged with possession because it's easier to convict. Have you thought about this?

Gray: Basically, I think that the prosecutors are right. We have people who are so overwhelmed that they have to reduce the sentences by plea-bargaining. However, they are all small pushers. They are all little guys. And a lot of them are selling small amounts of drugs in order to support their habits, because the drugs are so artificially expensive.

Reason: What has been the response of your colleagues to your speaking out on this issue?

Gray: Anyone who talks about it with me in the elevator or in the judges' lunchroom agrees that what we're doing is not working. Publicly, judges are pretty conservative people. A lot of them don't see themselves as social workers. A lot of them are concerned about their effectiveness and getting reelected, so they are just not going to say publicly what they believe privately.

That was really brought home to me when I gave four forums sponsored by the American Bar Association. After doing so, I received a letter from the present chief justice of the Supreme Court of a Southern state. He wrote, "Dear Jim: You're right. The War on Drugs isn't working. You're also right that it's fully appropriate for a sitting judge to discuss it because of what our position is in society. And I see these cases all the time coming across my desk. What we are doing simply isn't working. But I gave up a lucrative law practice for this present job. I love my job and if I were to speak publicly, I would have to spend all my time justifying myself. I just don't think I could do it."

Reason: You write that the only people whose positions have improved under the drug war are those who make more money selling drugs and those who make money enforcing the drug laws. Are you alleging a sort of bootlegger-Baptist coalition, where lawbreakers and prohibitionists end up on the same side of an issue?

Gray: De facto, yes. It was not set up that way. Just like it wasn't set up to discriminate against minorities. But it has evolved into an amazing alliance between the drug lords on the one hand, who are making just obscene amounts of money, and various officials who are getting paid money to enforce this. They both have a financial interest and incentive in continuing with the status quo.

When I was running for Congress a few years ago, I met individually with two sitting congressmen from Orange County to try to get their support. They both said that the War on Drugs isn't working, but the problem is even worse than I thought because most federal agencies get extra money to fight the War on Drugs. It's not just the obvious ones like the U.S. Customs Service and the DEA. It's the little guys too, the Bureau of Land Management, the Bureau of Indian Affairs. They are addicted to drug war funding.

January 2002

Best of Both Worlds

Milton Friedman reminisces about his career as an economist and his lifetime "avocation" as a spokesman for freedom.

Interviewed by Brian Doherty

MILTON FRIEDMAN NEEDS LITTLE INTRODUCTION. His career as one of the world's preeminent economists and advocates of freedom has won him many accolades, best-selling books, and a Nobel Prize.

It has also brought him much satisfaction. Now, in what he is acutely conscious are probably the last years of his life, he and his wife and longtime writing partner Rose Friedman are working on their memoirs.

I met Friedman in January in his elegant high-rise San Francisco condo, with an absorbing view of both the Pacific Ocean and the San Francisco Bay. His study is filled, but not cluttered, with his own books and economics reference works. While some Great Men in his position in life might refuse nuisances like interviewers entirely, Friedman is friendly and mostly forthcoming, speaking with the slow assurance of a lifelong professor and teacher very comfortable with explaining things. He welcomed me cordially but with a distinct set of limits, both in time and in subject matter. He has a large project to finish, and not much time to finish it in; and he refuses to psychoanalyze himself, largely avoids indulging in discussion of personalities, and wants to save some stories for his memoirs.

Friedman is used to discussing policy, but except for his assessment of the new Congress' potential, we wandered far afield into reminiscence; assessment of his intellectual development; and his thoughts

on the history, significance, and successes of the intellectual movement for freedom that he has served so staunchly.

Reason: You've long advocated many of the ideas the new Congress
is pushing, such as balanced budget amendments and flat taxes. Do you
think Congress will make your dreams come true?

Milton Friedman: I'm skeptical. The talk is good. But I expected
so much out of the Reagan administration and was disappointed. I'm a
great admirer of Ronald Reagan himself, and I suspect he would have
gotten much more done if it hadn't been for the Cold War and the problem of Nicaragua and El Salvador.

But nonetheless, there's no doubt that while he talked about cutting down the size of government, he did not succeed. He did slow it
down—you've got to give him credit for some achievements. But not
the massive reduction that he hoped for and planned for. That makes
me hesitant now.

Congress wants to talk in this direction. Would they really want to
move in that direction? The most important reform would be term limits, six-year limits. Because from an economic point of view, one of the
worst features of our system is that you have a new tax law every year
or every two years. However bad the tax law is, if you didn't change it
for five years it would do less harm. Why do you keep changing it? Because that's the most effective way to raise campaign funds. Lobbyists
will pay you to put loopholes in; they will pay you to take them out.

If you can get a flat tax with no exemptions or deductions—the
Armey plan I suppose would be fine—its main advantage would not be
the greater equity of a flat tax or less interference in private incentives.
It would be to end this business of changing the whole tax system every
few years and keeping prosperous these hordes of tax lawyers.

Reason: You were involved in the development of the withholding
tax when you were doing tax work for the government in 1941-43?

Friedman: I was an employee at the Treasury Department. We were
in a wartime situation. How do you raise the enormous amount of taxes
you need for wartime? We were all in favor of cutting inflation. I wasn't
as sophisticated about how to do it then as I would be now, but there's
no doubt that one of the ways to avoid inflation was to finance as large
a fraction of current spending with tax money as possible.

In World War I, a very small fraction of the total war expenditure was financed by taxes, so we had a doubling of prices during the war and after the war. At the outbreak of World War II, the Treasury was determined not to make the same mistake again.

You could not do that during wartime or peacetime without withholding. And so people at the Treasury tax research department, where I was working, investigated various methods of withholding. I was one of the small technical group that worked on developing it.

One of the major opponents of the idea was the IRS. Because every organization knows that the only way you can do anything is the way they've always been doing it. This was something new, and they kept telling us how impossible it was. It was a very interesting and very challenging intellectual task. I played a significant role, no question about it, in introducing withholding. I think it's a great mistake for peacetime, but in 1941-43, all of us were concentrating on the war.

I have no apologies for it, but I really wish we hadn't found it necessary and I wish there were some way of abolishing withholding now.

Reason: You've also had some history of advising candidates and presidents. How did you get involved in the Goldwater campaign?

Friedman: Through Bill Baroody at the American Enterprise Institute. The American Enterprise Institute was originally the American Enterprise Association, and had established a board of academic advisers to advise them on their publications. I had been a member of that I think since its inception, and Baroody arranged sometime in the early '60s a number of dinners at his house at which Goldwater was present. Baroody was the brain trust for Goldwater. I was also at some of those dinners, so I got to meet Goldwater. And then when the campaign came along, Baroody asked me to serve as economic adviser. I didn't go on the campaign trail. I sat at home and wrote memos.

Reason: Were you impressed with Goldwater's acumen?

Friedman: It depends on what you mean by acumen. There's no doubt whatsoever that he's a man of principle and strong character. His IQ is perfectly reasonable but it's not outstanding among the various politicians I've met, and that shows why IQ is not a good measure. The highest IQ was Richard Nixon's and he was a terrible president.

While I was never a governmental official, I was a member of an economic advisory group that Nixon appointed of which Arthur Burns was chairman. I saw Nixon from time to time when he was president, until he imposed price controls. I saw him only once after that.

Reason: Did you stop giving him advice?

Friedman: I kept giving him advice from *Newsweek*, but not personally.

Reason: Do you have a clear memory of how your political philosophy formed? Was it any specific teacher you encountered, book you read, or experience?

Friedman: I'm sure it was a combination of all of those. I was exposed as an undergraduate at Rutgers to two very strong influences: Homer Jones, who was a student of Frank Knight's from Chicago, and Arthur Burns. They both had a considerable influence on me as an undergraduate in my thinking and my writing.

But it would be hard to say what philosophy that left me with. One of the things I regretted all my life is that when I graduated from Rutgers and came home, I wrote out a statement of my beliefs. I put that away in a drawer somewhere in my mother's home and I've never been able to find the damn thing! I'd love to have it! So I can't really tell you what I believed at that time.

But obviously my ideas were not very well formed. I was an innocent youngster and what I was impressed by, of course, was the Great Depression, and the belief that somehow or another there ought to be something that can prevent any such thing from happening.

Thanks to Homer, I was offered a scholarship at the University of Chicago and I went to Chicago and studied with Frank Knight, Jacob Viner, Henry Schultz, and so on. The atmosphere in Chicago in 1932 was very lively and active and encouraging. Of course, I got a very good grounding in economic theory and statistics as well.

Next year, I managed to get a fellowship to Columbia. I spent a year at Columbia mainly to study with Harold Hotelling, who was a mathematical economist and statistician.

Then I went back to Chicago for one year and was a research assistant to Henry Schultz. There were a group of students in Chicago who were very, very important. George Stigler, Allen Wallis, Rose Director, and myself. We ate almost every lunch and dinner together. We spent all the time discussing economics, both economic theory and economic policy. And we were very close for the rest of our lives. George died about two years ago. Allen, I'm glad to say, is still alive.

In the 1930s, both Rose and I at separate times went to Washington and worked on the New Deal, but we were technical statisticians and economists, not anything that had any policy role.

Throughout my career, I spent most of my time on technical economics. This policy stuff has been a strict avocation. If you really want to engage in policy activity, don't make that your vocation. Make it your avocation. Get a job. Get a secure base of income. Otherwise, you're going to get corrupted and destroyed. How are you going to get support? You're only going to get support from people who are ideologically motivated. And you're not going to be as free as you think you're going to be.

One of the most important things in my career is that I always had a major vocation which was not policy. I don't regard what I've done in the field of monetary policy as on the same level as what I've done about trying to get rid of the draft or legalizing drugs. One is a technical byproduct of scientific work, and so that's the only sense in which my vocation has affected my policy. But by having a good firm position in the academic world, I was perfectly free to be my own person in the world of policy. I didn't have to worry about losing my job. I didn't have to worry about being persecuted.

I think you'll make a mistake if you're going to spend your life as a policy wonk. I've seen some of my students who have done this. And some of them are fine, and some of them, especially those who have gone to Washington and stayed, are not.

Reason: How did you come to enter the world of policy writing?

Friedman: What really got me started in policy and what led to *Capitalism and Freedom* was, in an indirect way, the Mont Pelerin Society. The first Mont Pelerin Society meeting was in 1947 in Switzerland. Hayek arranged it. It was his idea.

Mont Pelerin was the first time that I came into contact with people like Hayek, Lionel Robbins, and the European contingent of that time. That widened my perspective about issues and policy.

The Mont Pelerin Society was people who were deeply concerned about issues. It was people with whom you shared a basic common belief, who at home were isolated. Its great contribution was that it provided a week when people like that could get together and open their hearts and minds and not have to worry about whether somebody was going to stick a knife in their back—especially for people in countries where they were isolated.

The reason the Society ever happened was that Hayek had written *The Road to Serfdom*, which attracted the attention of the Volker Foundation, and it was the Volker Foundation that financed the American participation in the Mont Pelerin Society. A Swiss group financed the Swiss and European participation.

In the middle '50s, the Volker Foundation undertook a program of summer institutes for junior academics who were favorably inclined toward a free-market point of view or were interested in such issues. *Capitalism and Freedom* was based on a series of lectures that I gave at one of those seminars. Those seminars forced me to systematize my thoughts and present them in a coherent way. And they also provided a very good audience because the people who were there were lively, outspoken, didn't hesitate to criticize. It was a very good audience. There was a lot of free time as well for discussions outside of the formal seminar. And I learned a great deal, not only from the students who were there, but also the fellow lecturers.

And then my wife, Rose, took the transcribed tapes of the lectures and reworked them and that's what became *Capitalism and Freedom.*

Reason: Did you have any hesitation about publishing that book?

Friedman: None whatsoever. Why should I have had any hesitation? Remember, I was a tenured professor.

Another thing that helped form my policy orientation was when Hayek came to Chicago in 1950. He attracted quite a number of very able students, Sam Peltzman, Ron Hamowy, Ralph Raico, Shirley Letwin. There were quite a group of them. Hayek drew very high quality people. I was an adviser to their *New Individualist Review* and contributed articles to it. They were a very lively group that had organized discussion sessions and so on, which was part of the atmosphere.

I was persuaded at that time in the early 1960s that we were on the verge of developing a strong libertarian movement. These were libertarians, all of them, though Hayek would not have labeled himself a libertarian. As you know, he always avoided the term *conservative*, too. He would call himself an Old Whig. The others would have called themselves libertarians.

That's how I was able to develop my own ideas. What shaped them was the interaction with all these other people at lunches and dinners and lectures.

Ayn Rand was receiving increasing attention at that time. I believed a big upsurge in the libertarian philosophy and views was pending. And to some extent it was. You had the Randian group, and the Murray Rothbard group. But the developing libertarian movement was repressed by the Vietnam War and what it led to. You've only got room for one big movement at a time.

Reason: Why do you think you had more initial success as a public proselytizer—you had a regular column in *Newsweek*—than other prominent libertarians?

Friedman: I really don't know how to answer that. I was basically trained in economic science. I was interested in the history of thought and where it came from. I thought I was going back to some fundamentals rather than creating anything new. Ayn Rand had no use for the past. She was going to invent the world anew. She was an utterly intolerant and dogmatic person who did a great deal of good. But I could never feel comfortable with her. I don't mean with her personally—I never met her personally. I'm only talking about her writings.

Rothbard was a very different character. I had some contact with Murray early on, but very little contact with him overall. That's primarily because I deliberately kept from getting involved in the Libertarian Party affairs; partly because I always thought Murray, like Rand, was a cult builder, and a dogmatist. Partly because whenever he's had the chance he's been nasty to me and my work. I don't mind that but I didn't have to mix with him. And so there is no ideological reason why I kept separate from him, really a personal reason.

Reason: In seeing yourself as harkening back to 19th-century liberalism, you never became a system-builder like Rand or Rothbard. . . .

Friedman: Exactly. I'd rather use the term *liberal* than *libertarian*.

Reason: I see you occasionally use the word *libertarian*.

Friedman: Oh, I do.

Reason: As a concession to accepted usage?

Friedman: That's right. Because now *liberal* is so misinterpreted. So I am a Republican with a capital "r" and a libertarian with a small "l." I have a party membership as a Republican, not because they have any principles, but because that's the way I am the most useful and have most influence. My philosophy is clearly libertarian.

However, *libertarian* is not a self-defining term. There are many varieties of libertarians. There's a zero-government libertarian, an anarchist. There's a limited-government libertarianism. They share a lot in terms of their fundamental values. If you trace them to their ultimate roots, they are different. It doesn't matter in practice, because we both want to work in the same direction. I would like to be a zero-government libertarian.

Reason: Why aren't you?

Friedman: Because I don't think it's a feasible social structure. I look over history, and outside of perhaps Iceland, where else can you find any historical examples of that kind of a system developing?

Reason: One could argue the same thing about minimal-state libertarianism: that historically it seems not to be stable.

Friedman: I agree. I wrote an article once arguing that a free society is an unstable equilibrium. Fundamentally, I'm of the opinion that it is. Though we want to try to keep that unstable equilibrium as long as we can! The United States from 1780 to 1929 is not a bad example of a limited-government libertarianism that lasted for a long time.

Reason: Is feeling like part of a larger movement important to you? Would you have been able to do the work you did had you not felt part of a community of like-minded scholars?

Friedman: I've been very fortunate in being part of two communities of scholars: the community of economists on the one hand, and the community of libertarians on the other. And that combination has been very productive so far as I'm concerned, but I can't really tell you why. One thing is that it's very hard for somebody on his own to be sure that he's thought of all the angles. Discussion among people helps an enormous amount. And particularly able, good people.

If you have a person isolated in an environment unfriendly to his ideas and thoughts, he tends to turn bitter and self-directed. But the same person with three or four other people around—it doesn't have to be a lot of people—will be in a wholly different position since he will receive support from the others.

You remind me of one incident where in a sense the two worlds interacted. Back in the 1960s, my daughter was an undergraduate at Bryn Mawr, and I was invited by Haverford, I think it was, to spend three days giving talks on mathematical economics. Absolutely no policy involved, pure mathematical economics. And because my daughter was at Bryn Mawr, I agreed.

After I had agreed, they asked if I would also be willing to give a chapel talk on political matters. I said sure and I gave a title, something having to do with freedom. Then I discovered that chapel at Haverford was compulsory. I wrote to the president and said that I was very much disturbed at giving a talk on freedom to a compulsory audience.

When it was time to go to the chapel, I asked the president, "How do they count attendance?" And he said, "At the beginning of the hour there are people going around in the balcony and looking down. Everybody has an assigned seat, and they count."

When I got up to talk, I spoke up to the people in the balcony and said that those who were counting attendance, please let me know when they're through because I don't like the idea of speaking about freedom to a compulsory audience. I'm going to sit down and give the people who want to leave the chance to leave. And I did. Now, the students hadn't really thought that I was going to do it and when I did, about one or two people got up to leave and the rest of them booed them because obviously, I was talking on their level. As a result, I've seldom had a student audience who were so completely on my side as that group, even though the political atmosphere at Haverford was very much to the left. That's one of the greatest coups I've ever had as a public speaker.

Reason: Do you think you've become more radically libertarian in your political views over the years?

Friedman: The difference between me and people like Murray Rothbard is that, though I want to know what my ideal is, I think I also have to be willing to discuss changes that are less than ideal so long as they point me in that direction. So while I'd like to abolish the Fed, I've written many pages on how the Fed, if it does exist, should be run.

Murray used to berate me for my stand on education vouchers. I would like to see the government out of the education business entirely. In that area, I have become more extreme, not because of any change of philosophy, but because of a change in my knowledge of the factual situation and history.

I used to argue that I could justify compulsory schooling on the ground of external effects. But then I discovered from work that E.G. West and others did, that before compulsory schooling something over 90 percent of people got schooled. The big distinction you have to make is between marginal benefit and average benefit. The marginal benefit from having 91 percent of people in school rather than 90 percent does not justify making it compulsory. But if in the absence of compulsory education, only 50 percent would be literate, then I can regard it as appropriate.

Some issues are open and shut. Tariffs, property rights. No, not property rights, because you have to define property rights. But education is not open and shut. In *Capitalism and Freedom* we came out on the side of favoring compulsory schooling and in *Free To Choose* we came out against it. So I have become more radical in that sense. Murray used to call me a statist because I was willing to have government money involved. But I see the voucher as a step in moving away from a government system to a private system. Now maybe I'm wrong, maybe it wouldn't have that effect, but that's the reason I favor it.

Reason: Would you agree with the proposition that you have been the most successful and important proselytizer for libertarianism?

Friedman: I don't think that I've had the most influence. I think the most influential person was Hayek. The effect of *The Road to Serfdom* was really critical. In another area, Bill Buckley has certainly been very important on national policy.

Buckley's not a libertarian. But he's also not a socialist. And if you look at the political scene, his *National Review* has had a tremendous influence in providing a base for collaboration between the libertarians on the one side and the free-market conservatives on the other. That was epitomized in its most obvious form by Frank Meyer when he was with *National Review*. They've helped that coalition to form and hold together and have influence; Bill Buckley played an enormously important role.

I might have more public influence than ideologues like Rand or Murray Rothbard, the libertarians in that strict sense. And I believe that the reason is because they have been so intolerant.

Reason: You wrote an essay in *Liberty* about the intolerance of Rand and Ludwig von Mises. You say you never met Rand. . . .

Friedman: I was never to my knowledge in the same place as she was; I was in Chicago, she was in New York. I'm sure if I had been in New York, I would have met her. It was not because of any objection on my part. I think she was a fascinating woman and had a great influence. As I always have said, she had an extremely good influence on all those who did not become Randians. But if they became Randians, they were hopeless.

Reason: But you knew Mises personally. Did you see the intolerance that you find in his method also in his personal behavior?

Friedman: No question. The story I remember best happened at the initial Mont Pelerin meeting when he got up and said, "You're all a bunch of socialists." We were discussing the distribution of income, and whether you should have progressive income taxes. Some of the people there were expressing the view that there could be a justification for it.

Another occasion which is equally telling: Fritz Machlup was a student of Mises', one of his most faithful disciples. At one of the Mont Pelerin meetings, Fritz gave a talk in which I think he questioned the idea of a gold standard; he came out in favor of floating exchange rates. Mises was so mad he wouldn't speak to him for three years. Some people had to come around and bring them together again. It's hard to understand; you can get some understanding of it by taking into account how people like Mises were persecuted in their lives.

Reason: You don't link yourself openly to certain aspects of the libertarian political movement. . . .

Friedman: Well, you have to be more specific. Being very specific, I have not wanted to join the Libertarian Party simply because I have accumulated good working relationships with people in the Republican Party, and I think I can be more effective by being a Republican. That's the only reason. There are no other cases in which I have had any problem with the libertarian movement.

Reason: You certainly have a respectability and presence that most people and organizations labeled libertarian don't have. . . .

Friedman: That's because of one thing only: I won the Nobel Prize. What, are you kidding yourself?

Reason: Your status preceded your winning the Nobel.

Friedman: I did have some of it, yes. It's because I have a firm root in something other than ideology. Because I was firmly based in a scientific academic discipline. I wasn't simply a preacher or an ideologue or an unconnected philosopher.

But I think the libertarian movement is doing fine. I think that *Reason* magazine has been remarkably good; it has been very effective. It takes many kinds of people to make a movement. And one of the most

important things are publications. In any activity you have manufacturers, wholesalers, and retailers; and all three are essential and necessary. There are only a relatively small number of manufacturers
of ideas. But there can be a very large number of wholesalers and
retailers.

As I look around me I'm impressed by the fact that there's increasing attention paid to libertarian ideas. If you look at the picture now,
compared with 30 years ago, there's no comparison. Now you've got
much more. As far as journals are concerned, then we had the Foundation for Economic Education's *Freeman*; for a while we had the *New
Individualist Review* in Chicago, but that was about it. Bill Buckley established *National Review*, which is in a different corner.

But look at the situation today. You have *Reason* magazine, you have
Liberty magazine. You've got all of this stuff that spouts out from the
Cato Institute and the Competitive Enterprise Institute and a half doz-
en other think tanks. In fact, I think there are too damn many think
tanks now.

Reason: Why do you say there are too many?

Friedman: You don't have the talent for it.

Reason: Do you consider yourself in the libertarian mainstream on
foreign policy issues?

Friedman: I don't believe that the libertarian philosophy dictates a
foreign policy. In particular I don't think you can derive isolationism
from libertarianism. I'm anti-interventionist, but I'm not an isolation-
ist. I don't believe we ought to go without armaments. I'm sure we
spend more money on armaments than we need to; that's a different
question.

I don't believe that you can derive from libertarian views the notion
that a nation has to bare itself to the outside without defense, or that a
strong volunteer force would arise and defend the nation.

Reason: What did you think about the Gulf War?

Friedman: I always had misgivings about the Gulf War, but I never
came to a firm decision. It was more nearly justified than other recent
foreign interventions, and yet I was persuaded that the major argument used to support it was fallacious.

After all, if Iraq took over the oil, it would have to do something
with it. If they don't want to eat it, they'd have to sell it. I don't think
the price of oil would have been much affected. The more important

consideration was the balance of power with Iran and Iraq. I have mixed feelings about that war; I wouldn't be willing to write a brief on either side.

Reason: What would you regard as your most important accomplishment?

Friedman: It depends on what you mean. I wrote an essay on methodology in 1953. It was published in my book *Essays on Positive Economics*. I had been working on it for years before that, so it goes way back to the middle '40s. It started to generate a lot of comments, but I decided I would rather do economics than talk about how economics are done. So I made a distinct point of not replying to any criticism of that essay. And I think that's why it's so commented on.

That methodology article has probably been reprinted more often and referred to more often than anything else I've written, though I would by no means regard it as the most important thing I've ever done.

In terms of sheer technical quality there's no doubt in my mind that the best thing I ever did was *The Theory of the Consumption Function* which, from a scientific point of view, is a carry on from the methodology article. I regard the theory of the consumption function as a demonstration of applying the methodology I explained there. But also it has a neatness about it and a specific theorem which has generated an enormous amount of work since then. When things like that originally come out, the status quo says, "Oh, that's a bunch of nonsense, we can't possibly work with that," but give it time. And by now it's part of conventional economics.

In the realm of policy, I regard eliminating the draft as my most important accomplishment.

Reason: Have you retired from economics?

Friedman: Well, not from economics, but from that kind of work. There's been a tremendous advance in specialization in economics, particularly in the econometrics area. I was just looking at recent working papers published by the Federal Reserve Bank of Chicago. These are clearly built on work of mine, going back to the 1970s. But there's been a new development in econometrics that I haven't kept up with. The techniques they've adopted here are all different from ours. I'm not an expert in them anymore; I really couldn't deal with this material on the level on which they are dealing with it, although I can understand the thrust of what they're doing.

I'm not making any pretense of trying to do any more basic, fundamental economics work. I believe that almost all important contributions of a scientist are made in the first 10 years after he enters the discipline. Not the first 10 years of his professional life; he may shift from
one discipline to another. And I've been impressed as I've been going
over my memoirs, that my basic contributions all have their roots in
the early years of my work. I was reading over some preliminary professional papers in the 1950s, and I could see there the whole future of
the next 30 years of work that I did; it was all outlined in there.

You add things to it, you change it, but the fundamental ideas come
early. The 1940s-'60s was when I did my most important economic
work, even though it wasn't all published then.

Reason: I read an article recently in the *Washington Monthly* that
repeated all the silly ideas about inflation that you've been fighting
your whole career. Are battles like this ever won?

Friedman: No. All battles are perpetual. You go back in the literature of economics, and you'll find the same kind of silly statements
100 years ago, 200 years ago. And you'll find the same sensible statements the other way.

Reason: Are those kind of mistakes still made among professional
economists?

Friedman: If you look at the views of the profession as a whole,
no. There's a great deal of agreement among economists, contrary to
what people may think. You won't find much difference of opinion
on the proposition that raising the minimum wage will cost jobs. You
won't find much difference of opinion on the desirability of free trade.
And you won't find any difference of opinion on the idea that you
cannot have inflation without monetary expansion. There's no doubt
that there's very widespread agreement about those simple ideas.

Reason: How do you make that consensus spread to the general
public?

Friedman: You just have to keep on trying to do it. There's no
short cut. There's no way in which you're going to end the discussion,
because new generations arise; every group has the same crazy ideas.
I get a great many letters from people who think that the way to solve
budget problems and fiscal problems is to simply print money and
pay off the debt. And there's almost no way of making those people

realize just what a bunch of nonsense that is.

I'm inclined to think that there's no field so rife with cranks as currency and money, but I'm sure there are other fields that are just as bad. I'm just ignorant of them.

June 1995

Stand and Deliver Revisited

The untold story behind the famous rise—and shameful fall—of Jaime Escalante, America's master math teacher

Jerry Jesness

THANKS TO THE POPULAR 1988 MOVIE *Stand and Deliver*, many Americans know of the success that Jaime Escalante and his students enjoyed at Garfield High School in East Los Angeles. During the 1980s, that exceptional teacher at a poor public school built a calculus program rivaled by only a handful of exclusive academies.

It is less well-known that Escalante left Garfield after problems with colleagues and administrators, and that his calculus program withered in his absence. That untold story highlights much that is wrong with public schooling in the United States and offers some valuable insights into the workings—and failings—of our education system.

Escalante's students surprised the nation in 1982, when 18 of them passed the Advanced Placement calculus exam. The Educational Testing Service found the scores suspect and asked 14 of the passing students to take the test again. Twelve agreed to do so (the other two decided they didn't need the credit for college), and all 12 did well enough to have their scores reinstated.

In the ensuing years, Escalante's calculus program grew phenomenally. In 1983 both enrollment in his class and the number of students passing the A.P. calculus test more than doubled, with 33 taking the exam and 30 passing it. In 1987, 73 passed the test, and another 12 passed a more advanced version ("BC") usually given after the second year of calculus.

By 1990, Escalante's math enrichment program involved over 400 students in classes ranging from beginning algebra to advanced calculus. Escalante and his fellow teachers referred to their program as "the dynasty," boasting that it would someday involve more than 1,000 students.

That goal was never met. In 1991 Escalante decided to leave Garfield. All his fellow math enrichment teachers soon left as well. By 1996, the dynasty was not even a minor fiefdom. Only seven students passed the regular ("AB") test that year, with four passing the BC exam—11 students total, down from a high of 85.

In any field but education, the combination of such a dramatic rise and such a precipitous fall would have invited analysis. If a team begins losing after a coach is replaced, sports fans are outraged. The decline of Garfield's math program, however, went largely unnoticed.

Movie Magic

Most of us, educators included, learned what we know of Escalante's experience from *Stand and Deliver*. For more than a decade it has been a staple in high school classes, college education classes, and faculty workshops. Unfortunately, too many students and teachers learned the wrong lesson from the movie.

Escalante tells me the film was 90 percent truth and 10 percent drama—but what a difference 10 percent can make. *Stand and Deliver* shows a group of poorly prepared, undisciplined young people who were initially struggling with fractions yet managed to move from basic math to calculus in just a year. The reality was far different. It took 10 years to bring Escalante's program to peak success. He didn't even teach his first calculus course until he had been at Garfield for several years. His basic math students from his early years were not the same students who later passed the A.P. calculus test.

Escalante says he was so discouraged by his students' poor preparation that after only two hours in class he called his former employer, the Burroughs Corporation, and asked for his old job back. He decided not to return to the computer factory after he found a dozen basic math students who were willing to take algebra and was able to make arrangements with the principal and counselors to accommodate them.

Escalante's situation improved as time went by, but it was not until his fifth year at Garfield that he tried to teach calculus. Although he felt his students were not adequately prepared, he decided to teach the class anyway in the hope that the existence of an A.P. calculus course would create the leverage necessary to improve lower-level math classes.

His plan worked. He and a handpicked teacher, Ben Jimenez, taught the feeder courses. In 1979 he had only five calculus students, two of whom passed the A.P. test. (Escalante had to do some bureaucratic sleight of hand to be allowed to teach such a tiny class.) The second year, he had nine calculus students, seven of whom passed the test. A year later, 15 students took the class, and all but one passed. The year after that, 1982, was the year of the events depicted in *Stand and Deliver*.

The *Stand and Deliver* message, that the touch of a master could bring unmotivated students from arithmetic to calculus in a single year, was preached in schools throughout the nation. While the film did a great service to education by showing what students from disadvantaged backgrounds can achieve in demanding classes, the Hollywood fiction had at least one negative side effect. By showing students moving from fractions to calculus in a single year, it gave the false impression that students can neglect their studies for several years and then be redeemed by a few months of hard work.

This Hollywood message had a pernicious effect on teacher training. The lessons of Escalante's patience and hard work in building his program, especially his attention to the classes that fed into calculus, were largely ignored in the faculty workshops and college education classes that routinely showed *Stand and Deliver* to their students. To the pedagogues, how Escalante succeeded mattered less than the mere fact that he succeeded. They were happy to cheer Escalante the icon; they were less interested in learning from Escalante the teacher. They were like physicians getting excited about a colleague who can cure cancer without wanting to know how to replicate the cure.

The Secrets to His Success

How did Escalante attain such success at Garfield? One key factor was the support of his principal, Henry Gradillas.

Escalante's program was already in place when Gradillas came to Garfield, but the new principal's support allowed it to run smoothly. In the early years, Escalante had met with some resistance from the school administration. One assistant principal threatened to have him dismissed on the grounds that he was coming in too early (a janitor had complained), keeping students too late, and raising funds without permission. Gradillas, on the other hand, handed Escalante the keys to the school and gave him full control of his program.

Gradillas also worked to create a more serious academic environment at Garfield. He reduced the number of basic math classes and eventually came up with a requirement that those who take basic math must concurrently take algebra. He even braved the wrath of the community by denying extracurricular activities to entering students who failed basic skills tests and to current students who failed to maintain a C average.

In the process of raising academic standards at Garfield, Gradillas made more than a few enemies. He took a sabbatical leave to finish his doctorate in 1987, hoping that upon his return he would either be reinstated as principal of Garfield or be given a position from which he could help other schools foster programs like Escalante's. He was instead assigned to supervise asbestos removal. It is probably no coincidence that A.P. calculus scores at Garfield peaked in 1987, Gradillas' last year there.

Escalante remained at Garfield for four years after Gradillas' departure. Although he does not blame the ensuing administration for his own departure from the school, Escalante observes that Gradillas was an academic principal, while his replacement was more interested in other things, such as football and the marching band.

Gradillas was not the only reason for Escalante's success, of course. Other factors included:

The Pipeline. Unlike the students in the movie, the real Garfield students required years of solid preparation before they could take calculus. This created a problem for Escalante. Garfield was a three-year high school, and the junior high schools that fed it offered only basic math. Even if the entering sophomores took advanced math every year, there was not enough time in their schedules to take geometry, algebra II, math analysis, trigonometry, and calculus.

So Escalante established a program at East Los Angeles College where students could take these classes in intensive seven-week summer sessions. Escalante and Gradillas were also instrumental in getting the feeder schools to offer algebra in the eighth and ninth grades.

Inside Garfield, Escalante worked to ratchet up standards in the classes that fed into calculus. He taught some of the feeder classes himself, assigning others to handpicked teachers with whom he coordinated and reviewed lesson plans. By the time he left, there were nine Garfield teachers working in his math enrichment program and several teachers from other East L.A. high schools working in the summer program at the college.

Tutoring. Years ago, when asked if Garfield could ever catch up to Beverly Hills High School, Gradillas responded, "No, but we can get close." The children of wealthy, well-educated parents do enjoy advantages in school. Escalante did whatever he could to bring some of those advantages to his students.

Among the parents of Garfield students, high school graduates were in the minority and college graduates were a rarity. To help make up for the lack of academic support available at home, Escalante established tutoring sessions before and after school. When funds became available, he arranged for paid student tutors to help those who fell behind.

Escalante's field-leveling efforts worked. By 1987, Gradillas' prediction proved to be partially wrong: In A.P. calculus, Garfield had outpaced Beverly High.

Open Enrollment. Escalante did not approve of programs for the gifted, academic tracking, or even qualifying examinations. If students wanted to take his classes, he let them.

His open-door policy bore fruit. Students who would never have been selected for honors classes or programs for the gifted chose to enroll in Escalante's math enrichment classes and succeeded there.

Of course, not all of Escalante's students earned fives (the highest score) on their A.P. calculus exams, and not all went on to receive scholarships from top universities. One argument that educrats make against programs like Escalante's is that they are elitist and benefit only a select few.

Conventional pedagogical wisdom holds that the poor, the disadvantaged, and the "culturally different" are a fragile lot, and that the academic rigor usually found only in elite suburban or private schools would frustrate them, crushing their self-esteem. The teachers and administrators that I interviewed did not find this to be true of Garfield students.

Wayne Bishop, a professor of mathematics and computer science at California State University at Los Angeles, notes that Escalante's top students generally did not attend Cal State. Those who scored fours and fives on the A.P. calculus tests were at schools like MIT, Harvard, Yale, Berkeley, USC, and UCLA. For the most part, Escalante grads who went to Cal State–L.A. were those who scored ones and twos, with an occasional three, or those who worked hard in algebra and geometry in the hope of getting into calculus class but fell short.

Bishop observes that these students usually required no remedial math, and that many of them became top students at the college. The moral is that it is better to lose in the Olympics than to win in Little League, even for those whose parents make less than $20,000 per year.

Death of a Dynasty
Escalante's open admission policy, a major reason for his success, also paved the way for his departure. Calculus grew so popular at Garfield that classes grew beyond the 35-student limit set by the union contract. Some had more than 50 students. Escalante would have preferred to keep the classes below the limit had he been able to do so without either denying calculus to willing students or using teachers who were not up to his high standards. Neither was possible, and the teachers union complained about Garfield's class sizes. Rather than compromise, Escalante moved on.

Other problems had been brewing as well. After *Stand and Deliver* was released, Escalante became an overnight celebrity. Teachers and other interested observers asked to sit in on his classes, and he received visits from political leaders and celebrities, including President George H.W. Bush and the actor Arnold Schwarzenegger. This attention aroused feelings of jealousy. In his last few years at Garfield, Escalante even received threats and hate mail. In 1990 he lost the math department chairmanship, the position that had enabled him to direct the pipeline.

A number of people at Garfield still have unkind words for the school's most famous instructor. One administrator tells me Escalante wanted too much power. Some teachers complained that he was creating two math departments, one for his students and another for everyone else. When Escalante quit his job at Garfield, John Perez, a vice president of the teachers union, said, "Jaime didn't get along with some of the teachers at his school. He pretty much was a loner."

In addition, Escalante's relationship with his new principal, Maria Elena Tostado, was not as good as the one he had enjoyed with Gradillas. Tostado speaks harshly about her former calculus teachers, telling the *Los Angeles Times* they're disgruntled former employees. Of their complaints, she said, "Such backbiting only hurts the kids."

Escalante left the program in the charge of a handpicked successor, fellow Garfield teacher Angelo Villavicencio. Escalante had met Villavicencio six years previously through his students—he had been a math teacher at Griffith Junior High, a Garfield feeder. At Escalante's request and with Gradillas' assistance, Villavicencio came to Garfield in 1985. At first he taught the classes that fed into calculus; later, he joined Escalante and Ben Jimenez in teaching calculus itself.

When Escalante and Jimenez left in 1991, Villavicencio ascended to Garfield's calculus throne. The following year he taught all of Garfield's AB calculus students—107 of them, in two sections. Although that year's passing rate was not as high as it had been in previous years, it was still impressive, particularly considering that two-thirds of the calculus teachers had recently left and that Villavicencio was working with lecture-size classes. Seventy-six of his students went on to take the A.P. exam, and 47 passed.

That year was not easy for Villavicencio. The class-size problem that led to Escalante's departure had not been resolved. Villavicencio asked the administration to add a third section of calculus so he could get his class sizes below 40, but his request was denied. The principal attempted to remove him from Music Hall 1, the only room in the school that could comfortably accommodate 55 students. Villavicencio asked himself, "Am I going to have a heart attack defending the program?" The following spring he followed Escalante out Garfield's door.

Scattered Legacy

When Cal State's Wayne Bishop called Garfield to ask about the status of the school's post–Escalante A.P. calculus program, he was told,

"We were doing fine before Mr. Escalante left, and we're doing fine after." Soon Garfield discovered how critical Escalante's presence had been. Within a few years, Garfield experienced a sevenfold drop in the number of A.P. calculus students passing their exams. (That said, A.P. participation at Garfield is still much, much higher than at most similar schools. In May of 2000, 722 Garfield students took Advanced Placement tests, and 44 percent passed.)

Escalante moved north to Sacramento, where he taught math, including one section of calculus, at Hiram Johnson High School. He calls his experience there a partial success.

In 1991, the year before he began, only six Johnson students took the A.P. calculus exam, all of whom passed. Three years later, the number passing was up to 18—a respectable improvement, but no dynasty. It had taken Escalante over a decade to build Garfield's program. Already in his 60s when he made his move, he did not have a decade to build another powerhouse in new territory.

Meanwhile, Villavicencio moved to Chino, a suburb east of Los Angeles. He had to take a pay cut of more than $7,000, since his new school would pay him for only six of his 13 years in teaching. (Like many districts, the Chino Valley Unified School District had a policy of paying for only a limited number of years of outside experience.) In Chino, Villavicencio again taught A.P. calculus, first in Ayala High School and later in Don Lugo High School.

In 1996 he contacted Garfield's new principal, Tony Garcia, and offered to come back to help revive the moribund calculus program. He was politely refused, so he stayed at Don Lugo. Villavicencio worked with East Los Angeles College to establish a branch of the Escalante summer school program there. This program, along with more math offerings in the district's middle schools, allowed Villavicencio to admit even some ninth-graders into his calculus class.

After Villavicencio got his program running smoothly, it was consistently producing A.P. calculus passing scores in the 60 percent to 70 percent range. Buoyed by his success, he requested that his salary be raised to reflect his experience. His request was denied, so he decided to move on to another school. Before he left, Don Lugo High was preparing to offer five sections of AB calculus and one section of BC. In his absence, there were only two sections of AB and no BC.

Meanwhile, after seeing its calculus passing rate drop into the single digits, Garfield is experiencing a partial recovery. In the spring of 2001, 17 Garfield students passed the AB calculus exam, and seven passed the BC. That is better than double the number of students passing a few years ago but less than one-third the number passing during the glory years of Escalante's dynasty.

And after withering in the absence of its founder, the Escalante program at East Los Angeles College has revived. Program administrator Paul Powers reports that over 1,000 high school students took accelerated math classes through the college in the year 2000.

Although the program now accepts students from beyond the college's vicinity, the target pupils are still those living in East L.A.

Nationally, there is no denying that the Escalante experience was a factor in the growth of Advanced Placement courses during the last decade and a half. The number of schools that offer A.P. classes has more than doubled since 1983, and the number of A.P. tests taken has increased almost sixfold. This is a far cry from the Zeitgeist of two decades ago, when A.P. was considered appropriate only for students in elite private and wealthy suburban public schools.

Still, there is no inner-city school anywhere in the United States with a calculus program anything like Escalante's in the '80s. A very successful program rapidly collapsed, leaving only fragments behind.

This leaves would-be school reformers with a set of uncomfortable questions. Why couldn't Escalante run his classes in peace? Why were administrators allowed to get in his way? Why was the union imposing its "help" on someone who hadn't requested it? Could Escalante's program have been saved if, as Gradillas now muses, Garfield had become a charter school? What is wrong with a system that values working well with others more highly than effectiveness?

Barn Building

Lyndon Johnson said it takes a master carpenter to build a barn, but any jackass can kick one down. In retrospect, it's fortunate that Escalante's program survived as long as it did. Had Garfield's counselors refused to let a handful of basic math students take algebra back in 1974, or had the janitor who objected to Escalante's early-bird ways been more influential, America's greatest math teacher might just now be retiring from Unisys.

Gradillas has an explanation for the decline of A.P. calculus at Garfield: Escalante and Villavicencio were not allowed to run the program they had created on their own terms. In his phrase, the teachers no longer "owned" their program. He's speaking metaphorically, but there's something to be said for taking him literally.

In the real world, those who provide a service can usually find a way to get it to those who want it, even if their current employer disapproves. If someone feels that he can build a better mousetrap than his employer wants to make, he can find a way to make it, market it, and perhaps put his former boss out of business. Public school teachers lack that option.

There are very few ways to compete for education dollars without being part of the government school system. If that system is inflexible, sooner or later even excellent programs will run into obstacles.

Escalante has retired to his native Bolivia. He is living in his wife's hometown and teaching part time at the local university. He returns to the United States frequently to visit his children. When I spoke to him he was entertaining the possibility of acting as an adviser to the Bush administration. Given what he achieved, he clearly has valuable advice to give.

Whether the administration will take it is another question. We are being primed for another round of "education reform." One-size-fits-all standardized tests are driving curricula, and top-down reforms are mandating lockstep procedures for classroom instructors. These steps might help make dismal teachers into mediocre ones, but what will they do to brilliant mavericks like Escalante?

Before passing another law or setting another policy, our reformers should take a close look at what Jaime Escalante did—and at what was done to him.

July 2002

Gulf Lore Syndrome

Why are the Gulf War vets getting sick?
You won't find out by reading
the *New York Times* and *USA Today.*

Michael Fumento

"For Some, a Day of Betrayal," ran a headline in Denver's *Rocky Mountain News* the day before Veterans Day. A Persian Gulf vet said to be suffering the effects of the mysterious Gulf War Syndrome (GWS) was profiled, and the story by reporter Dick Foster contained a startling figure: "Cancers have developed in Gulf veterans at three to six times the rate among the general population." That news must have shot around Colorado faster than a Scud missile. Many vets probably spent their Veterans Day searching for lumps, bumps, sores, or anything else that might be a sign of cancer.

Three days later, a study appeared in the *New England Journal of Medicine.* Using the latest data available, it reported the cancer rate of Persian Gulf vets was slightly below that of comparable vets who didn't deploy to the Gulf, and far lower than that of the comparable civilian population.

Welcome to the world of Gulf Lore Syndrome. It is a world in which science is replaced by rumor, in which vets are presented as medical experts while real medical experts are ignored. It is a dimension in which authoritative review studies by eminent scientists are scorned and disdainfully labeled "Pentagon studies" because they reach the "wrong" conclusions—even if done by civilian organizations. Yet incredible accounts of such symptoms as skin-blistering semen and glowing vomit are taken as gospel. It is a "reality" constructed by crusading reporters, activists, demagogic congressmen, and, sadly, by Persian Gulf vets who have become convinced they are the victims of a conspiracy deeper and broader than anything on *The X-Files*. The sick vets live in this world of Gulf Lore Syndrome. Until reality is allowed to reach them, they will remain trapped in it.

I have been writing on GWS since 1993, and to the best of my knowledge I was the first writer to say that there is no Gulf War Syndrome in the accepted sense of the term. Since then, studies by some of the most prestigious scientists in the country have backed up that position. The early studies included two by the Department of Defense, one by the National Institutes of Health (NIH), and a preliminary report by the Institute of Medicine (IOM), an arm of the National Academy of Sciences. All said that the term Gulf War Syndrome was a misnomer. All said that the various theories of what might be making Persian Gulf vets sick lacked any scientific basis. And every one of these studies' conclusions bounced off the reporters, the activists, and the sick vets like bullets off an M1 tank.

Some things have changed: When I began writing on the topic there were perhaps a hundred news reports about GWS; there are now over 4,000. Back then there were a few thousand Persian Gulf vets who claimed to have the illness; now, depending on who's counting, there are anywhere from 40,000 to more than 100,000. GWS studies continue to appear. The most recent include:

• The final report from the Institute of Medicine, which said in October that there is no "scientific evidence to date demonstrating adverse health consequences linked with [Gulf War] service other than [about 30] documented incidents of leishmaniasis [a parasitical disease caused, in this case, by sand fly bites], combat-related or injury-related mortality or morbidity, and increased risk of psychiatric [problems from] deployment."

• A draft copy of the final report of the Presidential Advisory Committee on Gulf War Veterans' Illnesses (commonly called the PAC), leaked in November to the *New York Times* and the *Washington Post*, which found "no support for the myriad theories proposed as causes of illnesses among Persian Gulf war veterans, or even evidence there is a 'Gulf War Syndrome,'" according to the *Post*.

• The article in the November 14 *New England Journal of Medicine*, which found that Persian Gulf vets had the same death rate from disease as nonPersian Gulf vets, and a much lower rate than the comparable civilian population. An accompanying article looked at hospitalizations, finding Persian Gulf vets and nonPersian Gulf vets hospitalized at the same rate.

Will these findings make any difference? Within days of the PAC draft report's release, President Clinton announced a doubling of the budget to investigate GWS. A few weeks later, he announced that the PAC final report would not be a final one after all, that he was going to keep the committee going albeit perhaps dumping some old members and assigning new ones. Rep. Chris Shays (R-Conn.) called two days of highly publicized hearings to denounce the government and parade one sick soldier after another to testify before his congressional panel, each claiming that his symptoms were beyond doubt the result of GWS. Apparently, science is still reaching the wrong conclusion.

Myths Fit to Print
What pulled me back into the fray was the recent series of revelations concerning the demolition of bunkers at Khamisiyah, Iraq. The unit that blew up those bunkers was the 37th Engineer Battalion (Combat) (Airborne). In May, the Pentagon said U.N. inspectors had found that one of those bunkers and a nearby open pit contained Iraqi rockets marked to indicate a nerve gas called sarin. Thus, while the Pentagon could (and did) continue to say that there had been no offensive use of chemical weapons against U.S. troops, it was now clear that American soldiers had been close enough to exploding chemical weapons to be exposed to them. The 37th was my sister unit when I was in the 27th Engineers at Ft. Bragg, a decade earlier. I had lived in the same barracks and worn those same silver wings that mark the Army's proud elite, the paratrooper. I knew these soldiers in ways other reporters did not. What they would tell me in weeks of interviews taught me a great deal about GWS.

I interviewed eight of these men, beginning with former Pfc. Brian Martin. Martin is by far the most prominent 37th Engineer vet, having appeared on *60 Minutes* twice, on *Nightline, Geraldo, Montel Williams,* and *Tom Snyder,* and having been quoted by news wires, newspapers, and magazines, including the Associated Press, Gannett, the *Detroit News, Newsday, Playboy,* and one of a series of articles by the *New York Times*'s Philip Shenon. Martin, 33, is also co-president (with his wife) of International Advocacy for Gulf War Syndrome. Being a disabled vet is his life; indeed, his Web page lists his occupation as "disabled veteran," while his e-mail address is "dsveteran."

Martin is quick with a sound bite, such as, "I used to jump out of airplanes and now I can't even jump up and down." Sometimes he walks with a cane; other times he uses a wheelchair. We talked about our old brigade a bit. He explained to me the process of destroying the bunkers at Khamisiyah, and then I asked him to tell me about his symptoms. That was the first hint that something was seriously amiss about Pfc. Martin.

His long list of symptoms included such things as lupus—an auto-immune disease rarely found in men—and "early Alzheimer's." Sensationalist reporters just eat up things like this, but to a medical writer such symptoms were like flapping red flags.

Then the red flag unfurled. Martin told me what he would later tell a congressional panel headed by Shays on September 19, 1996. After returning from the Gulf, he told the panel, "during PT [physical training] I would vomit Chemlite-looking fluids every time I ran; an ambulance would pick me up, putting IVs in both arms, rushing me to Womack Community Hospital. This happened *every* morning after my return from the war." (Emphasis as noted in the official transcript.)

Chemlites are tubes that, when snapped, glow. In two conversations with me, Martin repeatedly referred to his vomit as being "fluorescent" and said these daily vomits lasted from "March 11 to December 31," 1991. Thus, we are dealing with a man who insists both that his vomit glows and that his NCOs and officers heartlessly insisted that he do physical training for 10 months, knowing that "every morning" he would end up in the hospital with IV tubes in his arms.

If Martin volunteered the vomiting story during both of my interviews with him, it's very likely he told it to every other reporter who interviewed him. Yet they all used Martin as a credible witness, omitting this peculiarity from their accounts.

There are two reporters that we know with certainty did this, because they attended the September 19 hearings and wrote about Martin's testimony. One was AP reporter Donna Abu-Nasr. I called her and asked why she didn't mention the glowing vomit remark. "I didn't notice it," she said. Did she think it impugned Martin's credibility? No, she said. "You have to remember he's been on talk shows, and they've written a lot about him." She then said, "Are you going to quote me?" I told her that was my job as a reporter, but I wouldn't if she insisted. Not good enough. "I think that's very dishonest of you," she said, and hung up.

The other reporter who covered the hearing was John Hanchette at Gannett News Service, the chain that owns *USA Today*. Hanchette, a 1980 Pulitzer Prize winner, has probably written more articles on GWS—over 80—than any other single reporter, sometimes alone and sometimes with Norm Brewer. Given his reputation and sheer volume, he's certainly had a big impact on the perception of GWS. The titles of his stories show his slant: "Active-Duty Soldiers Tear into Pentagon Over Gulf Syndrome"; "Are Gulf Veterans Getting Needed Treatment?"; "Several Gulf Units Plagued by Unusually High Illness Rate"; "White House Panel: Pentagon Can't Be Trusted in Persian Gulf War Syndrome Probe"; "Persian Gulf Illnesses—the Lingering War"; "Gulf War Parents with Birth Defect Children: All They Want Are Answers."

In his coverage of Martin's testimony, Hanchette chopped Martin's symptom list down to nine, omitting the glowing vomit. Nor is that all he did.

Rather than merely attributing the laundry list of symptoms to Martin, Hanchette wrote that these symptoms were supported by "federal medical exams," making Martin's symptom list sound far more credible. But I had called Martin's doctors (with numbers Martin provided), and while Department of Veterans Affairs rules prohibit them from talking about any specific patient, I got around this by asking them if any of their patients had the various symptoms Martin claimed. Often, the answer was no. Some of the illnesses the doctors said they had not observed in any of their patients—such as lupus— were among those Hanchette listed as confirmed by Martin's "federal medical exams." What exams could Hanchette possibly have been referring to?

I politely called Hanchette four times just to say I wanted to talk about his story. He didn't call back. I called twice more to say that I had reason to believe he had engaged in unethical conduct and that I wanted to give him a chance to respond. He still hasn't called back.

So I called Hanchette's editor, Jeffrey Stinson. In defending his reporter, Stinson noted twice that Hanchette was a Pulitzer winner, called my questions "a crock," and said he really couldn't comment further without seeing the relevant material. I faxed over Martin's testimony, Hanchette's write-up, and a list of questions. Stinson's response: "Our stuff is good; it's accurate. You're full of it, pal. Bye." Then he hung up.

60 Minutes of Alarm

Martin always has a good tale to tell. Hanchette and others have reported his claim that 95 percent of the weaponry in the Khamisiyah bunkers was U.S.-made. But such a survey would have been an exhaustive undertaking and hardly the job of the battalion commander's driver, which was what Martin was. Hanchette and others have written about the videotape Martin claims to have shot of the bunker ordnance. Actually, his company commander shot it; Martin's copy was a low-tech dubbing made by aiming his video camera at a TV set as his commander's tape played. But Martin's tallest tale is his claim that after the Khamisiyah bunker exploded and chemical alarms went off, the 37th soldiers did not put on their protective gear. Indeed, said Martin, they didn't even have access to it. That's the version *Newsday,* AP, the *Detroit News,* and others went with. It makes the military look very negligent and supports the allegation that these men were exposed to nerve gas.

Ed Bradley and *60 Minutes* built a whole segment around the allegation, broadcast in August. Bradley is the reporter who kicked off the Alar scare back in 1989 with his completely unfounded claim that the pesticide was "the most potent cancer-causing agent in our food supply." In the August show, Bradley told viewers the chemical weapons expert for the battalion, former Sgt. Dan Topalski, "put his suit on right away. Others did not. He is the only man in this group who is not sick."

Pretty damning stuff—were it true. But there were five other vets from the 37th Engineer Battalion who appeared on that *60 Minutes* broadcast, and each of them told me they and every soldier they saw were at "MOPP 4," meaning fully suited. I also called the battalion executive officer, Maj. Randy Riggins, now retired. Bradley's portrayal "was a total farce," he said.

Riggins added that Martin was "really going over the edge." The enlisted men I interviewed were mostly less charitable to Martin

("He's full of shit," was the most common refrain) though they were all thankful that Martin had drawn attention to GWS.

Ed Bradley even explained why the soldiers didn't suit up. "With continued use," he said, the gear "didn't last long, and since there had been so many false alarms, they were running out of suits." The next clip showed Topalski saying the battalion commander had issued "a directive that people would go into a mask-only posture and seek the cover of a tent or poncho liner, and people were not to use their suits unless specifically told to do so."

But Bradley used that quote wildly out of context. Topalski wasn't talking about Khamisiyah, but about Rhafa, Saudi Arabia, where the battalion had been encamped previously. "I had told them [*60 Minutes*] specifically that we were not told that at Khamisiyah, we were told that at Rhafa," Topalski said to me.

Did the vets make it absolutely clear to Bradley that they had put on their protective suits? "When we were talking to Ed Bradley, yes, we did tell him that we went to MOPP 4 when we were at Khamisiyah," former Specialist 4 Dan Cook told me. Former Sgt. Christian Toulious says he also told Liza McGuirk, the producer of the *60 Minutes* segment.

Bradley led his audience to believe all the vets' symptoms began after the Khamisiyah blast. "They're sick," he said, "and so are dozens more from their unit with the same symptoms thousands of other Gulf War veterans have: headaches, stomach ailments, nerve damage." And, said Bradley, "All of these men point to the day it happened, the day they blew up the huge warehouse containing the deadly nerve gas sarin." In fact, several of the vets he interviewed, including Martin, told me they had symptoms months before the Khamisiyah demolition.

And although Bradley said that the suited-up Topalski was "the only man in this group who is not sick," Topalski told me, "I never once told Bradley I was healthy. I said I had a lot of problems, but I said they could be attributable to something else" besides the Khamisiyah blast. The other vets I interviewed confirmed he had said this. He said he also told this to producer McGuirk, three weeks before the show aired. Yet Bradley's false statement was left in.

I called McGuirk, who told me she had no reason to think that Martin wasn't a credible witness. When I told her that some of the other vets claimed she ignored vital information they gave her, she said, "I'm not going to talk to you any further. I'm afraid I have to get off the phone." She hung up. Ed Bradley did not return my calls.

Syndrome Over Science

To doctors, bizarre symptom claims like glowing vomit are a ready indicator that they are dealing with a patient suffering hysteria. "It's an old joke around ER; we ask if people's stools glow in the dark or if their hair hurts," Dr. Scott Kurtzman, assistant professor of surgery at the University of Connecticut School of Medicine, told me. But to the media, such symptoms are the makings of a great story. Kate McKenna's article, "The Curse of Desert Storm," in the March 1996 *Playboy*, didn't mention Brian Martin's vomit but said that he is "often confined to a wheelchair" because of "a diarrhetic condition that has damaged his spine." Perhaps the makers of Kaopectate should advertise that it may be effective in preventing spinal injury.

McKenna and other reporters have also alerted us to the claim by Persian Gulf vets' wives (including Kimberly Martin) that their husbands' semen is burning and blistering them. "Shooting fire," they call it. *Life* magazine mentioned it in a cover article about vets' kids ("The Tiny Victims of Desert Storm"), later a finalist for a National Magazine Award. Hanchette and Brewer at Gannett built a whole article around it, declaring, "Sometimes the semen causes blisters, rashes, and itching on exterior skin." They didn't write that somebody reported such an occurrence; they just stated it as a fact.

Skin blistering from semen, like Elvis sightings, has provided lots of claims but never any verifications. I talked to several VA doctors, all of whom said they've heard about the phenomenon but have never actually seen any such blistered or burned skin. In fact, some women do develop allergic reactions to semen, according to Dr. David Bernstein, an allergist at the University of Cincinnati Medical Center, who has studied the "burning sperm" claims. He says the reaction is typically simply redness of the skin inside or outside the vagina. But blistering? "Personally, I've never seen that," Bernstein said politely. But Dr. Marvin Ligator, director of the toxicology and epidemiology department at the University of Texas Medical Branch, burst out laughing when I asked him about it. As to whether something the vets were exposed to could cause any seminal reaction at all, Ligator said,

"There are chemicals we know of that get into semen, but I've never heard of anything that causes burns or irritation." Bernstein concurred with Ligator.

Such bizarre symptoms may sound absurd. But to a vet who hears them through the grapevine and then sees them validated in print, they're horrifying. "There's been one soldier who died because his brain turned to mush," a 37th Engineer vet told me. "A softening of the brain matter is very well known" as a symptom of GWS, he explained.

A key component of Gulf Lore Syndrome entails suspending the laws of science whenever necessary. Consider the first death widely attributed to GWS, that of Army Reservist Michael Adcock. Adcock died in 1992 at the age of 22 from what began as a lymphoma (cancer of the lymph glands) and then spread to the rest of his body. Without doubt he believed—as his mother Hester testified before Congress—that he had contracted the lymphoma from exposure to something in the Gulf. His last words, she said, were, "Mama, fight for me. Don't let this happen to another soldier." The congressmen listened solemnly, and the media faithfully reported the story. But Army Surgeon General spokeswoman Virginia Stephanakis told me that Adcock "had rectal bleeding [the first symptom of his lymphoma] six days after arriving, and the family blamed it on the Gulf." It is universally accepted by the medical community that lymphomas take years to develop, perhaps 10 or more years on average. Not months, not weeks, and certainly not days.

Likewise, former Navy Seabee (combat engineer) Reservist Nick Roberts claims to have contracted his lymphoma within weeks of what he claims was a nerve gas attack. Roberts is almost as popular with reporters as Brian Martin. The AP, *USA Today*, States News Service, the *Atlanta Journal and Constitution*, and *Esquire* in its cover story on GWS have all portrayed Roberts as a prototypical GWS victim, using such headlines as "Walking Wounded" and "Trail of Symptoms Suggests Chem-Arms." I've talked to Roberts, and I'm sure he's convinced of what he says. But his claim is a medical impossibility, and none of the stories about him bothered to make that clear.

Roberts appeared before Shays's committee on the same day as Martin, so I called Robert Newman, the Shays staffer who invited them both to testify. I asked Newman first about Martin's daily spewing of glowing vomit. "In the overall scheme of things," Newman told me, "that's got to be a minor point." Well, OK. What about Roberts's lymphoma? "Do you know how long it takes a lymphoma to develop?" I asked Newman. "It takes a long time to develop," Newman said. "So you're willing to concede that Roberts's lymphoma couldn't have had anything to do with exposure from something in the Gulf?" I asked. "I'm not going to concede anything," he said.

No, he certainly wasn't. It is part of the strategy of the lore spreaders that you never, ever admit that any vet's claims are incredible, or that even a single veteran anywhere might be suffering psychosomatic illness. Newman ended our conversation by saying, "You caught me at a bad time because I'm in another crisis. Call me tomorrow." I did, and several times after that. We never talked again.

It is bad enough that the media and Congress always treat Persian Gulf vets as experts in self-diagnosis, but they're even considered experts in diagnosing others. Roberts told a congressional panel in November 1993 that of the 33 members in his military reserve unit, 10 in addition to him have been diagnosed with lymphomas. Were that true it would probably be the most amazing cancer cluster in history. He also held up a list of what he said were 173 cancer-stricken Gulf veterans, and the media duly reported his comments. Yet five months later, an update of the Persian Gulf Registry showed only eight lymphomas out of all the Gulf vets in the country, with 38 cancers of all types.

There have been reports of mysterious illness clusters throughout the GWS scare. Vets or their spouses will call other vets, essentially doing their own epidemiological study. Often they conclude that they are suffering an abnormal amount of illness. They then contact the media, who publicize these "findings," gingerly referring to them as "unofficial investigations."

The Institute of Medicine looked at three such reports, including one involving Nick Roberts' reserve Seabee unit. In all three cases, the IOM found that, while the symptoms tended to be the same among the three groups, these were classic psychosomatic manifestations. The outbreak studies, said the IOM, "were not successful in demonstrating that these symptoms occurred at a higher rate among PGW [Persian Gulf War] veterans than among [other] PGW-era veterans, or that these symptoms could be linked to specific medical diagnoses or exposures."

The most famous of the self-diagnosed clusters occurred in Mississippi, involving alleged defects in the babies of vets. These reports added a whole new dimension to the disease. Among the heart-wrenching stories built around the "cluster" were "Gulf Syndrome Kills Babies," "A Town in Torment," and *Ladies Home Journal*'s "What's Wrong with Our Children?"

The basic story, as *Nightline*'s reporter told it, was, "In Waynesville, Mississippi, 13 of 15 babies born to returning members of a National Guard Unit were reported to have severe and often rare health problems." It didn't say the report was "prepared," as it were, by the parents themselves. The Mississippi Department of Health investigated the alleged cluster and found that of 54 births to returning Guardsmen in that state, both major and minor defects were well within the expected range. There were also no more premature or low-birth-weight children than would be expected.

Since then, several birth-defect and miscarriage studies have looked for exceptional rates among the offspring of Persian Gulf vets. They have found none. In addition, all live births to Persian Gulf vets are being tracked, with birth defects compared to those in the offspring of non-deployed soldiers. When last analyzed, the children of the Gulf War vets had the same percentage of birth defects as the children of the comparison soldiers.

But of all the media outlets that originally reported on the alleged Mississippi cluster, only CNN later told its audience of the state's report. So the "Town in Torment" remains a staple of Gulf Lore. Dr. Russell Tarver, who headed up the study, told me, "It's unconscionable to frighten people out of reproducing unless you have some good data to support that contention." He called it "a crime against those veterans."

A Little Knowledge

Look, the vets did their job in the Gulf. These men and women are not supposed to be medical experts, and it's not their fault the media and Congress insist on treating them as such. Yet the medical knowledge on the part of the non-vet GWS advocates is just as appalling. Consider a 1996 article by Maggie O'Kane in the British newspaper the *Guardian*. She wrote that American Dr. Howard Urnovitz "says the syndrome can be successfully treated with an antibiotic called doxycycline, which attacks the cocktail of viruses that many experts say has led to the illness."

Later in the article O'Kane quotes GWS activist James Tuite II, former GWS investigator for Sen. Don Riegle (D-Mich.). "There's no doubt this treatment is working, but the problem is that viruses can develop an immunity to some antibiotics like doxycycline," said Tuite, "and if they stop taking them then the disease can come back."

No, actually antibiotics can't cure viruses at all; antibiotics treat only bacteria. I guessed that what Dr. Urnovitz had said is that doxycycline could treat secondary bacterial infections that sometimes arise when a person is suffering from a virus. He confirmed this to me. "This was not a very well-vetted story," he told me, though—as we'll see—he was glad for the publicity.

Who are these people who don't know what an antibiotic does? Well, Maggie O'Kane is one of her country's most influential GWS reporters. She has repeatedly written on the subject and even produced a TV documentary. Twice named Journalist of the Year, O'Kane won the 1996 James Cameron Award for reporting "of the highest quality"; the judges specifically cited her GWS coverage, calling her a "truth-seeking missile."

Tuite is America's most influential GWS activist, although the media outlets that cite his claims ("our government is ultimately responsible for more casualties than Saddam Hussein," he told the Presidential Advisory Committee, because of "what they've been concealing for the past five years") have usually treated him as a neutral observer.

Denise Nichols' September 19 testimony before Congress was on the same level of medical expertise. Nichols, a former Air Force nurse, is a Persian Gulf vet and Colorado coordinator of the Desert Storm Veterans Coalition. She told Shays' committee that she had transmitted GWS to one of her children. "My own daughter, along with the child of another Colorado veteran, has been diagnosed with congenital cataracts, which she did not have before my return from the Gulf," she testified. Somehow, a nurse didn't know that congenital means "from or at birth"; her doctor was telling her that her daughter did not "catch" her cataracts as a result of her mother's Gulf duty.

Or consider *Rocky Mountain News* reporter Dick Foster's claim that Persian Gulf vets have a cancer rate of three to six times that of the civilian population. Asked for his source, he cited William L. Marcus's congressional testimony in June 1996. The figure Marcus gave was not for cancers as a whole but for one specific cancer of the bone marrow called multiple myeloma. Marcus gave no overall cancer figure.

Is even the multiple myeloma figure accurate? Five days before the hearings, Centers for Disease Control and Prevention (CDC) Director David Satcher sent a letter to Shays with information explaining in detail why the data from which Marcus was drawing "are not adequate to assess whether service in the Gulf War resulted in increased risk for" tumors or death from cancer. A Department of Veteran's Affairs (VA) representative who testified before the committee concurred. The data were too limited not only to say just how many Gulf vets had cancer, but also to determine what a normal rate of cancer would be. Both sides of Marcus' equation, then, were useless. What we can say is that as of the end of 1996, of 52,000 vets from the Persian Gulf Registry who had been medically evaluated, only two had been diagnosed with multiple myeloma.

As for Marcus, he's not an epidemiologist or statistician but an Environmental Protection Agency (EPA) toxicologist who took it upon himself as a private citizen to do his own calculations. He has not authored a study that has appeared in a peer-reviewed journal; he's authored no study at all. No one has checked his numbers. But once Marcus was given the stamp of "expert" by Congress, Foster felt free to use his data. Foster then extrapolated from one type of cancer to all cancers. Now Foster's own article is on the Nexis and Dialog computer databases for any enterprising reporter to pull up and reuse.

Similarly, the 37th's Toulious told me he was frightened by the sudden upsurge in Persian Gulf vet deaths he'd heard about. "Who told you that?" I asked. It was Maj. Denise Nichols, he told me, the woman whose daughter got her congenital cataracts by contagion. "She's great," Toulious told me. "She's awesome." Sure enough, Nichols has been going to GWS meetings and saying that from the end of the war to November 1995, 2,900 Persian Gulf vets had died, yet by May 1996, the number had skyrocketed to 4,291. Local newspapers dutifully wrote it up.

I called Nichols to ask her source for the figures, and she specified an office at the VA. I called that office and talked to spokesman Terry Jemison, who explained Nichols' data are a splicing of "two different numbers." The first number was deaths from all causes among veterans of Operation Desert Storm itself, about 700,000 people. The second number was deaths among anyone who had served in the Gulf region since 1990, over a million people. Obviously a bigger base number of people is going to yield more deaths.

Jemison told me there are even wilder numbers in circulation, "numbers that we not only can't corroborate, but can't even figure out the source for." He cited the case of reserve Air Force nurse Cpt. Joyce Riley, director of the American Gulf War Veterans Association, who says she contracted GWS from her patients. She made a speech saying 10,000 to 12,000 Persian Gulf vets have now died. Her speech has since been posted on the Internet. She also says that the U.S. government invented not only the biological weapons that cause GWS but the AIDS virus as well.

For the Gulf vets, rumor is often their reality. Thus two months before this article even appeared, activists were calling vets and telling them not only that it had appeared but providing allegedly exact quotes. Brian Martin called to berate me for having written that despite his claims of being sick he was able to mow his lawn. "That's bullshit," he said. Yes, more so than he knew. In late December, I debated Denise Nichols on a Denver talk show. She said Christian Toulious was very upset with me for having "twisted" his words around. Yet the first time I ever quoted Toulious is in the article you're reading, which had just gone into galleys the day before. The only Toulious quotes it contained coincidentally related to Denise Nichols and consisted of "She's great," and "She's awesome!" I wonder which quote she thinks is twisted?

I later called Toulious, who confirmed he had heard my article had appeared and had misquoted him. He apologized for having been angry at me and says that he's now become utterly exasperated with the rumor mill. "I just have two words for all these people," he said. "Prove it." Wise words, indeed.

Post Gulf, Ergo Propter Gulf

Much of what drives the GWS myth is the simplest of fallacies: that if something happens after a given event, it must have been caused by that event. The GWS fallacy works like this: The vets were obviously healthy when they went to the Gulf, or they wouldn't have been sent. Now they're sick. Therefore it must have been something in the Gulf that made them ill.

Appearing on *Nightline*, Sen. John D. (Jay) Rockefeller IV (D-W.Va.) invoked the fallacy repeatedly with such statements as: "They were totally healthy when they went over to the Persian Gulf. No problems whatsoever. They come back and all of the sudden their children are [born] defective, they can't have children, or they [the children] die."

So what happened to these vets? It depends not just on whom you ask, but what day you happened to ask them. Consider just the headlines from some of the stories authored or co-authored by Hanchette:

"Experimental Drugs on Gulf Troops Rapped by Panel"

"Key to Gulf War Syndrome May Be Flies"

"Doctor Says Gulf Illnesses Stem from Vaccines"

"CIA Document: Scud Fuel May Be Involved in Gulf War Illnesses"

"U.N. Intelligence Representatives Show Iraq Could Have Spread Deadly Aflatoxin"

Just can't make up our minds, can we? It's not uncommon for a vet or activist or reporter to insist that one thing is absolutely, definitely the cause of GWS, and later to insist that something else is absolutely, definitely the cause. Sometimes the media or activists will even use a sort of shotgun approach.

Nightline's GWS show in October, which left no doubt that GWS was both real and spreading, first indicated the cause was nerve gas. That nerve gas symptoms couldn't possibly spread from person to person was apparently considered inconsequential. The *Nightline* reporter then proceeded to blame pyridostigmine bromide (PB) pills the vets had taken. Then it was exposure to fumes from oil wells. Again, neither of these could possibly cause symptoms that are communicable, but that too seemed not to matter.

Vets and their families will often be influenced by these shifting fads, as in the case of Michael Adcock, the Persian Gulf vet who died of cancer. In May 1993, the fad cause of GWS was multiple chemical sensitivity, and that month Adcock's mother, Hester, told the *Washington Times*, "Beyond a shadow of a doubt, I believe Michael died of multiple chemical exposure" in the Gulf. She cited oil well fires, fresh paint on vehicles, and lead in the diesel fuel used in lanterns and heaters. Six months later the fad cause of GWS was nerve gas, and Mrs. Adcock testified before Congress, doubtless sincerely, that her son's disease was from nerve gas released by a Scud missile the day before his first symptom of lymphoma appeared.

Though the fads come and go, the main two so far have been PB and Iraqi chemical weapons. PB was given to many of the troops because of evidence from animal experimentation that it could provide some protection if they were hit by one type of nerve gas. A Nexis search shows no fewer than 175 stories implicating PB as a possible cause of GWS.

But the focus on PB has more to do with confusion over terms than with science. Time and again, the media have described PB using the fear-triggering word *experimental.* Hanchette and Brewer at Gannett did so in two different articles, calling it "unlicensed" in a third. The soldiers "had no idea they were taking an investigational drug," Ed Bradley told *60 Minutes* viewers, with a follow-up quote from a vet in combat fatigues saying, "We've been used as guinea pigs."

What virtually no one out there in media- and activist-land says is that PB was "experimental" or "investigational" only insofar as its ability to prevent illness from nerve agents went. The drug itself comes from a class of pharmaceuticals that has been in use since 1864. Far from being "unlicensed," it was licensed by the FDA in 1955 to treat a neuromuscular disease called myasthenia gravis. Moreover, the dose given to myasthenia gravis patients ranges from 360 to 6,000 milligrams daily. In contrast, U.S. soldiers in the Gulf were given a one-week supply of PB, with three 30-milligram pills to be taken daily.

This is why both the NIH and IOM panels rejected out of hand the notion that PB could be causing illness among Persian Gulf vets, with the NIH saying that even at the massive doses taken by the myasthenia gravis sufferers, PB has shown "no significant long-term effects." Yet one newspaper, in attributing the ills of Persian Gulf vet Carol Picou to the PB pills, went so far as to tell its readers that PB has never even been tested on women and was only the subject of a single test on men.

The second main culprit, nerve gas, has become a popular GWS suspect for reasons more psychological than scientific. "Chemical weapons are not useful as tactical weapons," FDA specialist Peter Procter told a wire service reporter during the 1990 Gulf buildup. Only 3 percent of Iranians gassed during the Iran-Iraq war died. It was hardly because Hitler was a humanitarian that he refrained from using sarin, the new nerve gas his scientists had invented, but rather because his experts convinced him that the old-fashioned high explosive shells and rockets were far more effective. But the received wisdom among American civilians, soldiers, reporters, and even government officials is that chemical weapons are incredibly efficient killing machines, so much so that they are regularly lumped into the category "weapons of mass destruction," alongside hydrogen bombs.

Such weapons are mostly effective "as weapons of terrorism," the FDA's Proctor said six years ago. "The greatest fear among the soldiers on the line," wrote one reporter shortly before the Persian Gulf ground war began, "is the likelihood that the enemy artillery will be firing rounds of mustard gas and nerve gas." Thus, it's only natural that Gulf War vets seeking a cause for their symptoms would convince themselves that they must have been gassed.

But there are many problems with the gassing scenario. One is that, as the October IOM report stated, "there are no confirmed reports of clinical manifestations of acute nerve agent exposure." True, some vets are now claiming they remember being gassed, but not one of them reported to clinics then.

Chemical alarms went off constantly during the war, supposed evidence of gas attacks. But chemical alarms are made to be hypersensitive, for obvious reasons. Even a "confirmed" gas detection doesn't necessarily indicate the presence of gas; it's just a more specific test than the initial one.

The news that sarin nerve gas weapons were blown up at Khamisiyah with U.S. troops standing three miles away gave a new boost to the chemical weapons theory. The Gulf Lore Syndrome machine went into overdrive, led by *New York Times* reporter Philip Shenon. He churned out article after article, many on the front page, filled with speculation on the long-term effects of nerve gas poisoning and featuring sad interviews with members of the 37th. Later, the Pentagon stated the obvious, that the cloud containing debris from the explosion must have floated somewhere, possibly over a large number of troops. This led to such amazing headlines as "Gulf War Gassed 15,000?"

But as such a cloud spread, it would naturally thin and degrade to nothingness. It's like pouring a small dose of arsenic into a reservoir serving 15,000 people and claiming they've all been "exposed" to a deadly poison. The most important fact is that no soldier in the 37th, the unit that was right there, reported any acute symptoms of nerve gas poisoning. Not even Brian Martin. Thus, we're being told that exposure so slight that nobody even knew about it at the time is now causing terrible, widespread harm. We are also told that there's no scientific evidence as to whether this is possible.

In fact, the Persian Gulf Illnesses Investigation Team, the same Department of Defense-appointed group which first posted the news about Khamisiyah on the Internet, also released a "Report on Possible Effects of Organophosphate 'Low-Level' Nerve Agent Exposure." Sarin gas is an organophosphate. The report states, "The concept of low-agent exposure is not realistic. These are highly volatile substances and disappear quickly." Further, "it is hard to imagine an open-air situation in which low concentrations would not disappear to zero levels within moments." Not days, not hours. Moments.

The report then surveys the scientific literature on nerve gas exposure. Among these was a test on over 1,400 subjects, from which a National Academy of Sciences panel concluded there were no long-term effects. These subjects were exposed to a range of gas levels from low, symptomless doses all the way to those that caused acute illness. Another report on 297 cases of accidental exposure among workers manufacturing nerve agents found that about a fifth initially had symptoms, but all "eventually returned to work fully functional."

The Investigation Team notes the unlikelihood of "illnesses from very low levels of exposures in the presence of overwhelming evidence that those illnesses do not occur with high and longer levels of exposure. This would be incompatible with empirical science and the principles of biology and pharmacology." The October 1996 IOM report also concluded "there is no available evidence in human or animal studies to date that exposure to nerve agents at low levels that do not produce any detectable acute clinical or physiological manifestations results in any chronic or long-term adverse health effects."

All this evidence has been virtually ignored by the media. "I have tried in my stories to point it out," one Pentagon reporter with a major TV network told me on condition of anonymity. But his editors just aren't interested in such things. "They're much more interested in stories saying 'Mounting Evidence Indicates Pentagon Not Forthcoming' or in vets saying the Pentagon has something to cover up." The other problem, he says, is that "our editors are bamboozled by the *New York Times*." The *Times*' problematic role in covering GWS isn't hard to document. Despite its numerous front-page stories telling readers that GWS is real, it buried the October IOM report on page A17 under a misleading headline: "Poor Records Hampered Inquiry on Gulf War Ills, Panel Says." The IOM did say that, but it was a minor point, making up just four paragraphs of the 65-paragraph executive summary.

As to the IOM's conclusion that there is no real GWS, the *Times* gave that one cryptic paragraph: "The committee said ample evidence showed that some veterans were genuinely sick with a variety of symptoms, most notably fatigue, headache, skin conditions, muscle and joint pain, and loss of memory or attention problems. But, it said, all these abnormalities were probably not caused by a single event."

That's it. Readers could conclude that GWS resulted from multiple chemical attacks, or a combination of such attacks and drugs. In fact, a *Times* reader could conclude anything or nothing about what the IOM had really said.

Medicine and "*Miracles*"

Journalists aren't the only ones feeding the vets good stories that don't quite add up. Dr. Howard Urnovitz is one doctor beloved by vets who believe they have GWS. Last year he said his discovery of a mystery virus in Persian Gulf vets explains how, "Like rubella, it is being passed on as a virus and can, we believe, explain the birth defects in children of the veterans."

Urnovitz is not, however, a disinterested scientist. Although he may believe what he's saying, he also appears to be appealing to the vets' fears to raise money for his biotech company, Calypte Biomedical of Berkeley, California. After all, as Calypte's Web page (ChronicIll-lnet) informs readers, "ChronicIllnet feels that much of the current breakthroughs in understanding IMMUNE SYSTEM IMBALANCE SYNDROMES, such as cancer, will come from the MIRACLES occurring with the new treatments being explored in Persian Gulf War related illnesses." (Emphasis theirs.)

No responsible physician would use the term miracle to describe his treatments; that's huckster terminology. As it happens, miracle is a hypertext link. If you click on it, the link takes you to a story about a Gulf vet who claims that his GWS symptoms were cured by doxycycline. Somehow a general-purpose antibiotic developed in 1966 doesn't seem like the sort of thing that will lead to a cure for cancer.

But it's not just cancer that these "miracle" cures will finish off. "If we can find a cure for Gulf War Syndrome," Urnovitz said at a 1996 symposium in Denver, "we'll be able to cure cancer and AIDS and chronic fatigue syndrome and other immune system disorders. They're all linked together." Maybe that cure will start your car on a cold winter morning, too.

Another doctor who is revered by sick Persian Gulf vets and has testified before the Presidential Advisory Committee is Garth Nicolson. Nicolson is a highly regarded cancer researcher who says he and his wife Nancy, a molecular biophysicist, left the M.D. Anderson Cancer Center in Houston to pursue a cure for GWS after his stepdaughter, a Gulf War vet, fell ill.

Like Urnovitz, the Nicolsons claim great success with doxycycline. Unlike Urnovitz, the Nicolsons blame not a virus but a bacterium, specifically mycoplasma fermentans (MF). They claim that using a special form of the polymerase chain-reaction (PCR) test, they have detected MF in about half of the vets with GWS symptoms. With PCR you take some blood from a person and use a chemical procedure to enlarge parts of the DNA of an organism (such as MF) that you think might be in the blood. If you use the chemical that would enlarge the DNA of MF and it works, then you know the MF is there. If the chemical doesn't enlarge it, you don't have MF. So far, so good.

But the same sensitivity that makes PCR a useful tool in finding what's in blood also makes it liable to find what's not there. Improperly cleaned and sterilized equipment will have all sorts of DNA strands on it that didn't come from the blood of the specified patient. In the most famous case of PCR contamination, Dr. David Ho—recently named *Time*'s "Man of the Year" for his promising work on AIDS—published a study in the mid-'80s which, using PCR, detected the AIDS virus in numerous people who had tested negative in the standard blood test. It was a frightening result, but no one could duplicate his findings and Ho was forced to admit that his testing must have suffered contamination.

As with Ho's results, other doctors are finding they cannot duplicate Nicolson's PCR work on MF. This includes the man universally acknowledged as the leading expert on MF, Dr. Shyh-Ching Lo of the Armed Forces Institute of Pathology. "We've never found one" Persian Gulf vet with the bacterium, says Lo. "The Nicolsons claim their technique is different," allegedly using "a special form of PCR that's more sensitive," says Lo. Specifically, they claim their test can better find MF when it's hiding in the nucleus of the cell only. Lo says that's possible, "but we never truly get the detail of how [the Nicolsons] process PCR. They just give us the statements of their results." In late December, Garth Nicolson announced that he will divulge his testing technique, but he had not done so at this writing.

I asked Nicolson if there were any scientists who had duplicated his work. He named only one, Aristo Vojdani, himself a GWS advocate and doctor who specializes in multiple chemical sensitivity. MCS is an alleged ailment that mainstream organizations, such as the American Medical Association, find questionable, if not outright nonsense. Vojdani is also now among the shrinking number of researchers claiming that silicone breast implants are harmful.

The other way of judging the merit of the Nicolsons' PCR work would be to see where it has been published. One National Institutes of Health MF expert, who asked not to be identified, conceded that Nicolson had indeed published in this area, but only in "garbage journals." Indeed, of the seven pieces Nicolson sent me, six were in journals that specialize in MCS or related fields. The seventh was in the *Journal of the American Medical Association*—but it was only an unrefereed letter to the editor.

None of which conclusively proves that the Nicolsons' research is invalid. But even if their unique test does detect MF, it may have no connection to Gulf War Syndrome. For one, nobody knows how many perfectly healthy people carry around MF in their bodies, just as we carry around myriad types of benign and even helpful bacteria.

More important, medical science so far has identified MF as a probable cause of just one health problem, rheumatoid arthritis. There is also some evidence it may be involved in acute respiratory problems. Sure, some Gulf vets have complained of aching joints and others of breathing troubles. But what of the 100-plus other problems they claim?

Further, the very idea of MF as a biological weapon, as the Nicolsons claim it was, is ludicrous. The purpose of biological weapons is to cripple, kill, and terrorize on the battlefield—not to cause aching joints in vets years later.

Nor does it help the Nicolsons' credibility that they suggest they are targets of a conspiracy because their work threatens the GWS coverup. Garth told the *Houston Press*, an alternative weekly, that while he and his wife were at M.D. Anderson, their faxes and letters were repeatedly intercepted, and their phone had been tapped so many times that "it was a record." Nancy also claims there have been six attempts on her life, but "assassins told her they saw her face and just couldn't pull the trigger."

I asked Garth about this. "We had an armed agent who came into the hospital and opened an aluminum briefcase with a silenced Beretta [sub-machine gun] who identified himself as a defense intelligence agent and said to stop our work," he told me. Were there witnesses? He said yes but wouldn't supply their names. "Frankly, I don't want to discuss this because it detracts from what we're talking about," he said.

That's a matter of opinion. What's sad is that the vets are buying into such conspiracy theories. One of those vets is the 37th's Dan Topalski, who was told by Nicolson's lab that he and his wife were positive for MF. Topalski is terrified for himself and his spouse, and the other 37th vets are terrified for him. I called Topalski and told him that the nation's most eminent MF researcher, Dr. Shyh-Ching Lo, said he didn't think much of Nicolson's work. But Topalski told me that Lo was one of the government conspirators. "He was employed by Tanox Biosystems of Houston as their resident medical expert," he told me, "where he developed MF for warfare use." His source for this information? "Nancy Nicolson," he replied. "They both worked there in 1988."

Tanox informed me that they had never heard of either Lo or Nicolson. They claim their only research is in developing allergy treatments, and indeed they hold patents in this area. Nancy Nicolson, according to the *Mail on Sunday,* the British newspaper that interviewed her, also likes to talk about how Queen Elizabeth and Prince Phillip visited her, how the pope gave her a gold ring, and how her family has enough money to bring down the American economy.

The Mystery Solved

Of the many reasons the media perpetuate Gulf Lore Syndrome, one is that reporters—and readers—love a mystery. Indeed, a Nexis search in November found 630 stories referring to the "mystery" of GWS. The allure of a mystery is often such that it refuses to die no matter how much light is shone on it. So it is with GWS. But there is no mystery.

Why are there so many sick Persian Gulf vets? First, because there are so many Persian Gulf vets, period. Take 697,000 vets, add their spouses and children, and you have a pool of well over a million people. In such a pool you're going to have every illness in the book. Because modern medicine is not an exact science, you're also going to have a certain number of illnesses for which no firm cause is identified.

"Among approximately 697,000 people over a period of several years, there will be poorly understood ailments and a number of obscure diseases," as the October IOM report put it. The question is, Are Gulf War vets having these illnesses at an extraordinary rate? The flat answer is *no*: no more deaths (except vehicle accidents), no more cancers, no more birth defects, no more miscarriages. Persian Gulf vets have these problems because everybody has these problems. The difference is the media have convinced them that a neighbor's miscarriage is just a miscarriage, but their miscarriage is GWS.

Indeed, for all the talk of the "commonality" of symptoms of GWS, I have compiled a list of over 100, including hair loss, graying hair, weight gain, weight loss, irritability, heartburn, rashes, sore throat, kidney stones, sore gums, constipation, sneezing, leg cramps, insomnia, herpes, and "a foot fungus that will not go away." It is no exaggeration to say that every ailment any Persian Gulf vet has ever gotten—or that anybody has ever gotten—has been labeled a symptom of GWS.

According to Dr. Edward Young, former chief of staff at the Houston VA Medical Center, one of the three centers set up to investigate ailments among Gulf War vets, "We're talking about people who have multiple complaints. And if you go out on the street in any city in this country, you'll find people who have exactly the same things, and they've never been to the Gulf." In an interview with the *Birmingham Daily News,* he said, "It really rankles me when people stand up and call it 'Persian Gulf Syndrome.' To honor this thing with some name is ridiculous." Although Young later asked that the comments not be printed, the American Legion, the most powerful GWS lobbying group, got hold of them and complained to the VA. The VA unceremoniously yanked Young from his position, later citing his lack of compassion. As Shays staffer Robert Newman told me, "Nobody wants to go against vets; it's a very strong lobby." Amen.

Yet it's an oversimplification to say that vets are having exactly the same symptoms as anybody else. They appear to suffer more from illnesses commonly associated with stress—that is, psychosomatic ones.

Doctors have long understood that one can induce symptoms in many people by giving them reasons they should feel sick. David Murray, now with the Statistical Assessment Service in Washington, D.C., used to demonstrate this by telling his social anthropology students they might have suffered minor food poisoning at lunch and that, if so, they should go to the nurse's office. "Within five minutes there would be shifting of seats and belching and one or two people would walk out the door," says Murray. "Eventually a third of the class would have left or be complaining of illness."

Nothing enrages activists—or many sick vets—like suggesting that Gulf War vets are suffering psychosomatic illness. Responding to the Presidential Advisory Commission's conclusion, Denise Nichols told the *New York Times,* "I am appalled that after five years [the government] is still busy denying physical damage . . . this is not stress."

But "psychosomatic" does not refers to the symptom; it refers to its origin. You can get diarrhea because you're worried about tomorrow's final exam or because you ate a week-old taco. In the first case it is psychosomatic; in the second it is organic, meaning it came from some source other than stress. In either case, you're sick. Telling someone their symptoms are probably psychosomatic isn't an insult; it's just an explanation. Nor is there anything exotic about it; stress-induced symptoms—often more severe than organic ones— have been experienced by nearly everyone.

What is the source of this GWS stress? That has been muddled by the misapplication of the term, post-traumatic stress disorder (PTSD), coined to explain psychological (including psychosomatic) problems of Vietnam vets who had trouble adjusting to civilian life. *Nightline*, in October, said GWS couldn't possibly be PTSD because this wouldn't explain why vets' wives were sick.

Exactly right. What the vets and their wives are suffering is what I call current traumatic stress disorder. It isn't their experience in the Gulf that is haunting them, but rather what they're seeing on *Nightline* and other TV shows, what they're reading in the papers, what they're hearing from congressional demagogues and from activists, and finally what they hear from their fellow vets in conversations and Internet chatter. The Gulf War vets are sick for the same reason Murray's students became sick. They are bombarded with the message that they ought to be sick.

Epidemic Hysteria

Medical historian Edward Shorter of the University of Toronto calls related cases of psychosomatic illness "epidemic hysteria." As a historian, he finds the GWS phenomenon tragic yet "fascinating." Says Shorter, "Just as cholera is spread by water droplets, epidemic hysteria is spread by the media."

In his 1992 book on epidemic hysteria, *From Paralysis to Fatigue*, Shorter recounts the similar history of a 19th-century syndrome called "spinal irritation," originally diagnosed by a handful of British doctors. Once informed they had this mysterious ailment, the patients, usually young women, would present an often bizarre array of symptoms, including temporary blindness, paralysis (of the sort Brian Martin appears to suffer), constant vomiting, dribbling saliva, and painful menstruation. Doctors used a wide array of treatments, including leeching, putting caustic agents on the skin, and applying magnets. "The more convincing and resolute the treatment," wrote Shorter, "the greater the success in cases of psychosomatic illness." "Spinal irritation" eventually spread to the United States, where it continued to afflict Americans for decades.

In November, the CDC announced that a study to be published in 1997 showed that Gulf vets from a Pennsylvania National Guard unit were three times more likely than comparable troops who didn't deploy to the Gulf to complain of such symptoms as chronic diarrhea, joint pain, skin rashes, fatigue, and memory loss. "This is absolutely a breakthrough study," said Matt Puglisi, an official with the American Legion. "For those who were more skeptical" than the Legion, he said, "and wanted scientific proof, now we've got it." *New York Times'* Shenon also played the story this way, in several articles with titles like, "The Numbers Support Gulf War Syndrome Claims." But this was far from the smoking gun GWS activists were hoping for and claimed to have found. All of these are classic psychosomatic symptoms. Combined with studies showing the Gulf vets have no higher rates of things not generally related to psychosomatic illness, such as cancer and death, the symptoms are actually further evidence that GWS reflects epidemic hysteria. Lost in the fuss over the CDC study was the statement from one of the authors to the Associated Press that "we have found there is nothing unique to the Persian Gulf, other than having gone there."

The GWS epidemic appears to have begun in mid-1992 as true PTSD among reservists who had such complaints as "hair loss, joint aches, severe bad breath, and fatigue." As reservists they were not as psychologically prepared to fight as were the active-duty soldiers; moreover, the reservists had to return to civilian jobs almost as if nothing had happened. At that point *USA Today*—the same newspaper that launched what proved to be the phony black church-burning epidemic of 1996—went into action, dubbing the symptoms "Gulf War Syndrome" and broadcasting them throughout the country.

A study of reservists found no extraordinary health problems, just illnesses attributed to stress. But Gulf Lore Syndrome was up and running. That's when the active-duty soldiers began to fall ill. By late 1993, CNN and others were seizing upon the alleged Mississippi birth defect cluster to say that GWS could be inherited. Gulf Lore Syndrome now included children.

By early 1994 some vets were linking their spouses' illnesses—including such things as irregular menstruation—to GWS. The media ran headlines like, "Gulf War Syndrome Spreading to Veterans' Families," and suddenly complaints about GWS symptoms began increasing among vets' wives. By late 1996 GWS had reached a point where people were contracting it from objects that had been in the Gulf. *Nightline* said Brian Martin's daughter got it from his military gear. CNN did a spot in November about a woman who contracted it from an Army surplus duffel bag.

For a year and a half, GWS remained strictly an American problem. By December 1993, however, the *Guardian* was reporting British cases. Eventually, GWS crossed to the continent. In a February 1996 article, Hanchette and Brewer began, "As recently as 15 months ago, asking the military about [GWS] often triggered this response: If there really is a sickness emanating from that war, why are our allies free of all symptoms?" To which the Gannett reporters responded: "Not any more." Well, here's a question for Hanchette and Brewer. Pick your favorite cause of GWS—chemical weapons, Scud fuel, sand flies, MCS—and explain why it would affect Americans three years before hitting soldiers in other countries.

"It's absolutely unmistakable" that "the symptoms are thoroughly psychosomatic," Shorter says. "The syndrome has no scientific status. It's entirely driven by political needs and the media's needs for sensationalism."

That's not entirely fair. Reporters like John Hanchette and Ed Bradley have probably convinced themselves they're doing vets a favor. They're not. Nor are the demagogic congressmen or the angry activists. You don't do people a favor by terrorizing them over their own health and that of their spouses and children. You don't do people a favor by replacing science with nonsense and reality with rumors.

It's been almost six years since the men and women who served us honorably in the Gulf War survived assault. They're still under assault, only now their enemy is more insidious, and, judging from the fear I saw in them, more successful.

March 1997

Billions Served

Nobel Peace Prize Winner and "Father of the Green Revolution" Norman Borlaug is still fighting world hunger — and the doomsayers who say it's a lost cause.

Interview by Ronald Bailey

WHO HAS SAVED MORE HUMAN LIVES than anyone else in history? Who won the Nobel Peace Prize in 1970? Who still teaches at Texas A&M at the age of 86? The answer is Norman Borlaug.

Who? Norman Borlaug, the father of the "Green Revolution," the dramatic improvement in agricultural productivity that swept the globe in the 1960s.

Borlaug grew up on a small farm in Iowa and graduated from the University of Minnesota, where he studied forestry and plant pathology in the 1930s. In 1944, the Rockefeller Foundation invited him to work on a project to boost wheat production in Mexico. At the time Mexico was importing a good share of its grain. Borlaug and his staff in Mexico spent nearly 20 years breeding the high-yield dwarf wheat that sparked the Green Revolution, the transformation that forestalled the mass starvation predicted by neo-Malthusians.

In the late 1960s, most experts were speaking of imminent global famines in which billions would perish. "The battle to feed all of humanity is over," biologist Paul Ehrlich famously wrote in his 1968 bestseller *The Population Bomb*. "In the 1970s and 1980s hundreds of millions of people will starve to death in spite of any crash programs embarked upon now." Ehrlich also said, "I have yet to meet anyone familiar with the situation who thinks India will be self-sufficient in food by 1971." He insisted that "India couldn't possibly feed two hundred million more people by 1980."

But Borlaug and his team were already engaged in the kind of crash program that Ehrlich declared wouldn't work. Their dwarf wheat varieties resisted a wide spectrum of plant pests and diseases and produced two to three times more grain than the traditional varieties. In 1965, they had begun a massive campaign to ship the miracle wheat to Pakistan and India and teach local farmers how to cultivate it properly. By 1968, when Ehrlich's book appeared, the U.S. Agency for International Development had already hailed Borlaug's achievement as a "Green Revolution."

In Pakistan, wheat yields rose from 4.6 million tons in 1965 to 8.4 million in 1970. In India, they rose from 12.3 million tons to 20 million. And the yields continue to increase. Last year, India harvested a record 73.5 million tons of wheat, up 11.5 percent from 1998. Since Ehrlich's dire predictions in 1968, India's population has more than doubled, its wheat production has more than tripled, and its economy has grown nine-fold. Soon after Borlaug's success with wheat, his colleagues at the Consultative Group on International Agricultural Research developed high-yield rice varieties that quickly spread the Green Revolution through most of Asia.

Contrary to Ehrlich's bold pronouncements, hundreds of millions didn't die in massive famines. India fed far more than 200 million more people, and it was close enough to self-sufficiency in food production by 1971 that Ehrlich discreetly omitted his prediction about that from later editions of *The Population Bomb*. The last four decades have seen a "progress explosion" that has handily outmatched any "population explosion."

Borlaug, who unfortunately is far less well-known than doomsayer Ehrlich, is responsible for much of the progress humanity has made against hunger. Despite occasional local famines caused by armed conflicts or political mischief, food is more abundant and cheaper today than ever before in history, due in large part to the work of Borlaug and his colleagues.

More than 30 years ago, Borlaug wrote, "One of the greatest threats to mankind today is that the world may be choked by an explosively pervading but well camouflaged bureaucracy." As *Reason*'s interview with him shows, he still believes that environmental activists and their allies in international agencies are a threat to progress on global food security. Barring such interference, he is confident that agricultural research, including biotechnology, will be able to boost crop production to meet the demand for food in a world of 8 billion or so, the projected population in 2025.

Meanwhile, media darlings like Worldwatch Institute founder Lester Brown keep up their drumbeat of doom. In 1981 Brown declared, "The period of global food security is over." In 1994, he wrote, "The world's farmers can no longer be counted on to feed the projected additions to our numbers." And as recently as 1997 he warned, "Food scarcity will be the defining issue of the new era now unfolding, much as ideological conflict was the defining issue of the historical era that recently ended."

Borlaug, by contrast, does not just wring his hands. He still works to get modern agricultural technology into the hands of hungry farmers in the developing world. Today, he is a consultant to the International Maize and Wheat Center in Mexico and president of the Sasakawa Africa Association, a private Japanese foundation working to spread the Green Revolution to sub-Saharan Africa.

Borlaug is Distinguished Professor in the Soil and Crop Sciences Department at Texas A&M and still teaches classes on occasion. Despite his achievements, Borlaug is a modest man who works out of a small windowless office in the university's agricultural complex. A few weeks before the interview, Texas A&M honored Borlaug by naming its new agricultural biotechnology center after him. "We have to have this new technology if we are to meet the growing food needs for the next 25 years," Borlaug declared at the dedication ceremony. If the naysayers do manage to stop agricultural biotech, he fears, they may finally bring on the famines they have been predicting for so long.

Reason: What are you currently working on?

Norman Borlaug: Since 1984, I've been involved in the Sasakawa Africa Association. Our program has devised the best package of farming practices we could with the best seed available, the best agronomic practices, the best rates and dates of seeding, the best controls for weeds and insects and diseases, and put them into test plots in 14 countries. We have found that there is a large food production potential in these African countries which are now struggling with food shortages. The package of practices that we have devised uses modest levels of inputs so the cost is not particularly high compared to their traditional ways of farming. The yields are at the worst double, nearly always triple, and sometimes quadruple what the traditional practices are producing. African farmers are very enthusiastic about these new methods.

Reason: Could genetically engineered crops help farmers in developing countries?

Borlaug: Biotech has a big potential in Africa, not immediately, but down the road. Five to eight years from now, parts of it will play a role there. Take the case of maize with the gene that controls the tolerance level for the weed killer Roundup. Roundup kills all the weeds, but it's short-lived, so it doesn't have any residual effect, and from that standpoint it's safe for people and the environment. The gene for herbicide tolerance is built into the crop variety, so that when a farmer sprays he kills only weeds but not the crops. Roundup Ready soybeans and corn are being very widely used in the U.S. and Argentina. At this stage, we haven't used varieties with the tolerance for Roundup or any other weed killer [in Africa], but it will have a role to play.

Roundup Ready crops could be used in zero-tillage cultivation in African countries. In zero tillage, you leave the straw, the rice, the wheat if it's at high elevation, or most of the corn stock, remove only what's needed for animal feed, and plant directly [without plowing], because this will cut down erosion. Central African farmers don't have any animal power, because sleeping sickness kills all the animals—cattle, the horses, the burros and the mules. So draft animals don't exist, and farming is all by hand and the hand tools are hoes and machetes. Such hand tools are not very effective against the aggressive tropical grasses that typically invade farm fields. Some of those grasses have sharp spines on them, and they're not very edible. They invade the cornfields, and it gets so bad that farmers must abandon the fields for a while, move on, and clear some more forest. That's the way it's been going on for centuries, slash-and-burn farming. But with this kind of weed killer, Roundup, you can clear the fields of these invasive grasses and plant directly if you have the herbicide-tolerance gene in the crop plants.

Reason: What other problems do you see in Africa?

Borlaug: Supplying food to sub-Saharan African countries is made very complex because of a lack of infrastructure. For example, you bring fertilizer into a country like Ethiopia, and the cost of transporting the fertilizer up the mountain a few hundred miles to Addis Ababa doubles its cost. All through sub-Saharan Africa, the lack of roads is one of the biggest obstacles to development—and not just from the standpoint of moving agricultural inputs in and moving increased grain production to the cities. That's part of it, but I think roads also have great indirect value. If a road is built going across tribal groups and some beat-up old bus starts moving, in seven or eight years you'll hear people say, "You know, that tribe over there, they aren't so different from us after all, are they?"

And once there's a road and some vehicles moving along it, then you can build schools near a road. You go into the bush and you can get parents to build a school from local materials, but you can't get a teacher to come in because she or he will say, "Look, I spent six, eight years preparing myself to be a teacher. Now you want me to go back there in the bush? I won't be able to come out and see my family or friends for eight, nine months. No, I'm not going." The lack of roads in Africa greatly hinders agriculture, education, and development.

Reason: Environmental activists often oppose road building. They say such roads will lead to the destruction of the rain forests or other wildernesses. What would you say to them?

Borlaug: These extremists who are living in great affluence . . . are saying that poor people shouldn't have roads. I would like to see them not just go out in the bush backpacking for a week but be forced to spend the rest of their lives out there and have their children raised out there. Let's see whether they'd have the same point of view then.

I should point out that I was originally trained as a forester. I worked for the U.S. Forest Service, and during one of my assignments I was reputed to be the most isolated member of the Forest Service, back in the middle fork of the Salmon River, the biggest primitive area in the southern 48 states. I like the back country, wildlife and all of that, but it's wrong to force poor people to live that way.

Reason: Does the European ban on biotechnology encourage elites in developing countries to say, "Well, if it's not good enough for Europeans, it's not good enough for my people"?

Borlaug: Of course. This is a negative effect. We always have this. Take the case of DDT. When it was banned here in the U.S. and the European countries, I testified about the value of DDT for malaria control, especially throughout Africa and in many parts of Asia. The point I made in my testimony as a witness for the USDA was that if you ban DDT here in the U.S., where you don't have these problems, then OK, you've got other insecticides for agriculture, but when you ban it here and then exert pressures on heads of government in Africa and Asia, that's another matter. They've got serious human and animal diseases, and DDT is important. Of course, they did ban DDT, and the danger is that they will do the same thing with biotech now.

Reason: What do you see as the future of biotechnology in agriculture?

Borlaug: Biotechnology will help us do things that we couldn't do before, and do it in a more precise and safe way. Biotechnology will allow us to cross genetic barriers that we were never able to cross with conventional genetics and plant breeding. In the past, conventional plant breeders were forced to bring along many other genes with the genes, say, for insect or disease resistance that we wanted to incorporate in a new crop variety. These extra genes often had negative effects, and it took years of breeding to remove them. Conventional plant breeding is crude in comparison to the methods that are being used with genetic engineering. However, I believe that we have done a poor job of explaining the complexities and the importance of biotechnology to the general public.

Reason: A lot of activists say that it's wrong to cross genetic barriers between species. Do you agree?

Borlaug: No. As a matter of fact, Mother Nature has crossed species barriers, and sometimes nature crosses barriers between genera—that is, between unrelated groups of species. Take the case of wheat. It is the result of a natural cross made by Mother Nature long before there was scientific man. Today's modern red wheat variety is made up of three groups of seven chromosomes, and each of those three groups of seven chromosomes came from a different wild grass. First, Mother Nature crossed two of the grasses, and this cross became the durum wheats, which were the commercial grains of the first civilizations spanning from Sumeria until well into the Roman period. Then Mother Nature crossed that 14-chromosome durum wheat with another wild wheat grass to create what was essentially modern wheat at the time of the Roman Empire.

Durum wheat was OK for making flat Arab bread, but it didn't have elastic gluten. The thing that makes modern wheat different from all of the other cereals is that it has two proteins that give it the doughy quality when it's mixed with water. Durum wheats don't have gluten, and that's why we use them to make spaghetti today. The second cross of durum wheat with the other wild wheat produced a wheat whose dough could be fermented with yeast to produce a big loaf. So modern bread wheat is the result of crossing three species barriers, a kind of natural genetic engineering.

Reason: Environmentalists say agricultural biotech will harm biodiversity.

Borlaug: I don't believe that. If we grow our food and fiber on the land best suited to farming with the technology that we have and what's coming, including proper use of genetic engineering and biotechnology, we will leave untouched vast tracts of land, with all of their plant and animal diversity. It is because we use farmland so effectively now that President Clinton was recently able to set aside another 50 or 60 million acres of land as wilderness areas. That would not have been possible had it not been for the efficiency of modern agriculture.

In 1960, the production of the 17 most important food, feed, and fiber crops—virtually all of the important crops grown in the U.S. at that time and still grown today—was 252 million tons. By 1990, it had more than doubled, to 596 million tons, and was produced on 25 million fewer acres than were cultivated in 1960. If we had tried to produce the harvest of 1990 with the technology of 1960, we would have had to have increased the cultivated area by another 177 million hectares, about 460 million more acres of land of the same quality—which we didn't have, and so it would have been much more. We would have moved into marginal grazing areas and plowed up things that wouldn't be productive in the long run. We would have had to move into rolling mountainous country and chop down our forests. President Clinton would not have had the nice job of setting aside millions of acres of land for restricted use, where you can't cut a tree even for paper and pulp or for lumber. So all of this ties together.

This applies to forestry, too. I'm pleased to see that some of the forestry companies are very modern and using good management, good breeding systems. Weyerhauser is Exhibit A. They are producing more wood products per unit of area than the old unmanaged forests. Producing trees this way means millions of acres can be left to natural forests.

Reason: A lot of environmental activists claim that the BT toxin gene, which is derived from *Bacillus thuringiensis* and which has been transferred into corn and cotton, is going to harm beneficial insects like the monarch butterfly. Is there any evidence of that?

Borlaug: To that I [respond], will BT harm beneficial insects more than the insecticides that are sprayed around in big doses? In fact, BT is more specific. There are lots of insects that it doesn't affect at all.

Reason: It affects only the ones that eat the crops.

Borlaug: Right.

Reason: So you don't think that putting the BT gene in corn or cotton is a big problem?

Borlaug: I think that whole monarch butterfly thing was a gross exaggeration. I think the researchers at Cornell who fed BT corn pollen to monarch butterflies were looking for something that would make them famous and create this big hullabaloo that's resulted. In the first place, corn pollen is pretty heavy. It doesn't fly long distances. Also, most monarchs are moving at different times of the season when there's no corn pollen. Sure, some of them might get killed by BT corn pollen, but how many get killed when they are sprayed with insecticides? Activists also say that BT genes in crops will put stress on the pest insects, and they'll mutate. Well, that's been going on with conventional insecticides. It's been going on all my life working with wheat. It's a problem that has been and can be managed.

Reason: But the Cornell researchers went ahead and published their paper on the effects of BT corn pollen on monarch butterflies in the laboratory.

Borlaug: Several of us tried to encourage them to run field tests before it was published. That's how science gets politicized. There's an element of Lysenkoism [Lysenko was Stalin's favorite biologist] all tangled up with this pseudoscience and environmentalism. I like to remind my friends what pseudoscience and misinformation can do to destroy a nation.

Reason: Some activists claim that herbicide-resistant crops end up increasing the amount of herbicide that's sprayed on fields. Do you think that's true?

Borlaug: Look, insecticides, herbicides, and fertilizer cost money, and the farmer doesn't have much margin. He's going to try to use the minimum amount that he can get by with. Probably in most cases, a farmer applies less than he should. I don't think farmers are likely to use too much.

Reason: What other crop pests might biotech control in the future?

Borlaug: All of the cereals except rice are susceptible to one to three different species of rust fungi. Now, rusts are obligate parasites. They can only live under green tissue, but they are long-lived. They can move in the air sometimes 100, 500, 800 miles, and they get in the jet stream and fall. If the crop variety is susceptible to rust fungi and moisture is there and the temperature is right, it's like lighting a fire. It just destroys crops. But rice isn't susceptible—no rust. . . . One thing that I hope to live to see is somebody taking that block of rust-resistance genes in rice and putting it into all of the other cereals.

Reason: Do biotech crops pose a health risk to human beings?

Borlaug: I see no difference between the varieties carrying a BT gene or a herbicide resistance gene, or other genes that will come to be incorporated, and the varieties created by conventional plant breeding. I think the activists have blown the health risks of biotech all out of proportion.

Reason: What do you think of organic farming? A lot of people claim it's better for human health and the environment.

Borlaug: That's ridiculous. This shouldn't even be a debate. Even if you could use all the organic material that you have—the animal manures, the human waste, the plant residues—and get them back on the soil, you couldn't feed more than 4 billion people. In addition, if all agriculture were organic, you would have to increase cropland area dramatically, spreading out into marginal areas and cutting down millions of acres of forests.

At the present time, approximately 80 million tons of nitrogen nutrients are utilized each year. If you tried to produce this nitrogen organically, you would require an additional 5 or 6 billion head of cattle to supply the manure. How much wild land would you have to sacrifice just to produce the forage for these cows? There's a lot of nonsense going on here.

If people want to believe that the organic food has better nutritive value, it's up to them to make that foolish decision. But there's absolutely no research that shows that organic foods provide better nutrition. As far as plants are concerned, they can't tell whether that nitrate ion comes from artificial chemicals or from decomposed organic matter. If some consumers believe that it's better from the point of view of their health to have organic food, God bless them. Let them buy it. Let them pay a bit more. It's a free society. But don't tell the world that we can feed the present population without chemical fertilizer. That's when this misinformation becomes destructive.

Reason: What do you think of Worldwatch Institute founder Lester Brown and his work?

Borlaug: I've known Lester Brown personally for more than 40 years. He's done a lot of good, but he vacillates, depending on the way the political and economic winds are blowing, and he's sort of inclined to be a doomsayer.

Reason: He recently said, "The world's farmers can no longer be counted on to feed the projected additions to our numbers." Do you agree with that?

Borlaug: No, I do not. With the technology that we now have available, and with the research information that's in the pipeline and in the process of being finalized to move into production, we have the know-how to produce the food that will be needed to feed the population of 8.3 billion people that will exist in the world in 2025.

I don't like to try to see further than about 25 years. In 1970, at the Nobel Prize press conference, I said I can see that we have the technology to produce the food that's needed to the year 2000, and that we can do it without destroying a lot of the environment. Modern agriculture saves a lot of land for nature, for wildlife habitat, for flood control, for erosion control, for forest production. All of those are values that are important to society in general, and especially to the privileged who have a chance to spend a lot of long vacations out looking at nature. I say we can produce enough food with the technology available and what's in the process of being developed, assuming that we don't have all this agricultural progress destroyed by the doomsayers. That is, we will be able to produce enough food in 2025 without expanding the area under cultivation very much and without having to move into semi-arid or forested mountainous topographies.

Reason: It seems that every five years or so, Lester Brown predicts that massive famines are imminent. Why does he do that? They never happen.

Borlaug: I guess it sells. I guess what he writes has a lot to do with raising funds.

Reason: Brown notes that India tripled its wheat yields in the past three decades, but he says that will be impossible to do again. Do you think he's right?

Borlaug: No. The projections in food production in India continue to go up on the same slope. When we transferred the Green Revolution wheat technology to India, production was 12 million tons a year. Last year it was 74 million tons, and it is still going up. Once in a while production may go down by a couple of million tons when there's a drought, but in general it continues to go up. Also, the increase in production has occurred with very modest increases in cultivated area. A lot of wild land has been saved in India, China, and the United States by high-yield technology.

India has produced enough and sometimes has a surplus in grain. The problem is to get it into the stomachs of the hungry. There's a lack of purchasing power by too large a part of the population. There are still many hungry people, not dying from starvation, but needing more food to grow strong bodies and maintain health and work effectively. The grain is there in the warehouses, but it doesn't find its way into the stomachs of the hungry.

Reason: What do you think of Paul Ehrlich's work?

Borlaug: Ehrlich has made a great career as a predictor of doom. When we were moving the new wheat technology to India and Pakistan, he was one of the worst critics we had. He said, "This person, Borlaug, doesn't have any idea of the magnitude of the problems in food production." He said, "You aren't going to make any major impact on producing the food that's needed." Despite his criticisms, we succeeded, of course.

Reason: When an alleged expert like Ehrlich is being negative like that, does that discourage people? Does it hurt the efforts to boost food production?

Borlaug: Sure, because we were funded by a foundation. . . . They'd hear his criticisms, and I'm sure there were some people at Rockefeller saying, "Maybe we shouldn't fund that program anymore." It always has adverse effects on budgeting.

Reason: Why do you think people still listen to Ehrlich? One can go back and read his doomsday scenarios and see that he was wrong.

Borlaug: People don't go back and read what he wrote. You do, but the great majority of the people don't, and their memory is short. As a matter of fact, I think this [lack of perspective] is true of our whole food situation. Our elites live in big cities and are far removed from the fields. Whether it's Brown or Ehrlich or the head of the Sierra Club or the head of Greenpeace, they've never been hungry.

Reason: You mentioned that you are afraid that the doomsayers could stop the progress in food production.

Borlaug: It worries me, if they gum up all of these developments. It's elitism, and the American people are vulnerable to this, too. I'm talking about the extremists here and in Western Europe. . . . In the U.S., 98 percent of consumers live in cities or urban areas or good-size towns. Only 2 percent still live out there on the land. In Western Europe also, a big percentage of the people live off the farms, and they don't understand the complexities of agriculture. So they are easily swayed by these scare stories that we are on the verge of being poisoned out of existence by farm chemicals.

Bruce Ames, the head of biochemistry at Berkeley, has analyzed hundreds and hundreds of foods, including all of the basic ones that we have been eating from the beginning of agriculture up to the present time. He has found that they contain trace amounts of many completely natural chemical compounds that are toxic or carcinogenic, but they're present in such small quantities that they apparently don't affect us.

Reason: Would you say the Green Revolution was a success?

Borlaug: Yes, but it's a never-ending job. When I was born in 1914, the world population was approximately 1.6 billion people. It has just turned 6 billion. We've had no major famines any place in the world since the Green Revolution began. We've had local famines where these African wars have been going on and are still going on. However, if we could get the infrastructure straightened out in African countries south of the Sahara, you could end hunger there pretty fast. . . . And if you look at the data that's put out by the World Health Organization and [the U.N.'s Food and Agriculture Organization], there are probably 800 million people who are undernourished in the world. So there's still a lot of work to do.

April 2000

Typing Errors

The standard typewriter keyboard is Exhibit A in the hottest new case against markets. But the evidence has been cooked.

Stan Liebowitz and Stephen E. Margolis

LIKE A MODERN HORROR MOVIE VILLAIN who keeps coming back from the dead, a false story can take on a life of its own: Eskimos have hundreds of words for snow, Millard Fillmore ordered the first bathtub for the White House, that sort of thing. Even after they are shown to be false, some stories are repeated, embellished, and occasionally built into entire belief systems. These fictions may ordinarily be little more than curiosities or mere affronts to our concern for the truth. But our concern here is with one such story that is put forward as part of a case against the effectiveness of free markets and individual choice. This story has consequences.

Our story concerns the history of the standard typewriter keyboard, commonly known as QWERTY, and its more recent rival, the Dvorak keyboard. Pick up the February 19 edition of *Newsweek* and there is Steve Wozniak, the engineering wunderkind largely responsible for Apple's early success, explaining that Apple's recent failures were just another example of a better product losing out to an inferior alternative: "Like the Dvorak keyboard, Apple's superior operating system lost the market-share war." Ignoring for the moment the fact that just about all computer users now use sleek graphical operating systems much like the Mac's graphical interface (itself taken from Xerox), Wozniak cannot be blamed for repeating the keyboard story.

It is commonly reported as fact in newspapers, magazines, and academic journals. An article in the January 1996 *Harvard Law Review*, for example, invokes the typewriter keyboard as support for a thesis that pure luck is responsible for winners and losers, and that our expectation of survival of the fittest should be replaced by survival of the luckiest.

But this is just the tip of the iceberg. In the *Los Angeles Times*, Steve Steinburg writes, regarding the adoption of an Internet standard, "[I]t's all too likely to be the wrong standard. From QWERTY vs. Dvorak keyboards, to Beta vs. VHS cassettes, history shows that market share and technical superiority are rarely related." In the *Independent*, Hamish McRae discusses the likelihood of "lock-in" to inferior standards. He notes the Beta and VHS competition as well as some others, then adds, "Another example is MS-DOS, but perhaps the best of all is the QWERTY keyboard. This was designed to slow down typists. . . . " In *Fortune*, Tim Smith repeats the claim that QWERTY was intended to slow down typists, and then notes, "Perhaps the stern test of the marketplace produces results more capricious than we like to think."

In a feature series, Steven Pearlstein of the *Washington Post* presents at great length the argument that modern markets, particularly those linked to networks, are likely to be dominated by just a few firms. After introducing readers to Brian Arthur, one of the leading academic advocates of the view that lock-in is a problem, he states, "The Arthurian discussion of networks usually begins at the typewriter keyboard." Other prominent appearances of the QWERTY story are found in the *New York Times*, the *Sunday Observer*, the *Boston Globe*, and broadcast on PBS's *News Hour with Jim Lehrer*. It can even be found in the *Encyclopaedia Britannica* as evidence of how human inertia can result in the choice of an inferior product. The story can be found in two very successful economics books written for laymen: Robert Frank and Philip Cook's *The Winner-Take-All Society* and Paul Krugman's *Peddling Prosperity*, where an entire chapter is devoted to the "economics of QWERTY."

Why is the keyboard story receiving so much attention from such a variety of sources? The answer is that it is the centerpiece of a theory that argues that market winners will only by the sheerest of coincidences be the best of the available alternatives. By this theory, the first technology that attracts development, the first standard that attracts adopters, or the first product that attracts consumers will tend to have an insurmountable advantage, even over superior rivals that happen to come along later. Because first on the scene is not necessarily the best, a logical conclusion would seem to be that market choices aren't necessarily good ones. So, for example, proponents of this view argue that although the Beta video recording format was better than VHS, Beta lost out because of bad luck and quirks of history that had nothing much to do with the products themselves. (Some readers who recall that Beta was actually first on the scene will immediately recognize a problem with this example.)

These ideas come to us from an academic literature concerned with "path dependence." The doctrine of path dependence starts with the observation that the past influences the future. This conclusion is hard to quibble with, although it also seems to lack much novelty. It simply recognizes that some things are durable. But path dependence is transformed into a far more dramatic theory by the additional claim that the past so strongly influences the future that we become "locked in" to choices that are no longer appropriate. This is the juicy version of the theory, and the version that implies that markets cannot be trusted. Stanford University economic historian Paul David, in the article that introduced the QWERTY story to the economics literature, offers this example of the strong claim: "Competition in the absence of perfect futures markets drove the industry prematurely into standardization on the wrong system where decentralized decision making subsequently has sufficed to hold it."

According to this body of theory, if, for example, DOS is the first operating system, then improvements such as the Macintosh will fail because consumers are so locked in to DOS that they will not make the switch to the better system (Rush Limbaugh falls for this one). The success of Intel-based computers, in this view, is a tragic piece of bad luck. To accept this view, of course, we need to ignore the fact that DOS was not the first operating system, that consumers did switch away from DOS when they moved to Windows, that the DOS system was an appropriate choice for many users given the hardware of the time, and that the Mac was far more expensive. Also, a switch to Mac required that we throw out a lot of DOS hardware, where the switch to Windows did not, something that is not an irrelevant social concern.

A featured result of these theories is that merely knowing what path would be best would not help you to predict where the market will move. In this view of the world, we will too often get stuck, or locked in, on a wrong path. Luck rules, not efficiency.

Most advocates of this random-selection view do not claim that everything has been pure chance, since that would be so easy to disprove. After all, how likely would it be that consecutive random draws would have increased our standard of living for so long with so few interruptions? Instead, we are told that luck plays a larger role in the success of high-technology products than for older products. A clear example of this argument is a 1990 Brian Arthur article in *Scientific American*. Arthur there distinguishes between a new economics of "knowledge based" technologies, which are supposedly fraught with increasing returns, and the old economics of "resource based" technologies (for example, farming, mining, building), which supposedly were not. "Increasing returns" (or "scale economies") means that conducting an activity on a larger scale may allow lower costs, or better products, or both.

Traditional concepts of scale economies applied to production—the more steel you made, the more cheaply you could make each additional ton, because fixed costs can be spread. Much of the path-dependence literature is concerned with economies of consumption, where a good becomes cheaper or more valuable to the consumer as more other people also have it; if lots of people have DOS computers, then more software will be available for such machines, for instance, which makes DOS computers better for consumers. This sort of "network externality" is even more important when literal networks are involved, as with phones or fax machines, where the value of the good depends in part on how many other people you can connect to.

What Arthur and others assert is that path dependence is an affliction associated with technologies that exhibit increasing returns—that once a product has an established network it is almost impossible for a new product to displace it. Thus, as society gets more advanced technologically, luck will play a larger and larger role. The logical chain is that new technologies exhibit increasing returns, and technologies with increasing returns exhibit path dependence. Of the last link in that chain, Arthur notes: "[O]nce random economic events select a particular path, the choice may become locked-in regardless of the advantages of the alternatives."

This pessimism about the effectiveness of markets suggests a relative optimism about the potential for government action. It would be only reasonable to expect, for example, that panels of experts would do better at choosing products than would random chance. Similarly, to address the kinds of concerns raised in Frank and Cook's *Winner-Take-All Society*, the inequalities in incomes that arise in these new-technology markets could be removed harmlessly, since inequalities arise only as a matter of luck in the first place. It does not seem an unimaginable stretch to the conclusion that if the government specifies, in advance, the race and sex of market winners, no harm would be done since the winners in the market would have been a randomly chosen outcome anyway.

Theories of path dependence and their supporting mythology have begun to exert an influence on policy. Last summer, an amicus brief on the Microsoft consent decree used lock-in arguments, including the QWERTY story, and apparently prompted Judge Stanley Sporkin to refuse to ratify the decree. (He was later overturned.) Arguments against Microsoft's ill-fated attempt to acquire Intuit also relied on allegations of lock-in. Carl Shapiro, one of the leading contributors to this literature, recently took a senior position in the antitrust division of the Justice Department. These arguments have even surfaced in presidential politics, when President Clinton began referring to a "winner-take-all society."

Stanford University economist Paul Krugman offered the central claim of this literature boldly and with admirable simplicity: "In QWERTY worlds, markets can't be trusted." The reason that he uses "QWERTY worlds," and not DOS worlds, or VHS worlds, is that the DOS and VHS examples are not very compelling. Almost no one uses DOS anymore, and many video recorder purchasers thought VHS was better than Beta (as it was, in terms of recording time, as we have discussed at length elsewhere).

The theories of path dependence that percolate through the academic literature show the possibility of this form of market ineptitude within the context of highly stylized theoretical models. But before these theories are translated into public policy, there really had better be some good supporting examples. After all, these theories fly in the face of hundreds of years of rapid technological progress. Recently we have seen PCs replace mainframes, computers replace typewriters, fax machines replace the mails for many purposes, DOS replace CP/M, Windows replace DOS, and on and on.

The typewriter keyboard is central to this literature because it appears to be the single best example where luck caused an inferior product to defeat a demonstrably superior product. It is an often repeated story that is generally believed to be true. Interestingly, the typewriter story, though charming, is also false.

The Fable

The operative patent for the typewriter was awarded in 1868 to Christopher Latham Sholes. Sholes and his associates experimented with various keyboard designs, in part to solve the problem of the jamming of the keys. The result of these efforts is the common QWERTY keyboard (named for the letters in the upper left hand row). It is frequently claimed that the keyboard was actually configured to reduce typing speed, since that would have been one way to avoid the jamming of the typewriter.

The rights to the Sholes patent were sold to E. Remington & Sons in early 1873. Remington added further mechanical improvements and began commercial production in late 1873. Other companies arose and produced their own keyboard designs to compete with Remington. Overall sales grew, but slowly.

A watershed event in the received version of the QWERTY story is a typing contest held in Cincinnati on July 25, 1888. Frank McGurrin, a court stenographer from Salt Lake City who was purportedly the only person using touch typing at the time, won a decisive victory over Louis Taub. Taub used the hunt-and-peck method on a Caligraph, a machine with an alternative arrangement of keys. McGurrin's machine, as luck would have it, just happened to be a QWERTY machine.

According to popular history, the event established once and for all that the Remington typewriter, with its QWERTY keyboard, was technically superior. Wilfred Beeching's influential history of the keyboard mentions the Cincinnati contest and attaches great importance to it: "Suddenly, to their horror, it dawned upon both the Remington company and the Caligraph company officials, torn between pride and despair, that whoever won was likely to put the other out of business!" Beeching refers to the contest as having established the Remington machine "once and for all." Since no one else at that time had learned touch typing, owners of alternative keyboards found it impossible to counter the claim that Remington's QWERTY keyboard arrangement was the most efficient.

So, according to this popular telling, McGurrin's fluke choice of the Remington keyboard, a keyboard designed to solve a particular mechanical problem, became the very poor standard used daily by millions of typists.

Fast forward now to 1936, when August Dvorak, a professor at the University of Washington, patented the Dvorak Simplified Keyboard. Dvorak claimed to have experimental evidence that his keyboard provided advantages of greater speed, reduced fatigue, and easier learning. These claims were buttressed when, during World War II, the U.S. Navy conducted experiments demonstrating that the cost of converting typists to the Dvorak keyboard would be repaid, through increased typing speed, within 10 days from the end of training. Despite these claims, however, the Dvorak keyboard has never found much acceptance.

In many regards this is an ideal example. The dimensions of performance are few, and in these dimensions the Dvorak keyboard appears to be overwhelmingly superior. The failure to choose the Dvorak keyboard certainly seems to demonstrate that something is amiss. On top of all that, it's a charming tale that is easy to tell, and the moral seems easy to find.

Unfortunately, what is amiss here is not the market choice, but the tale itself. The standard telling of this story turns out to be false in almost every important respect.

Tainted Evidence for Dvorak

The belief that the Dvorak keyboard is superior to QWERTY can be traced to a few key sources. A book published by Dvorak and several co-authors in 1936 presented Dvorak's own investigations, which might charitably be called less than objective. Their book has the feel of a late-night television infomercial rather than scientific work. Consider this from their chapter about relative keyboard performance:

"The bare recital to you of a few simple facts should suffice to indict the available spatial pattern that is so complacently entitled the universal [QWERTY] keyboard. Since when was the universe lopsided?

The facts will not be stressed, since you may finally surmount most of the ensuing handicaps of this [QWERTY] keyboard. Just enough facts will be paraded to lend you double assurance that for many of the errors that you will inevitably make and for much of the discouraging delay you will experience in longed-for speed gains, you are not to blame. If you grow indignant over the beginner's role of innocent victim, remember that a little emotion heightens determination. Analysis of the present keyboard is so destructive that an improved arrangement is a modern imperative. Isn't it obvious that faster, more accurate, less fatiguing typing can be attained in much less learning time provided a simplified keyboard is taught?" Unfortunately, their statement that they will not stress the facts appears truthful.

Dvorak and his co-authors claimed that their studies established that students learn Dvorak faster than they learn QWERTY. But they compared students of different ages and abilities (for example, students learning Dvorak in grades 7 and 8 at the University of Chicago Lab School were compared with students learning QWERTY in conventional high schools), in different school systems, taking different tests in classes that met for different lengths of time. One doesn't need to be a scientist to realize that such comparisons are not the stuff of controlled experiments. Even in their studies, however, the evidence is mixed as to whether students learning Dvorak retain an advantage, since the differences seemed to diminish as training progressed.

But it is the Navy study that is the basis for the more extravagant claims of Dvorak's advocates. That is the study that supposedly established that the entire retraining cost is recaptured 10 days after the *start* of retraining.

Since several academic authors, including Paul David, have made reference to this Navy study, we assumed it would not be too difficult to find. But when we started to look for it, it seemed to have disappeared from the face of the earth. After trying our own libraries, we tried the Navy Library, the Martin Luther King Library, the Library of Congress, the National Archives, the National Technical Communication Service, and so forth. The librarians were more helpful than we had any right to expect, but the results of their efforts seemed to indicate that we would not find the Navy study.

Had any of the modern authors who referred to the Navy study as supporting Dvorak's keyboard ever actually read it? This appears to be one of those cases in which one author relies on another's account, who in turn is relying on another's, and so on, without any of them reading the original. Yet the Navy study is a primary source of many of the claims for the Dvorak keyboard. This is certainly not a high watermark in scholarship.

We had about given up hope when we located a copy of the study held by an organization called Dvorak International, headquartered in the attic of a farmhouse in Vermont. The report does not list the authors. The report's foreword states that two prior experiments had been conducted but that "the first two groups were not truly fair tests." This certainly raised our suspicions. Might those earlier tests have been ignored because the results were inconsistent with the results the authors desired? This suspicion was later reinforced when we read about a 1953 study for the Australian Post Office. In the early phases of the Australian study, the experiments showed no advantages for Dvorak. But then adjustments were made in the test procedure to "remove psychological impediments to superior performance." We can only guess how the proponents of the Dvorak keyboard, who conducted the experiments, might have removed those nasty impediments.

As to the experimental design of the Navy study, we can only state that if the experimental controls seemed bad in the early studies authored by Dvorak and his associates, the Navy study seems even worse.

First, 14 Navy typists were retrained on *newly overhauled* Dvorak typewriters for two hours a day. We are not told how the typists were chosen, although we are told that they had initial typing speeds of 32 words per minute, well below the Navy's standard of competence. Yet in spite of their poor typing skills, the typists had IQs only two points below average and dexterity skills 15 points above average. Based on these abilities, this group of typists should have been expected to type at far above minimal competency. After completing 83 hours on the new keyboard, we are told that the typing speed for this group had increased to an average of 56 net words per minute, a 75 percent increase.

A second part of the experiment consisted of the *retraining* of 18 typists on the QWERTY keyboard. These typists reported a 28 percent increase in typing speed from their initial speed of 29 words a minute.

Although this evidence looks like a slam-dunk for Dvorak, it is not.

First, it is not clear how the QWERTY typists were picked, or even if members of this group were aware that they were part of an experiment. The participants' IQs and dexterity skills are not reported for the QWERTY retraining group. Were their abysmal typing scores surprising, given their inherent abilities? It is difficult to have any sense whether this group is a reasonable control for the first group. Nor do we know if the QWERTY typewriters were newly overhauled. Nor do we know who retrained these typists.

Even worse, there is clear evidence that the results were altered through a series of inappropriate data manipulations. For example, the initial typing scores for the QWERTY typists were measured differently from the initial scores of the Dvorak typists so as to greatly disadvantage the QWERTY results. The report states that, because three typists in the QWERTY group had initial net scores of zero words per minute (!), the beginning and ending speeds were calculated as the average of the first four typing tests and the average of the last four typing tests. This has the effect of raising the measured initial typing speed, and lowering the measured ending speed. In contrast, the initial experiment using Dvorak simply used the first and last test scores. Using numbers reported in the footnotes of the report, we were able to calculate that this truncation of the reported values at the beginning of the test reduced the measured increase in typing speed on the QWERTY keyboard by almost half. The effect of the truncation at the end of the measuring period also decreases the reported gains for the QWERTY typists, though the size of this distortion cannot be determined from the report. The important thing, however, is that the numbers appear to be cooked in favor of Dvorak.

How can we take seriously a study which so blatantly seems to be stacking the deck in favor of Dvorak? And, indeed, there appears to have been good reason for that deck stacking.

We discovered that the Navy's top expert in the analysis of time and motion studies during World War II was none other than . . . drum roll please . . . Lieut. Com. August Dvorak. Earle Strong, a professor at Pennsylvania State University and a one-time chairman of the Office Machine Section of the American Standards Association, reports that the 1944 Navy experiment was conducted by Dvorak himself. Strong was heavily involved with these issues. He was the author of a key test of the typewriter keyboard commissioned by the General Services Administration.

As if the potential for bias were not great enough, we also discovered that Dvorak had a financial stake in this keyboard. He not only owned the patent on the keyboard but had received at least $130,000 from the Carnegie Commission for Education for the studies performed while he was at the University of Washington, a rather stupendous sum for the time.

Of course, the purported Navy results, if true, would be quite remarkable. After those first 10 days in which the investment is made and recovered, the faster typing continues every working day in the life of the typist. This would imply that the investment in retraining repays itself at least 23 times in one year. Does it seem even remotely possible that employers with large typing pools would turn down investments with returns of 2,200 percent a year?

Evidence Against Dvorak

Naturally, these false results were going to get found out. As many businesses and government agencies contemplated changing keyboards in the mid 1950s, the General Services Administration commissioned Strong's study to confirm the earlier results. This study provides the most compelling evidence against the Dvorak keyboard. It was a carefully controlled experiment designed to examine the costs and benefits of switching to Dvorak. It unreservedly concluded that retraining typists on Dvorak was inferior to retraining on QWERTY.

In the first phase of the experiment, 10 government typists were retrained on the Dvorak keyboard. It took well over 25 days of four-hour-a-day training for these typists to catch up to their old QWERTY speeds. (Compare this to the Navy study's results.) When the typists had finally caught up to their old speeds, the second phase of the experiment began. The newly trained Dvorak typists continued training and a group of 10 QWERTY typists (matched in skill to the Dvorak typists) began a parallel program to improve their skills. In this second phase the Dvorak typists progressed less quickly with further Dvorak training than did QWERTY typists training on QWERTY keyboards. Thus Strong concluded that Dvorak training would never be able to amortize its costs. He recommended instead that the government provide further training in the QWERTY keyboard for QWERTY typists.

The GSA study attempted to control carefully for the abilities and treatments of the two groups. The study design directly paralleled the decision that a real firm or a real government agency might face: Is it worthwhile to retrain its present typists? If Strong's study is correct, it is not efficient for current typists to switch to Dvorak. The study also implied that the eventual typing speed would be greater with QWERTY than with Dvorak, although this conclusion was not emphasized.

Much of the other evidence that has been used to support Dvorak's superiority actually can be used to make a case against Dvorak. We have the 1953 Australian Post Office study already mentioned, which needed to remove psychological impediments to superior performance. A 1973 study based on six typists at Western Electric found that after 104 hours of training on Dvorak, typists were 2.6 percent faster than they had been on QWERTY. Similarly, a 1978 study at Oregon State University indicated that after 100 hours of training, typists were up to 97.6 percent of their old QWERTY speed. Both of these retraining times are similar to those reported by Strong but not to those in the Navy study. But unlike Strong's study neither of these studies included parallel retraining on QWERTY keyboards. As Strong points out, even experienced QWERTY typists increase their speed on QWERTY if they are given additional training.

Ergonomic studies also confirm that the advantages of Dvorak are either small or nonexistent. For example, A. Miller and J. Thomas, two researchers at the IBM Research Laboratory, writing in the *International Journal of Man-Machine Studies*, conclude that "no alternative has shown a realistically significant advantage over the QWERTY for general purpose typing." Other studies based on analysis of hand-and-finger motions find differences of only a few percentage points between Dvorak and QWERTY. The consistent finding in ergonomic studies is that the results imply no clear advantage for Dvorak, and certainly no advantage of the magnitude that is so often claimed.

QWERTY's Competition

Remington's early commercial rivals were numerous, offered substantial variations on the typewriter, and in some cases enjoyed moderate success. This should come as no surprise. Entrepreneurs in the late 19th century would have realized that the typewriter market was potentially vast, in the same way that Netscape, AT&T, and Microsoft are drooling over the potential of the Internet at the end of the 20th century.

The largest and most important QWERTY rivals were the Hall, Caligraph, and Crandall machines, which sold in relatively large numbers. Two other manufacturers offered their own versions of an ideal keyboard: Hammond in 1893 and Blickensderfer in 1889. Many of these companies went on to success in the typewriter market, although, in the end, they all produced QWERTY keyboards. So manufacturing prowess was not a problem for QWERTY's rivals.

In the 1880s and 1890s typewriters were generally sold to offices not already staffed with typists. Potential typists were learning to type from scratch. A manufacturer that chose to compete using an alternative keyboard had a window of opportunity, since standards were not yet established. As late as 1923, typewriter manufacturers operated placement services for typists and were an important source of typists to businesses. A keyboard that allowed more rapid training and faster typing should have done well. And switching old typewriters to a new keyboard was not particularly expensive—only $5.00 for resoldering in the 1930s.

There were also direct tests of these competing keyboards. Typing competitions, it turns out, were quite common in the late 1800s. The Cincinnati contest was not the rare event claimed by Beeching, and McGurrin was not the world's only touch typist. Once again, the facts have been twisted to make a better tale. We did a search in the *New York Times* in 1888 and 1889. We found numerous typing contests and demonstrations of speed involving many different machines, with various manufacturers claiming to hold the speed record.

In February 1889, under the headline "Wonderful Typing," the *New York Times* reported on a typing demonstration given the previous day in Brooklyn by Thomas Osborne of Rochester, New York. The *Times* reported that Osborne "holds the championship for fast typing, having accomplished 126 words a minute at Toronto August 13 last." In the Brooklyn demonstration he typed 142 words per minute in a five-minute test, 179 words per minute in a single minute, and 198 words per minute for 30 seconds. He was accompanied by George McBride, who typed 129 words per minute blindfolded. Both men used the non-QWERTY Caligraph machine.

The *Times* offered that "the Caligraph people have chosen a very pleasant and effective way of proving not only the superior speed of their machine, but the falsity of reports widely published that writing blindfolded was not feasible on that instrument." Note that this was just months after McGurrin's Cincinnati victory.

There were other contests and a good number of victories for McGurrin and Remington. On August 2, 1888, just weeks after the Cincinnati contest, the *Times* reported a New York contest won by McGurrin with a speed of 95.8 words per minute in a five-minute dictation. In light of the received history, according to which McGurrin is the only person to have memorized the keyboard, it is interesting to note the strong performance of his rivals. May Orr typed 95.2 words per minute, and M. Grant typed 93.8 words per minute. Again, on January 9, 1889, the *Times* reported a McGurrin victory under the headline "Remington Still Leads the List."

Clearly, typists other than McGurrin could touch type, and machines other than Remington were competitive. These events have largely been ignored. But if we are interested in whether the QWERTY keyboard's existence can be attributed to more than happenstance or an inventor's whim, these events are crucial. The other keyboards did compete. They just couldn't surpass QWERTY. So we cannot attribute the success of the QWERTY keyboard either to a lack of alternatives or to the chance association of this keyboard arrangement with the only touch typist or the only mechanically adequate typewriter.

There is further evidence of QWERTY's viability in its survival throughout the world. As typing moved to countries outside the United States, any QWERTY momentum could have been only a minor influence, yet the basic configuration has been adopted with only minor variations in virtually all countries with similar alphabets. What's more, the advent of computer keyboards, which can easily be reprogrammed to any configuration, lowers the cost of converting to Dvorak to essentially zero (not counting retraining). Yet few computer users have adopted the Dvorak keyboard.

Epilogue

The vitality of markets is that they allow competing alternatives to demonstrate their capabilities. The primary players in this drama are entrepreneurs, a group largely missing from the economic theories that claim to establish the potential for this new kind of market failure. These game-theory models limit firms to an artificially narrow choice of actions, while actual entrepreneurs look for ways to overcome supposed "lock-in." In theory, for instance, there's no such thing as a training course. Entrepreneurs, as we have argued in other writings, are the ones who will bring about the demise of an inefficient standard. Producers of alternative keyboards were motivated to cash in on the success allowed in a market-based economy. That they failed suggests that the non-QWERTY arrangements held no real advantage.

The QWERTY keyboard cannot be said to constitute evidence of any systematic tendency for markets to err. Very simply, no competing keyboard has offered enough advantage to warrant a change. The story of Dvorak's superiority is a myth or, perhaps more properly, a hoax.

In April 1990, we published a more detailed version of this material in a *Journal of Law and Economics* article titled "The Fable of the Keys." This journal is well known and has published some of the most influential articles in economics. In the six years since we published that article there has been no attempt to refute any of our factual claims, to discredit the GSA study, or to resurrect the Navy study. Unless some new evidence is produced to support a claim of QWERTY's inferiority to Dvorak, how can it even be said that there are two sides to a legitimate scientific disagreement over the keyboard?

Yet the QWERTY myth continues to be cited as if it were the truth. Krugman's book has a 1994 copyright. Frank and Cook's copyright is 1995. In a 1992 article in *Industrial and Corporate Change,* Paul David cites the QWERTY example, as do Michael Katz and Carl Shapiro in their Spring 1994 article in the *Journal of Economic Perspectives.*

In a 1995 article on chaos theory, Michael Schermer goes on at length about the need for examples of path dependence. With that, he devotes an entire section, titled "The QWERTY Principle of History," to repeating the myth of Dvorak superiority. The *Social Science Citation Index* for 1994 shows a total of 28 citations to Paul David's 1985 *American Economic Review* article presenting the QWERTY myth (the very large majority of these are uncritical uses of the QWERTY story). And there is no sign of abatement. The Citation Index for the first two-thirds of 1995, which is all that is available as of this writing, shows 25 citations. If academics keep using a false example, authors of popular articles can hardly be held to higher standards of scholarship.

Apparently the theory of path dependence and lock-in to inferior technologies is in trouble without the QWERTY example. Apparently the cost of giving up this example is greater than the discomfort associated with its illegitimate use. Apparently the typewriter example is of such importance to many writers because it can so easily persuade people that an interventionist technology policy is necessary. How else to explain its continued use in this literature? Since an interventionist technology policy is no more likely to benefit consumers than are the myriad other government interventions in the market, we should not be surprised that good examples are largely fictional.

July 1996

Dense Thinkers

"New Urbanism," the latest fad in urban planning, promises less traffic, better air, and lower taxes. Here's what it really delivers.

Randal O'Toole

IN 1992, RESIDENTS OF PORTLAND, OREGON, were terrified that their growing city was fast becoming the Pacific Northwest's version of Los Angeles—as they saw it, a congested, polluted city with too many cars and too little sense of community. The threat was considered so serious that a traditional anti-growth response—a tough, comprehensive land-use plan limited to the actual city boundaries—wasn't enough. To prevent the paving of Portland, area voters signed off on the creation of Metro, a regional planning authority with dictatorial land-use planning powers over 24 cities and three counties.

To hear Metro boosters describe it, Portland-area residents can now rest easy. The concrete landscape of Southern California won't be copied any time soon in the Beaver State. Far from it. Though Metro's experts predict that the region's population will grow by 75 percent in the next few decades, the agency has a plan that will accommodate these newcomers while promoting "livable neighborhoods," "protecting open space," "reducing dependence on the automobile," and maintaining "affordable housing" and lower infrastructure costs. All in all, an idyllic package: better neighborhoods, pedestrian-friendly streets, cheaper housing, and lower taxes.

What will it take to reach such goals? Only the community's desire—as codified in Metro's planning and zoning laws—to squeeze more people and more businesses into smaller spaces under tighter

regulatory control. Metro's regional plan restricts development outside of an urban growth boundary that allows only a 6 percent expansion of the urbanized area for at least two decades. The plan also
doubles or triples the population density of many neighborhoods by
rezoning them to require apartments, row houses, or other high-density housing whenever new construction is undertaken.

Additionally, Metro sets strict population targets for each of the 24
cities and three counties under its dominion, forcing them to convert
10,000 acres of prime farmlands, golf courses, city parks, and other
open spaces to high-density residential or commercial uses. Finally,
Metro plans to spend billions of dollars to build 100 miles of rail transit lines to free residents from their cars.

Reduced congestion, better air quality, lower taxes. No wonder
Portland has gotten great national press and praise. There's only one
little problem: Metro's own data say the plan is doomed to failure.

Details, Details

Consider, for instance, Metro's bold, confident prediction that its plan
will double public transit usage. Since transit currently carries less
than 2.5 percent of Portland-area trips, doubling that doesn't get you
very far toward a car-free utopia. Similarly, Metro expects at best a
modest decline in auto usage, from 92 percent of urban trips to 88
percent. In fact, given the 75 percent population increase that Metro
predicts over 50 years, that translates into *five* cars driving around for
every *three* cars today. Accordingly, planners estimate that traffic congestion will triple or quadruple and that air pollution will increase.

Then there's the tax question. Metro wants to pay for the rail lines
it says will lure people out of autos by adding billions of dollars to local property taxes. And to promote high-density development in an
area already glutted with apartments, Portland and other area cities
are giving developers millions of dollars in tax breaks and other subsidies that will ultimately come out of residents' pockets. Meanwhile,
housing prices are skyrocketing because of the artificial land shortage
created by the urban growth boundary, giving Portland the least affordable housing in the nation after only San Francisco.

Oh, and there's one more thing. Remember how Metro was supposed
to save Portland from becoming Oregon's answer to L.A.? In 1994, Metro
planners studied the nation's 50 largest urban areas to see which one was

closest to the future they envisioned for Portland—one with higher population densities and fewer roads. It turned out that the metropolitan area—defined as all of the land in and around a city whose population density exceeds 1,000 people per square mile—with the highest population density also had the fewest miles of freeway per capita. Its name: Los Angeles. While the *city* of Los Angeles proper has a lower density than New York City, the Los Angeles metro area is nearly one-third denser than the New York metro area, which includes—among other places—northeastern New Jersey and Long Island. Far from being the incarnation of evil, auto-dependent sprawl, L.A. was the model to emulate.

To their credit, Metro planners did fess up to this unexpected and uncomfortable finding, daring to write, "With respect to density and road per capita mileage, [Los Angeles] displays an investment pattern we desire to replicate" in Portland. Of course, saying this out loud would have meant instant death for their plans, if not their persons. So the document in which this conclusion is reached is available only to people willing to pay $10 for a 60-page booklet filled with eyeball-glazing graphs and statistics.

Here's another irony: Despite such glaring and self-evident contradictions, Portland has become a shining beacon for urban planners, who envy Metro's Singapore-like regulatory authority. Places ranging from Minneapolis–St. Paul (with a metro population of about 3 million) to Missoula, Montana, (43,000) have adopted plans based on the Portland model.

Suburban Renewal

Welcome to the crazy world of the New Urbanism, the latest fad in urban planning. The New Urbanism is a broad-based movement of planners, architects, environmentalists, central city governments, downtown business interests, transit agencies, and engineering and construction firms that has coalesced over the past 10 years. Proponents seek to recreate the high-density cities of the 19th and early 20th centuries. To impose their will, New Urbanists take particular aim at suburbs and the automobiles that helped make them possible. Indeed, a more appropriate name for the movement might be Suburban Renewal, since the New Urbanists' chief goal is to convert the suburbs—invariably regarded as banal, ugly, sterile, and inefficient—

into something like inner-city areas.

A recent Sierra Club study, "The Dark Side of the American Dream," is representative of New Urbanist thinking. "The automobile way of life is unhealthy, anti-social, and unsustainable," claims the report, which was partly funded by the U.S. Environmental Protection Agency (EPA). The New Urbanism, in contrast, seeks to create neighborhoods "where jobs, shopping, services, and recreation are all nearby" so that people can get around without cars. Low-density suburban development—pejoratively termed "sprawl"—leads to "increased congestion, longer commutes, increased dependence on fossil fuels, crowded schools, worsening air and water pollution, lost open space and wetlands, increased flooding, destroyed habitat, higher taxes and dying city centers."

None of these claims is documented, which isn't surprising, because none of them is true. What *is* true is that the Sierra Club, the American Planning Association, and other New Urbanists have definite ideas about how the suburbs should be rebuilt. Their plans usually call for the following:

• Urban growth boundaries to restrict suburban expansion.
• Prescriptive zoning and development subsidies to force higher-density development inside growth boundaries. Prescriptive zoning mandates higher densities whenever building or rebuilding occurs. If your house burns down, you may even be required to build an apartment in its place.
• Discouraging driving through "traffic calming" measures such as narrow streets, parking limits, roadway barriers, and zoning codes that require shopping malls to turn their parking lots into apartments. There may also be rules requiring employers to write up plans to reduce workers' auto commuting.
• A focus on hugely expensive—and hugely ineffective—rail transit to the exclusion of highway construction or expansion.

New Urbanists firmly believe they can change people's behavior by redesigning the cities in which they live. That's not an indefensible notion, but it's not as easy as it sounds. Consider the fate of Laguna West, a widely touted Sacramento suburb designed by California architect and New Urban guru Peter Calthorpe. Calthorpe thinks suburbanites suffer from a "sense of frustration and placelessness." To fix this, he designs what he calls "pedestrian pockets" or "transit-oriented developments" that plug people into where they live.

As envisioned by Calthorpe, Laguna West would have consisted of a "transit center" surrounded by high-density apartments and condominiums. A ring of single-family homes on small lots would surround the high-density core. Scattered throughout would be stores, offices, and other commercial uses. Most people would be able to walk to shopping, and many would be able to walk to work or the transit center.

But Laguna West was a financial failure. No one wanted to live in the high-density area, and as a result its developer went bankrupt. Instead, a new builder put low-density housing in the core. While those houses were actually salable, their presence also meant that most transit riders had to drive to the transit center. Since Calthorpe provided no parking at the transit center, drivers parked in front of other people's homes. The homeowners objected and successfully lobbied to have the transit center moved outside of the development. Meanwhile, residents do all of their shopping at a conventional strip mall outside the development. The only commercial use inside Laguna West—a quick oil-change joint—hardly testifies to people's decreased dependence on the auto.

If it's hard to design a successful suburb from scratch, it's that much more difficult to shift residents from already established patterns of land use and behavior. But urban planners all over the country are trying to impose New Urban ideals on existing suburbs and cities. Metro even hired Calthorpe to show them how pedestrian pockets and transit-oriented developments could be scattered throughout the Portland area.

Congestion as "Positive Urban Development"

The vision of a place where people walk to the grocery store and take the train to work certainly has its charms. But far from delivering urban zones from the curse of "auto-dependent" lifestyles, New Urbanist policies have consistently led to significant increases in highway congestion; deteriorating air quality (because autos pollute more in slow-moving, congested traffic); dramatic infrastructure shortfalls as sewer, water, schools, and other systems designed for low-density cities must be rebuilt for higher densities; rapidly increasing housing prices as land becomes scarce; and disappearing urban open spaces such as parks and golf courses as developers turn them into residential and other developments. Such negative outcomes are not accidental. Indeed, they are the predictable, inevitable, and often *intended* consequences of New Urbanist plans.

Consider the New Urbanist claim that increased population density will reduce traffic congestion. The idea makes some intuitive sense: If people are closer to one another, to jobs, and to shopping, they won't need to drive so much to get to their destinations. But the reality is that while higher population density may slightly reduce per capita driving, it vastly increases congestion and pollution. Say, for instance, that doubling density reduces per capita driving by 10 percent. Two hundred percent as many people each driving 90 percent as much results in 180 percent as many cars. Unless the road network is expanded by 80 percent—which New Urbanists would oppose—80 percent more traffic produces a huge increase in congestion.

Real-world experience suggests that 10 percent less per capita driving with a doubling of density is about the best that can be expected. In fact, it may be overly optimistic. What's more, Census Bureau and Federal Highway Administration data show little correlation between density and the number of miles people drive. The Miami, Ft. Lauderdale, and West Palm Beach metropolitan areas all cover about the same number of square miles. Miami has twice the density of West Palm Beach, and per capita driving is indeed about 10 percent less in Miami. But residents of Ft. Lauderdale, whose density is halfway between those of Miami and West Palm Beach, drive more than residents of both areas.

In Portland, planners have used a sophisticated computer model to predict the effects of their plans on driving habits. Under their most optimistic scenarios, by the year 2040, auto use will drop from 92 percent of all area trips to 88 percent. Since planners assume a 75 percent increase in population, this translates to a massive expansion in traffic and congestion—they figure three to four times the current number of congested road miles.

But that's OK, say Metro officials in one of their we've-got-to-destroy-the-village-in-order-save-it moments, because congestion actually "signals positive urban development." Indeed, though they rarely talk about it in public, a major short-term New Urbanist goal is to *increase*, not reduce, congestion. After all, clogged, slow-moving traffic might encourage a few people to get out of their cars, while punishing those who do not.

Minnesota's Twin Cities Metropolitan Council takes a similar view of increased congestion. In addition to planning the Minneapolis–St. Paul region, the council runs the area's public transit system. Bus ridership has declined by 40 percent in the past 25 years, while highway traffic has greatly increased, with further increases projected. So what does the Metropolitan Council plan to do? Build no more roads for at least 20 years. The council wants to promote ridership on its buses by increasing highway congestion to intolerable levels. "As traffic congestion builds," says the council's Transportation Plan, "alternative travel modes will become more attractive." Of course, as congestion builds, alternative places to live will become more attractive too.

If New Urbanist attitudes toward traffic congestion are muddled— they seek to alleviate traffic congestion by increasing it—their attitudes toward commuting are no less contorted. As with the assumed relationship between density and miles driven, the real world refutes New Urbanist claims that low-density suburban development forces people to spend more time commuting. Census data show that, regardless of the year or the urban area's size, commuters spend an average of 20 to 25 minutes getting to work. This is as true in Los Angeles (with a metro area population of 12 million) as it is in Houma, Louisiana (68,000).

Indeed, if New Urbanists were really concerned about long commutes, they would advocate more road construction and less emphasis on mass transit: The average public transit commuter travels a shorter distance yet spends more time commuting than the average driver. The first-, second-, and third-longest average urban commute times are in New York, Washington, and Chicago—which, not coincidentally, are the urban areas with the first-, second-, and third-highest shares of commuters riding mass transit.

A similar paradox undergirds New Urbanist air quality policies. Since automobiles pollute the air, New Urbanists convinced Congress to deny federal highway funds to cities with significant air pollution problems. Not only does that policy make it tough for congested areas to build bigger highways, it almost certainly makes pollution worse in those cities. That's because most auto pollution is a function of congestion and density: Cars use more energy and pollute more when they drive slowly or in stop-and-go traffic than when they drive fast in free-flowing traffic. The best prescription for reducing air pollution, then, is to reduce congestion by adding highway capacity or making other improvements to speed up traffic.

Dirty air is also a function of density, which promotes the concentration of dangerous levels of pollutants. The EPA rates urban air pollution as extreme, serious, moderate, marginal, and none. Not surprisingly, the worst pollution is found in the urban areas with the densest populations. Thus, the New Urban prescription of increased density with few new roads doubly increases urban air pollution.

Sprawling Costs
Worsened air quality is a price New Urbanists apparently are willing to pay. But when it comes to what they call "the costs of sprawl," they're not so generous. As with most of their core beliefs, New Urbanist cost analyses of suburban development rely more on faith than on empirical data. Hence, a 1974 Council on Environmental Quality report arguing that low-density development imposed higher costs for urban services—roads, sewers, schools, and the like—than higher densities remains a holy text among the New Urbanist faithful. That the document was based entirely on speculative and unverified estimates doesn't seem important; neither does the fact that numerous studies since that time have found that taxes and urban service costs are actually higher in high-density areas.

A 1992 Duke University study, for example, analyzed data from 247 counties that contain well over half the population of the United States. The researchers found that, above a density of 250 people per square mile (which is a rural density), costs rose as densities increased. In fact, urban service costs in areas of 24,000 people per square mile—a density typical of the core of older cities such as Philadelphia and Boston—were nearly 50 percent greater than in areas of 250 people per square mile.

But even if a new high-density development did impose lower costs than a low-density development, it does not follow that it costs less to rebuild a low-density suburb to high densities than it would to simply build a new low-density suburb. That's because infrastructure such as sewers, water, roads, and schools are built for the densities they serve. Suddenly doubling densities means tearing up streets for utilities, widening roads (or increasing congestion), and buying land for new schools.

Residents of San Diego know all about that. In 1980, the city adopted a New Urban plan that discouraged development outside of an urban ring and promoted "infill" development in the core area ("infill" is the development of vacant lots and redevelopment of existing residential areas to higher densities.) Ten years later, the sewage system was regularly breaking down, traffic congestion had significantly increased, and the city estimated that it needed $1 billion to bring urban infrastructure up to its 1980 levels. Ironically, the Sierra Club cited San Diego as one of the nation's worst examples of sprawl.

In a related way, New Urbanists get it backward when it comes to housing and living costs: Policies they think will lead to cheaper housing and living costs actually make things more expensive. In low-density cities such as Houston and Minnesota's Twin Cities, land represents a tiny fraction of the value of a home. In higher-density cities, it's common for land to account for half or more of the value of a home. This means that people of a given income level in a high-density city can afford less house than they might buy in a low-density area. That's one reason why the suburbs are so popular—you tend to get more house (and property) for the money.

The same basic economic reality affects retailing as well. A major reason why megastores and supermarkets gravitate to the outskirts of areas is that land is cheaper and allows for bigger buildings. The New Urbanist dream of shopping at a corner market may be quaint, but it ignores two basic things people look for in stores: good prices and a wide selection of products, neither of which is characteristic of small shops (as any inner-city grocery shopper will tell you). Stores get bigger when they can serve more people. When they get bigger, they can offer a greater variety of products, fresher produce, and lower prices than small stores. Corner grocery stores might serve the occasional emergency need for a quart of milk or six-pack of beer. But most people will do most of their shopping where choices are greater and costs are lower—which means that they will shop by car.

In spite of New Urbanist claims, such residential and retailing mobility hasn't led to unchecked sprawl. According to the U.S. Department of Agriculture, more than 95 percent of the lower 48 states remains undeveloped. In fact, the vast majority of Americans live in the less than 3 percent of the country that is urbanized (defined by the Census Bureau as more than 1,000 people per square mile). The only open spaces that are truly threatened are golf courses, u-pick farms, and large suburban backyards. All are targeted by New Urbanists for "infill" development. Portland is even selling park lands at discount prices to entice developers into building high-density apartments.

The Congestion Coalition

Despite its theoretical and practical failings, the New Urbanism is quietly sweeping the nation. Portland's Metro recently passed the most restrictive plan ever adopted for a U.S. city. The legislatures of Maryland, Minnesota, and Washington have enacted "smart growth" or "growth management" laws, both New Urbanist euphemisms. Pressure groups in Denver, Phoenix, Albuquerque, Tampa, and other cities are demanding and getting New Urbanist plans for their communities. If you live in a metropolitan area, your city planning bureau is probably infested with New Urbanists.

This success is all the more remarkable given the manifest and widely recognized failure of grand, utopian planning schemes. As Jane Jacobs' *The Death and Life of Great American Cities* showed, the urban renewal movement in the 1950s and '60s destroyed living communities and replaced them with sterile monuments to human arrogance. In *Nowhere to Go*, Fuller Torrence credibly blames much of the homeless problem on planners who demolished the low-income apartments where many of these people lived. Planners also created many of the public housing disasters of the past few decades. The history of urban planning is a lesson in the law of unintended consequences.

How do the New Urbanists respond to the failure of their forebears? They not only admit that past planners made mistakes, they themselves blame most urban ills on previous generations of planners. Their perverse, if savvy, solution is to give planners *more* power, so they can correct past mistakes through even stronger rules and regulations.

New Urbanist supporters include planners, environmentalists, federal bureaucrats, central city officials, downtown businesses, and construction companies. Their motivations range from idealism to economic self-interest, but all have a stake in maintaining or rebuilding tightly packed urban cores. Together, they also have the clout to get things done.

Planners and environmentalists are among the idealists in what can be dubbed the "congestion coalition." Recognizing that traffic congestion is one of the major concerns of urban residents, most New Urbanist planners no doubt think their convoluted approach will eventually alleviate the situation. (To put a more cynical spin on their designs, they can at least rest assured that increases in congestion caused by their plans will lead to calls for more planners.) Environmentalists' idealism is less concerned with urban quality of life per se than with preserving what they see as pristine wilderness; New Urbanist nostrums of denser urban areas and less automobile usage are means to that end.

By themselves, however, planners and environmentalists are not powerful enough to persuade anyone to implement the New Urbanism. That's where the other members of the congestion coalition come in. If planners and environmentalists supply the vision, bureaucrats, local officials, downtown businesses, and contractors provide the money and the might to make New Urbanist dreams a reality.

A number of friendly federal agencies directly finance the New Urbanist agenda. For instance, as part of its Transportation Partners program, the EPA gives several hundred nonprofit organizations money to lobby for transit and pedestrian ways and against highways. The avowed goal of the program is to reduce the number of "vehicle miles traveled." (In true New Urbanist fashion, the claims to success are meager at best: The EPA boasts these "partners" reduced annual vehicle travel by 1.25 billion miles in 1997. That's a questionable figure, but even if valid, it represents less than 0.1 percent of all urban driving.)

The U.S. Department of Transportation (DOT) also supports the New Urbanism. The Federal Transit Administration, the branch of the department charged with promoting transportation planning, strongly influences urban spending because New Urbanists convinced Congress that cities receiving federal transportation funds should be forced to create regional transportation plans. The onerous planning process gives New Urbanists plenty of opportunities to skew the results their way. For example, federal transit officials grade local transportation planners for the effort they make at getting cyclists, pedestrians, and transit riders—but not auto drivers—involved in the planning process. The transportation bill recently passed by Congress provides $20 million a year in local grants similar to the EPA's Transportation Partners program.

New Urbanism is also supported by DOT and Department of Housing and Urban Development requirements that urban areas have metropolitan planning organizations (MPOs) representing most or all local governments. Originally conceived as clearinghouses for federal grants, many MPOs function instead as political safety valves. As Brookings Institution economist Anthony Downs notes in *Stuck in Traffic*, a regional planning agency "can take controversial stands without making its individual members commit themselves to those stands. Each member can claim that 'the organization' did it or blame all the other members."

Urban Godsends

That's exactly what has happened in Portland, where Metro has ultimate planning authority over two dozen cities and three counties. Metro requires these cities and counties to rezone existing neighborhoods to meet its population targets. Far from resisting such targets, many cities view them as a way to increase their tax base by packing more residents into their jurisdictions, and some even asked for higher ones. But when neighborhoods object to being rezoned, they are told, "We don't have a choice. Metro is making us do it."

The turn to MPOs is a godsend especially to officials in large cities seeking to consolidate, if not increase, their power, which has been on the wane for most of the postwar period. Since 1950, nearly all urban growth has been outside big cities. That massive population shift toward suburbs and mid-size cities has made it tougher for traditional central cities to generate tax revenue and to qualify for pork-barrel spending tied to population. The MPOs change all that.

Because of its relative size, the strongest player in any MPO is invariably the largest city in the region. The MPO gives such cities an instrument to redirect development dollars their way and to get revenge on the suburbs (tellingly characterized as "godawful trash" by one Portland City Council member). The same holds true for downtown business interests: Like their public-sector counterparts, they resent the shopping malls, office campuses, and modern factories that have grown up in the suburbs. For central city officials and businesses, then, the New Urbanism represents the latest ploy to maintain their way of life.

Of course, it's unlikely it will succeed any more than the billions of federal and local dollars already spent trying to maintain particular urban areas. The problem with most central cities is that they were built in an age when primitive transportation and communications dictated high densities; people had to live near one another. The "decline" of cities that officials worry so much about is due to the fact that cars, telephones, and electricity make it possible for people to live in lower densities—and most choose to do so.

Fretting over urban "decline" is misguided in another sense too. Downtown interests, argues Joel Garreau in the brilliant *Edge City*, "believe settlement patterns to be a zero-sum game": Any gain in the suburbs represents a loss for downtown. Yet Garreau notes that even as suburbs have boomed, American "downtowns have been going through their most striking revivals of this century. From coast to coast . . . downtowns are flourishing."

To be sure, most recent downtown growth has been in the areas of arts and entertainment. This fails to impress downtown traditionalists, who still think downtowns should be the main retail and commercial centers of a city. So New Urbanist prescriptions, such as limits on new shopping malls and parking restrictions in existing malls, are appealing to downtown businesses. If new stores can't open in the suburbs, goes this line of thought, they'll have to set up shop downtown.

Such zero-sum thinking undergirds what is perhaps *the* defining characteristic of the New Urbanism: an undying reverence for light-rail networks. Central city officials and downtown interests know that, if transportation dollars go into highways, they will be spent in the suburbs, where most growth is taking place. But if those funds are spent on a rail transit system, the vast majority will be spent in the central city because most, if not all, rail lines will radiate from a downtown.

Light rail not only restores to downtown some of its former central-ity, it represents a huge pork-barrel project for the fifth member of the congestion coalition: the civil construction industry. With the Inter-state Highway System effectively completed and strong resistance to new roads in the cities, the construction industry has been looking for work. What better opportunity exists than to rebuild the rail systems that moved urbanites in the pre-automobile age?

New Urbanists spuriously claim that light rail is more efficient than highways. For the construction industry, the attraction of rail systems is that they cost much more to build than highways. A typical ur-ban freeway costs about $5 million to $10 million per lane-mile, or $20 million to $40 million per mile of four-lane road. By comparison, Portland just opened a new light-rail line that cost $55 million per mile—and is planning a new line that will cost a whopping $100 mil-lion per mile. (That neither of these lines will carry as many people as a single freeway lane is the sort of consideration that never seems to make it onto the planner's ledger sheet.)

Light rail isn't always as expensive as in Portland, but its costs when finished are almost always far greater than when originally proposed. For the construction industry, then, rail is not only less controversial than highways. Because of typical cost overruns and "gold-plating," rail adds up to huge profits for a wide variety of consulting, engineer-ing, and building firms.

Light rail does nothing to reduce congestion; in fact, because most transit systems sacrifice more-popular bus routes once they introduce less-popular trains, it typically *increases* congestion. But that is not the construction industry's concern. So long as New Urban interests can channel money toward rail, the construction industry will be only too happy to finance the political campaigns of New Urbanist city officials and any ballot measures that might be required to obtain local rail funding.

The Metro Dilemma

Given the strength of the congestion coalition, it's no surprise that the New Urbanism has gotten as far as it has. While the movement has visible critics—including Joel Garreau, Peter Gordon of the Univer-sity of Southern California, and John Charles of the Portland-based Cascade Policy Institute—sometimes it seems as if it is an unstoppable civic juggernaut. Beyond underscoring its inconsistencies and misrepresentations, one way of challenging the New Urbanism is to recognize its place in the urban planning tradition.

Far from being the "scientific" and "rigorous" school of thought its proponents claim, the New Urbanism is best understood as simply the latest attempt by planners to pass narrow, essentially moral judgments on American cities. Beginning with the "City Beautiful" movement in the late 19th century, planners believed that good design would lead to a "new urban man" who would be a morally upright member of the community. Given the proper architectural circumstances, planners theorized, urban residents would work hard and not turn to crime; social ills such as drunkenness would disappear.

Early land-use planners believed that the crowded, dirty cities where houses were mingled with factories and commercial uses should be replaced by low-density residential areas separated from other uses. There, workers would be free from easily transmitted diseases and have cleaner air. A few decades later, in the 1920s, early transportation planners hoped that good roads would revitalize downtowns—threatened even then by "sprawl"—by reducing congestion and attracting new investments. But all the freeways did is give residents and employers a quicker escape from the crowded central cities.

New Urbanism has learned well the lesson that roads let people go where they want to go. They've wedded that insight to the early land-use planners' goal of improving people's moral behavior. The immoral behavior New Urbanists want to end now is driving, which they see as wasteful, noxious, and anti-social. Interestingly, to stop people from driving, they are trying to turn entire urban areas into the crowded, mixed-use cities that 19th-century planners found so degrading. "The politics of stasis," says interstate highway historian Mark Rose, "has displaced the politics of growth." What hasn't changed is the belief that people cannot or should not be left to their own devices when it comes to deciding where and how to live their lives.

If the New Urbanists put the actual quality of life of urban residents ahead of their theories about quality of life, they would chart a vastly different course. The best prescription for the central cities is to let them depopulate as people move out to the suburbs. As their densities fall, they will become more attractive places to live. This has happened in Cleveland, the former national joke which has become one of the more livable cities in the Midwest. But such a policy bruises the egos of the city officials who want to maintain political hegemony over the suburbs; it also fails to satisfy the demands of the rest of the congestion coalition.

So the New Urbanists turn instead to regional planning, growth boundaries, suburban "densification," congestion-inducing road policies, and light-rail transit. This is a prescription for destroying not only the central cities but the suburbs as well. As baby boomers retire and telecommuters increase, fewer and fewer people will need to live in urban areas. If the New Urbanists succeed in making the suburbs as unlivable as many central cities already are, people living in cities and suburbs are likely to become "exurbanites," moving out to rural areas. Exurbanization will be sprawl with a vengeance, as people forbidden to live on quarter-acre suburban lots happily move to five-to-40-acre rural lots.

A recent survey of Portland residents should give the New Urbanists pause, even as it apparently confirms their agenda. The poll found that most Portlanders do in fact support Metro's plan. But then the poll asked where people would live if they had a choice: the city, the suburbs, or rural areas. The same majority said "rural areas." That response might seem odd, but it's in keeping with the New Urbanism, which produces in abundance everything its adherents claim to oppose: congestion, pollution, unaffordable housing, and higher taxes.

January 1999

Copy Catfight

How intellectual property laws stifle popular culture

Jesse Walker

ON AUGUST 19, 1999, IN LOS ANGELES, a mild act of censorship took place. Twentieth Century Fox, the colossus behind the cult series *Buffy the Vampire Slayer*, sent a letter to Alexander Thompson, a 35-year-old data processor and devoted *Buffy* fan. Thompson had spent countless hours transcribing each episode of the show, complete with descriptions of the scenery and action, and had posted the results on the World Wide Web, to his fellow fans' delight. Joss Whedon, the show's writer and producer, had praised Thompson for the job he'd done, even autographing one of the transcripts.

Whedon, however, did not own the copyright to his work. Fox did. And Fox, the company told Thompson, "has a legal responsibility . . . to prevent the unauthorized distribution of its proprietary material."

In other words, Thompson had to remove his transcripts from his Web site or face a lawsuit.

As far as repression goes, this no doubt sounds trivial. Fox is clearly being stupid—Thompson's transcripts were a resource for fans, not a substitute for the show—but the company was within its legal rights as the owner of the *Buffy* program. What it did was obnoxious, silly, and bad business, but it's hardly a threat to free speech. Right?

Don't be too sure. There is an inherent conflict between intellectual property rights and freedom of speech, a tension between your right to control a story you've written and my right to use it as raw material for my own work. Thanks to two trends, that tension is turning rapidly into a collision—one where more than the convenience of online *Buffy* fans is at stake.

On one hand, as information has grown more valuable, copyright and trademark law has become increasingly restrictive. At the same time, there has been, in the words of MIT media studies professor Henry Jenkins, an "explosion of grassroots, participatory culture," a new high-tech folkway that not only draws on pop culture but appropriates from it more easily than ever before, and disseminates itself on a wider scale.

Now the companies atop the culture industry, from Fox to Disney to LucasFilm, are starting to notice this alternate universe of fans, parodists, and collagists. They don't quite understand what they're finding, and for the most part they don't like it. And they've got the government on their side.

In theory, a copyright is simply an incentive to create: Compose something original, the Constitution says, and we'll make sure you get a chance to profit from it. Trademark law is even simpler. It's a protection against fraud and consumer confusion, a recognition that Nike shoes are a particular product, and that if I start selling some homemade slippers as "Nikes," I am deceiving my customers.

Copyrights, unlike trademarks, have always posed problems, even if you think they're necessary. They are, after all, government-granted monopolies; as such, they should be strictly limited and carefully watched. If someone wants to extend their reach, he'd better have a compelling argument for doing so, and lawmakers should approach his proposal with due skepticism.

Instead, Congress acts as a rubber stamp for copyright holders, especially the big campaign donors in the entertainment industry. At the dawn of the republic, copyrights lasted for just 14 years and could be renewed for another 14. This period has been gradually extended, especially lately: It has been lengthened 11 times in the last 40 years, most recently by the Sonny Bono Copyright Term Extension Act of 1998.

Before the Bono Act, new or recent works copyrighted by individuals were protected for life plus 50 years. Afterward, protection lasted for life plus 70 years. Corporate-owned copyrights were also extended by two decades, to 95 years, as were all copyrights for works produced before 1978. The push for the new law was spearheaded by Disney, whose most famous character, Mickey Mouse, was scheduled to enter the public domain in 2004, with Pluto, Goofy, and the rest following shortly thereafter. Disney is notoriously jealous with its cartoon cast: In one of the most famous copyright cases of the '70s, it successfully halted sales of *Air Pirates Funnies*, a risqué underground comic by Dan O'Neill featuring the Disney characters, even though the comic was clearly a *Mad*-style parody.

The prospect that just anyone would be allowed to produce his own Mickey merchandise was evidently unthinkable at Disney HQ, and the company exploited its connections to get the copyright extension passed. The very day Senate Majority Leader Trent Lott became a co-sponsor of the bill, the Center for Responsive Politics reports, the Disney Political Action Committee donated $1,000 to his campaign chest; within a month, it had also sent $20,000 in soft money to the National Republican Senatorial Committee. And Disney had help: Other entertainment giants, from Time-Warner to the Motion Picture Association of America, joined the lobbying effort, as did some well-known songwriters, such as Bob Dylan, and heirs of dead songwriters, such as George and Ira Gershwin.

The irony was rich: Disney, which draws heavily on public-domain characters and stories in its own products (Aladdin, the Little Mermaid, Mulan), was fighting to keep the cultural commons closed. And Dylan regularly bases his work on the chord structures, and sometimes lyrics, of older folk songs—"The Girl from the North Country" on "Scarborough Fair," "I Dreamed I Saw St. Augustine" on "I Dreamed I Saw Joe Hill Last Night." Yet there he was, demanding royalties from his music until 70 years after his death.

Meanwhile, the Gershwin heirs, who didn't even write the songs that keep them wealthy today, found themselves essentially arguing that the 20-year extension would somehow be a further incentive to their dead ancestors' creativity, a claim that smacks of either spiritualism or desperation.

"It's a joke," declares David Post, a professor of law at Temple University. "It's a disgrace. There is no better example that I can imagine, literally, of Congress caving in to small, highly focused special interests. There is no conceivable public benefit from the additional 20 years. Zero." Copyrights don't bother Post, but retroactive extensions of them, which by definition cannot affect the original creator's incentives, do. "Congress was bought," he continues. "This was the sale of legislation in the crudest form. They should be ashamed."

If the Bono bill's intended consequences are bad, its unintended effects are arguably worse. When it's unclear who owns a copyright—for an old B movie, say, or a cult writer's early short stories, or an ancient R&B record—that discourages companies from reissuing the work, even if there's considerable interest in reviving it. The potential legal hassle is simply too daunting.

Last October, the U.S. District Court for the District of Columbia rejected a suit alleging the Bono bill was unconstitutional; the plaintiffs have appealed the case, and it should be heard again by next August. One plaintiff, 56-year-old Eric Eldred of East Derry, New Hampshire, operates Eldritch Press, a popular Web site filled with digitized editions of old volumes, ranging from H.L. Mencken's *In Defense of Women* to books about boats. "I'm not interested in putting up works by Stephen King," he says. "I'm interested in books that are down a couple of tiers: books that are interesting, but that publishers don't find profitable to reprint." The new law threw some roadblocks in his way.

Consider *Horses and Men*, a 1923 collection of short stories by Sherwood Anderson. The book has long been out of print; the rights to it are owned by the Sherwood Anderson Trust, which makes money by putting out scholarly editions of Anderson's work. Many of the stories in *Horses and Men* will not be reprinted in any of their Anderson anthologies, and those that are will often have the punctuation "corrected" to reflect modern usage. Eldred would like to put the original book up on his Web site, so people can read the out-of-print tales and so they can compare Anderson's original punctuation to the new version. He expected the book to pass into the public domain in 1998, allowing him to do just that. But thanks to the Bono bill, the copyright won't expire for another 20 years.

And that's no aberration. Another 1923 book, Robert Frost's *New Hampshire*, has been out of print for more than 70 years; several of the poems have not been reprinted, and many of those which have been reprinted now include—this seems to be a theme—different punctuation marks. (It's also, Eldred notes, an attractive book in itself, with handsome woodcuts he'd like more people to see.) "Our real battle is not with the traditional publishers," Eldred explains. "It's not with people who want to make money publishing books. It's with people who want to lock up books."

A law that keeps old books out of the public domain does the same for old movies. One vocal opponent of the copyright extension is Sinister Video, a small company that specializes in reissuing old exploitation flicks. "There are literally thousands of works, particularly in the area of motion pictures, that are sitting on the shelf waiting for the freedom of the public domain," the company noted in a statement. "The large companies that own the rights to them have no intention of ever making most of those works available again on a widespread basis." Thanks to the Bono Act, "Copyrights on all works will be extended so that the major companies can continue to exploit the small percentage of works that are still profitable to them—the rest be damned!" Damned indeed: In 20 years, a lot of those "protected" movies will have physically disintegrated. (For that reason, a film preservation group and a movie archive have joined Eldred's suit against the Bono law.)

For those who can't wait for those movies to enter the public domain, there is a loose distribution network that might satisfy them. But it exists in a gray area: not quite illegal, but always subject to the possibility that someone will decide a tape violates his copyright. For the most part, the videos are available only by mail order, though some specialty stores carry them as well.

One such store is Cinefile Video, a film buff's nirvana located next to Los Angeles' famous Nuart theater. Founded last May by four refugees from another video shop, Cinefile carries tapes that range from obscure industrial films to footage from Orson Welles' unfinished *Don Quixote*, from Italian horror-porn to classic Soviet silent cinema, from ancient TV specials to Grade Z movie trailers. "We'll buy anything that we find that we know you just can't find anywhere else," reports co-owner Hadrian Belove, "even if I don't particularly like it. There's a certain respect I have for the archival value of having such really weird tapes."

Most of the store's wares are regular copyrighted tapes, though many of them have gone out of print. Some have copyrights that have expired; others were never copyrighted; with others, no one's sure who owns the rights at all, and someone decided to release the films anyway. Some are foreign movies that don't have official distributors in the United States, thus giving Americans the right to sell dubs of them on demand.

And then, Belove concludes, "There are certain companies that own things and purposefully don't release them, either because they think they're embarrassing or—who knows?—because of some vindictive streak." Disney, for example, will not allow anyone to sell or rent *Song of the South*, a 1946 film of Uncle Remus stories that is periodically damned for its alleged racism. It is indisputably illegal to carry those movies, and Cinefile will not stock them. Belove does have his own copies of several such tapes, however, and often personally lends them to his store's customers for free—thus moving the transaction out of the marketplace and out of the reach of the company lawyers.

Song of the South, of course, would be covered by a copyright whether or not the Bono bill was in effect. Disney's efforts to suppress it indicate that the trouble with intellectual property laws goes deeper than the length of time a work can be monopolized. It can erode free speech to monopolize a work at all.

The most dangerous thing about restrictive copyright laws isn't what they do to old works. It's what they do to new ones. Copyright has traditionally been tempered by the doctrine of "fair use," which allows a limited amount of appropriation for the purpose of parody or criticism. (That is why book critics, for example, do not have to get permission to quote the texts they are reviewing.) Fair use is not dead: In the 1994 case *Campbell v. Acuff-Rose Music, Inc.*, the Supreme Court ruled unanimously that the rap group 2 Live Crew had the right to parody the old Roy Orbison hit "Oh, Pretty Woman," declaring that "a parody's commercial character is only one use to be weighed in a fair use enquiry," and that the new record was clearly "commenting on the original or criticizing it, to some degree."

Unfortunately, the courts have not been consistent friends of fair use. Two years after the *Campbell* decision, for instance, Dr. Seuss Enterprises successfully convinced a federal district court to issue an injunction against *The Cat NOT in the Hat!*, an O.J.-oriented parody by "Dr. Juice." Splitting every hair in sight, the court ruled that the parody defense applied only when there was "a discernible direct comment on the original." And Dr. Juice's book, the court ruled, was lampooning the Simpson case, not *The Cat in the Hat*; Seuss' story merely provided a narrative framework. The U.S. Court of Appeals for the 9th Circuit agreed: "While Simpson is depicted 13 times in the Cat's distinctively scrunched and somewhat shabby red and white stove-pipe hat," it ruled, "the substance and content of *The Cat in the Hat* is not conjured up by the focus on the Brown-Goldman murders or the O.J. Simpson trial." Therefore, the book was bannable.

Nor is fair use consistently protected for the purpose of criticism. There is a long tradition of letting critics and scholars quote passages from books. There is much less precedent for quoting, say, a 30-second excerpt from a movie on a CD-ROM, or 10 seconds of a song in an online journal, partly because CD-ROMs and Web sites have not been around that long and partly because the courts seem to regard sounds and images as somehow different from text. The editors of one recent critical collection, *The Many Lives of the Batman*, discovered that they could not freely quote images from comic books, a tricky problem if one wants to make an argument about the placement of words or images within a panel or the relation of one panel to another. "If you can't quote what you're talking about," comments MIT's Jenkins, a contributor to the Batman anthology, "then at a certain point it becomes impossible to talk about it at all. You cut off certain ideas from being heard."

One of the most common sparks for a copyright fight is the practice of sampling, in which parts of older records are spliced and recycled in newer tunes. In 1991, for instance, the long-forgotten '70s pop star Gilbert O'Sullivan, discovering that rapper Biz Markie had appropriated three words from his song "Alone Again (Naturally)," successfully sued, not for a share of the royalties, but to suppress Biz Markie's record altogether.

These days the issue extends far beyond music. "We now live in a culture that is based on sampling," Jenkins argues, "with new means of poaching and redoctoring images. It's a new aesthetic." Where samizdat artists once had to make do with photocopiers and audio cassettes, they now can use videotapes, camcorders, Photoshop, digital film editing, recordable CDs, MP3 files, and the Internet. The result has been an explosion of amateur films, fiction, and music, all of which can be "published" for a minimal investment by putting them on the Web.

The most active amateurs are probably the members of various fan subcultures. I own, for example, a CD called *Do It Again: The Kover Kontroversy Kontinues*, a collection of songs composed by the British rock band the Kinks and performed by members of an Internet fan group, the Kinks Preservation Society. The contributors live everywhere from Holland to Hawaii to Brazil; some recorded straightforward remakes, while others reworked the songs in interesting ways—translating the lyrics into Portuguese, say, or adding a reggae rhythm, or splicing in a verse from the folk standard "Wayfaring Stranger." The performers never bothered to get the rights to the songs, figuring that wouldn't be necessary for a communal, noncommercial, low-circulation project. Legally speaking, that isn't necessarily so. Fortunately, the band doesn't seem to mind, recognizing the project as an informal tribute, not a commercial competitor. ("I personally gave Dave [Davies, the band's guitarist] a copy of the CD," reports Paul Wykes, who organized the project, "and he seemed thrilled by it.")

Not every copyright owner is so tolerant. Devotees of *Star Trek, Star Wars,* and the like have long produced their own fiction set in their favorite show's or movie's universe. In the last decade, this genre of writing has moved almost entirely out of the realm of small presses and zines and onto the Internet—where, being much more visible, it is also much more vulnerable to a copyright infringement challenge. This is a particular problem for fan filmmakers, a once-tiny group that has grown tremendously now that they can use relatively cheap camcorders, editing software, and computer animation instead of low-tech, silent Super 8 film—and now that their work can be viewed not just in living rooms and at science fiction conventions but on any computer screen hooked to the World Wide Web.

Thus, a Web surfer with the right software—most of it available for free—can download an astonishing array of homemade epics, varying widely in tone and quality:

• *Star Wars: The Remake* is a mimetic recreation of the first *Star Wars* film, compressed into 15 soundless minutes. Made in 1980, this specimen from an earlier generation of fan filmmaking will be utterly incoherent to viewers who have not seen the original movie, and will be rather impressive, in an odd way, to viewers who have.

• *Kung Fu Kenobi's Big Adventure* is a seven-and-a-half-minute short by one Evan Mather, with musical and visual allusions to everything from *Mission: Impossible* to *A Charlie Brown Christmas.* Performed by *Star Wars* action figures against a computer-generated animated background, this film is 50 times as inventive as *The Phantom Menace* and about 100 times as entertaining. My favorite scene: a recreation of the Jedi Council meeting in *Menace*, on a set made out of Legos. The Jedi knight played by Samuel Jackson rises and delivers a speech, sampled directly from a rather different film starring Jackson, *Pulp Fiction*:

"Blessed is he who, in the name of charity and good will, shepherds the weak through the valley of darkness, for he is *truly* his brother's keeper. And I will strike down upon thee with *great* vengeance and *furious* anger"—Yoda interrupts: "*Anger* leads to *hate*."

Kung Fu Kenobi violates more copyrights than I could count. All the dialogue is taken directly from the soundtracks of other films. All the characters are lifted from other films, too. And I doubt Mather paid any licensing fees for the music. But it's an original work in itself, a funny movie that appeals even to ogres like me who don't care much for *Star Wars*. Mather has made several other pictures, each of them built, in different ways, on pop culture allusions; his latest is titled *Buena Vista Fight Club*.

• *Star Wars: A Newfangled Hope* is too big to put on the Web, but individual sites have screened it as a streaming video at pre-advertised times. It consists of the first *Star Wars* film in its entirety, with a new soundtrack dubbed over the old one. I haven't seen it, but according to the Mos Eisley Multiplex, an online guide to *Star Wars* fan cinema, it presents a world in which "Ben Kenobi's a hairdresser, Luke is one horny dope, Threpio endlessly sings showtunes and Darth has a major high-school crush on Leia."

Redubbing—an honored comic technique ever since Woody Allen turned a Hong Kong spy flick into *What's Up, Tiger Lily?*, if not earlier—is a favorite method among fan directors. The most common target appears to be the *Phantom Menace* trailer, which exists online in countless guises.

• *Macbeth Episode 5: MacDuff Strikes Back*, an English project by some New Jersey high school students, is a 17-minute featurette reminiscent of the cult video *Green Eggs and Hamlet*. By any rational standard, it is a bad movie: It fuses *Macbeth* and the *Star Wars* films rather haphazardly, it's sometimes impossible to make out what the actors are saying, and the filmmakers didn't bother concealing the fact that they were shooting inside a school.

But it would take a cold-hearted snob indeed not to appreciate this movie, or at least the spirit behind it. There's a message on the directors' Web site, a few sentences that sum up the spirit of the micro-moviemaking movement: "If you have a video camera lying around, and better yet some editing equipment (pretty cheap for computers nowadays), go experiment. Be your own director. Go Hollywood . . . use a skateboard for dolly shots, or a fishing rod for special effects. It's fun. . . ."

That is, ultimately, the best argument for letting movies like this exist. It's not just that there's a sizable subculture that wants to watch them, and it's not just that sometimes a director like Evan Mather will make something so fun that even nonfans will enjoy the results. These movies are a first rung in the art of filmmaking, a chance for budding actors, writers, and directors to learn the rudiments of their craft. If those young auteurs want to adopt bits of the *Star Wars* mythos in their films, well, why shouldn't they? *Star Wars* is a part of our culture; it's a shared experience. And as Jenkins points out, "If something becomes an essential part of our culture, we have a right to draw on it and make stories about it. . . . The core question is whether First Amendment protections include a right to participate in our culture." And not just to participate, but to criticize: A law that prohibits a *Star Trek* devotee's homages to his favorite show also restricts a *Star Trek* hater's right to parody the program's militarism, its view of sex roles, or its vision of the future.

There's a common-sense issue here, too. It is legal, after all, to write or improvise one's own *Star Wars* adventures using action figures; that is, indeed, what the toys are for. It is legal to record those playlets on film or video; this is known as "making a home movie." Shouldn't it be legal to show those home movies to anyone you please? Especially if it's all done on a non-profit, amateur basis, with no threat of direct, head-to-head competition with the official *Star Wars* pictures?

LucasFilm has taken an inconsistent approach to its online imitators. Some fan films—such as Kevin Rubio's *Troops*, a *Cops*-inspired parody I have not seen—have received Lucas' warm praise. Others, such as the Australian-made *The Dark Redemption*, have received letters from lawyers telling them to shut down their sites, or else.

If copyrights have grown more restrictive over the years, trademarks have been transformed even more radically. Once restricted to pre-venting customer confusion and protecting businesses' reputations, they are increasingly treated as property that no one may appropriate at all. In 1996, for example, the New York Racing Authority sued Jeness Cortez, a painter whose work often depicted the Saratoga Race Course and, thus, various Racing Authority trademarks.

In that case, the courts upheld Cortez's First Amendment rights. In other cases, artists have not been so lucky. In one infamous incident, the Rock and Roll Hall of Fame successfully sued photographer Chuck Gentile over a poster depicting its museum at dusk. The Hall of Fame not only alleged that the poster's title—"The Rock and Roll Hall of Fame and Museum in Cleveland"—violated one of its trademarks; it claimed that *the building's design itself* was a protected mark, thus in essence claiming a property right in the way part of the Cleveland skyline looks. The U.S. District Court for Northern Ohio sided with the museum and issued an injunction against Gentile's poster. The U.S. Court of Appeals for the 6th Circuit later tossed out the injunction, but the museum is still pushing its case in the district court.

In part, this shift reflects the increased popularity of "dilution" laws over the last several decades, culminating with the Federal Trademark Dilution Act of 1995. Under this rule, it is illegal to produce, say, Microsoft brand ramen noodles, even though that other Microsoft isn't in the noodle business, lest the lousiness of your pasta undermine the software company's reputation. When dealing with a famous mark, such as Microsoft, the dilution doctrine makes some sense: There is, after all, a reasonable argument that commercial misrepresentation is afoot. The courts have stretched the doctrine out of shape, however, applying it with little regard for whether the trademark in question is famous enough for "dilution" to be a possibility.

Furthermore, the very definition of trademark has been expanding for the last 10 years. Writing in the *Yale Law Journal*, Mark Lemley of the University of Texas notes that "companies have successfully claimed trademark rights in the décor of their restaurant, the 'artistic style' in which they paint, the design of their golf course, the shape of their faucet handle, the diamond shape of a lollipop, the 'unique' registration process of their toy fair, the shape of their mixer, and the design of their personal organizers." At some point, this stops being anything more than a way to club your competition.

The fiercest trademark battles, though, involve words, not images. As e-commerce sweeps the Internet, domain names—those ugly streams of letters that end with "org" or "net" or "com"—have become more valuable, and some companies have become upset over URLs that bear too great a resemblance to theirs. Many of the resulting conflicts don't even make it to court: The very threat of legal action is enough to cow the alleged transgressor into dropping its address, even if he'd probably prevail before a judge. "A lot of this is just bullying," comments Temple University's David Post. "A lot of these claims are totally spurious." But the simple cost of defending themselves is often too much for those on the receiving end of a legal threat. The plaintiffs in such suits tend to have more money and lawyers at their disposal.

Besides, given the vagaries of the justice system, the defendant just might lose. Late in 1999, a judge ordered etoy.com, a Web site run by some European performance artists, to take down its site or pay a fine of $10,000 a day. Its URL, the court ruled, violated the trademark held by the online retailer eToys.com—even though etoy had been around since 1994, well before eToys existed. If the older site is finally saved, its rescuer will probably be public opinion, not the common sense of a judge or jury. Two weeks after the injunction, eToys suggested that it may voluntarily withdraw its suit, its reputation battered by constant protest on the Internet. (At press time, the case is not yet closed.)

Now Congress has gotten involved, passing the infamous "cybersquatting" law in late 1999. Cybersquatting is the practice of registering someone else's trademark (or a famous person's name) as a domain name, usually in hopes of selling the domain to the trademark holder later. The new law prohibits such speculation, imposing fines of up to $100,000 and, in the process, undermining the adjudication process already hammered out by the members of the International Corporation for Assigned Names and Numbers, a.k.a. ICANN. Civil libertarians worry that it will also intrude on our right to use trademarks in real sites' addresses—that if I devote a site to criticizing Shell Oil and call it www.shelloil.org, or even www.shelloilstinks.org, I may be breaking the new law.

While it would be a good idea to repeal the cybersquatting and dilution laws, one could probably avoid even more trademark battles with more prosaic measures. Post suggests expanding the range of domain names: If eToys.com could have called itself eToys.toys, he argues, the problem might never have emerged in the first place. There is also, he adds, a case for adopting the so-called "English system," in which a lawsuit's loser pays the winner's legal costs. Such an arrangement poses some problems of its own, but it would clearly discourage frivolous, bullying suits.

For centuries, our popular myths have enshrined the "romantic" or "heroic" author, conjuring new books out of nothing but his solitary genius. This image is popular with nonwriters, because many of them do not know how writing is done, and it is popular with writers, because it flatters us. It is, however, untrue. Every book, film, and song in the world draws on an existing cultural commons. Creativity rarely, if ever, means inventing something out of nothing. It means taking the scraps and shards of culture that surround us and recombining them into something new.

When the government tells us we can't use those scraps without permission from Disney, Fox, or the Sherwood Anderson Trust, it constrains our creativity, our communications, and our art. It tells us that we cannot draw on pop songs the way we once drew on folk songs, or on TV comedy the way we once drew on vaudeville; it says we cannot pluck pieces from *Star Wars* the way George Lucas plucked pieces from foreign films and ancient legends. The consequences are staggering. Imagine what would have happened if, 100 years ago, it had been possible to copyright a blues riff. Jazz, rock, and country music simply could not have evolved if their constituent parts had been subject to the same restraints now borne by techno and hip hop.

Few would argue that artists shouldn't be able to make a living from their work, or that customer confusion is a good thing. But we've stood those ideas on their heads. Rather than promoting enterprise and speech, copyrights and trademarks often restrain them, turning intellectual property law into, in Jenkins' words, "protectionism for the culture industry."

Fortunately, the state simply isn't big enough to enforce every intellectual deed on the books. You can still find Alexander Thompson's *Buffy* transcripts on the Web, even though he's taken them down: Several fellow fans had already downloaded them and posted them to sites of their own. Copies of *The Dark Redemption* are still floating around—if the movie itself isn't online, people willing to sell you tapes are. Even *The Cat NOT in the Hat!* persists, not as a book but as a frequently forwarded e-mail. The overzealous enforcement of copyrights and trademarks may chill speech, but it won't kill it.

But the chilling is bad enough. Americans are not mere passive consumers, dully absorbing images invented in distant corporate laboratories. We hatch our own ideas and compose our own stories, drawing on pop culture without absorbing it blindly. We should look with disfavor on any law that tells us to shut up and get back on the couch.

March 2002

Stand-Up Guy

Comedian Drew Carey on network censors, Hollywood guilt, and why he likes eating at Bob's Big Boy

Interview by Nick Gillespie and Steve Kurtz

COMEDIAN DREW CAREY has become a full-fledged media sensation: His self-titled television show, which airs Wednesdays at 9 p.m. EST on ABC, is beginning its third season ensconced in the Nielsen top 20 (and locked in a ratings war with NBC's *Third Rock from the Sun*); his cable specials, most recently HBO's *The Mr. Vegas All Night Party*, command huge audiences; and his book *Dirty Jokes and Beer: Stories of the Unrefined* (for which he reportedly received a $3 million advance) hit stores in September.

Carey's appeal stems in large part from his Everyman status. The *Washington Post* once described him, not inaccurately, as "a tubby dork in a crew cut and thick-rimmed glasses . . . [who is] lovably and goofily awkward. . . . Part of Carey's charm is that he manages to seem out of place in every setting." In his sitcom, which shares certain blue-collar affinities with shows such as *Roseanne* and *Grace Under Fire*, his character is an assistant personnel manager at a Cleveland department store. He is the consummate working stiff, besieged on all sides by an indifferent employer, hostile co-workers, aimless friends, and a strong sense of his own inadequacy and lack of success. From this potentially grim reality, Carey squeezes immense humor (and precious little sentimentality).

Carey's appreciation for the exasperations of everyday life is matched by a delightful sense of the absurd (his show sometimes features elaborate dance numbers) and an eagerness to strip away all sorts of pretensions and self-serving myths. Consider his take on the Hard Rock Hotel and Casino in Las Vegas and its ubiquitous slogan, "Save the Planet": "[That's] the most pandering corporate slogan I've ever heard," he writes. "'Save the Planet.' You can't get away from it. It's on every sign, every chip, every matchbook: 'Save the Planet.' Like you can really save the planet from people in the first place, and if you wanted to, you could do it by drinking and gambling at the Hard Rock. 'Hey, not only am I getting shit-faced drunk and picking up cute chicks, I'm saving the planet. . . . Every time I play craps there, when I roll the dice I yell, 'Save the Planet!' Then, win or lose, I loudly announce, 'I don't care if I win or not, I just want the planet to be safe,' while I count my hundred dollar chips."

Although Carey openly disdains Hollywood activism—he winces at the mention of people such as Alec Baldwin and Barbra Streisand—there is a proto-political message in much of his humor. As the Hard Rock example suggests, Carey believes that people are far more resistant to soothing, feel-good rhetoric than its practitioners may fully grasp. In an age of ubiquitous and self-serving spin, that is no small point.

Reason: Much of your humor pokes fun at liberal Hollywood sensibilities. What kind of response does that provoke from your peers?

Drew Carey: People look at me like a drunk uncle: "Oh, that Drew!" Everybody in Hollywood loves symbolic gestures. Have you been to the Hard Rock Casino in Vegas? There's nothing save-the-planetish about it. Hollywood people are filled with guilt: white guilt, liberal guilt, money guilt. They feel bad that they're so rich, they feel they don't work that much for all that money—and they don't, for the amount of money they make. There's no way I can justify my salary level, but I'm learning to live with it.

I've got to say that I don't see myself as some sort of political type like Alec Baldwin or Barbra Streisand. I don't want to come across like that. I'd be embarrassed if that was the way I came across. I should watch what I say about Streisand: She could call a congressman, not have my garbage picked up anymore, change my zoning laws, totally screw me over.

When I did *Comic Relief,* I did it to be on the show; it's a badge of honor as a comedian to do that show. *Comic Relief* does a lot of good, but homeless people really bug the hell out of me. They're smelly, they're always asking me for money. I mean, I like to help out, but I also do this in my act where I say, "I don't know how much money we raised to help the homeless tonight, but the food backstage was great." And it was: all gourmet-catered, all the drinks were free, not a homeless guy in sight. Everyone in Hollywood comes to these things and then says, "Look how we cured homelessness." They feel guilty if they party and there's not a good reason for it. If you had the same show with all the best comedians and no charity involved, they'd be like, "Uh-oh, can't do that." They want to make themselves look good—a lot of it is about feeding egos. My publicist always calls me with charity appearance requests, and I turn them down now. I told her I'm not doing any more charity where I show up and say, "Hi, I'm Drew Carey for the American Cancer Society."

Reason: So you're in favor of cancer?

Carey: No (laughs). I'm in favor of *not* inflating your ego, of only doing good deeds to pump yourself up. Which is about as anti-Hollywood, as anti-celebrity as you can get.

Still, I wish there were more organizations like [Comic Relief]. Then the government wouldn't step in all over the place. Then you could decide for yourself to help the homeless or not help the homeless.

Reason: What's your basic attitude toward government?

Carey: The less the better. As far as your personal goals are and what you actually want to do with your life, it should never have to do with the government. You should never depend on the government for your retirement, your financial security, for anything. If you do, you're screwed.

Reason: But you were in the Marines reserve, weren't you?

Carey: That's all the government should be: Army, Air Force, Navy, Marines (laughs). P.J. O'Rourke once said the government has passed enough laws—it should just stop. It oversteps its bounds so often. Giving it a little bit of power is like getting a little bit pregnant, or thinking that a little bit of sex will do you for a long time—it just doesn't work that way.

Reason: Is that the case with TV content ratings?

Carey: I'm not against ratings per se. I think more information is always good. But I certainly don't think the government has to step in and set guidelines for how shows should be rated.

Reason: Former Sen. Paul Simon (D-Ill.), one of the main forces behind ratings, said that if TV people didn't "clean up its act," the government would have to do it for them.

Carey: He's a bowtied prick. What right does he have to tell me what I can and cannot watch? Change the channel if you don't like what's on TV! The government is really into "protecting" people. The Federal Communications Commission (FCC) says you can't broadcast certain words and certain pictures. It says it's protecting citizens. But I'm sitting in my home with DirecTV and can watch whatever I want. I can afford the best pornography—laser-disc porn! The government's not protecting me from anything.

All the government's doing is discriminating against poor people. It thinks poor people are like cows, that poor people can't think straight: If we let them hear dirty words or see dirty pictures, there's going to be *madness*! If you're poor and all you can afford is a 12-inch black-and-white TV and can't pay for cable—you're so protected! You'd probably be happier if you could see some pornography, a pair of titties, once in a while on free TV. But a pair of titties on free TV? The government figures if you saw that, you'd just explode!

Reason: You devote a chapter of your book to ABC's own network censor, filled with examples of what was and wasn't approved for your show. The focus on particular words is both pathetic and hilarious: In one case, he asked you to change *dwarf* to *little person*; in another, he asked you to substitute *hooker* or *prostitute* for *whore*; in a third, he passed on *butt wipe* but OK'd *butt weasel*.

Carey: People who have read the book have said that's their favorite chapter. You just don't normally get that sort of inside look at the process.

Reason: Do you ever catch the censor cursing?

Carey: Yes, yes: "What the fuck's going on? You can't say that!"

Reason: Would the use of blue language make your television show better?

Carey: There'd be more stuff to joke about, and it would make the show funnier. As it is, there are certain parts of life you can discuss and certain parts you can't. If my character stubs his toe really bad, he can't say, "Aw fuck, I stubbed my toe!" He has to say, "Ooch, ooch,

ooch."

Reason: Why is cursing funnier?

Carey: It's not always. But comedy's all about exaggeration. To do that sometimes you need the strongest words you can use. In the book, I tell this joke about a man and a woman who meet in a bar. They're both divorced because their spouses thought they were too kinky. So they go back to the woman's place and she goes to her bedroom and puts on black leather boots, a miniskirt, comes out with a riding crop and some handcuffs. The guy's putting on his coat and heading out the door. "Hey, where you going? I thought we were going to get kinky," she says. "Hey," he says, "I fucked your dog, I shit in your purse. I'm outta here!" That just isn't funny if you say, "I had sex with your dog and defecated in your purse."

Reason: What do you think about comedians like Bill Cosby who crusade against dirty comics?

Carey: He has a market and I have a market. I don't care if my jokes are appropriate for a kid.

Reason: While you're Cleveland's favorite son, you write longingly of your years living in Las Vegas, a city which many people see as the embodiment of vice and excess, of everything that's wrong with America. What do you like about Vegas?

Carey: Vegas is everything that's *right* with America. You can do whatever you want, 24 hours a day. They've effectively legalized everything there. You don't *have* to gamble if you don't want to. There's tons of churches in Vegas, too: You'll see a church right next to a casino. But a lot of people like gambling, so they make money off it. Nobody forces you to put money in a machine and pull the handle. But the fact is they *allow* it. Nevada's one of the most conservative states in the Union, but you can do what you want in Vegas and nobody judges you.

And they've got great schools in Vegas (laughs).

Reason: So why do so many people dump on Vegas?

Carey: I think a lot of people are afraid of freedom. They want their lives to be controlled, to be put into a box: "Be here at 9, leave at 5, we'll take care of you." People like that cradle-to-grave concept because it says you don't have to think too much, you don't have to worry too much, because someone else is looking out for you. But that also means you can't do as much as you want.

You have to do what someone else says is right, what someone else thinks you should do. Why should someone else put a limit on how much fun I can have, how much I can accomplish?

Reason: You write about the 1970s—something else people heap scorn on—in a similar vein.

Carey: Again, a lot of people don't like people having fun. And the '70s were all about doing as much debauchery and having as much fun as you possibly could: Fuck anybody you wanted, do any drug you wanted to.

Reason: I take it you favor drug legalization?

Carey: Yeah. But every time you bring that up, people always ask, "Oh, you think they should sell heroin and crack in stores?" Sure: Smoke crack, die, get out of my way. As long as I don't have to pay for it (laughs). There's always the argument that not everyone is as responsible as you are, that we have to protect everyone from people who would smoke crack and not be responsible. Like we're doing now, right? Liquor prohibition led to the rise of organized crime in America, and drug prohibition has led to the rise of the gang problems we have now.

Reason: Prohibition also leads to another topic: the Kennedys. In an earlier draft of your book, you had an entire chapter devoted to that brood. What is it that you hate about them?

Carey: There were a lot of questions about language in the book. I said, "Look, give me some of the bad language, and I'll take out the whole Kennedy chapter." Plus, the publisher wasn't sure it would pass the lawyers. I read in *USA Today* that a Kennedy has never lost an election in Massachusetts. I wrote about what it would take for a Kennedy to lose one: They bust into a bank, pistol whip the manager, fuck the teller up the ass, take turns posing for pictures. And nobody would say a thing: "Those Kennedy's are great, aren't they? I can't believe a Kennedy fucked *me* up the ass!" They can get away with anything.

Reason: Your comic persona and TV show successfully blend a working-man shtick and a willingness to play with dramatic conventions and audience expectations. What's the appeal of those things?

Carey: I try not to lose touch with [working people]. I go back to Cleveland a lot. I love the normalcy of Cleveland. There's regular people there. I like [the TV show] *King of the Hill* because it's about normal people. I *don't* miss the economic insecurity, the living paycheck to paycheck. Twice when I was living in Vegas, I almost lost my rent money playing blackjack, got down to my last two dollars.

I'm glad I don't have to deal with that anymore. But I don't want to lose touch with things like eating in Bob's Big Boy. I feel comfortable here.

The show is very easy to relate to [in that way]. I wanted to do a show based on what my life would be like if I had never become a comedian. I would have had some bullshit degree, some general job, going nowhere. People laugh to forget their troubles, and to forget their troubles they like to look at people who aren't doing better than they are. Nothing's funny about someone who's successful. People who are happy and adjusted just aren't funny. Even when people are rich and successful on TV shows, there's always some trouble—you have to poke holes in them, throw them out of a job, put a pie in the face.

Like I said, all comedy is based on exaggeration, big or small, whatever you can get away with. In a promotional bit for the show, Mimi [a character from the show] and I are walking down a dirt road with fishing poles, like Andy and Opie on *The Andy Griffith Show*. The original script was that she would push me in the water and I'd be floundering like I couldn't swim. When we did the filming, I said, "Wouldn't it be funnier if I just floated like I was dead?" And it's funnier that way because it went the extra mile.

What also helps our show is that we never take ourselves seriously. Here's a show that can wink at itself. Everyone involved knows we're just a sitcom. You'll never see a "very special episode" of the show. The episode featuring Speedy the Crippled Dog is the most we're going to do.

Reason: Your book is different from most celebrity tomes. It's not simply an autobiography or a reprinting of your stand-up routines, although it has some of both. You've got a half-dozen short stories, a section on how the network censor operates, an entire chapter devoted to penis jokes, and then some. How did the book's form come about?

Carey: I didn't want to do what every other celebrity does. I couldn't imagine sitting down and writing my thoughts on the universe. Who cares? Really, who gives a shit what a comic thinks about life in general?

I only wanted to do short stories. I loved the old stories in *National*

Lampoon, like the original story the movie *Vacation* was based on. I used to laugh at them until I cried. I like short stories, and I don't think I'm good enough to write a novel (laughs). The publisher was hoping to get Drew on beer, Drew on dating, that sort of thing. I wanted to do the stories, and I wanted to do a chapter on how ABC's standards and practices works. So I gave the publisher some of the other stuff to make them happy. The important thing is that it's all meant to be funny.

Reason: You cast aspersions on celebrities who unveil dark secrets, but you also mention that you were molested as a boy and that you tried to commit suicide during your Vegas years.

Carey: The reason I mentioned that stuff is that I wanted to tell people that you can get over it, that you don't have to be embarrassed by it. I mean, I'm very well-adjusted in real life. Well, pretty well. Most parts, anyway. You could ask my girlfriends (laughs).

What I don't like are celebrities who use it as their crutch all the time, who use it as a calling card: "Hi, I'm fill-in-the-blank and I was molested." Shut up already, man. It's one thing to mention it and move on. I have two pages on being molested when I was 9 in the book, and *The Globe* had this big story: "Drew Carey Bombshell!" They didn't mention one thing about the chapter called "101 Big Dick Jokes."

Reason: You have the only hit show on ABC in recent memory, but you've also been quick to point out that network shows are nowhere near as big as they used to be. Why is that?

Carey: DirecTV, maybe. The network shows are fine; it's just that there's so many other things to watch. We'll never see national shows with 45 shares again. Before, you never had a choice. You had to watch *M*A*S*H,* or whatever was on the three big networks. Now, if I don't come across a regional sports show or a history special I want to watch, *maybe* I'll watch *M*A*S*H,* or whatever's the best of what's broadcast. I don't even watch the local affiliates here in Los Angeles anymore. When I first got DirecTV, the installer told me I needed an antenna to pick up the local broadcast channels. I had him put one in, but I never turn them on.

Reason: How are the networks responding?

Carey: They can't assume everyone is going to watch the new "fall season," that people will tune into something right when it goes on the air. My show was like that. You have to get used to it; some people still don't [like the show], which is fine with me. We had kind of a slow growth in audience. The TV season is a year-long thing now, and the networks are starting to look at it that way, thanks to cable, satellites, and competition.

Reason: A lot of people in your position must hate the competition. Since viewers have more options, they're tougher to hold onto.

Carey: Some people don't like competition because it makes them work harder, better. I'm competitive at everything. When I play poker, I don't like losing the pot. The first Monopoly game I played with my brothers, I hated losing so much, I just had to beat them. I love beating people (laughs). But it's a natural driving force, a way of testing yourself, of measuring how you're doing. It's insane to [hate competition]. How can people not know that competition makes everything better?

Reason: You've got the book out. The show's starting its third season. What's next on your plate?

Carey: I'll tell you what's going to be the most depressing day in my life: when my book gets thrown in the discount bin with a "50 Percent Off" sticker on it. This year, I'm going to try an experiment with my creative process. When the show's in production, we work for three weeks at a time and then take a week off. When I'm working, I'm going to avoid all media. No newspapers, no magazines, no movies, no radio, no TV. I'm just going to do creative work. During the week off, I'll catch up. When I read a headline like "Mideast Talks Stalled by Bombing," I wonder what the hell I could possibly miss: Talk about the '70s! They just keep that headline handy; they probably even just use the same photo.

November 1997

E Pluribus Umbrage

The long, happy life of America's anti-defamation industry

Tim Cavanaugh

THE SEXUAL ABUSE SCANDAL OF 2002 is arguably the gravest crisis in the history of the American Catholic Church. Sexual dysfunction, hypocrisy, institutional self-regard, Soviet-style secrecy, pathological hostility to plain dealing—even the infamous 19th-century nativist fable *The Awful Disclosures of Maria Monk* couldn't support so many anti-Catholic stereotypes.

In the midst of this emergency, the Catholic League for Religious and Civil Rights, the nation's most prominent Catholic advocacy organization, alerted its 300,000 members to a grave threat to the faith: a *King of the Hill* episode in which cartoon housewife Peggy Hill impersonates a nun. Even for the perpetually outraged Catholic League, this was minor stuff. But it's the kind of distorted controversy found in a strange and often lucrative segment of the political economy.

Call it the anti-defamation industry, the anti-discrimination lobby, or maybe the umbrage market. From politically connected lobbying behemoths to one-man shoestring operations using a Kinko's fax machine, the United States hosts a Mad Monster Party of advocacy groups dedicated to rebutting every real and imagined racial or ethnic slur. It's a field that attracts the talented and the warped, passionate crusaders and transparent self-promoters. It creates media stars and villains.

And if the nit-picking interest group has become a cliché, anti-discrimination's capacity for driving legal and legislative agendas is no joke. Pandering to imagined Hibernian hypersensitivities has already resulted in the construction of an Irish Hunger Memorial on prime real estate in New York City's Battery Park and a gratuitous curriculum requirement that Empire State public schools teach the Irish famine as an attempted genocide by the British government. The Anti-Defamation League (ADL) of B'nai B'rith boasts that its model hate crimes legislation has inspired actual laws in Wisconsin and elsewhere. One of President Bush's first initiatives after the September 11 attacks was to get a series of photo ops with representatives of Arab and Muslim anti-discrimination groups.

It's hard to place a valuation on the anti-discrimination industry. The 89-year-old Anti-Defamation League is the trailblazer, with an annual take of more than $40 million and a $400,000 salary for storied director Abraham Foxman. The National Council of La Raza rakes in a cool $16 million per year, a combination of government grants, public support, and other revenues. The Polish American Congress pulls down more than $5 million—despite its leader's habit of making wildly impolitic public statements (more on this later). The venerable Sons of Italy runs a nearly $200,000 Commission for Social Justice.

Tactics pioneered by the Anti-Defamation League are used by anti-discrimination groups that butt heads with the ADL itself. The American-Arab Anti-Discrimination Committee budgets "in the area of a million dollars," according to an official, as does James Zogby's Arab American Institute. The Council on American-Islamic Relations (CAIR) describes its budget as between $2 million and $4 million. The Rev. Jesse Jackson's Rainbow/PUSH Coalition famously declines to disclose its finances at all.

All Against All

The number of unincorporated one- or two-person social justice advocacy operations out there is beyond count. If you've noticed an absence of "No Latvians Need Apply" notices at local businesses, you can thank either the Latvian Truth Fund, which defends "the legal and civil rights of persons born in Latvia or of Latvian descent," or the American Latvian Association, which "defends the interests of Latvian Americans." There are Indian-American groups combating misrepresentations of Ganesha, Italian-American committees who condemn *Mickey Blue Eyes*, and Irish organizations bent on eliminating Barry Fitzgerald–style stereotypes.

Funny though they may be, such groups turn honest (or dishonest) differences into pseudo-crusades and portray an America that, contrary to abundant evidence, has made no progress against the bigotries of the past. "These groups serve a vital function," says Robert Alan Goldberg, a University of Utah history professor and author of *Enemies Within*, a study of conspiracy theories in America, "but somebody has to sound the fire bell when they pour gasoline on the fire and get into thrust and counterthrust with other groups."

Virtually all anti-discriminationists describe themselves as opponents of bigotry in all its forms. But despite some areas of agreement, such as support for "hate crimes" legislation, the anti-discrimination industry is the Hobbesian nightmare in a nonprofit setting. Arab and Muslim groups struggle with the ADL for mind share in the Arab-Israeli conflict. The Serbian Orthodox Church combats not only anti-Serb stereotypes in the entertainment industry but also the Hague War Crimes Tribunal and the de facto pro-Croat teachings of Our Lady of Medjugorje. The Polish American Congress alienates the Jewish community in Chicago. Italian Americans battle American Indians every Columbus Day.

Advocacy groups also come into conflict with people they putatively represent. The Anti-Defamation League is frequently criticized by liberal Jews. A recent *Sports Illustrated* poll suggested most Native Americans tolerate or even support the Indian team nicknames advocacy groups have fought for many years. William Donohue, president of the Catholic League, battles his own church's liberals. Many or most Italian Americans regard Mafia films as, at worst, too abstracted from reality to cause much alarm.

Nevertheless, institutional logic demands eternal vigilance. "Simply said, there are careers, status, jobs and influence to be had as long as racism exists," writes Laird Wilcox in his 1998 book *The Watchdogs*, which details incidents of strong-arm tactics by anti-discrimination groups. An anti-discrimination group has little motive to report improvement, or even stasis, in cultural relations, because that would lessen the perceived need for the group.

Nor is there incentive to declare victory and go home, even when victory clearly has been won. The Polish American Congress is still operating decades after Mike Stivic endured his last Polish joke on *All in the Family*. Both the ADL and the Simon Wiesenthal Center are famous for fund raising letters warning of what the ADL calls "a rising tide of anti-Semitism here and around the world" and the Wiesenthal Center describes as "a frightening new wave of antisemitism and extremism—often mixed with Holocaust denial." The Catholic League's Donohue defines anti-Catholicism as the "anti-Semitism of the elites" and asserts "there is a contempt for Christianity among our elites in this country that has no rival."

If this perpetually rising tide is troubling, it's useful in forming cultural identity, particularly where such identity is fading or never existed in the first place. Asian Americans of all backgrounds now attach themselves to the World War II–era internment of Japanese Americans. Large numbers of Irish Americans dwell on the relatively mild bigotry their ancestors endured two presidents and countless CEOs ago. "It's easy to pick on the Irish, since we're easily dismissed as a minority or ethnic grouping of no particular significance," writes the *Richmond Times Dispatch*'s Tom Mullen. "You can say what you like about the Irish—especially Irish Catholics—but woe be unto you if you say anything critical about African-Americans or gays or any other group that has suffered from any kind of bigotry."

Even if we concede that historical suffering of a group confers political coherence on that group's descendents, few anti-discrimination groups have the serious historical roots of, say, the National Association for the Advancement of Colored People or the American Indian Movement. Self-described ethnic groups whose experience of America has been almost entirely positive can get into the act. *Don't talk to me about slavery; my ancestors were traumatized by* The Katzenjammer Kids! This may explain why anti-discrimination is a growth industry even—or especially—while identity politics fades into history, more Americans decline to identify themselves by ethnicity, and actual discrimination is, by virtually all measures, at historically low levels.

Toilet Trouble

"We are not humorless," says Ajay Shah. "There are things that are clearly humorous, and you have to be willing to take a joke." Shah, convener of American Hindus Against Defamation (AHAD), is speaking of Apu, the Indian Quik-E-Mart owner on *The Simpsons.* Shah occasionally has been called upon to object to this characterization of a penny-pinching subcontinental; he sees Apu as a creation more of affection than calumny. "I get two or three incidents reported every month," he says. "You have to make a judgment whether it's worth pursuing or just trivial."

In the anti-discrimination economy, AHAD is a penny stock, with no paid staff, office, or telephone. AHAD convenes on a case-by-case basis. Its targets have included an Aerosmith album cover depicting a disfigured Krishna, Sanskrit shlokas in an orgy scene in the movie *Eyes Wide Shut,* and, most famously, a Seattle design shop selling toilet covers with pictures of Ganesha and Kali. In all these cases, AHAD's strategy of engagement with offenders, backed up by e-mail campaigns and the hint of boycotts, resulted in removal of the offending images.

"In all of our protests we have never asked for monetary compensation," says Shah, "because if we can educate people, we'll become a major organization whom they'll come to before they start a project."

AHAD has come under fire from both left and right. In a screed for the Indian Web site Rediff.com, writer Varsha Bhosle attacks Shah's "ingrained Hindu obsequiousness," which allowed the Seattle designer to escape "without a scratch." In Bhosle's view, AHAD is a lily-livered Gandhian group that deserves "a nice Islamic-style whipping."

Liberals, on the other hand, condemn AHAD's affiliations with both the million-dollar advocacy outfit Vishwa Hindu Parishad of America, which has ties to India's ruling BJP party, and the nationalist group Rashtriya Swayamsevak Sangh, whose mission includes "strengthening the [Hindu] society by emphasizing and inculcating a spirit of unity, so that no one can dare challenge it." Both groups supported the demolition of the Ayodha mosque and say attacks on Christian missionaries result from "anger of patriotic Hindu youth against anti-national forces."

"The issues we pick have no political overtones," counters Shah. "We take up issues offensive to Hindus . . . once people denigrate your symbols, it's a matter of time before they say, 'If people worship these symbols, they're worth ridiculing.'" Shah notes that his group participates in pluralism efforts and meets with the Council on American-

Islamic Relations. "Hindus are very liberal," he says. "We see nothing wrong with people choosing their own lifestyles. If there is a libertarian religion, it's Hinduism."

Upping the Anti

This easygoing spirit is a rarity among anti-discrimination groups. "The issue," Wilcox writes in *The Watchdogs*, "is the abominable record . . . with respect to individual rights . . . misrepresentations and lies, exploitation of normal human sympathy for the underdog, flagrant double standards, hidden agendas, unprincipled methods, and unconscionable use of law enforcement to advance their own ends."

Not surprisingly, the 9/11 attacks pushed these tendencies to the forefront while giving urgency to anti-discrimination efforts. CAIR tallies anti-Muslim incidents, which it says tripled in the last year. The group issues news alerts with headlines that are witty ("Ann Coulter Attacks, Dates Muslims"), breathless ("House Leader Calls for Ethnic Cleansing of Palestinians"), or mendacious ("First Lady Says She Can't Empathize With Palestinian Mothers").

The post-9/11 backlash, the Afghan war, endless intifadas, and the Bush administration's hysterical terrorist threat warnings have inspired an unbroken string of columns, speeches, and television appearances from CAIR, the American-Arab Anti-Discrimination Committee (ADC), and the Arab American Institute (AAI). The rising profile of these groups never goes unchallenged. The ADL's Foxman, who accuses the AAI's Zogby of "crude anti-Semitism," campaigned to get Zogby's son ousted from a position in the Clinton State Department. Leaders of other Arab and Muslim groups have been subject to similar attacks.

"They're saying don't let me on television because I'm bad," says ADC spokesman Hussein Ibish. "Pipes and Emerson rehash a version of anti-Semitism: 'There is a plot out there to destroy our Christian way of life; they may look like us, but they worship a hostile and alien god.' This is *political* anti-Semitism, recast against another Semitic group to exclude that group from the political process."

Ibish is referring to Middle East expert Daniel Pipes, head of the Middle East Forum, and Steven Emerson, self-dramatizing MSNBC terrorism expert. The dustup between Pipes and his Saracen adversaries is one of the oddest offshoots of the war on terrorism. Pipes has condemned CAIR as "'moderate' friends of terror." AAI founder Zogby has been the subject of a rant in Pipes' *Middle East Quarterly*. Ibish, Pipes writes, is "Anti-American, anti-Semitic, inaccurate and immoral."

Pipes' Web site carries exposés about CAIR. CAIR shoots back with a special "Who Is Daniel Pipes?" feature on its own site. Like all pissing contests, it ends with everybody getting wet. Pipes mass e-mails alerts about his run-ins with various interlocutors ("Pipes on 'Hardball'—hits one back to the pitcher," "Pipes on O'Reilly Factor, dukes it out with host," "Pipes vs. Zakaria on MSNBC's 'Hardball'"). His enemies are even more energetic. Here is how Mohammed Alo, a young writer at toledomuslims.com, describes a Pipes appearance on the defunct talk show *Politically Incorrect*:

"Host Bill Maher and the other guests quickly argued that Pipes is the one that needs to be controlled and kept out of the public stage. Even they noticed his outright hatred and anti-Muslim sentiments. You could faintly hear an audience member shout out 'Pipe down Pipes!'

"Pipes was humiliated. His plans were foiled once again. Bigotry was on display, but failed to reign supreme. Hooray for America. Pipes will forever remain in the garbage bin of history, and rightfully so."

Needless to say, very little of this has to do with fighting discrimination. "We're a civil rights organization, but much of what we do is devoted to foreign policy," says Ibish. "Much of the discrimination Arab Americans face stems from disagreements between Arab Americans and the rest of society over our policies toward the Middle East. Until we can create a more reasonable foreign policy, we'll face defamation in the form of films, television, discrimination in the workplace. . . . I believe this absolutely."

Nevertheless, Arab-American leaders concede that animosity toward their ethnicity may be less than advertised. "Is there a generalized antagonism?" says Zogby. "No. Was there a problem immediately after 9/11? Yes . . . the country doesn't have much tolerance for hearing Arabs whine. There are people who try to make politics out of whining. I choose not to be a professional victim, because I don't think it's true and because people don't have much tolerance for it."

Victimization politics also holds tactical disadvantages. Anti-Semitism remains a concept with much more punch than such recently diagnosed maladies as "Anti-Arabism" or "Islamophobia." Reference to the Holocaust is still sufficient to shout down any discussion about the plight of Arab Americans. "I don't think anything in the Arab experience can resonate similarly, because I don't think anything in the Arab experience is similar," admits Ibish. "But since we can't counter that emotional appeal honestly, we can question its relevance to the Arab-Israeli conflict."

Big Trouble in Little Poland

For an odder case of emotional appeal turned into political ordnance, consider the City of Big Shoulders, where the slow-motion implosion of the Polish American Congress (PAC) mirrors the political decline of Chicago's Polish community.

Since 1996 PAC President Edward Moskal has been making statements that can charitably be called ill-considered. "The spilled blood of those Jews, however torrential it may have been, cannot wash away the blood of their Christian neighbors," Moskal wrote in a 1996 article that defended a commemorative cross at Auschwitz. (Elsewhere in the piece, he averred that Jews collaborated with Poland's Soviet occupiers.) He dismisses evidence of Polish collaboration with the Germans as "twisted history," an assault on Polish sovereignty. Moskal ridicules attempts by Poland's leadership to offer restitution to Jews and implies Jan Nowak-Jezioranski, generally considered a resistance hero, was a Nazi collaborator.

Moskal's impatience with talk of Polish guilt is partly understandable.

"[Poles] see themselves as victims, which they were," says Guy Billauer, director of the National Polish-American-Jewish-American Council, which broke with PAC in 1996. "They have a right to think that way. But [the Moskal controversy] has opened our eyes. We believe it's hard to reform somebody who holds these views. It's like mending fences with Arafat."

"I think people should welcome the opportunity to discuss these issues with somebody who speaks his mind," counters PAC spokesman T. Ron Jasinski-Herbert, "rather than saying the right things and thinking all the bullshit inside." Whatever Moskal's true feelings may be (he did not consent to an interview for this article), his comments have diminished both membership and clout for PAC, an umbrella group for 3,000 religious, fraternal, and political orders.

The situation came to a head during this year's Democratic primary in the 5th Congressional District, which pitted former state legislator Nancy Kaszak against combative Clinton administration apparatchik Rahm Emanuel. Because of demographic changes and redistricting in Chicago's 30th Ward, the Polish-American voting bloc is declining. "We do have a valid gripe," says Jasinski-Herbert. "If we lose this one we have no more Polish representatives from the largest Polish community outside Poland."

But it may not have helped when, a few weeks before the election, Moskal gave Kaszak a contribution and then denounced Emanuel as a "millionaire carpetbagger" with divided U.S.-Israeli loyalties, accusing Emanuel's Polish supporters of accepting "30 pieces of silver to betray Polonia." "The country from which Poles come struggled for democracy," Moskal said. "While the country . . . to which [Emanuel] gave his allegiance defiles the Polish homeland."

Kaszak publicly rejected Moskal's endorsement. Emanuel insisted that Kaszak go further and order Moskal to "cease and desist." The incident received wide media play, and in the weeks after Moskal's comments Emanuel closed an eight-point deficit in polls to win the primary. The loss of Polish-American political clout turned out to be a self-fulfilling prophecy.

Celtic Twilight

But what is ethnic cleansing or the Holocaust compared to the scourge of stage Irishmen? For Ultan O'Broin, founder of San Francisco's Celtic Tiger Anti-Defamation League, the great issues of the day include *Angela's Ashes, Fighting Fitzgeralds, Darby O'Gill and the Little People,* and presumably the *Star Trek* episode wherein Kirk beats the stuffing out of an arch-rival tellingly named Finnegan.

O'Broin, an Irishman working in Silicon Valley, publishes articles excoriating "Oirish" stereotypes and ridiculing the dumb Americans who fall for them. "In the last decade, the Republic of Ireland has undergone a sea change," he writes, noting that "Ireland has the highest per capita ownership of Mercedes-Benz automobiles in Europe." Yet "stereotyping continues in the United States." His proposed solution—one of them, anyway—is simple: "Americans (and Irish Americans) need to go to Ireland to see for themselves. They should protest the negative stereotyping. Then they might be more than welcome to celebrate what it really means to be Irish today."

The Celtic Tiger Anti-Defamation League (CTADL) claims to have attracted 150 members, and the group's proposals for anti-stereotype legislation have been given a sympathetic hearing by San Francisco's mayor and legislators. As with soccer and Islam, the CTADL's small base alone may qualify it as one of America's fastest-growing organizations.

But the politics of Hibernian equality are thorny, even among Hibernians. Consider the sad case of Francis Boyle, a law professor at the University of Illinois at Urbana-Champaign. Boyle, described by legendary activist Philip Berrigan as "a lawyer of the quality of Thomas More or Gandhi . . . the most competent and impassioned advocate of international law in the U.S.," claims he experienced discrimination when he objected to the bar crawls graduate students hold every St. Patrick's Day. "A bar crawl 'in honor' of St. Patrick, the Patron Saint of Ireland, and one of the great figures of Western Judeo-Christian Civilization, is completely sacrilegious," he says.

Boyle's objections, he says, made him a target. "It's clearly a hostile work environment for me," he says. "I've been subject to ridicule by students and student organizations. This is a hostile environment based on my race—I'm of Irish nationality and a citizen of the Irish Republic—and on my religion—I'm Catholic."

Indeed, Boyle claims the harassment got so bad that he complained to the U.S. Department of Justice's Civil Rights Division, noting that "it doesn't cost me anything" to have the government investigate his claims. Yet when pressed for details, Boyle becomes as vague as Van Morrison lyrics. "I got nasty e-mails," the professor says, giving no hint of their contents. "They ridiculed me for being Catholic and ridiculed Catholicism. Two years ago, they even made a T-shirt ridiculing me." Was this ridicule based on religion or ethnicity, or do Boyle's students and colleagues just dislike him? Without examples, it's impossible to say.

It's also hard to see a legal case, given that "Irish" is nowhere recognized as a racial category. Sacrilege is an even tougher case, since nothing in Catholic canon law prohibits getting loaded on St. Patrick's Day. Boyle is having none of this. "My secretary, who has a high school education, and isn't even Catholic, understands this," he snaps, abruptly ending the interview.

Perhaps a professor who claims discrimination while offhandedly insulting his secretary is not the ideal client, but shouldn't Boyle and the Celtic Tigers be able to find common ground? Alas, the professor's claim to Irish citizenship is based on Ireland's notorious grandparent loophole—a practice to which the Tigers, who loathe Irish Americans, strongly object. "This citizen stuff is complete nonsense," says CTADL spokesman William O'Herlihy. "Why not grant American citizenship to anyone in Ireland who has an American grandchild?" Thus even apparent allies cannot escape the anxiety of small differences.

Bald Sopranos

The Irish are not the only long-assimilated European immigrant group that still has it tough. "I'm a lawyer, but my dad was a shoemaker," says Ted Grippo, the chatty and amiable founder of Chicago's American-Italian Defense Association (AIDA). "Since 1930, we've had over 800 Mafia-type movies. I can't tell you how many times I've been asked if I'm connected." Fed up, Grippo is taking aim at Tony Soprano and the gang at the Bada-Bing—who themselves comically raised the issue of defamation in a recent episode about Columbus Day protests organized by Native Americans.

Grippo's familiarity with HBO's hit series would surprise the show's most ardent fans. "In *The Sopranos*, there are two groups of Italians: the mob guys and the other people. Of that second group—Dr. Cusamano, the parish priest, the restaurant owner, the kids, the wife, Dr. Melfi—they're all a bunch of slobs. Compare that to when Carmela met the Jewish psychiatrist or the African priest. Both of them were noble people, full of conscientious advice." As Grippo describes the subtlest details of *Sopranos* plots, you suspect he may be a secret fan, but the show's ethnic dynamic trumps everything for him.

Last year, Grippo brought legal action against Time Warner, citing a clause in the Illinois constitution that condemns "communications that portray criminality, depravity or lack of virtue in . . . a person or group of persons by reference to religious, racial, ethnic, national or regional affiliation." While the suit was dismissed, AIDA attracted 160 members. Grippo expects to have 200 or 300 members "pretty quickly. We're edging toward a paid staff. Within the next year we'll have some permanent staff."

Italian-American anti-discrimination has a long pedigree and one great event: the rise of Joe Colombo's Italian-American Civil Rights League (IACRL). Colombo, who gave his name to the reputed "Colombo Crime Family," formed the group in 1970, after son Joe Jr. was charged with melting down $500,000 in U.S. coins for their silver content. Within a year the IACRL attracted 100,000 members, boasting a multimillion-dollar budget and a five-room office suite on Madison Avenue. Pop culture Goliaths such as Alka-Seltzer's "Mamma mia, datsa somma spicy meat-a-balls" slogan and Macy's "Godfather Game" fell to the group's wrath. New York Gov. Nelson Rockefeller and U.S. Attorney General John Mitchell attended a "Unity Day Rally" at Columbus Circle. Thanks to the IACRL, the terms *Mafia* and *Cosa Nostra* are never uttered in the film version of *The Godfather*. Colombo's vision grew to include an IACRL-run hospital and rehab center and Camp Unity, a 250-acre retreat for underprivileged kids. In early 1971 he attained that benchmark of Nixon-era success, an appearance on *The Dick Cavett Show*.

The dream ended just as quickly after Colombo was fatally shot at the second Unity Day Rally in 1971; the league did not outlive him. Mob fans speculate the assassination was ordered by either Colombo rival Joe Gallo or boss Carlo Gambino, who feared the league's potential for drawing attention to discreet Gambino activities.

Richard Capozzola, a retired Florida high school teacher who worked for the IACRL, disputes both theories. "In the two years I was with the League, I worked closely with Joe; I never saw any criminal actions or heard so much as a profanity," he says. "There is no other group that has a label pinned to its people . . . Michael Milken, Marc Rich, Allie Tannenbaum, Crazy Eddie Antar—those were all criminals. But if you want to get your backside kicked, write about them and call them the Kosher Nostra."

At his site ItalianInfo.net, Capozzola publishes a 3,000-word essay defending the legacy of Colombo and the IACRL (whose "accomplishments overshadowed what all national Italian American organizations had tried to do for over SIXTY YEARS"). He speculates that Colombo's assassination was ordered by the government as part of its long-term project to denigrate Italian Americans. "The assassination of Joe Colombo, in my view, was a capstone to the unjust and unethical treatment that Italian Americans are subject to in everyday life."

Capozzola still speaks out against "Uncle Tomassos" like Joe Pesci, Paul Sorvino, and *Sopranos* creator David Chase. "I love my country, but I sure don't love Hollywood," he says. His hope is that there might someday be an organization that weeds out anti-Italian slurs as assertively as the Anti-Defamation League obliterates anti-Semitism.

Hate for Sale

Anti-discrimination efforts do not occur in a vacuum. Even hypochondriacs get sick, and the anti-discrimination lobby exists in part because real discrimination exists. If the ADL's picture of an anti-Semitic Arab lobby is vivid, that's because pro-Arab sentiments frequently do slide into hoary anti-Jewish tropes, a fact the more honest Arab advocates, such as the ADC's Ibish, acknowledge.

To the surprise (if not disappointment) of Arab-American advocates, the post-9/11 backlash against Arabs and Muslims was more scattered and restrained than ubiquitous talk about internment camps and midnight roundups had led us to expect. But it would take a true Pollyanna to dismiss the troubles of Muslims in America when citizen and noncitizen alike are being deprived of such fancy Western niceties as the right to legal counsel.

Moreover, hate crime is often real crime. American Hindus Against Defamation is part of a political awakening that followed the murder of 30-year-old Navroze Mody by the Jersey City "Dotbusters" gang; agitation from the Indian community clearly helped push that case to a successful prosecution. (On the other hand, prominent civil rights advocate Helen Zia formed American Citizens for Justice after the murder at a strip club of 27-year-old Vincent Chin in 1982—a crime now widely described as a racially motivated killing, though the circumstances are murkier than advocates admit.)

But does a crime become worse because it's a hate crime? Are Americans too dumb to recognize bigotry unless a professional identifies it? Do anti-discrimination organizations actually make any difference?

Anti-discrimination groups are untroubled by such airy-fairy questions. Virtually all support broader federal hate crime laws. Ted Grippo's lawsuit against *The Sopranos* is amusing but not uncommon. Even the Celtic Tiger ADL, which seems at first like a Swiftian hoax, is dead serious about expansive hate crime laws.

"We would like to see local legislation or guidelines enacted to prevent negative stereotyping in the local media and at officially sanctioned events or by anyone in receipt of public contracts," says CTA-DL spokesman O'Herlihy. "If 24 Hour Fitness can draw the wrath of the oversized persons lobby . . . then I don't see why those that are offended by the negative stereotyping of *their* culture shouldn't be given serious thought too."

Nonlegislative strong-arming is even more common. The Anti-Defamation League of B'nai B'rith pressures Internet service providers that don't police bulletin boards and libraries that display objectionable books. It once attempted to ban a textbook that "[leaned] over backward to provide a flattering portrait of Islamic civilization."

Laird Wilcox, a civil rights activist who fell out with ADL while researching fringe groups, devotes more than a quarter of *The Watchdogs* to ADL abuses. Among other things, he claims a documentary he worked on in the 1980s was faked by ADL staffers posing, with fake names and mustaches, as white supremacists.

The ADL's public record is daunting enough. In 1993 the group was fined for employing an off-duty San Francisco police officer to spy on other civil rights groups. Last year the ADL was fined nearly $10 million for defaming a Colorado couple with baseless charges of anti-Semitism. The organization defends its copyright on the word *anti-defamation*, taking action against groups such as the Anarchists Anti-Defamation League and Russell Means' American Indian Anti-Defamation Council.

Other civil rights groups, Wilcox contends, might behave similarly with a $40 million budget. "They're not hesitant to suppress free speech when they don't agree with it," he says, "but on the whole they're no worse and probably better than the ADL."

A League of Their Own

The endearing thing about Bill Donohue is that he genuinely seems to enjoy hurting people. The president of the Catholic League for Religious and Civil Rights peppers his press releases with blistering jabs at luminaries who stumble into anti-Catholic offense: "LARA FLYNN BOYLE ADMITS TO HER STUPIDITY . . . HEATHER GRAHAM'S SEXUAL HANG-UPS . . . Yo, Sly, ever think about getting out of the ring once and for all?" (The last is a reference to Sylvester Stallone's canceled series *Father Lefty*.)

Donohue specializes in invidious comparisons of the "If they said the same thing about blacks/Jews . . ." type. Some samples:

"Sadly, there is also a market for Jew-bashing cards. Millions of people hate gays. Ditto for Muslims. White racists abound. But there are no cards, thank God, that attack these groups. Just Catholics."

"If a group of white anti-black bigots dressed up as Al Jolson and mocked African Americans, no one would excuse them. . . . "

"For starters, would [the Brooklyn Museum of Art] include a photograph of Jewish slave masters sodomizing their obsequious black slaves?"

In an interview for this story, Donohue is energetic, engaging, and unapologetic about his aggressive personal style. "We're not located in Kansas City," he says (a dig at the liberal *National Catholic Reporter*, which is headquartered there). "New York is a rough town. The people I debate are smart, quick, and tough. I'm not some pious little bluenose, backwoods kid."

Invoking the image of sodomite Jewish slave masters is, in Donohue's view, fair play. "Why is that an invidious comparison?" he says. "Why isn't it analogous? I want a level playing field."

The Catholic League was formed in 1973 and turned over to Donohue's leadership 20 years later. Donohue's genius was to change the terms of the discussion, to present the Catholic League not as a socially conservative group but as the champion of an abused religious sect in a relentlessly bigoted environment. Everywhere the Catholic League looks—art museum, multiplex, TV set—an abyss of nearly Elizabethan Catholic bashing gazes back; the league fights back with press releases, letter writing campaigns, boycott threats, and an annual "Index of Anti-Catholicism."

This strategy invites a good deal of media mockery of the "wait 'til the Catholic League gets a load of this" variety. "When any other group complains, they're against discrimination," Donohue says. "When Bill Donohue leads a protest, it's censorship. He's against free speech." This charge clearly rankles Donohue, who insists—against considerable evidence—that he opposes governmental decency policing. "I don't want the government to be the agent of resolution," Donohue says. "I'd rather see somebody bashing my religion than see the government exercising censorship."

This last claim should not be taken at face value. Donohue's opposition to government intervention is such that when WNEW's *Opie and Anthony* radio show staged a live sex act in St. Patrick's Cathedral this August, Donohue's first action was to file a complaint with the Federal Communications Commission (FCC), demanding that WNEW's license be revoked. The Catholic League has in the past filed FCC protests against a San Diego radio station and a WB Network quiz show; in 1998 Donohue went after the FCC itself, when a subscriber to the commission's e-mail digest posted "a joke that poked fun at nuns." As is often the case, government intervention is in the eye of the beholder.

But these were minor dustups compared to this year's revelations that Boston's Archdiocese housed a de facto pederasty ring that was protected by the church hierarchy. Suddenly the Catholic League was in an odd position. While the rest of the country was talking about child-abusing priests and their accomplices in the bishopric, the Catholic League was still denouncing harmless chestnuts about high-strung nuns and wacky confessional mixups.

"When this happened in Boston, I thought carefully, do I want to get involved in this thing?" says Donohue, who acknowledges having waited out the early stages of the controversy. "The reason we talk more about it now is that this thing blew up. And I wanted to have a voice of somebody who loves the church, who hates the abuse that's going on in the church, and will oppose the efforts of the left and the right—especially the left—to impose an agenda."

Donohue decisively inserted himself into the debate in March, briefly becoming a ubiquitous presence on talk shows and managing partly to direct the battle back toward a familiar enemy: Catholic liberals. He has become one of the major proponents of the thesis that the root of the problem was excessive tolerance for gays in the priesthood.

This, however, doesn't address a main cause of public outrage: not just that child abuse occurred but that a self-interested church hierarchy was willing to act as an accomplice. In April a widely publicized Vatican meeting of U.S. cardinals produced a lawyerly and mealy-mouthed set of proposals; at a June meeting, America's bishops, who had already emerged as the villains in the public mind, produced "zero tolerance" guidelines that made no mention of their own responsibility. It doesn't take a Catholic basher to be struck by the fact that a church uniquely confident in its opposition to stem cell research, condom use, and war in Iraq is somehow unable to take a strong stand against raping children.

Despite promises that he would not "defend the indefensible" or "carry water for the church," Donohue inevitably has had to speak carefully about Church pusillanimity and promise that real reform is on the way. Damage control is an uncomfortable job for him. In his element, Bill Donohue is a happy warrior, not an apologist. Witness a telling exchange with James Carville on CNN's *Crossfire*:

> **Donohue:** Most of the damage was done in the 1970s and the early 1980s. The cultural and sexual revolution that this country went through in the '60s, '70s, and early '80s had negative consequences all over. I'm not excusing it. I'm giving you. . . .
>
> **Carville:** I know. But I lived through the cultural revolution. And I didn't fondle no Boy Scout.

The fight has not gone out of Bill Donohue; he just wasn't born to be somebody else's straight man. Donohue promises, however, that if and when the scandal settles down, "I am gonna say to people: 'It's not OK to beat up on us just because we created our own problems.'"

Let a Thousand Flowers Bloom

One thing you can say for anti-discrimination groups: By their very existence, they negate the idea of America as a homogeneous, or even harmonious, society. This alone constitutes a public service. The Council on American-Islamic Relations, for example, keeps close track of the war on terrorism's erosion of civil liberties, if only because its constituents are directly impacted. Between the tyranny of common interest and the tyranny of special interests, at least you still have the freedom to name your poison.

"We like these groups," says Chip Berlet, a senior analyst at Cambridge, Massachusetts–based Political Research Associates. "It's a good question why a person who is sensible would like these groups, but it's because we don't think it's that annoying to ask whether people are being treated fairly—and to be able to do that without people running into a corner and ignoring each other. I want people to find a way to speak out in a way that is civil."

It's hard, though, to see how accusations of bigotry, sniping over political agendas, or appeals to courts and legislatures help promote civility. Anti-discrimination groups may in fact be most valuable when they are most combative, most obdurate, most willing to give up phony abstractions about equality for all and openly fight each other for crumbs of public attention.

Your meaningless cacophony could be somebody else's Whitman-esque symphony. It would also be somebody else's highly remunerative business, providing gainful employment for executives, clerks, and boards of directors. In this sluggish economy, isn't that enough? Even when there's little to gripe about, Americans from all walks of life can still come together and complain. We may be one nation after all.

December 2002

35 Heroes of Freedom

Celebrating the people who have made the world groovier and groovier since 1968

***

The *Reason* Staff

"THINGS ARE A LOT GROOVIER NOW," declared former *Reason* Editor-in-Chief Robert W. Poole back in 1988, on the occasion of *Reason*'s 20th anniversary. During the magazine's first two decades, he pointed out, all sorts of political and cultural changes had occurred, most of them unambiguously for the better. The Vietnam War was history, stagflation had been vanquished, and technology that enabled everything from cleaner, more fuel-efficient cars to automated teller machines to videocassette recorders had vastly improved everyday life. As important, "numerous personal freedoms we take for granted were very tenuous in 1968." By 1988, the women's movement had revolutionized the home and workplace, gays were out of the closet for good, and the acceptance of other alternative lifestyles and generally rising standards of living had created a far looser, more liberated society.

No one could have predicted that the *next* 15 years would be the freest in human history (or that most of us would acknowledge such phenomenal progress with little more than a shrug). Half a billion people or more have escaped the gray hand of totalitarian communism, and the percentage of people living in poverty is declining worldwide. The Soviet empire is kaput, and so are the Cold War proxy battles that poisoned relations around the world. South Africa's revolting apartheid system is no more, and South America, though a basket case in many ways, boasts mostly democratic governments. Globally, economic freedom is on the rise, bringing with it an invigorating, intoxicating mix of goods, people, and cultures. Scientific breakthroughs continue to enrich lives, alleviate suffering, and improve the environment. The digital revolution has given rise to new means of expression, commerce, and community.

The ideas that have always animated this magazine—that the good society is one in which people are as free as possible to pursue happiness on their own terms; that economic and civil liberties are indivisible; that markets and borders and societies should be open and that governments should be limited; that there is no one best way to run a country, a business, a family, a life—have moved from the fringes of the debate to the center, in some cases even becoming the conventional wisdom.

While there is no shortage of threats to life and liberty—from international terrorism to poverty-inducing trade barriers to the deadly war on drugs—these are indeed high times for a magazine devoted to exploring the promises of "Free Minds and Free Markets." For all of its many problems, the world we live in is dizzying in its variety, breathtaking in its riches, and wide-ranging in its options. Malcontents on the right and left who diagnose modernity as suffering from "affluenza" or "options anxiety" will admit this much: These days we've even got a greater choice of ways to be unhappy. Which may be as close to a definition of utopia as we're likely to come.

What follows is *Reason*'s tribute to some of the people who have made the world a freer, better, and more libertarian place by example, invention, or action. The one criterion: Honorees needed to have been alive at some point during *Reason*'s run, which began in May 1968. The list is by design eclectic, irreverent, and woefully incomplete, but it limns the many ways in which the world has only gotten groovier and groovier during the last 35 years.

Nick Gillespie

John Ashcroft. If Donny and Marie Osmond were a little bit country and a little bit rock 'n' roll, the current attorney general is little bit J. Edgar Hoover and a little bit Janet Reno. Whether it's prosecuting medical marijuana users, devoting scarce resources to arresting adult porn distributors, or using tax dollars to create USA PATRIOT Act propaganda Web sites, Ashcroft has unintentionally managed to create an unprecedented coalition of conservatives, liberals, and libertarians around a single noble cause: the protection of civil liberties.

Jeff Bezos. The world's greatest bookstore may yet go belly up, but Amazon's founder has revolutionized commerce and made all hard-to-find tomes easier to track down—especially if you live 1,000 miles from the nearest B. Dalton's. Now he's doing the same with clothes, toys, electronics, and more. His Segway enthusiasm notwithstanding, Bezos runs a company that consistently leads the pack in collaborative software, customer service, recommendations, you name it.

Norman Borlaug. The "father of the Green Revolution" is one Nobel Peace Prize winner (1970) who fully deserved the honor. Not only did he help raise crop yields in the developing world so that literally billions of people didn't starve, he remains an outspoken critic of environmentalists who attack the biotechnology that will help wipe out world hunger, of international development programs that often do more harm than good, and of kleptocrats who fill their own stomachs while their citizens starve.

Stewart Brand. By introducing the *Whole Earth Catalog* in 1968, he helped give birth to the most individualist wing of the hippie counterculture. "We are as gods," the first issue announced, "and might as well get good at it. So far, remotely done power and glory—as via government, big business, formal education, church—has succeeded to the point where gross defects obscure actual gains. In response to this dilemma . . . personal power is developing—power of the individual to conduct his own education, find his own inspiration, shape his own environment, and share his adventure with whoever is interested. Tools that aid this process are sought and promoted by the *Whole Earth Catalog.*" A couple decades later, he helped create one of the first great Internet communities, the Well.

William Burroughs. Along with Jack Kerouac and Allen Ginsberg, a member of the Beat Holy Trinity that helped to irrevocably loosen up Eisenhower's America. Not only is his fiction (*Junky, Naked Lunch, Nova Express*) relentlessly anti-authoritarian, he proved that you can abuse your body in every way imaginable and still outlive the entire universe.

Curt Flood. The Moses of free agency in professional sports, the star St. Louis Cardinals outfielder started the process that led to athletes' getting paid something close to what they're actually worth. While he never personally made it to the Promised Land of fan-alienating fat contracts, his principled martyrdom helped all American workers to finally shrug off the Organization Man mentality.

Larry Flynt. Where Hugh Hefner mainstreamed bohemian sexual mores, hard-core porn merchant Flynt brought tastelessness to new depths, inspiring an unthinkable but revealing coalition between social conservatives and puritanical feminists—and helping to strengthen First Amendment protections for free expression along the way.

Milton Friedman. The 91-year-old Nobel Prize-winning economist didn't just co-author *Free to Choose*, the book that pumped up Arnold Schwarzenegger's mind. He's brought libertarian ideas both to a mass audience and to the elite ranks of policy makers, helped to end the draft and discredit wage and price controls, popularized the privatization of schooling and pensions, and made criticism of the war on drugs respectable.

Barry Goldwater. The iconic Arizona senator offered "a choice, not an echo" in his laughably doomed 1964 presidential campaign. He bridged the tradition of Western individualism with the then-barely-glimpsed future of Sunbelt anti-governmentism, inspiring later revolts such as California's Prop. 13. Though he might have used nukes in Vietnam, he more likely would have pulled out; he also helped convince Nixon to resign. A maverick to the end, he even supported gays in the military.

F.A. Hayek. He mapped the road to serfdom during World War II and paid a steep price—decades-long professional isolation—for daring to suggest that social democracy had something in common with collectivist tyrannies of the right and left. The economist-cum-philosopher lived to see his arguments vindicated by the failure of the Third Way and even took home a Nobel Prize in 1974. Building on the work of that other great Austrian economist, Ludwig von Mises, and combining a respect for inherited wisdom with an understanding that freedom is fundamentally disruptive, Hayek showed that the uncoordinated actions of individuals generate wonders—market prices, language, scientific progress—that the deliberate designs of central planners never could.

Brian Lamb. The Great Stone Face of C-SPAN has produced more must-see TV than anyone else in the history of the medium. There's no reason to pick a favorite among the likes of *Booknotes, Washington Journal*, and all the other C-SPAN fare, but his greatest contribution may well be his first: turning a surveillance camera on the den of iniquity known as the U.S. House of Representatives.

Vaclav Havel. Havel demonstrated definitively that the simple act of speaking truth to totalitarians, while being willing to suffer the consequences, is more potent than a thousand tanks. He pushed artistic boundaries, defended the right of rock stars to be filthy, helped engineer the most magical of the Communist-toppling revolutions, and then remained an influential moral voice long after his regional counterparts faded away.

Robert Heinlein. The author of compelling science fiction with individualist themes was the entry point for millions of readers into rabid, late-night arguments about rights, responsibilities, the state, and *really* alternative sexual practices. If you don't grok *Starship Troopers, Stranger in a Strange Land, The Moon Is a Harsh Mistress*, and *Time Enough for Love*, you just plain can't grok anything.

Jane Jacobs. There's Jane Jacobs the scholar, whose books (especially *The Death and Life of Great American Cities*) undermined the ideas of planners who either hated the city or thought they could mold it into a grand monument without regard for how the people who lived in it preferred to live their lives. And then there's Jane Jacobs the activist, who went to the barricades to keep people like Robert Moses from ripping out the heart of the particular cities she lived in. Few others did as much to defend the lives people forged for themselves against the static visions planning elites love to impose.

Alfred Kahn. As head of the defunct Civil Aeronautics Board during the Carter years, "the architect of deregulation" pushed for free markets in the airline industry, ushering in an age in which virtually every slob in America could afford to fly and providing an unassailable example of markets delivering better prices and greater safety than government regulation. Snobs sniff that Kahn turned once-classy airlines into buses in the sky, which is just one more reason to praise him.

Rose Wilder Lane. The daughter of Laura Ingalls Wilder, Lane extensively edited and shaped that great alternative history of American settlement, the *Little House* books, which place the family, community, and commerce—rather than male adventure, escape, and violence—at the heart of our national experience. She was a prolific author in her own right and, along with Isabel Patterson and Ayn Rand, one of the three godmothers of modern libertarianism. Lane's *The Discovery of Freedom: Man's Struggle Against Authority* remains a powerful statement about the evolution and necessity of individual rights.

Madonna. As one of the first music video megastars, the Material Girl led MTV's glorious parade of freaks, gender-benders, and weirdos who helped broaden the palette of acceptable cultural identities and destroy whatever vestiges of repressive mainstream sensibilities still remained. Along the way, her continuous self-fashioning has brought so many avant-hip trends to the masses that we can even forgive her current fake English accent and children's-book-author phase.

Nelson Mandela. Mandela cheerfully served a prison sentence that would have left Jesus bitter and spiteful. Sprung from jail, he showed remarkable forbearance and amity in overseeing South Africa's post-apartheid transition, creating a model for how the world might finally push past centuries-old racial strife. His quest for personal freedom continued into his ninth decade, when he divorced the murderous Winnie and happily remarried.

Martina Navratilova. The dominant tennis player (male or female) of her day, Martina defected from Czechoslovakia in 1975 to pursue personal and professional freedom, writing, "I honestly believe I was born to be an American." As the first superstar athlete to admit she was gay and the first woman to play tennis like a man, Martina did more than inspire movies like *Personal Best*; she smashed stultifying stereotypes like so many poorly hit lobs.

Willie Nelson. One of the great crossover artists in popular music, the Texas legend pulled off a Martin Luther King Jr.-like achievement by uniting hippies and rednecks in a single audience. An inadvertent hero to tax resisters everywhere, Nelson brought the battle against puritanism to the very roof of the Carter White House, where he famously smoked dope to relieve his—and our—national malaise.

Richard Nixon. Between waging secret wars, enacting wage and price controls, and producing Watergate, Tricky Dick did more than any other single individual to encourage cynicism about government and wariness of presidential power.

Les Paul. Paul was a terrific jazz guitarist who invented the solid-body electric guitar in 1947, helping usher in America's most liberating cultural invention of the latter 20th century, rock 'n' roll. He pioneered multitracked recording and built the first eight-track, which put the *D* into *DIY* while allowing bands like the Beatles to make lasting works of art.

Ron Paul. Paul is the only member of Congress who always votes according to the principles they all should follow. First, he asks if the program is authorized by the Constitution. If it is, he then consults his campaign promises, which include pledges to never raise taxes or increase spending. Look for his votes in the *nay* column.

Ayn Rand. While her private life outstripped them in terms of melodrama, there's no denying that novels such as *The Fountainhead* and *Atlas Shrugged* introduced libertarian ideas to millions of readers in a vivid, compelling way, encouraging them to reject the cult of self-sacrifice, oppose the demands of collectivism, and question the rule of experts. In contrast to the half-hearted, pusillanimous defenses of capitalism offered by conservatives, she explained why a system of peaceful, voluntary exchange is morally right as well as efficient.

Dennis Rodman. As a cross-dressing, serially pierced, tattoo-laden, multiple National Basketball Association championship ring holder, the Worm set an X-Men-level standard for cultural mutation. His flamboyant, frequently gay-ish antics place him in apostolic succession to a madcap handful of athletes such as Joe Namath, Rollie Fingers, and Muhammad Ali, all of whom challenged the lantern-jawed stiffness that had traditionally made sports stars such dull role models.

Louis Rossetto. The genius behind *Wired* magazine didn't merely chronicle the digital revolution that continues to shape our world: He helped to conceptualize and realize it. Long after the tech bubble burst, his crucial insight—that new technologies are undermining all existing authorities and empowering end users in new and subversive ways—remains a guide to the future.

Julian Simon. In books such as *The Ultimate Resource* and *The State of Humanity*, the late "Doomslayer" patiently and exhaustively collected the data proving that neo-Malthusians such as Paul Ehrlich and Lester Brown were blowing smoke about environmental degradation and overpopulation. More impressive still: This oracle of optimism suffered from depression much of his adult life.

Thomas Szasz. Since the 1961 publication of *The Myth of Mental Illness*, the great and tireless critic of the therapeutic state (and longtime *Reason* contributing editor) has never stopped pointing out the coercive implications of politicizing medicine and medicalizing politics.

Margaret Thatcher. The much-maligned Iron Lady set the pace for the rollback of nationalized industries throughout Western Europe, doing the heavy lifting needed to change England from the Sex Pistols' land of "no future" to today's Cool Britannia. More important, she outsmarted the racist "repatriation" crowd that put her into office through pro-small-business policies that helped complete the Pakistanization of the U.K. On top of it all, she was the only reliable supporter of the U.S. in the Cold War's final stages.

Clarence Thomas. After surviving the Hiroshima of confirmation hearings, Thomas has emerged as an all-too-rare advocate on the Supreme Court for federalism, the enumerated powers doctrine, and a constrained view of the Commerce Clause. He's also a reliable defender of freedom of speech in such diverse contexts as advertising, broadcasting, and campaign contributions.

The Tiananmen Square martyr. By putting his life on the line in front of his government's tanks, he provided not only one of the most memorable images of the last 35 years but one of the most inspiring too. The free China of the future owes him a statue or two.

Ted Turner. By launching CNN, the socialist idiot savant created the 24-hour news cycle, familiarized audiences around the world with the idea of globalization, proved the necessity of cable television, and inspired countless imitators who have collectively reshaped and improved the news media by giving voice to more and more viewpoints. Bonus points: After 50 years of confrontation via the Olympics, Turner's ironically titled Goodwill Games flop provided a hint that the Soviet Union likely would end with not a bang but a whimper.

Evan Williams. With a little luck and a lot of technology, Williams did as much as anyone in history to provide the once-scarce freedom of the press to millions of individuals, through his co-founding of Pyra Labs, which introduced easy-to-use Blogger technology and free-as-air Blogspot hosting to the masses.

The Yuppie. This widely reviled Reagan-era social construct opened up to ordinary people countless pleasures and pursuits once reserved for the upper class, from "gourmet" food to good-looking cars to nicely designed furniture to fancy-pants literary devices to an obsession with Tuscany. In striving "upward," Yuppies spurred a massive exfoliation of choice at all levels of American society.

Phil Zimmerman. By inventing and distributing Pretty Good Privacy, a free, easy, and damn-nigh uncrackable e-mail encryption program, he gave dissidents everywhere the ability to communicate without fear—all while challenging his own government's attempt to control that ability. He's living proof that a single individual with a good idea can make a huge difference.

December 2003

contributors

Peter Bagge is a comic book artist best known for the influential underground comic *Hate*. His work has appeared in magazines ranging from *Spin* to *Details* to *Hustler* and his *Adventures of Bat Boy* comic strip appears in the *Weekly World News*.

Ronald Bailey is *Reason*'s science correspondent and the author of *Eco-Scam* and the forthcoming *Liberation Biology: A Moral and Scientific Defense of the Biotech Revolution*. He is the editor *The True State of the Planet, Earth Report 2000*, and *Global Warming and Other Eco-Myths*. He is a member of the Society of Environmental Journalists and the American Society for Bioethics and Humanities.

Joe Bob Briggs is a Texas satirist and TV personality whose next book, *Profoundly Erotic: The Movies That Changed Sex*, is a sequel to *Profoundly Disturbing: Shocking Movies That Changed History*, from which "Kroger Babb's Road Show" was drawn.

Drew Carey is a comedian and television star.

Tim Cavanaugh is *Reason*'s web editor. He was the editor of the late satiric Web site Suck.com and his work has appeared in the *Washington Post*, the *San Francisco Chronicle*, the *Beirut Daily Star*, *Mother Jones*, *San Francisco Magazine*, *Agence France-Presse*, *Wired*, *Newsday*, *Salon*, and many other publications.

Brian Doherty is a senior editor at *Reason* and author of *This Is Burning Man*. His essays and reviews on culture and politics have appeared in dozens of magazines and newspapers, including the *Washington Post*, the *Wall Street Journal*, *Spin*, and the *Los Angeles Times*.

Edith Efron (1922-2001) had a long and varied career in journalism, writing for publications ranging from the *New York Times Magazine* to *TV Guide*. She was the author of several books, including *The News Twisters*, a study of media bias in the 1968 presidential election, and *The Apocalyptics*, an exposé of junk science and its effects on environmental policy.

Charles Paul Freund is a senior editor at *Reason*. A former documentary filmmaker and assistant editor at the *Washington Post*'s Outlook section, his work has appeared in the *New York Times*, the *International Herald Tribune*, the *Village Voice*, *Esquire*, *Columbia Journalism Review*, *American Photographer*, *Film Comment*, *American Film*, the *New Republic*, and in newspapers throughout the United States.

Michael Fumento is a senior fellow with the Hudson Institute and the author of five books, including *Fat of the Land: The Obesity Epidemic and How Overweight Americans Can Help Themselves* and *BioEvolution: How Biotechnology Is Changing Our World*. A former Army paratrooper and *Reason* science correspondent, he is a nationally syndicated columnist with Scripps Howard News Service.

Glenn Garvin spent two decades covering Latin America for newspapers including the *Miami Herald* before becoming the *Herald*'s television critic in 2002. He is the author of *Everybody Had His Own Gringo: The CIA and the Contras*, and, with Ana Rodriguez, *Diary of a Survivor: Nineteen Years in a Cuban Women's Prison*.

Nick Gillespie is editor-in-chief of *Reason*. His work has appeared in the *Los Angeles Times*, the *New York Times*, *Salon*, *Slate*, *Suck*, the *Wall Street Journal*, the *Washington Post*, and many other places.

Christopher Hitchens is a columnist for *Vanity Fair* and the author of many books, including *Blood, Class and Empire: The Enduring Anglo-American Relationship*, *A Long Short War*, and *Why Orwell Matters*.

Jerry Jesness is the author of *Teaching English Language Learners K-12*. He teaches various subjects at the Discipline Alternative Educational Program in Los Fresnos, Texas, and is a member of the Education Consumers Consultants Network.

Steve Kurtz is a lawyer turned screenwriter whose scripts include *Serious Business* and *The Producer*. He is the author of *Steve's America*, available at www.stevesamerica.com.

Stan Liebowitz and Stephen E. Margolis are coauthors of *Winners, Losers and Microsoft: Competition and Antitrust in High Technology*. Liebowitz is a professor of economics in the School of Management at the University of Texas at Dallas and the author of *Rethinking the Network Economy*. Margolis is a professor of economics at North Carolina State University. His publications include articles on markets for physicians' services, monopolistic competition, and efficiency concepts in law and economics.

Mike Lynch served as *Reason*'s Washington editor and national correspondent between 1996 and 2002. He is currently a financial planner for Barnum Financial Group, an office of MetLife, in Shelton, Connecticut.

Michael McMenamin is a longtime contributor to *Reason* and lawyer who lives in Cleveland, Ohio. He is working on a book about the Martha Stewart trial with Kelly Breckenridge, the pen name of a financial analyst on Wall Street.

Virginia Postrel is the author of *The Substance of Style* and *The Future and Its Enemies* and an economics columnist for the *New York Times*. From 1989 to 2000, she was editor of *Reason*.

Rhys Southan is a former *Reason* intern, the co-author of the musical *Who Is Jim Holt?*, and the co-director of the film festival favorite *Sean Connery Golf Project*. He maintains the *World Star Gazette* (www.worldstargazette.com).

Jacob Sullum, a senior editor at *Reason* and a syndicated columnist, is the author of *Saying Yes: In Defense of Drug Use* and *For Your Own Good: The Anti-Smoking Crusade and the Tyranny of Public Health.* His weekly column is carried by newspapers across the country, including the *New York Post,* the *Washington Times,* and the *Orange County Register.* His work has appeared in the *New York Times,* the *Wall Street Journal, USA Today, National Review,* and *Cigar Aficionado.*

Jesse Walker is managing editor of *Reason,* author of *Rebels on the Air: An Alternative History of Radio in America,* and co-director of the documentary film *Talking Butts.* His work has appeared in the *New York Times,* the *Wall Street Journal,* the *Washington Post,* and many other publications.

Matt Welch is a columnist for Canada's *National Post.* He launched the first independent English-language newspaper in the post-Communist East Bloc, has contributed to publications ranging from *AlterNet* to *The American Spectator* to the *Columbia Journalism Review,* and is a seven-time award winner from the Greater Los Angeles Press Club. His work is archived at www.mattwelch.com, where he maintains a popular weblog.

About the Editor

ASKS THE *WASHINGTON POST*: "Which monthly magazine editor argues that the spread of pornography is a victory for free expression? And that drugs from marijuana to heroin should not only be legalized, but using them occasionally is just fine? And is also quite comfortable with gay marriage? The answer is Nick Gillespie."

The 41-year-old Gillespie joined *Reason*'s staff in 1993 as an assistant editor and ascended to the top slot in 2000. His work has appeared in the *New York Times*, the *Washington Post*, the *Wall Street Journal*, the *Los Angeles Times*, *Slate*, *Salon*, and many other publications.

He is a frequent commentator on radio and television networks such as National Public Radio, CNN, C-SPAN, Fox News Channel, and MSNBC. Prior to joining *Reason*, he worked as a reporter at several New Jersey newspapers and as an editor at several Manhattan-based music, movie, and teen magazines. He is almost certainly the only journalist, living or dead, to have interviewed both Ozzy Osbourne and the 2002 Nobel laureate in economics, Vernon Smith.

In 1996, Gillespie received his Ph.D. in English literature from the State University of New York at Buffalo. He holds an M.A. in English with a concentration in creative writing from Temple University and a B.A. in English and Psychology from Rutgers University. He lives in the Washington, D.C. area with his wife and two sons.

About Reason Foundation

Reason magazine and *Reason Online* (reason.com) are published by the Los Angeles–based Reason Foundation, a 501(c)(3) nonprofit educational and research group that advances a free society by developing, applying, and promoting the libertarian ideas of individual liberty, free markets, and the rule of law.

In addition to publishing *Reason* and *Reason Online*, the foundation operates the Reason Public Policy Institute, a nonpartisan public policy think tank promoting choice, competition, and a dynamic market economy as the foundation for human dignity and progress.

For more information, go to reason.org and rppi.org.